Ethics & Organizations

Ethics & ORGANIZATIONS

edited by
MARTIN PARKER

SAGE Publications
London • Thousand Oaks • New Delhi

First published 1998

SAGE Publications Ltd
6 Bonhill Street
London EC2A 4PU

SAGE Publications Inc
2455 Teller Road
Thousand Oaks, California 91320

SAGE Publications India Pvt Ltd
32, M-Block Market
Great Kailash – I
New Delhi 110 048

British Library Cataloguing in Publication data

A catalogue record for this book is available from the British Library

ISBN 0 8039 7496 5
ISBN 0 8039 7497 3(pbk)

Library of Congress catalog card number 98–61101

Typeset by M Rules
Printed in Great Britain by The Cromwell Press Ltd,
Trowbridge, Wiltshire

Contents

Notes on authors

Peter Anthony retired early from Cardiff Business School and has since been contributing to postgraduate management courses at King's College London and the Universities of Lancaster and Glamorgan. His more recent work includes *Managing Culture* and *The Foundation of Management.* His current interests include developments in management morality.

Joanna Brewis is Senior Lecturer at the University of Portsmouth Business School. She has a BSc (Hons) in management sciences and a PhD in management, both from UMIST. Joanna specializes in teaching organizational behaviour and research methodology across a variety of undergraduate and postgraduate degree programmes. Her current research interests focus on gender, sex and sexuality in organizations, as reflected in her doctoral thesis, which examined the power effects of and resistances to various knowledges around sex at work, using an analysis developed from Foucault. Joanna has published in journals including *Gender, Work and Organization*, *Management Learning* and *Human Relations.*

John Desmond is currently Lecturer in Marketing at Heriot-Watt University. Prior to this he worked at the University of Glasgow and at Manchester Business School. He is interested in a whole host of areas and is easily diverted from the true vocation of the marketing academic. He enjoys nothing better than dabbling in other people's specialisms and then beating a hasty retreat. In addition to ethics, current interests include 'taste' in advertising, perceptions of the 'hyper-real', critical communications and the search for newer (and better) metaphors for marketing.

Stephen Fineman is Professor of Organizational Behaviour in the University of Bath's School of Management. His recent research includes major qualitative studies of industrial managers' values and responses to environmental pressures and of the way the environment is socially constructed and regulated. He has published widely, recent books being *Emotion in Organizations* (Sage, 1993), *Organizing and Organizations* (Sage, 1993) and *Experiencing Organizations* (Sage, 1996).

Karen Legge is currently Professor of Organizational Behaviour, Warwick Business School, University of Warwick. Previously she worked at Manchester Business School, MRC/ESRC Social and Applied Psychology

Unit, University of Sheffield, at the Management School, Imperial College and at the Department of Behaviour in Organizations, Lancaster University. Karen is joint editor of the *Journal of Management Studies*, and is also a member of the editorial boards of *British Journal of Industrial Relations*, *Human Resource Management Journal, Gender, Work and Organization* and *Organization*. Her latest book is *HRM: Rhetorics and Realities* (Macmillan, 1995). She is presently working on a book with the provisional title *Postmodernity and the Ethics of Organizing,* a title which encapsulates her present research interests.

Hugo Letiche. How can one try to do *justice* to one's *self* in a short biographical note? After all, I'm writing it because Martin Parker said I *had* to. And I'm writing it much too late because it was a-*law*ed (*de facto*) to do so. Under my *duties* is a Professorship at CSTT Keele University and teaching at the Rotterdam School of Management (Erasmus University Graduate Business Faculty). I *just*-ify my academic work as the ethnographic description of organization and knowledge (work/management). My *others* include many of the contributors to this book who are a forum for discussion and attend (every once in a while) to my work (and I to theirs). In so far as there is a *subjectile* to academe, Keele has provided (welcome) space(s) that are too scarce and much needed.

Rolland Munro is Professor of Organisation Theory in the Department of Management at Keele University and Director of the Centre for Social Theory and Technology. Drawing on his ethnographies of large organizations, he has published a number of articles which rework notions of 'the social' in ways that avoid traditional dualisms such as self and society, or people and technology. He has co-edited two books, *Accountability: Power, Ethos and the Technologies of Managing* (Chapman and Hall, 1996) and *Ideas of Difference: Social Spaces and the Labour of Division* (Blackwell, 1997).

Glenn Morgan is Senior Lecturer in Organizational Analysis at Warwick Business School, The University of Warwick. He previously worked at Manchester Business School. He is author of *Organizations in Society* (Macmillan, 1990) and joint editor (with David Knights) of *Regulation and Deregulation in European Financial Services* (Macmillan, 1996). His current research interests include the comparative study of organizations, the regulation of the UK financial services industry and the management of innovation in the National Health Service. He has never taught a course on business ethics and is unlikely to do so in the future.

Martin Parker is a Senior Lecturer in Social and Organizational Theory at the University of Keele. He holds degrees in anthropology and sociology from the Universities of Sussex, London and Staffordshire and previously taught sociology at Staffordshire. His research and publications cover organizational and social theory, and the sociology of culture. He has edited *Postmodernism and Organisation* and *Towards a New Theory of Organisation* (both with John Hassard) and *The Dilemmas of Mass Higher Education* (with David Jary). He teaches a course on business ethics and rather hopes this volume will be both infuriating and useful for some of the students doing it.

Tom Sorell is Professor of Philosophy at the University of Essex. He has published extensively in applied ethics, the history of philosophy and the philosophy of science. He is author (with John Hendry) of *Business Ethics* (1994) and Associate Editor of *Business Ethics: A European Review*. In 1996–7 he was Faculty Fellow in the Ethics Programme, Harvard University.

Tony Watson teaches and researches about organizations, managerial work and industrial sociology at Nottingham Business School. His books range from *The Personnel Managers* (1977) to *In Search of Management* (1994) and *Sociology, Work and Industry* (1980, 1987, 1995). His current research is concerned with the way that day-to-day and strategic pressures are handled by managers, as individuals who have to manage their own lives, identities and biographies as well as work-based tasks. This work builds upon both his experience within industrial organizations and research work carried out in a range of different settings. A special interest is the potential for ethnographic research as a means of investigating the complexities and contradictions, pains and delights of organizational life. Whilst this work can most usefully be carried out within a non-representationalist epistemology, he feels that it still needs to engage with and utilize social science theory at the same time as learning from wider literary and philosophical endeavours.

Hugh Willmott is Professor of Organizational Analysis in the Manchester School of Management. He is currently working on a number of projects whose common theme is the changing organization and management of work, including a project in the ESRC Virtual Society programme and an ICAEW funded study of strategic reorientation. His most recent books include *Skill and Consent* (Routledge, 1992, co-edited), *Critical Management Studies* (Sage, 1992, co-edited), *Making Quality Critical* (Routledge, 1995, co-edited) and *Managing Change, Changing Managers* (CIMA, 1995, co-authored). *Making Sense of Management: A Critical Introduction* (Sage, co-authored) was published in 1996. *Management Lives* (Sage, co-authored) is to appear in 1998. Hugh has served on the editorial boards of *Administrative Science Quarterly*, *Organization*, *Organization Studies* and *Accounting, Organizations and Society*.

Edward Wray-Bliss is Lecturer in the Centre for Business and Management Studies, Edge Hill University College, Ormskirk. For his recently completed PhD (UMIST) and as his ongoing research and life interests, Edward is committed to a process of reflecting upon and challenging subordinating representations and relations reproduced in both mainstream, and 'critical', academic work. He is interested in generating links with others similarly exploring the crossings, conflicts, and connections between our ethical/political commitments and our academic practice.

Preface

The idea of an edited volume on ethics and organization theory was originally conceived some time ago when I was listening to papers by Tony Watson and Steve Fineman presented at the 1994 Labour Process Conference. Partly inspired by *Critical Management Studies* by Mats Alvesson and Hugh Willmott (Sage, 1992) I wanted this book to be one in which the chapters took account of each other. In other words, rather than the usual collection of monologues from a conference, this book was intended to be more like a written conversation between interested parties. After a great deal of correspondence over two years, the list of contributors and issues was finally settled and draft papers were presented at a workshop in Stoke-on-Trent in early 1997. All the authors were then asked to revise their chapters taking into account the arguments put forward within the other contributions. As a result, all the chapters in the volume attend to certain key themes and I have also edited them to maximize 'cross-fertilization'. Hopefully this has resulted in a collection which is intellectually challenging in terms of its attention to contradictions and similarities but also easier to use because of its thematic organization.

Grateful thanks are due to the following for their various contributions during the three and a half years it took to put it all together. Sue Jones (then at Sage) saw the potential of the initial idea and offered to subsidize the workshop, and Rosemary Nixon (now at Sage) saw it through and organized the cheque. Keele University's Department of Management helped to subsidize the workshop by covering the substantial amount I went over budget. The small audience at the workshop also helped the event go well by asking penetrating questions and drinking enough to ensure that I overspent on the budget and, to my shame, didn't get home that night. In addition, the various members of Keele's Centre for Social Theory and Technology have allowed me to ask my ethics question in so many seminars over the last three years that I no longer understand it myself. Finally, my heartfelt thanks to the contributors for putting up with the slow progress of this tortuous project, and responding so thoughtfully to my editorial comments. Despite the many differences between the contributors, this volume seems to exemplify the spirit of careful and collective intellectual enquiry which is becoming increasingly rare under the pressure to publish or perish.

Martin Parker

1 Introduction: Ethics, the Very Idea?

Martin Parker

ethics [*eth*iks] (n. pl.) scientific study of morals; system of morality

Ethics? I suppose the most common definition of ethics is the attempt to build a systematic set of normative prescriptions about human behaviour, codes to govern everyday morals and morality. In that sense it is a modern science that claims to be able to replace the holy books and traditions that supposedly guided our ancestors. That is to say, under the name of ethics philosophers and others have attempted to use the tools of reason to generate rules which should guide our judgement in particular and general circumstances. This project should, it seems, be the crowning glory of the rational scientific method and (if successful) would no doubt precede an era in which human unhappiness and cruelty would be substantially reduced, if not eliminated. If in doubt about our conduct, we could refer to a comprehensive dictionary of ethics, a code book, to discover what we should do, to whom and why. Otherwise, what would be the point of all this thinking, talking and writing?

However, the project of ethics (like so many others which began with grand ambitions) seems to have spent an awful lot of time going nowhere. As all of the authors in this volume suggest, though for very different reasons, the idea of foundational ethical codes is one that cannot (and perhaps should not) be taken very seriously. For a start there are considerable problems in deciding what ethics contains, or rather, in deciding what content *should* fill the very contentious definitions I gave above. The tension between theorizing what people should do (prescriptive ethics) and explaining what people actually do (descriptive ethics, the anthropology of moralities) is a fracture that threatens the project from the very start. To begin with the former, if we stick with the notion that ethics is about producing prescriptions – 'golden rules' – then we immediately notice what a variety of rules philosophers have already presented us with. Aristotle's suggestions about the virtuous character, Kant's 'act as if your action were a general rule', the utilitarians' insistence on calculating the happiness of the greater number, Rawls's thought experiments about social justice, and so on, are by no means commensurable arguments that could somehow be 'solved' by reason. Indeed it seems that philosophers have drained oceans of ink over many years debating the relative merits of various frameworks and yet come no closer to any final adjudication. In any case, why should we listen to them? There are many 'reasonable' attempts to formulate ethical prescriptions which have nothing much to do with philosophy – religious movements, everyday conversations, political pronouncements, soap operas, mission statements and so on. Given this huge range of claims, and sources of these claims, one might well conclude that the search for the ethical 'one best way' is likely to be fruitless.

Yet if we move to the seemingly more solid terrain of description, of trying to explain everyday moralities, matters are no better simply because it is by no means clear how such description should be done. Descriptions are not innocent of theoretical prejudices after all, and there is simply no common agreement as to what sort of thing us humans are, and hence what would constitute a good description of us in the first place. Are we creatures of structural, cultural or linguistic determination? Are we the creations of one or many supernatural beings? Are we free agents who socially construct the worlds around us? Should we attend to speech acts, situated accounts, discourses, materials, concepts or historical contexts? Should we rely on sociology, anthropology, geography, cultural studies, history, psychology or biology? In sum, since we don't seem to agree on what being human means, then how could we agree on a description of what being human does? Again, as I suggested for philosophy, the recent history of the human sciences would seem to attest to a necessarily inconclusive conclusion.

But none of this confusion has stopped academics, and everyone else, talking and writing about ethics. Indeed it seems that the last few years have seen an active surfacing of ethical issues across a wide range of disciplines and, in terms of this volume, in management and organization theory in particular. I want to suggest a few reasons why this might be the case.

The first is the most general justification and has little to do with organization studies in particular. It is my perception that the general 'state of play' in the theoretical areas of the human sciences – that is to say debates around postmodernism, social constructionism, relativism and so on – has explicitly moved ethics to a new centrality. The recent writings of (amongst others, and in diplomatically alphabetical order) Bauman, Derrida, Foucault, Giddens, Habermas, Haraway, Irigaray, Levinas, Lyotard, Said and Sedgwick, together with the political philosophy of Rorty, Taylor and MacIntyre, all broadly support a turn to foregrounding questions of judgement. To put it simply, if there are no foundational grounds for epistemology or ontology then we either stop writing altogether or provide ethical-political reasons why we believe our writing is important. This is not to say that we will therefore discover foundations for ethics either, but simply to say that ethical-political claims of some sort are made – perhaps have to be made – to account for any saying and hence the possible reasons for making that saying. Of course, this should be seen not as a 'solution' to the various crises of the 'post', but rather as a recognition that the relativist point has been made forcefully and, if we still want to carry on doing intellectual work, we should attend carefully to our reasons for justifying it.

Apart from this general background of social theoretical undercurrents there seem to be a few reasons specific to organization studies that make this a key issue at the moment. One is the increasing importance of ethical issues in conventional organization studies and management science: debates around equal opportunities policies; gender, age, disability and ethnicity issues; social cost accounting; politically correct marketing; environmental responsibility; community involvement and sponsorship; business scandals; whistle-blowing; consumer redress; corporate governance; and so on. All these and other issues are being addressed in a huge explosion of material, particularly in the USA, on business ethics and corporate social responsibility. Many of the ideas and problems in these new textbooks, journals, newspaper articles and courses are also informed by a renewed moral emphasis from theorists and theologians of both right and left who have begun a critique of market-based liberal individualism and the enterprise culture in favour of 'back to basics' moral values based on notions of community, responsibility, citizenship and so on. In sum, ethical issues seem increasingly central in much writing about organizations and their social and natural environments.

Adding to this, or perhaps the cause of this, is the cultural or humanist turn in theories of organizations themselves. Many authors – evangelical gurus, TQM advocates, HRM writers – have been proposing for some time that the abstract and dehumanized rules of the bureaucratic organization are simply no longer appropriate. The search is on for ways to energize and capture the commitment of organization members. In an older language, this might be about moving from McGregor's 'theory X' to 'theory Y', or perhaps, more cynically, about replacing the Taylorist stick with the internalized carrot of false consciousness. According to this story, the well-motivated organizational member will have strongly felt values that can cope with the unsettling effects of rapid market change and the varied culture clashes of a global business context. This, of necessity, means that the engineering of beliefs becomes the task of the visionary manager. Moral-ethical principles are hence at the heart of this intervention – the belief in an organizational mission that supposedly replaces mere rule following. I am not necessarily suggesting that this is what is actually happening in organizations, but simply declaring that this new language of beliefs and values is symptomatic in itself. If managers are now being persuaded to act ethically, does this mean they were not previously? Do these ethical principles have any effect on practice and does this have emancipatory possibilities for the humanization of work organizations? More broadly, and perhaps the hardest question of all, are global liberal capitalism and these 'new' ethical business principles even compatible in organizational terms?

The final reason for a concentration on ethics is a simpler problem to pose. What are organization theory and management studies for? Over the last twenty years there has been a huge rise of 'management' and 'business' teaching and research within universities across the globe. Some of the teachers and researchers would like to think that they were providing a critical or liberal education and not merely being, in Baritz's phrase, 'servants of power'. Can this self-image be justified or is management education simply a performative feature of modern societies in which the development of technicist means obscures debate about ethical ends? If management educators are doing something worthwhile, what is it? Are they pursuing worthwhile, ends or merely developing social technologies (what Marxists would call ideologies) to lubricate the wheels of late capitalism?

Taking all these problems and issues together it seemed to me that a book on the ethics of organization theory would be particularly timely as an intervention into many current areas of debate and teaching. This volume hence draws together a wide range of social theoretical standpoints – Marxism, poststructuralism, feminism, institutional theory – together with empirical materials from organizations and attempts to think these issues through across a range of substantive areas – marketing, accounting, human resource management, the natural environment, management education and so on. Whilst there is a common agreement amongst the authors on the paucity and irrelevance of much contemporary business ethics, there are wide divisions about how, to put it rather cryptically, we should describe theorizing and theorize description. In a sense this could be said to come down to a debate between those who wish to foreground empirical contexts – whether local, institutional or historical – and those who prefer the close examination of 'texts' informed by contemporary social theory.

This is by no means a simple binary, but it has structured my organization of the volume as a whole. As a result, the chapters themselves are broadly arranged in three parts. The first part – 'Theories' – contains five chapters which, in various ways, foreground a particular form of thinking. In order, these are on analytic philosophy; Marxism; and feminism; followed by two chapters which deal with poststructuralist thought in rather different ways. The second part – 'Practices' – contains five more chapters on, respectively, human resource management; marketing; accounting; governance; and the environment. Though these chapters are, of course, explorations of theory, they are also examples of how we might take a particular organizational theme and subject it to critical scrutiny from the standpoint of a concern with the ethical. The final part – 'Implications' – contains chapters that take up general issues which follow from a concern with the ethics of organization. Again in order, these are on how the ethics of management practice might be studied; the consequences for management education; and finally whether a concern with ethics is itself an ethical position. I will now briefly summarize the concerns of the chapters, before making some short general remarks about the book.

Chapter 2 is written by Tom Sorell, the only professional philosopher in the book and the co-author of a text on business ethics. His central concern is to question the viability of business ethics in terms of its ability to communicate to business people themselves, but without 'overrationalizing' the ethics of business. In other words, how can business ethics find itself an audience that is prepared for some criticism of its practices, or that is capable of underpinning something like a professional code of conduct for management? Sorell notes how little business ethics has achieved in the world of business, partly because of its US bias but also because of its dominant focus on big organizations – on transnational corporations and not on the small firms which make up the majority of business organizations. The chapter goes on to suggest that, in pragmatic terms, a revised form of stakeholder theory might allow for a business ethics that is not simply 'beyond the fringe'. Sorell's cautious assessment of the future of business ethics is mirrored in his analytic carefulness with grand language, and his disavowal of abstract philosophy in favour of an applied ethics, or a reflexive politics, that can make sense to the actors involved. In a way that prefigures a major divide between the authors in this volume, Sorell is not particularly interested in epistemological or ontological issues, in the problems of objectivity or realism. Instead the issue becomes one of intelligibility, of the possibilities for persuading key actors that there is an issue here in the first place and of making business ethics into a viable project.

The following chapter is concerned with illustrating how Marxism, particularly humanistic Marxism, provides a way to theorize the ethics of capitalist organizations themselves. Edward Wray-Bliss and myself prefer to stress the writings of the early Marx on agency and creativity, and are hence suspicious of the economic determinism, or structuralism, which is associated with Marx's later writings. In suggesting this, however, we are setting ourselves up to 'open' Marx to this kind of reading and would certainly resist any suggestion that a 'true', 'correct' form of Marxism can be gleaned from his writings, or indeed the authoritarian practices of certain subsequent 'Marxists'. We then move through a series of key concepts – labour, alienation, the working class, revolution and socialism – in order to explore our reading of Marxism as, in some sense, an originary project for questioning contemporary capitalist organizations. Marxism can then be seen as an ethical project based on understanding the material and multiple bases of oppression and resistance within modernity. Importantly it is also an utopian vision which might be used to guide action toward desired goals, though for us an utopianism which must always be tempered by self-reflection on our own standpoint as academics and hence 'knowledge producers'. In other words, we suggest a continual questioning of where knowledge comes from, including our own, and whose interests it serves. Though we clearly have differences over the place that humanist language might have in such a project (see my concluding chapter for an illustration of this) this chapter serves to illustrate something about the continuing importance of engaging with Marxist thought if we are to be able to understand, and perhaps change, capitalist organizations.

Joanna Brewis's chapter, 'Who Do You Think You Are?', continues this theme by exploring the strengths and limitations of a feminist critique of contemporary patterns of organization. Brewis's chapter begins by introducing liberal, Marxist and radical feminisms – all of which she characterizes as largely reliant, though in different ways, on a code-based ethics. Like Marxism, there is a sense in which feminism can be articulated as a fundamental ethical project for critiquing organization, but (again like Marxism) it is a project that often relies on essentialism combined with forms of authoritarianism. In other words, it is possible to suggest that feminism might deny an openness to ethical alternatives because it relies heavily on already having defined the guilty and the victims. In order to begin to escape the solidities of a feminist ethical code Brewis suggests that a reading of Foucault's later writings allows us to recognize our inescapable location in discourse – patriarchal discourse for example – yet also encourages a kind of responsibilization of the self. Of course, when Foucault writes about 'the care of the self' he is neither denying discursive constitution nor celebrating individual agency. The point is rather that he is setting thought against essentialisms. Controversially, Joanna Brewis illustrates this through empirical examples which deny a feminist interpretation of women as 'victims' of sexual harassment. Rather than accepting easy finger pointing, she suggests, an ethics can only be approached as a reflexive practice, of gender for example. Such a practice should not be seen as relying on a metaphysics that would allow us to think of 'freedom' or 'constraint' as somehow outside the social context in which they are located. To care for oneself would involve not merely accepting an existing configuration of power, but neither would it be sufficient to imagine that one could heroically overturn one either. The reflexive fashioning of the self that follows might be a less ambitious project than required by many feminists (or indeed Marxists) but it avoids reliance on ethical codes, and prefigures many of the poststructuralist arguments in the two chapters that follow.

Hugh Willmott's chapter is the first of two that engage with poststructuralist arguments. In a sense, it can be argued that contemporary intellectual fashion has moved away from analytic philosophy, Marxism or feminism and towards a range of poststructuralist (or posthumanist, postfoundationalist) positions which are so characteristic of French thought over the last twenty years or so. 'Towards a New Ethics?' rehearses this move in arguing against humanist and foundationalist versions of ethics. Following the influential work of Zygmunt Bauman, Willmott explores the problems with codes of ethics for organizations and the way in which they can be articulated as preventing moral reflection, rather than encouraging it. Distinguishing between prescriptive, normative and analytic forms of ethical argument he suggests that poststructuralism can be seen as a contribution to normative ethics, though in a negative sense. This is done by questioning the basis of a structuralist or humanist ethics, and therefore (like Brewis) by suggesting that the idea of an ethical 'code' is itself the problem. The bulk of the chapter then discusses Ishiguru's novel *Remains of the Day* as a literary case study which illustrates many of the issues that Willmott wishes to engage with. In exploring the complicity of Stevens, the butler, with his employer's fascism, questions of 'professional' rule following, of duty, are counterposed with Max Weber's heroic individualist ethic and Bauman's formulation of the 'moral impulse'. Whilst Willmott clearly does not 'resolve' such a dualism – between structured codes and individual morals – he pushes us into questioning it. Importantly, he also questions why our modern insecurities about ego lead us into needing an/other for our assertions about ethics. A poststructuralist and posthumanist ethics would instead stress our connections with nature, with others, with that which is denied through foregrounding a particular form of ethical life. In that sense, Willmott proposes that a 'compassionate questioning' of dualisms – including that of 'ethical/unethical' – might be the best form of defence against authoritarianism.

Chapter 6, the concluding chapter of the 'Theories' part, again follows broadly poststructural lines. Hugo Letiche's method is more obviously 'textual' than Willmott's – involving as it does a close reading and rewriting of three authors – but his radical suspicion is certainly similar in intent. Letiche begins with a lecture given by Jacques Derrida, a key figure in poststructural thought. Derrida takes as his topic the relation between law and justice, or more precisely, the way in which speaking of justice as a law is itself an injustice. As with the tension between codes and morality discussed in the previous two chapters, this then becomes an issue of the relationship between concepts. The necessary singularity of justice to an/other is counterposed with the generalized collective violence that law – or ethics – must rely on. Letiche then moves on to discuss Zygmunt Bauman's depiction of the immorality of legislating ethics, and his 'solution' to Derrida's dilemma. For Bauman, the only way to rescue any sense of a 'postmodern ethic' in our fragmentary times is through refusing the easy acceptance of ethics as a solvable problem which can generate rules to constrain conduct. This results in an existential suggestion that what he calls the 'moral impulse' is the precondition for any form of being with others. Following the writings of Levinas, Bauman argues that recognizing, perhaps cherishing, this fundamental relation can provide for the possibility of a more genuine 'age of ethics' than the modern absolutism of certainty that preceded it. Throughout this exposition, Letiche shows how Bauman's position is based on deep assumptions about what it means to be 'really' human which are themselves not subjected to the kind of radical doubt that Bauman wishes to claim inheritance of, and that Derrida's writing exemplifies. Letiche therefore moves to introducing the work of another French philosopher, Gilles Lipovetsky, as a description of postmodern society which does not assume some existential substrate to all 'really human' action. Like Bauman, Lipovetsky describes postmodernity as the saturating experience of consumerism and radical individualism, but (unlike Bauman) he does not assume there is anything else than our shared experience of these forms. If there is an optimism in Lipovetsky's writing, it is the possibility of a 'third type of organizing' – one based, rather like Brewis's reading of Foucault, on a radical hedonism of the self. Not of course, Letiche concludes, that this resolves Derrida's paradox – how can we know justice? But then perhaps 'knowing justice' means always continuing to worry about such a question.

The following five chapters each take organizational functions or issues and debate the possibility of their ethics. Again, to reiterate my earlier point, this does not mean they are somehow atheoretical, but that they attempt to engage with an 'ethics of' something, rather than demonstrating an 'ethics with' (or 'ethics through') a particular conceptual framework – as the previous five chapters do. Karen Legge's chapter on human resource management sets itself up to adjudicate whether contemporary HRM practice is ethical according to four ethical frameworks – Kantianism, virtue theory, utilitarianism and contractarianism. Because of her engagement with 'classical' ethics, it might also be a helpful chapter for those readers who are uncertain about the different logics of these ways of thinking. Her answer is in two parts. First, it depends what you think HRM is – whether it is a new 'soft' humanist practice or a 'hard' form of relabelled management control. Secondly, it depends on how you interpret the different frameworks since it is by no means obvious that following a particular ethical code provides rules of evidence that would allow you to come to a self-evident conclusion. However, Legge's strategy of using a combination of empirical evidence and analytic philosophy, broadly suggests that utilitarianism comes out best. But again, this does depend on which version of utilitarianism you prefer. Yet Legge recognizes that the power of such an adjudication, of which ethics and which HRM, is that it exposes the impossibility of answering questions framed in such a manner. As I suggest in my concluding chapter, utilitarianism is in a sense the logic of organization, and the dominant theme in Legge's chapter is that the problem is not simply HRM, but contemporary capitalism itself. Whether there are alternatives to contemporary capitalism might take us back into Marxism again, but it (at least) encourages a re-evaluation of the boundary between 'ethics' and 'politics' where business is concerned.

In Chapter 8, John Desmond uses historical evidence and contemporary theory to look at the moral neutrality which is achieved by marketing. Again engaging with Bauman, Desmond uses the term 'adiaphorization' – a term which refers to the process of making something value-neutral. It can be argued that marketing is a dominant technology in contemporary society and organization, and one that has often justified itself on the basis of a story of liberating consumers from constraints, yet it achieves its effects through distancing, objectification, effacement, disassembly and so on. In other words, marketing itself stands as an example of the practical separation of face-to-face responsibility from the effects of the division of labour. Hence, despite its ostensible focus on liberal individualism and free markets, as a technology it effaces the face of the consumer. Just as Weber and Bauman described how bureaucratic forms of organization, characteristic of modernity itself, enable means to efface ends, so Desmond illustrates how marketing allows ethics to always be somebody else's problem. Indeed, despite the recent turn to social and relationship marketing, the practicalities of professional moral distancing still continue unhindered. The story of green marketing, or as it was cynically labelled by some, 'greenwash', neatly illustrates how a simulation of concern can itself be used to further spread market relations into new social spaces. How then can marketing be escaped? Since it seems that our very senses of moral community are often being shaped by marketing technologies, it is increasingly difficult to imagine a space 'outside' within which we could claim that justice and responsibility were genuine. Hence, Desmond concludes, the prognosis for an 'authentic' ethics does not look very promising – but then perhaps it never was.

'Ethics and Accounting', by Rolland Munro, continues the theme of investigating the 'effects' of using particular organizational technologies. Like Desmond, Munro is concerned to explore the general conditions of possibility that make (in this case) accounting a viable way of re-presenting organization. However, unlike Desmond, he wishes to suggest that we should consider ethics as a form of social technology too. Generalizing the metaphor of accounting, that is to say, providing an account of something, suggests that post-Kantian conceptions of ethics have been concerned with accounting for the self to the self. Yet this is clearly an odd kind of accountability since there is no external visibility here, simply a reflexive process of setting the self up to judge the self. In a way then, it might initially be possible to suggest that accounting is more 'neutral' than ethics, that it somehow allows for unbiased representations of truths about the world that can then provide clear guidance for organizational actors to strategize. But, of course, given the complicity of accounting in clearly political decisions – coal pit closures for example – and the rise of a 'social cost' accounting which is, in some way, supposed to clarify the stakeholders involved in specifying costs and benefits, it is increasingly difficult to accept that accounting is no more than a refined scientific method with numbers. In any case, as Bauman's arguments about the Holocaust and ethical distance amply illustrate, neutrality seems to effectively add up to the denial of responsibility which is itself a problematic position. Yet Munro does not leave it here, but goes on to explore the sense in which it is the very separation between people and technologies, between people and accounting, or between people and ethics, which is the problem here. The idea that any 'real', 'authentic' humanity could somehow be distilled 'before' technology is convenient, but flawed. The technologies themselves provide the very evidence that allows the self to be both constituted and interrogated. So the question then becomes reframed as how technologies make the self, and how any and all forms of technology rely on a process of 'obviation' (a term similar to adiaphorization) which makes some matters relevant, and others recede into insignificance. For Munro, a poststructuralist radical suspicion must include being suspicious of the technologies of fashioning the self, and hence questioning the will to be drawn to account, to oneself or others.

Chapter 10, on governance, begins as a challenge to both the abstractions of business ethics and those of poststructuralists. Glenn Morgan sets himself against what he sees as abstract philosophizing – perhaps like that exemplified in the previous chapter – and instead sponsors concrete analyses of how things like 'markets', 'exchange', 'ownership' and so on are produced in real social contexts. In that sense he wishes to radicalize contemporary institutional theory in order to produce empirical descriptions which are comparative in their intent. The epistemological basis of such an approach is social constructionist since the assumption is that there is no foundational basis for understanding the logic of the structures of governance and regulation within contemporary organization. This allows him to demonstrate that there are always alternatives, that things could always be otherwise because they often have been, that 'rules' are not timeless but matters of negotiation. This is then an ethics of denying the inevitability of the one best way of market capitalism, through practising a 'descriptive ethics' of comparison. The chapter moves through four domains of the institutionalization of rules – property rights, governance structures, conceptions of control, and rules of exchange – in order to demonstrate that there is a wide variety of ways of formulating such matters. Morgan concludes from this that it is always a dangerous generalization, both empirically and politically, to assume that there are any inevitable tendencies within modernity such as those that Bauman claims to identify. In practice, modern organization exemplifies an interplay between local and distant controls, between the local negotiation of face-to-face morality, and the institutionalization of abstract rules. For ethics then, as for practice, there can never be a formulation that is independent of these interplays. Yet, as Morgan honestly admits, his version of institutionalism is driven by the desire to sponsor and strengthen more communitarian, or mutualistic, ways of fashioning markets, properties and so on. Interestingly, through an argument which is largely hostile to abstraction, Morgan ends up by folding the ethical into the social in the same way that many of the other authors in this volume do. Though for different reasons, the key problem again becomes the claim to a separation between abstract ethics and everyday conduct.

The final chapter in this part underlines the problems with this claim even more forcefully, and also neatly illustrates how conceptions of the natural environment – the ultimate non-human limit – are inseparable from matters of their social construction. Stephen Fineman's 'The Natural Environment, Organization and Ethics' begins by further exploring Tom Sorell's 'alienation problem'. In order to 'capture' the environment for management purposes both romantic and scientistic versions of the green problem need to be translated into a language of 'means'. Yet, since the green problem is itself socially constructed through other interest groups who are often developing a generalized critique of consumer capitalism, it is difficult to see how an expansion of stakeholders to include rivers, trees and the planet can possibly impact on management action in anything other than a trivial manner. Yet again, the effects of 'adiaphorization', or 'obviation', that are defining of formal organization seem to disqualify the possibility of environmental ethics ever being more than merely a marketing or accounting problem. As Fineman neatly shows, using empirical materials, the green agenda is effectively too abstract and general to be of concern to practising managers, apart from as an agenda item that can be neatly packaged and dealt with. The tendency is hence for an understanding of the problem of 'greening' to become reframed as another way of doing 'business as usual'. Management rationality, the demands of satisfying stakeholders, the very structure of decision-making and responsibility in meetings all conspire to ensure that radical moralizing about the environment is unlikely to have a great deal of effect. As with all the other chapters in this part, Fineman refuses to assume that there are any easy solutions, or indeed that an environmental ethics could be considered independent of social contexts. Yet he refuses to conclude with quietism, suggesting that a continual questioning of ends, though perhaps not always under the alienating rubric of business ethics or global salvation, may itself help to change the context within which managerial decision-making takes place. In a sense, like Morgan, this would involve education about different modes of regulation, not an all or nothing project of pitting a heroic ethics of saving the world against an uncaring management and organization.

The final part – 'Implications' – contains three chapters which explore the general consequences of engaging with the ethics and organization problematic. The first, by Tony Watson, is an exemplary illustration of how a descriptive ethics of management might operate in practice. It is, in that sense, an exploration of the implications for management research that follow from understanding management and organization as already ethical through and through. Following a broadly ethnographic methodology, Watson illustrates how management and managers can be seen as always and already members of moral communities. In a Durkheimian sense, this is a matter not of inserting ethics into the social, but rather of recognizing that values, arguments, attitudes and opinions are the stuff out of which organizations are already made. Hence the abstractions of analytic philosophy, or the neatness of the case study, are replaced with everyday conversational materials within which managers engage with the practicalities of moral dilemmas. Watson's material is therefore shaped primarily by a framing already given by his respondents – as his subtitle anticipates. Importantly, this is a framing which echoes many of the problems dicussed in this volume: the tempting certainties of the language of the bottom line; the permanent problem of accounting for a moral self; and the means–ends dilemma of Bauman's bureaucratically engineered Holocaust. What Watson's chapter illustrates most clearly, however, is his sympathy with management and his refusal to engage in the abstract condemnations of a prescriptive ethics. Rather than echoing a vision of the general effacing of morality, this is instead an attempt to speak with the voices of managers, and then perhaps to hope that both 'they' and 'us' might then use that material for our own further reflections.

Chapter 13, by Peter Anthony, also engages with implications – in this case those for the practice of management education. Again like Watson's, his chapter is positioned as a counter-argument to some of the more philosophical or critical-theoretical formulations, including those in this volume. Expressing a broad affinity with a materialist Marxist standpoint on exchange and a Durkheimian emphasis on the embeddedness of morality, he sets himself up against postmodern abstracted 'idealism' and prescriptive critical management. Both, though arguably for different reasons, end up being irrelevant, unreal and elitist by ignoring the everyday material basis of patterns of exchange and the practical moralities of management. Instead, he suggests we should base a descriptive study, not a prescriptive sermon, on what managers actually do. Drawing on Hume's problematizing of the relationship between 'is' and 'ought' allows Anthony to suggest that, though a move to 'ought' is not disqualified out of hand, it is one that should (note the underlying imperative here) be made carefully and only after much reflection. In part this is also an acknowledgement that the concrete basis of production and exchange will not be changed by mere management education, however strident, but the reflexiveness of managers might. So, like Watson and Fineman, Anthony suggests that a careful, and sympathetic rather than scornful, study of the morality of everyday practices might allow both academic and student to learn through reflection. Whether we like it or not, managers are key figures in modernity, and educating this 'barbarian elite' should be undertaken with the same care and attention that we would expect other forms of moral education to exemplify.

My concluding chapter is concerned with exploring the 'set-up' that has produced the project of business ethics, and this book itself. I also use this opportunity to try to synthesize some of the arguments made by the various authors in this volume. When I began telling people that I was working on business ethics, they often responded by suggesting that this was merely a way of taking a moral high ground, of being disdainful of the unethical behaviours of others. Rather like being a vegetarian, the assumption is sometimes that this practice is itself an implicit criticism of carnivores. So, one of the agendas behind this concluding chapter is to discover in what sense attending to ethics is itself ethical. I begin by suggesting that the tension between moral philosophy and pragmatic managerialism is a trap which is impossible to resolve within its own parameters. Business ethics is, in that sense, a contradiction in terms because, as most of the other chapters attest, it embraces a division between ethical rules and the moral life which is so deeply problematic. I then try to suggest that this 'trap' is mirrored in sociological diagnoses of modernity itself and briefly illustrate this with reference to formulations of nostalgia and modernization in the works of Marx, Durkheim and Weber. However, rather than simply staying within this tense dualism, I then go on to propose that it might be possible to redescribe the problem in terms of modern and postmodern epistemologies. Being radically sceptical about the problem of knowledge might suggest that the search for 'ethics' is itself a flawed one, and I try to show just how flawed by interrogating the concepts of 'decision' and 'judgement' until they collapse under their own logic. Along with Willmott, Munro and Letiche I conclude by suggesting, paradoxically, that being 'against ethics' is perhaps itself the only position that might allow us to believe in the possibility of justice.

Broadly however, it seems to me that being 'against' ethics – as an imposed code – is what all the contributions to this volume offer. Whether this is because of the practical or epistemological problems with ethics, the general conclusion seems to be that we should try to be deeply suspicious about the project of business ethics itself, though of course not necessarily therefore embrace nihilism. The critical engagement with Zygmunt Bauman's exemplary work that runs through so many of the chapters seems to indicate a convergence on this kind of scepticism – though there is also a deep divide over how it should be expressed, and perhaps how radical it should be. In a way this becomes a question of what we are prepared to take as foundational: institutional differences, patterns of exchange, the practical realization of management, the structure of organizing; or, more minimally, some kind of 'moral impulse' as a precondition of being human; or, perhaps most minimally of all, the indeterminate flows of language. The 'problem' of ethics presents itself differently depending on what we accept that we can know, and hence what status these 'knowings' might have in our arguments. Finally, I want to point to the curious status that this volume has: neither business ethics, management science, sociology, anthropology nor philosophy. It occupies an unusual terrain, and I think hence has a strange strength and flavour. But, if we are all sceptics now, then for readers and writers to be sceptical about notions of academic discipline (think of the restraining connotations of this word) is a powerful way to generate knowledge and knowing in more creative ways. So, in that spirit, I hope you find the book useful for your own knowings.

Part 1: THEORIES

2 Beyond the Fringe? The Strange State of Business Ethics

Tom Sorell

Business ethics continues to have a marginal status in both the theory and the practice of commercial organizations at the end of the 1990s. As an approach to management or selling it has been adopted by relatively few companies, and even among firms which proclaim an interest in such a thing, there are minimalist interpretations of corporate responsibility. In many parts of the world – Eastern Europe and much of Africa and Latin America – business ethics in the form in which it is sometimes practised in America, Britain, Holland and Germany is entirely alien. Elsewhere – Japan, for example – communitarian practices associated with business ethics in the West are much harder to disentangle from mainstream business. In short, self-consciously ethical business is far from being business as usual. And just as it is untypical or marginal as a form of commercial activity, so business ethics is a fringe discipline in business schools (Freeman, 1991: Chapters 1–5). When it has a course to itself, it is frequently an elective rather than part of the compulsory curriculum, and in the USA, where it is longest established, it often rides on the coat-tails of mainstream subjects, such as strategic management or organization theory. Even in applied ethics, which is itself an outlying branch of moral philosophy, business ethics is peripheral. Legal and medical ethical questions are much more widely discussed by philosophers and political theorists than questions concerning (for example) profit-making and employment, and legal and medical ethics have a bigger audience not only amongst academics but also the general public.

Will the future be like the present and recent past, or is business ethics about to come into its own? An argument that it *should* move into the mainstream is easier to construct than an argument that it will do so. I shall concentrate on the prospects of business ethics as an academic discipline, and will not address what is probably the more interesting question of whether it is likely to become, or ought to become, more dominant in the practice of business. I shall argue that business ethics as an academic discipline need not be the unrealistic or utopian subject its critics sometimes claim it is, even when it draws on the resources of moral philosophy. It can be both realistic and morally critical, as a certain recent literature demonstrates. But even in its best current forms, it suffers from a cultural narrowness and from a fixation on big business.

Utopianism and the rhetorical task of business ethics

Is there any reason to think that, in the academic world, a tide, or at least a current, is running in the direction of business ethics? Signs of interest in applying critical theory to business may be relevant here (cf. Alvesson and Willmott, 1990). Critical theory, the approach to political thought associated with the Frankfurt school, has lately been taken up by a number of management academics who are impressed with its goal of arriving at emancipatory understanding. This sort of understanding is believed to be helpful when so much management theory and practice treat lower-level employees as simple vehicles for the execution of plans and strategies worked out at the top. It is also appropriate when career paths that lead to the top are not accessible to everyone with the same qualifications. Perhaps it can also throw light on the relation of business to the promotion of ever greater consumption. Critical theory is not alone in prompting ethical questions when applied to business. Feminist theory and ecology do the same (see Brewis, Chapter 4, and Fineman, Chapter 11 in this volume). Still, devotees of critical management studies are conscious of themselves as a minority (1990: 1–21), and so if their preoccupations give evidence of a new interest in business ethics in management theory, it is interest from the fringes of management theory. As for feminism and ecology, although they raise ethical questions about business, their formulations of the issues are alien to much academic business ethics. The fact is that academic business ethics is still largely the preserve of Anglo-American philosophers, whose methods of argument and general outlook can be as much at odds with those of feminist and ecological theory as mainstream management theory itself is. Even critical theory, in at least some of its versions, decries pretensions to objectivity in ways that many Anglo-American philosophers regard as self-refuting, question-begging, hopelessly obscure, or all three.

I will eventually suggest that despite the different atmospheres inhabited by critical management theory, feminism, and ecology on the one hand and most academic business ethics on the other, a *rapprochement* between them is not impossible, and traces of one may already be discernible. But I want to start with differences. The difference over objectivism (to which many chapters in this volume are hostile) is not, in my view, the most important of these. It is better to begin with the fact that, in contrast with at least some versions of critical theory, many academic business ethicists entirely set aside the question of whether capitalism as a form of economic organization is morally defensible (see Wray-Bliss and Parker, Chapter 3 in this volume). They assume that ethics and capitalistic business are in principle compatible, and even that some real businesses and business practices are examples of ethical business and ethical management. This sets the stage for a certain rhetorical task: namely that of showing why these examples are worth following in mainstream business, where the reasons have to be persuasive to business people and business school students with assumptions close to those of mainstream business. The reasons can be drawn from the conventional morality that people in business think they act upon outside the office, and often inside the office as well, and which business people agree they have to *justify* departing from when, as it seems to them, the demands of business make them do so.

Now the rhetorical task of academic business ethics just described is not its only task. There is also the more theoretical one of specifying systematically the meta-ethics and normative ethics appropriate to, for example, human resource management; marketing and advertising; competition; and financial reporting. The most general questions that arise in this connection include those to do with whether businesses or business people are the agents on whom ethical responsibilities fall; whether the ethical responsibilities of businesses can conflict; whether responsibilities vary according to local standards of business and ethics in different parts of the world; and whether carrying out these responsibilities requires a motivation consistent with or at odds with self-interest. These are important questions, and they connect the theory of business ethics to normative ethical theory and meta-ethics in general as well as to other areas of applied ethics. There is a special reason, however, why tackling these questions can be thought secondary to the rhetorical task of reaching more business people. The reason is that relations between academic ethicists and practitioners is much more uneasy in the case of business than in such areas as medicine, legal advocacy, police work or public administration. Not only means but also ends in business can seem morally problematic to ethicists, whereas there seems to be wide agreement that many of the purposes of lawyering, doctoring, administration, even political office-holding are morally valuable.[1] Mainstream business goals can look dubious to ethicists; and where they do not, they can look less weighty than moral goals even when what is in the balance is the survival of a business. As for the pronouncements of the ethicists, these can seem self-righteous or utopian to business people and to mainstream management academics.

Let us call what I am describing 'the problem of the alienation of ethicists from practitioners' or the *alienation problem* for short. Unless it is solved the goal of affecting practice is in danger of being compromised as it hardly ever is elsewhere in applied ethics. While a wholly ineffectual business ethics is not self-contradictory, and while there is still an intellectual point to systematizing the normative ethical justification for certain business practices and the meta-ethical questions already listed, the ethical point of doing so when no business people are listening is perhaps a little obscure. Yet the alienation problem is not easy to overcome. Worse, those who would solve it have to avoid the corresponding problem of overrationalizing business practice.

There are business ethicists who, perhaps for the sake of gaining credibility with the business community, are overzealous in arguing for the primacy of the obligation of maximizing shareholder return (Sternberg, 1994; Vallance, 1995). Call this the *overrationalization problem*. In order to overcome the alienation problem without succumbing to the overrationalization problem, business ethics has to tailor its standards not to business as usual, but to businesses that manage to be both morally out of the ordinary and profitable at the same time. This is the form of the rhetorical task that I have been suggesting is central to any business ethics that wishes to affect the practice it deals with.

Rhetoric without moral philosophy?

To get clearer on what the rhetorical task might involve, we need to look more closely at the ingredients of the alienation and overrationalization problems. A good guide to the alienation problem exists in a recent article by Andrew Stark (1993). 'Far too many business ethicists,' Stark says,

> have occupied a rarefied moral high ground, removed from the real concerns of and real-world problems of the vast majority of managers. They have been too preoccupied with absolutist notions of what it means for managers to be ethical, with overly general criticisms of capitalism as an economic system, with dense and abstract theorizing, and with prescriptions that apply only remotely to managerial practice. Such trends are all the more disappointing in contrast to the success that ethicists in other professions – medicine, law, and government – have had in providing real and welcome assistance to their practitioners. (1993: 38)

Stark backs up this claim with many effective quotations from the recent literature of business ethics. He traces the problem he is describing to a number of different factors, not the least of which is the dominance of American academic business ethics by moral philosophers. According to Stark, the moral philosophers have tended to emphasize the wrong question – 'Why should business be ethical?' – and have ignored or dissented unreasonably from the perfectly good answer that business people were giving to this question long before the moral philosophers came on the scene. Namely, that it *pays* business to be ethical, or that it is in the enlightened self-interest of business to be ethical. Not all business ethicists, not even all moral philosophers among the business ethicists, are tarred with the brush that Stark applies to the purists. He has praise for writers like Robert Solomon (cf. Solomon, 1992) who connect business with some traditional and not so traditional moral virtues. The traditional virtues – courage, wisdom, justice, self-control – are considered alongside 'toughness'. But Stark wishes that philosophers would turn from the question of the motivation of ethical practice to the principles that should guide it in the face of competing considerations, like the need to get more business, the need to pay off debt, and the need to pay dividends.

In an earlier article (Sorell, 1996) I expressed some sympathy for Stark's view, agreeing that some business ethics is too far removed from business to be any good. I went further, suggesting that there is a whole genre of applied ethics – 'armchair applied ethics' – that extends in an objectionable way the method of arguing *a priori* and by abstract counter-example that is justifiable in most of the rest of philosophy. In applied ethics there is an obvious value to leg-work – leaving one's armchair and finding out about the actual practice of business, medicine and law, including the questions that seem natural to practitioners, or urgent to them at different times. The value of the leg-work is that it increases the chances of a piece of applied ethics appearing relevant to practitioners, who are part of the natural audience of applied ethics. Resorting to leg-work, however, is not the same thing as going native, and there is no reason why applied ethicists should desert the role of moral critic when they get closer to the practices and practitioners they write about, substituting the norms of business people for their own wherever there is a discrepancy. There is no reason, in other words, why the principles proposed by business ethicists who are knowledgeable about business practice should not conflict with, and imply the need for the reform of, that very business practice. The reason why this last claim does not necessarily reintroduce utopianism is the very straightforward one that many business people are themselves self-critical and see that some standard business practices are, if not in fact dubious themselves, then like dubious practices. One reason why they are prepared to say that their business practices are *prima facie* dubious is that they can involve departures from practices they would find normal in personal morality. This is a very important piece of common ground between academic business ethics and business, and in my view one of the reasons why the rhetorical task of business ethics is practicable at all. The existence of such common ground also helps to explain why the problem of over-rationalizing business practice is avoidable: because business people do not themselves think that everything they do is all right. To meet them on their own ground it is not necessary to deny that all practices that seem questionable to outsiders *are* in fact questionable. What is required is some understanding of and respect for the reasons that make some of these practices seem legitimate or unavoidable.

Stark gestures at what he thinks is another piece of common ground in repeated references throughout his article to the parallels between, on the one hand, a profession of business or management and, on the other hand, other professions, such as government, law and medicine, which in Stark's view are not alienated or are less alienated from the corresponding branches of professional ethics. For example, enlarging on the impracticality of business ethics, Stark says that it

> is concerned with prescriptions that, however morally respectable, run so contrary to existing managerial roles and responsibilities that they become untenable. As a result, such work in business ethics hasn't 'taken' in the world of practice, especially when compared with the work of ethicists in other professions such as government, medicine or law. (1993: 43)

He goes on to call attention to some parallels between legal and business ethics: both generate moral demands that put particular strain on the relevant professionals in ways that, say, ethics for governments does not. The strategy of modelling business ethics on some more congenial branch of professional ethics strikes me as doubly ill-conceived. First, it is not at all clear that business is a 'profession' at all, let alone a profession in the sense that law and medicine are. Secondly, to ask for the same treatment for business as government gets from ethics sounds like a plea for permissiveness, and one of the things at issue when he claims that there is something wrong with business ethics is whether business ethics is or is not permissive enough. The fact, if it is one, that professional ethics lets politicians off the hook more readily than business people may not be a reason for agreeing that business ethics ought to be like ethics for politicians, or that political ethics should let *anyone* off the hook.

Further, the claim that business is one more profession like law or medicine is disputable in a number of ways. First, the status of law or medicine as a profession is based on, among other things, the existence of an agreed body of specialized medical and legal knowledge, which has been part of the university curriculum from before the Renaissance. To enter the profession it is usually necessary but not sufficient to have a university qualification. It is usually also necessary to pass examinations set and marked by current members of the profession. To be a member of the profession is usually to be on a publicly available list of practitioners recognized by the profession, from which one can have one's name taken off and so be excluded from the profession. Not all of the traditional professions – for example, architecture or engineering – follow the pattern of law and medicine in every particular, but they conform more closely than the would-be profession of business. Partly this is because business is so varied an activity. One can be in business shining shoes or in business manufacturing sixty different types of automobile. One can be in business with very little, sometimes no, education, and certainly without business school training. Indeed this is how most business has always been carried out. Even big business, which arguably demands more specialized knowledge than at any rate some small business, is open to the self-taught. There is no real analogue of being struck off a professional list, indeed no list in the first place except perhaps the Yellow Pages. Not even bankruptcy excludes one from business for long in most countries, and there is a vast amount of business conducted entirely clandestinely and out of the reach of law in black and grey markets. Only the finicky would deny the status of business to the building firm in the grey economy with two sets of books and more transactions in cash than through the banking system. The people who run the firm are certainly business people. But are they professionals? Not in the sense spelt out above, even though they may have specialized knowledge and have direct dealings with customers.

Again, many professions are in principle able to be practised solo. This means that in principle one practises in person and deals directly with clients, who know one personally, not just the firm one works for. One can be directly liable for negligence or error. One reason why the micro-level of legal and medical ethics – the level of one-to-one client dealings – is open to codification, and requires codification, is that it is to do with one-to-one relationships. These are professional relationships often carried out personally, and so test the limit between professional and personal which is at the heart of much professional ethics. They are often carried on with people who are ill or in trouble and therefore possibly vulnerable and dependent, and they standardly require trust and confidentiality, even some kinds of intimate contact. All of this is background for moral risk as well as moral responsibility. In business it is also possible for professional relationships to be personal, and to involve trust. Standardly, however, being vulnerable or in trouble is not quite the factor in being a customer that it is in being a lawyer's or doctor's client. Not that they can never be standard factors: after all, they may be in the funeral business. But an ethics for business in general would not have to cater for them in quite the same way as a code for lawyers and doctors, and a would-be ethics for business in general is what is under discussion.

The differences go on. Doctors and lawyers are often reimbursed according to a scale of rates fixed by fellow practitioners. There is no standard 'business person's' fee, still less one that is fixed by a body of business people. Doctors and lawyers practise in institutions – hospitals and law courts – that have a public identity of their own and can be run by the state rather than privately. Businesses are not public institutions, even when they are state-owned.

Moral sensibility and insensibility in business

So the idea of business as a profession seems an unpromising, even a pretentious, beginning for a business ethics that aims to overcome the alienation problem. A better place to start is with a sense of the moral problems derived from business itself. This sense may be acquired by talking to business people or joining their ranks, but it is also available in print. One such public source, perhaps a little notorious in American business ethics, is an article dating back to 1968. This is Albert Z. Carr's 'Is Business Bluffing Ethical?', a piece belonging to the dawn or early history of academic business ethics, or perhaps even its pre-history, since its author was not an academic. The foreword to the article says that

> Mr Carr became interested in this subject when he was a member of a New York firm of consultants to large corporations in many fields. The confidences of many stress-ridden executives made him aware of the extent to which tensions can arise from conflicts between a firm's ethical sense and the realities of business. He was struck also by the similarity of the special ethical attitude shown by many successful and stress-free businesspersons in their work to that of good poker players. (Carr, 1992: 1)

Carr argues that certain forms of deception in business are just as permissible as bluffing is within a card game. It is all right to bluff in poker, although it is not all right to do other things. Some of the other things are simply against the rules, such as playing with cards up one's sleeve or in secret partnership with another player. Others are ethically wrong, as when one gets one's opponent drunk or distracts him with loud talk when it's his turn to bet. Although these things are wrong, bluffing is permissible. In the same way, it is permissible in business to sell a product that one knows one could make to last longer, or to exert certain kinds of influence on politicians who can introduce legislation advantageous to one's business (1992: 2). It is permissible to do these things, but wrong to do other things, such as fix prices or spread malicious rumours about one's competitors. One reason why the things indicated are permissible, according to Carr, is that they are in keeping with people's expectations. Everyone who plays poker is prepared for bluffing, and the practices of lobbying legislatures and designing products not to last forever are to be expected in business as well.

Carr realizes that deception is not permissible in every context, even though everyone with even a little experience knows that other people lie. But then he thinks that not all kinds of human relations are the same, morally speaking. Thus he insists on 'a sharp distinction between the ethical systems of the home and the office' (1992: 7). The action of a business person that looks tawdry or compromising from the standpoint of private morality can be seen as a matter of 'game strategy' when viewed from a position within business itself. Or so Carr claims. What gives this sort of a position its use as a starting point for the rhetorical task of business ethics is that it was put forward by Carr himself with some sense of its appearing controversial, even to other business people. The article did in fact generate a large and mostly hostile correspondence from readers of *Harvard Business Review*, which is evidence that Carr was drawing the line between permissible and impermissible behaviour in a way that could be challenged by those inside as well as those outside business.

A natural point of entry is Carr's assumption that private morality and business morality belong to separate areas of activity that work by distinct rules. There are a number of straightforward ways of questioning this that are open to elaboration by a usable yet critical academic business ethics. First, how can the spheres be separate if the business person is the same person who has a family life and who engages in business activity? Secondly, and more important, both spheres are known to matter enormously to the people who occupy them – so much so that there is often serious competition from each sphere for the same person's time. Connected with the time spent in both spheres is what one might call the investments of one's self in each sphere – the extent to which one identifies oneself with one's job or one's home life. If one's identification with both one's job and one's home life is significant, then it is plausible to hold that following rules in one sphere that one cannot follow in the other is not just a psychological problem but a moral one, since one cannot occupy both spheres with integrity, and integrity may be part of living life honestly or flourishingly – where both honesty and flourishing have moral content. The fact that it may be possible for business people to keep the two spheres separate in the sense that activity in one is kept out of sight of the other sphere does not mean that they *are* separate or that one sphere does not have consequences with moral significance for the other. A person may manage to lead two quite separate lives – say by conducting a love affair, or through an occupation that requires very sustained play-acting – and yet still be morally responsible for betrayal in the one role and deception in the other. And this may be true though, for example, people enter marriage nowadays knowing that affairs are quite common, and though the play-acting part of one's life is forever led without the knowledge of people in the other part of one's life. Finally, the fact that a certain activity comes to be expected does not necessarily alter its moral character. Someone who is known to be a congenital liar does not cease to lie just because no-one believes him; and the fact that stealing is epidemic in a certain neighbourhood of town does not mean that when you enter that neighbourhood the normal prohibition on stealing lapses and you can take what you like.

Not only virtue theory but also utilitarianism can develop these points in ways that do not begin to impugn business activity *per se* (for similar arguments see Legge, Chapter 7 in this volume). Virtue theory represents certain difficult-to-acquire but cultivatable characteristics, such as courage, justice and self-control, as good to acquire because of the way they contribute to something else that is uncontroversially good: namely a flourishing human life. The person who approaches business activity as if it were a game like poker might experience strains on integrity, and these strains might be thought to interfere with flourishing. This line of thought is compatible with thinking that both business and its material rewards are part of the flourishing life. Utilitarianism represents as morally obligatory whatever practicable policy or action mostly increases the welfare of sentient beings. Welfare is understood as satisfied rational preference. The theory lends itself to arguments that say that the split life of the Carr-approved businessman is psychologically harmful if generalized and therefore better avoided on moral grounds. On the other hand, utilitarianism also lends itself to saying that if the Carr-type business person is able to compartmentalize his different spheres of activity to such an extent that he is never troubled about one from the standpoint of the other, there may be utility in cultivating the ability to keep the spheres separate. Either way it can say that business activity, even capitalism, is indispensable for maximizing human well-being.

A virtue theory or utilitarianism that is able to say some of the things just indicated is not a fawning or supine moral theory, unable to criticize business practice just because it has a good word *at all* to say about business. On the contrary, both utilitarianism and virtue theory are easily able to avoid both the alienation problem *and* the overrationalization problem. This is not to say that utilitarianism is incapable of generating a moral conclusion that will strike mainstream business as outrageous. For example, it could easily be adapted to showing that the sum total of welfare is most effectively increased by radical reforms of our treatment of animals, which might raise the costs of farming and the prices of agricultural products far above what is currently regarded as reasonable in the food production and retailing industries. The point is that utilitarianism does not necessarily have an anti-business thrust, even though as a formal moral theory it is a philosopher's invention. The same is true of virtue theory. Whether or not the same is true of every standard moral theory that philosophers recognize is less clear. Although it has its defenders as a vehicle for business ethics in the real world,[2] Kantianism, with its tradition of requiring motivation untainted by self-interest, may or may not be the exception that proves Stark's conclusion about the moral myopia and irrelevance of moral philosophy in relation to business (on Kant see Munro, Chapter 9 in this volume). But even if he is right about Kantianism, Stark is wrong about moral philosophy in general. Moral philosophy is no more incapable of articulating a real-world business ethics than it is of articulating the at first sight much more difficult justification for mass killing in war. The unworldliness of moral philosophy, in short, has been much exaggerated by critics like Stark.

Near-realistic business ethics

So far I have been pointing out the compatibility of very standard moral theories in philosophy with moral controversies among business people themselves. I now turn to a piece of mainstream business ethics and indicate how it avoids the twin pitfalls of alienation and overrationalization in a different but, once again, perfectly acceptable way. The standard piece of business ethics I have in mind is stakeholder theory, the approach to business ethics that has grown out of contesting the Friedmanite maxim that business ethics begins and ends with the responsibilities of managers to owners of a business, including stockholders (Friedman, 1997). Stakeholders are people at whose expense or for whose benefit a business may be run. Or, what I take to amount to the same thing, they are people whose welfare is importantly affected by the management of a business. Such people may be managers, employees, customers, suppliers, creditors, residents in the vicinity of the relevant firm's premises as well as stockholders (if the company is public) or outright owners. Less standardly included among stakeholders are a firm's competitors, one or more governments, even non-persons like local plants or landscapes affected by the firm's activities.

Perhaps the most sophisticated recent version of the theory is due to R. Edward Freeman (1997). Freeman is out to sketch a theory that challenges 'the basic idea of managerial capitalism': namely, that 'in return for controlling the firm, management vigorously pursues the interests of stockholders'. In this formulation 'vigorously' is a euphemism for 'single-mindedly' or 'ruthlessly'. Stakeholder theory conflicts with the thinking behind managerial capitalism because it identifies interests – those of stakeholders other than stockholders – that constrain the pursuit of stockholder interests. It also challenges the managerial capitalist definition of the purpose of the firm which, as Freeman understands it, is to maximize stockholder welfare as the best means of promoting the general welfare or as the best means of promoting property rights. His preferred version of stakeholder theory is more pluralistic not just about whose welfare is to be promoted but also about the grounds for welfare promotion. Freeman envisages a cluster of stakeholder theories with different and in principle compatible grounds for core precepts about how a company should be governed and what managers should do. Thus there might be a 'fair contracts' stakeholder theory, a 'feminist standpoint' stakeholder theory or an 'ecological' stakeholder theory, among others (1997: 73). The feminist standpoint stakeholder theory would, for example, outline a model of corporate governance faithful to the importance of 'caring and connection', while the ecological theory would do the same, in keeping with some general requirement of caring for the earth.[3] Evidently both of these approaches bring academic business ethics in the mode of Anglo-American philosophy closer to the area occupied by critical management studies, and this is the evidence of convergence or *rapprochement* that I alluded to at the beginning. The general form of Freeman's theory, moreover, is hospitable to further such approaches, since each of the cluster of stakeholder theories he envisages constructs its principles of corporate governance and management according to its own 'background disciplines of value creation'.

It is difficult not to feel at least a slight scepticism about Freeman's pluralism, however, especially at the level of the background theories. In his depiction of his proposal (Table 2.1), Freeman simply stipulates that even the feminist and ecological versions of stakeholder theory will draw on unspecified 'business theories'. What he does not explain is how he can be sure that feminism and ecology will be consistent with those theories, so that all play their role in centre stage – the normative core of stakeholder theory – rather

TABLE 2.1 *A reasonable pluralism*

	Corporations ought to be governed:	Managers ought to act:	The background disciplines of value creation are:
Doctrine of fair contracts	in accordance with the six principles	in the interests of stakeholders	business theories; theories that explain stakeholder behaviour
Feminist standpoint theory	in accordance with the principles of caring/connection and relationships	to maintain and care for relationships and networks of stakeholders	business theories; feminist theory; social science understanding of networks
Ecological principles	in accordance with the principle of caring for the earth	to care for the earth	business theories; ecology; other

than waging a fight to the finish in the wings. Few versions of feminism that I am aware of cohere very well with, for example, the value of competition, though nothing could be more central to standard business theory. The routineness of hierarchy, the strict divide of office from home: all these staples of conventional business thinking are at war with the main tenets of feminism, in particular a feminism inspired by Foucault that, in application to business, would focus on micro-relations (see Brewis, Chapter 4 in this volume). And the problem is arguably much more severe when it comes to making business theories and ecology cohere, for the ecological imperative that we consume less could not be further away from the most central assumptions of marketing (see Fineman, Chapter 11, and Desmond, Chapter 8 in this volume). The tensions in the idea of green business in fact go far beyond this obvious one, from the standpoint of ecological theory (Sorell and Hendry, 1994: 185–7).

Freeman himself elaborates a 'fair contracts' approach to stakeholding, intended to reflect the assumptions and methodology of the modern liberal theory of justice and property rights. This faces fewer risks of internal incoherence than its feminist and ecological counterparts, and uses principles readily intelligible to those who are familiar with market economics. For example, it is a ground rule of the approach that the conditions for entering, dissolving and renegotiating contracts should be clear to all parties. It is another ground rule that someone not party to a contract who is adversely affected by it should be able to become party to the contract, and so on. The guiding idea is that principles of corporate governance and management in a given firm ought to be acceptable if they could be agreed to by all stakeholders in ignorance of their actual stakes (Freeman, 1997: 73). Not only does this Rawlsian theory appear to escape entirely the objection that it is purist or otherworldly; it is supported by two lines of argument that I believe are particularly effective in converting business people to it. One of these lines of argument is legal, the other economic. Both kinds of argument are potentially very fruitful in discharging the rhetorical task that from the beginning I have been claiming is central to business ethics. The legal argument consists of a review of US court decisions whose joint effect is to make it a legal requirement for companies to consider the interests of the groups identified by stakeholder theory. The economic argument consists of considerations which show that, unless it is regulated, the behaviour of people in the market will tend to be monopolistic, free-riding, and externality creating. The legal constraints that outlaw these phenomena are in effect acknowledgements of the infringement of the corresponding interests: those of consumers, competitors, and fellow occupants of the market. The effect of the legal and economic arguments in a rhetoric directed at firms that are noncommittal about stakeholding is to suggest that the shape of the business environment is changing in such a way that business activity has to accommodate itself to the very interests that stakeholder theory talks about. This is no rhetoric based on the first principles of moral philosophy. It is more like a case of pointing to the handwriting on the wall. Business people do not need to be roused from their dogmatic slumbers to register this sort of message. It is the sort of message they are constantly attuned to. The point here is that it is a message that moral philosophy can be the messenger of.

Unfinished business

The last three sections can be summarized by saying that a relevant *and* critical academic business ethics is possible, and that some of its materials are ready to hand. But this conclusion does not justify complacency; and there are at least three different grounds for supposing that a satisfactory business ethics cannot entirely meet Stark's criticism or begin from Freeman's starting point.

First, business ethics has not solved the admittedly abstract and theoretical problem of showing why something is not worth doing in business (as elsewhere) just because it is right. Stark's complaint that this problem is too dominant in the business ethics literature may be justified; but to concede as much is not to concede that there is no problem, or that it does not require a solution. The most that Stark shows (though it is important enough to show this) is that the eager or even willing audience for this solution is unlikely to come from mainstream business, and it will alienate the business audience for business ethics if would-be solutions are talked about by ethicists to the exclusion of other things. Would-be solutions have a different audience, made up of moral philosophers, and these people are not the main or most important audience for business ethics. All that may be agreed to and yet it may still be necessary for business ethics to face the problem that Stark thinks is the height of purism. The problem is important because it seems to be part of a native conception of the moral that its reasons are not permissibly overridden. If they are overridden or ignored, then that is *wrong*, even if not overriding them and not ignoring them is bad in some sense – inconvenient, or financially costly, or stomach turning. Much of the business ethics that Stark approves of has resources for saying that moral reasons, while always important, *may* be overridden or ignored if the effects on a business are particularly bad. The business ethics Stark approves of also have resources for saying that when the reasons for doing what morality asks are not the reasons morality gives, but other reasons that come naturally in business, then so long as one does what morality asks one to do, something morally right and morally valuable has been done. But this line of thought, too, challenges a near-relation of the idea that moral reasons are unignorable and non-overrideable, namely that moral reasons promote the *highest* sort of value, not just some sort of positive value or other. These challenges to the idea of the moral may be legitimate, but it takes philosophy and abstraction to argue out the issue – and business ethics must make room for it, on pain otherwise of being accused of ducking the hard questions.

The second reason for thinking that much more work needs to be done – even in the part of business ethics that is relevant to business – is that not all business, and in fact rather little, is *corporate*. Another way of putting it is by saying that relatively little business in the world – even in the West – is big business. There is something pompous about the idea of applying stake-holding to the corner café, hardware shop, bakery or car repair shop; and yet these businesses are far more typical of businesses than Coca-Cola or Texaco. They are also just as capable as big business of wronging customers, suppliers and employees as others. Less may be expected legally of such businesses. In the European Community, for example, many of the requirements on worker democracy and redundancy simply fail to apply to businesses with fewer than 100 employees. They are often run by families with family members sometimes doubling as 'employees' and working hours that no non-family employee would be asked to work. They are a world apart from the businesses for which Freeman's theory is designed, however real-world that theory purports to be. Since it seems to me that legal exclusion from expensive legal requirements is morally justifiable for small businesses, especially on utilitarian grounds, I think there is a prospect at present of a uniform handling of small and big business. But the gap in business ethics that this implies could not be bigger.

Finally, there is the problem of cultural narrowness. Not all business is big business, and not all business is conducted in the American economic or legal environment, or an environment like it. Even the more general idea of a Western economic and legal environment is a bit of a fiction, since the business cultures of the main partners in the European Union are already quite distinct (Randelsome, 1993). An important aspect of the difference between American and non-American business ethics is the different background assumptions about the value of big government and the welfare state. Since much of the post-Cold-War world is participating in the same global market while retaining its faith in the ability of governments as well as the private sector to involve themselves legitimately in economic and social life, the distinction between public and private may identify something less than the sharp antagonism sometimes put over by business ethics in the style of neoclassical economics.

Arriving at a relevant business ethics that is able to overcome the distortions of traditional emphases on big business and American business, while facing up to its fair share of philosophical perplexity, is no easy matter. So even if business ethics leaves its place at the fringes of academic management and business practice and gravitates toward the centre, it seems to me that it is unlikely to reach maturity in the near future.

Notes

1 This is not to deny that lawyers sometimes treat legal ethics as organized scolding from philosophers, while health care professionals sometimes find the application of moral theory, as it is done in the leading textbooks, pretty sterile. See Smith (1990: 67–93). For criticism of philosophical medical ethics, see Hoffmaster et al. (1989).

2 Norman Bowie's projected *A Kantian Theory of the Firm* will make the case at book length.

3 Freeman cites two articles in which he and colleagues have collaborated on feminist work on the stakeholder concept: see Wicks et al. (1994); and Freeman and Liedka (1991).

References

Alvesson, M. and Willmott, H. (1990) *Critical Management Studies*. London: Sage.

Carr, A. (1992) 'Is Business Bluffing Ethical?' (1968), *Harvard Business Review*, 46. HBR reprint I-391-298.

Freeman, R.E. (1991) *Business Ethics: The State of the Art*. New York: Oxford University Press.

Freeman, R.E. (1997) 'A Stakeholder Theory of the Modern Corporation', in T. Beauchamp and N. Bowie (eds), *Ethical Theory and Business*, 5th edn. New York: Prentice-Hall. pp. 67–75.

Freeman, R.E. and Liedka, J. (1991) 'Corporate Social Responsibility: A Critical Approach', *Business Horizons,* 34: 92–8.

Friedman, M. (1997) 'The Social Responsibility of Business Is To Increase its Profits', in T. Beauchamp and N. Bowie (eds), *Ethical Theory and Business*, 5th edn. New York: Prentice-Hall. pp. 57–61.

Hoffmaster, B., Freedman, B. and Fraser, G. (1989) *Clinical Ethics*. Clifton, NJ: Humana.

Randelsome, C. (1993) *Business Cultures in Europe.* Oxford: Butterworth-Heinemann.

Smith, M.B.E. (1990) 'Should Lawyers Listen to Philosophers about Legal Ethics?', *Law and Philosophy*, 9: 67–93.

Solomon, R. (1992) *Ethics and Excellence*. New York: Oxford University Press.

Sorell, T. (1996) 'Armchair Applied Philosophy and Business Ethics', in C. Cowton and R. Crisp (eds), *The Theory and Practice of Business Ethics.* Oxford: Clarendon Press.

Sorell, T. and Hendry, J. (1994) *Business Ethics.* Oxford: Butterworth-Heinemann.

Stark, A. (1993) 'What's Wrong with Business Ethics?', *Harvard Business Review*, 71: 38–48.

Sternberg, E. (1994) *Just Business.* London: Little Brown.

Vallance, E. (1995) *Business Ethics.* Cambridge: Cambridge University Press.

Wicks, Gilbert D. and Freeman, R.E. (1994) 'A Feminist Reinterpretation of the Stakeholder Concept', *Business Ethics Quarterly*, 4.

3 Marxism, Capitalism and Ethics

Edward Wray-Bliss and Martin Parker

Defining Marxisms

It is much easier to find references to Marxism in books on ethics than it is to find references to ethics in books on Marxism. This is hardly surprising since the 'science' of historical materialism seemed to illustrate that what usually passed as ethics was better seen as ideology, as a mystification of the real which served particular class interests (Wood, 1991). In this chapter, this is not an understanding of Marxism that we wish to support, simply because we want to argue that Marxism can be seen as an ethical stance in itself – and a very powerful one at that. Specifically then, this chapter explores Marxist thought as a potential source of material with which to interpret, represent and understand oppression in capitalist organizations: in other words it opens up a space for a debate about the ethics of contemporary organizing. We argue that Marxism's radical and revolutionary stance, which stresses the potential of oppressed people to resist and transform oppressive structures, opens up opportunities for exploring the potential of resistance to limit, challenge and transform common characteristics of organizations and capitalism more generally. Marxism thus opens up possibilities for exploring not just personal, but also interrelational and structural forces and effects of resistance and oppression. In summary, we wish to argue for a Marxism which is humanist and respectful of agency, an interpretation usually associated with Marx's early, rather than late, writings (see for example Cowling, 1989).[1]

In writing this chapter we have been mindful of both the phenomenal wealth of primary and secondary Marxist literature, and the plethora of different, sometimes contradictory, interpretations of Marxist thought (see for example Willmott, Chapter 5, Anthony, Chapter 13, and Morgan, Chapter 10 in this volume). The various ghosts and spectres of Marx that occupy the human sciences are simply too numerous and any consideration of the totality of Marxist thought is well beyond the limits of this chapter. Accordingly, the discussion of Marxism that we engage in is unavoidably very partial, and any definition that we propose – no matter how broad – is always going to be contentious because we will be excluding other Marxisms from discussion. Even if it is impossible for us to definitively state what Marxism 'really' is, if it is to be discussed at all we need a broad working definition, so that we can understand at least what it is not. Of course any definition simultaneously opens up and closes areas for discussion: however, the definition we give is intended to narrow the discussion of Marxism to manageable proportions, but at the same time to open up Marxism to various interpretations which we tend to favour. So, we suggest that Marxist thought may be understood as attempting to provide the theoretical expression of class oppression within, and class resistance to, capitalism. However, this is not simply a matter of theory, but is also a practice aimed at the overthrow of capitalism and the development of a socialist society.

This definition is similar to Molyneux's: 'Marxism is not just the theory of the proletarian's resistance to capitalism and its struggle against capitalism; it is also, and above all, the theory of its victory' (1983: 14). That being said, Molyneux is concerned to present his definition as an identification of the 'real' Marxist tradition in order that he can identify unauthentic Marxisms – for example, Kautskyism, Stalinism, Third World nationalism, and Western Marxism (with the exception of Lukacs and Gramsci). As we have stated, this is not our purpose simply because we do not wish to argue that ours is the only correct understanding of Marxism. Yet it is also clear that Molyneux's attempt to identify an unauthentic Marxist tradition is not done for solely academic reasons but for practical reasons too. As a senior member of the UK's Socialist Workers' Party, his definition is partly aimed at party members to try and make them clearer about who they are and what they stand for, presumably so that they may be more effective politically. A difference between our own and Molyneux's approach then perhaps rests upon this issue. We consider it more defensible to base political action upon shared ethical values which are developed through reflexive and critical engagement with ideas. Molyneux (like other representatives of political parties more generally) emphasizes having the true knowledge, and hence following the 'party' line on particular issues. As we shall argue below, this seems to us unlikely to guarantee anything apart from more oppression, as the history of Marxism and totalitarianism this century seems to indicate (see for example Bauman, 1989 and the various discussions of his work elsewhere in this volume).

Our examination of Marxist thought is based upon this broad definition from which we draw out the central elements that organize the discussion. The various sections of the chapter explore the meanings of this definition and their relevance for ethics and organization. In particular we address the concepts of capitalism, labour, alienation, the working class, revolution, and finally socialist society. In each section we will explore possible interpretations that we believe are useful for our purposes, and distinguish these from others that we find unhelpful. As we will suggest, the idea of a Marxist ethic is itself subject to debate, and it cannot be assumed that different interpretations of Marxism will lead in the same ethical direction. Hence the tension between Marxist 'ethics', as a reflexive practice, and Marxist 'science', as an authoritarian imperative, is the key topic for the chapter, and we will make some comments on that in the conclusion.

Capitalism

Understanding Marxism's characterizations and critiques of capitalism, the form of oppression which capitalism embodies, and the arguments for resistance and change, are fundamental to any understanding of Marxist thought. However, exploring alternative understandings of the nature of oppression also has the potential to open up alternative understandings of the mechanisms by which people are oppressed. In other words, there are many answers to the question 'Why critique capitalism?' We will outline in this section two possible responses to this challenge, starting with one that we find least helpful for our purposes – scientific Marxism.

Perhaps the most dogmatic (or perhaps modernist) version of Marxism is that which is sometimes termed determinist or structuralist. It is one that combines an analysis of historically determined social and economic structures with a faith in a version of the scientific method. Under this heading of 'scientific Marxism' we include figures such as Althusser, Stalin, Engels and Kautsky because of their claim to a form of epistemological authority based on a conceptualization of the superiority of 'scientific' over other forms of knowledge (Seidman, 1994). This is not of course to say that their work is comparable on other grounds. For example, Stalin's use of the rhetoric of science to force through industrialization in Russia, and to justify brutal acts of oppression and butchery, is obviously quite different from Althusser's attempt to provide a scientific explanation for capitalism's collapse that was explicitly anti-Stalinist in its orientation and purposes. Accordingly, this homogenization of different Marxist practices and writings is done simply to collect together writers who base their arguments on science, whilst other aspects of their work are dissimilar.

For scientific Marxists capitalism is not 'bad' as such, in the sense that we might ethically condemn it. Rather it is understood as an immature state of societal form which, according to the laws of historical development known to the Marxist theorist, will inevitably be surpassed by a higher state of socialist, and then communist, society (McLellan, 1989). This effectively means that questions concerning the lived moralities of capitalism or the basis of knowledge and judgement are simply irrelevant because Marxist science claims to already have access to the truth. Variations of this view often involve a very particular reading of Marx's writings on history and economics and hence what we regard as a rather mechanical and teleological understanding of historical dialectics. Legitimation of this 'science' is frequently given through reference to Marx's later writings and Engels's popularization of Marxism after Marx's death (McLellan, 1975; though see Rees, 1994 for an alternative interpretation of Engels's influence). As Engels put it in his speech at Marx's grave: 'Just as Darwin discovered the law of development of organic nature, so Marx discovered the law of development of human history' (in McLellan, 1975: 73).

According to a scientific Marxist reading, capitalist society is still in the quagmire of pre-history (Marx and Engels, 1967). Contradictions endemic to the capitalist form of economic, social and political organization (such as the tendency for the rate of profit to fall, or capital's search for further accumulation which creates the conditions for revolutionary classes) lead to crisis. Further, any attempts within capitalism to resolve such problems inevitably lead to bigger crises, and hence eventually the collapse of the capitalist system and its transformation into a new, non-contradictory, form. Revolution is therefore an inevitable consequence of these structural contradictions, and hence of a materialist Hegelian movement of history. Within this account, individual agency is subsumed within, and determined by, historical and economic forces which doom the capitalist system to failure.

> What the bourgeoisie therefore produces, above all, are its own grave diggers. Its fall and the victory of the proletariat are equally inevitable. (Marx and Engels, 1967: 94)

> Centralization of the means of production and socialization of labour at last reach a point where they become incompatible with their capitalist integument. This integument is burst asunder. The knell of capitalist private property sounds. The expropriators are expropriated. (Marx in McLellan, 1975: 56)

Such an interpretation of Marxist thought should be familiar to many. It has been presented (and critiqued) so many times – often as an easy way for those with opposing views to disregard all else in Marxist thought by merely making reference to 'determinism' – that we do not intend to spend a great deal of time on it here. Accordingly we wish to only make three main points, concerning the elitism, the structuralism and the practice of this version of Marxism.

The first point is that determinist/scientific interpretations of Marxist thought are only helpful in so far as they highlight capitalism's inability to fully resolve its own problems on its own terms. This is certainly a useful way to question the attempts of 'business ethics' to provide a 'moral', or 'moralizing', solution to the endemic contradictions and exploitation in the employment relationship. However, scientific Marxism fails to offer any form of alternative to the subordinating effects of managerialist ethics. The subordination of people in organizations to the dictates and control of managerial authority is reproduced within scientific Marxism as a subordination to (reified) objective structures such as the economy and the authority of the intellectual or party (McLellan, 1989: 134–6, 299–303). In effect, any sense of the potential agency of the individual worker, taken from them in large part by vesting in management the control and organization of their activity, is taken yet again by the theorist. Creative autonomy is distrusted by management, by business ethicists, and by scientific Marxists. Rather than offering the potential for an alternative conceptualization of ethics that might challenge subordination and explore a self-directing and resisting subject, scientific Marxism reproduces the problem on another level. It mistrusts the activity and resistance of the oppressed and hence oppresses once again by excluding and silencing in theory those currently oppressed materially.

In addition, scientific Marxism, particularly as constructed by Althusser, perhaps its most sophisticated proponent (McLellan, 1975: 82), is unlikely to aid any examination of resistance as a locally motivated practice. Contrary to common conceptualizations of science, Althusser's scientific Marxism is distinctly non-empirical. The scientific Marxist was to be concerned with meta-theory, the 'creation of concepts which were a precondition for knowledge' (McLellan, 1989: 300), rather than the examination of actual subjects in social situations. The inevitability of revolutionary change, and the privileging of analysis at the structural level, leaves little if any space or purpose for an analysis at the level of an individual workplace. People in particular organizations, their difference, autonomy and agency, are subsumed within grand historical movements, the warring of structural antagonisms and the depersonalized effects of economics and technology. Vince's conversation with Dan, the working class hero of McIlvanney's book *The Big Man* (1990: 268), beautifully illustrates the point:

> 'No, no. You're compounding the problem. You did it wrong, Dan. You don't attack the individual. You attack the system.'
>
> 'The system. Where does it live? You got an address for it?'
>
> 'The individuals are irrelevant. Change the system, you'll change the individuals. It's the only way . . . The future,' Vince said. 'See you and me, Dan, we don't matter much. Only what we can contribute to what's comin'.'
>
> 'Ye're a slander on life,' Dan said. He thought of himself and was generous enough not to exempt others from his condition. 'We're only even money tae have a future. You don't like people, Vince. You want to turn them intae ideas. Any future that has to sacrifice the present to get there isny worth goin' to. Don't save me a ticket.'
>
> 'Well, one thing I'm sure –'
>
> 'Anybody who's sure doesn't know, Vince.'

Finally, any concern to explore the relationship between academic work and ethical-political activity, or to put it another way the relationship between a theory of ethics and a practice of ethics, is not helped by scientific Marxism. For example, although Althusser recast theoretical work as theoretical practice (McLellan, 1989: 300), this did not so much entail reflection on the problems of integrating theory and practice, but rather was premised upon reconceptualizing a very abstract theory *as* practice. Such reframings can perhaps be seen to more easily serve the purpose of legitimizing and justifying an academic non-engagement in practical politics, rather than contributing greatly to a discussion of how academic work, particularly of an ethically and politically oppositional nature, can challenge the practice it critiques. In other words, by attempting to provide an epistemological warrant for its work, rather than engaging with debates about ethics, or practical political intentions and effects, scientific Marxism effectively ends discussion, analysis and, ultimately, agency.

However, and as we indicated, Marxist thought does not have to be understood in this way. For a start, Marx's lifelong engagement in revolutionary politics, and radical polemical journalism, does not sit easily with the idea of interpreting Marx as predicting an inevitable revolution determined by objective historical forces. Similarly, Marx's own use of his concepts and theories in his journalistic work and correspondence displayed a flexibility and sensitivity that might be seen to contradict their use as ahistorical, rigid, 'scientific' tools (McLellan, 1980). Indeed Engels himself was moved to speak against attributing too much of a determining power to economic forces:

> Marx and I are ourselves partly to blame for the fact that the younger people sometimes lay more stress on the economic side than is due to it. We had to emphasize the main principle *vis-à-vis* our adversaries, who denied it, and we had not always the time, the place or the opportunity to give their due to the other elements involved in the interaction. (in McLellan, 1975: 41)

Further, it is unclear that Marx and Engels's use of the label 'scientific' for their ideas had quite the same positivist or modernist connotations that it has for many critical social scientists today. It has been suggested that the label 'science' encapsulated for Marx and Engels notions of usefulness, rather than objectivity. 'What Marx was concerned centrally to deny,' according to McLellan, 'was the validity of any doctrine that claimed to be able to give an "objective", neutral or static account of the world from an uninvolved position' (1975: 39). This is the meaning for McLellan of Marx's statement that 'the question of whether objective truth can be attributed to human thinking is not a question of theory but a *practical* question.' In summary then, Marx does not have to be read as a determinist, and cannot therefore be so easily disregarded by those seeking to develop a formulation of ethics from a post-scientific context. An alternative, and possibly more useful, way to understand Marxist thought is one that presents people not as passive and determined subjects of historical and economic forces, but as active, creative, and resistant human beings engaged in the construction of their world and themselves. Central to this, ethical humanist, understanding of Marx is the concept of labour.

Labour

In seeking to develop this version of Marxism, it is important to understand the concept of labour as a generality, not merely an activity carried out in work organizations. According to Marx, labour is what defines human beings as a species, labour is our 'species-being', our truly human function (in Simons, 1994: 62–4). Though animals create some of the most intricate and beautiful structures and habitats, they do so instinctively and only from within the bounds of necessity. Human beings, on the other hand, may create 'purposefully' (Walton and Gamble, 1979: 28), with conscious intention, free from the dictation of immediate need and according to some plan, design, or standard of beauty. For Marx the animal 'is its life activity. Man makes his life activity itself into an object of his will and consciousness' (in Simons, 1994: 63). By creating tools and structures in the outside world, by transforming 'nature' according to our plans, we objectify our species-life and realize our unique ability to create. Not only do we demonstrate our humanity through our acts of creation in the world, but we produce our humanity and hence produce ourselves.

> In his treatment of the objective world, therefore, man proves himself to be genuinely a species-being. This production is his active species-life. Through it nature appears as his work and his actuality. The object of labour is thus the objectification of man's species-life: he produces himself not only intellectually, as in consciousness, but also actively in a real sense and sees himself in a world he made. (1994: 63)

The most important creation of our labour is ourselves. We are self-creating beings, and we create ourselves through our interaction with the world and with other people (McLellan, 1975: 43).

> Labour is, in the first place, a process in which both man and Nature participate, and in which man of his own accord starts, regulates, and controls the material reactions between himself and Nature . . . By thus acting on the external world and changing it, he at the same time changes his own nature. He develops his slumbering powers and compels them to act in obedience to his sway. (in McLellan, 1980: 176)

Of course this formulation of labour as self/world creation may be understood as potentially problematic if it privileges economic activity over any other life activity, and if it retains the masculine and physical connotations generally ascribed to it – as Marx's use of 'man' might be taken to imply. After all, Marxism may easily be in danger of being reduced to a parochial and patriarchal system of thought, which resonates with Western industrial images of labouring males, and results in a heroization of masculine values of work, strength, and physical activity. Homo-erotic passages like the following from Marx and Engels serve to support such an accusation:

> When communist artisans associate with one another . . . the brotherhood of man is no mere phrase with them, but a fact of life, and the nobility of man shines upon us from their work hardened bodies. (in Brenkert, 1983: 16, emphasis added)

As feminists and others have pointed out, basic Marxist terms such as 'worker', rather than being gender neutral, more readily conjure up images of men, and are often seen to require explicit indexing if they are meant to apply to or include women (as in 'women workers'). Any version of Marxism that was based upon an exclusively masculine economic conceptualization of labour would seem to have little to say about women's labour in the private or public spheres (see Brewis, Chapter 4 in this volume). It is therefore important to acknowledge this tendency in Marxist language and thought, resulting from its own historical embeddedness, and then reframe the concept of labour in a way that does not limit its use to analysing public patriarchy.

This reframing can be encouraged through further exploration of its use in Marx's thought. For example, he suggests that in a communist society it would be possible to reduce necessary labour time, that is to say time that needs to be spent to reproduce human existence, so that people could work toward their own development and pleasure and that of others (Marx, 1993). In other words, according to Marx, people only realize their species-life when they are freed from public economic necessity, when they are able to produce according to their own standards and purposes (McLellan, 1980: 165). Indeed, he suggests that religion, morality, science, art and politics could be regarded as particular forms of production (1980: 118). Rather than an image of a world full of labourers as we may understand the concept today, Marx's 'utopia' is populated by people developing, producing, and creating themselves and their relations with others. The category of labour could then be broadly understood to include all instances of our engagement and relations with the world, self and others (for further exploration of this see, Arendt, 1958).

The conceptualization of labour as a *relationship* with others and the world is important in order to distinguish Marx's view of freedom from the individualism that characterizes much of professional moral philosophy (Brenkert, 1983). Self- and world creating labour in Marxist thought may then be understood not in the antagonistic and competitive way that the self-governed person is often understood, but rather in the communitarian sense that creation can only ever take place within a social context.

> Only within a community has each individual the means of cultivating his gifts in all directions; hence personal freedom becomes possible only within the community. (Marx and Engels, 1976 in Brenkert, 1983: 16)

The process of creation is an inescapably social act: only in relations with others do people generate the potential to create their world. It is only in connection with others and as a result of the acts of others that the potential for our own development and creation is generated. Thus Marx writes that even the development of something as material as our senses is a social product.

> The sensuous world around him is not a thing given from all eternity, remaining for ever the same, but the product of industry and of the state of society; and, indeed [a product] in the sense that it is an historical product, the result of the activity of a whole succession of generations, each standing on the shoulders of the preceding one . . . Even the objects of the simplest 'sensuous certainty' are only given . . . through social development, industry and commercial intercourse. (Marx and Engels in Brenkert, 1983: 48)

Creative labour is only achievable in relations of interdependence and cooperation. It is within this broader communal use of the term 'labour' that it then becomes a potentially useful concept for the articulation of resistance in organizations as itself a creative – and ethical – activity or labour, whereby workers construct and transform their relations with self, others and the world. The suggestion that we are labouring beings hence provides an existential basis for articulating a humanist version of Marxism. In that sense it moves us away from the negative authoritarianism of business ethics, which defines resistance as an antagonistic or antisocial reaction, to legitimate managerial authority – what Kjonstad and Willmott (1995) term 'restrictive ethics'. However, an argument about labour as the production of self and the world does not in itself provide any basis with which to compare the labour of workers and managers. Or, to put it another way, the understanding that we are self-creating rather than determined beings is usually viewed from within Marxism as an ontological, not an ethical, standpoint (Walton and Gamble, 1979: 27). This is why it is important to recognize that the ethical basis of Marxism's opposition to capitalism lies in its critique of the *particular* constructions of self and world that commodified economic labour tends to encourage.

> Men make their own history, but they do not make it just as they please; they do not make it under circumstances chosen by themselves, but under circumstances directly encountered, given and transmitted from the past. (Marx in McLellan, 1980: 137)

These particular circumstances and their effect on the possibility of self-creation are the basis of a Marxist understanding of oppression and hence the substance of the Marxist ethical critique. This critique is encapsulated within the concept of alienation.

Alienation

The idea of alienation is present throughout all of Marx's writings and is used in a variety of contexts, and a variety of ways, to criticize religion, philosophy, politics and economics. In common with many other Marxist concepts it has been subject to vigorous debate concerning its place, if any, in Marxist thought. While some scientific Marxists wish to disregard Marx's writings on alienation as philosophical abstractions, and consign such musings to an early immature Marx who was yet to find his scientific materialist voice, for others alienation is the unifying concept that makes his work a continuous 'meditation on themes begun in 1844' (see McLellan, 1980: 122).

Following our general approach to questions of definition, we are not concerned to divine what Marx 'really' meant by alienation or to revisit Hegel in order to work out precisely where Marx departed from his teacher. Rather, we wish to embrace the uncertainty, the undecidability, of the concept in order to argue that the relationship between different definitions of alienation makes it a useful way of opening up alternative representations of oppression and resistance. So, in general terms, alienation may be understood to refer to the situation where people are prevented from realizing their unique abilities to create their relations with the world and others, and thus to create themselves. 'Realizing' is understood here to signify both the subjective process within which one mentally realizes that one has a human potential to self-create, and the objective state within which one is able to make real this potential in the actual structures and relations in which one is located in the world. The consequent tensions and interrelations between subjective and objective, self and structure, in the concept of alienation, are useful in sensitizing us to the complexity of the subjective and objective features of oppression in organizations.

Marx's fullest writings on alienated labour, contained in his *Economic and Philosophic Manuscripts*, describe four main ways in which people are alienated within capitalism. First, the labour of the worker produces an alien world that acts to prevent and inhibit them from realizing their self- and world creating potential. This alien world refers to the immediate products that workers produce, which in capitalism are produced by the worker not as the externalization of their needs and values, as the externalization of their own being, but rather as subject to the demands and control of another. The immediate products of the worker's labour thus exist, legally and symbolically, as separate from the worker and confront them as a hostile and alien power (Simons, 1994: 60). Subsequently, these products are translated into profit and capital which themselves strengthen the organization, for example, as an objective construction that is (or seems to be) independent of the control of the worker (Phillips, 1991). Thus, through the act of their labour, the worker constructs objects, and an objective world, that paradoxically provides them with less ability to change this world, or to labour in a creative way that would produce the kind of relationship they might like to have with the world. Thus Marx writes: 'The more the worker exerts himself, the more powerful becomes the alien objective world which he fashions against himself, the poorer he and his inner world become' (in Simons, 1994: 60).

In addition to being unable to labour in this purposive or self-determined way because of structural alienation, Marx highlights how workers are also alienated subjectively, in consciousness. Through their taking part in the process of production, workers come to understand their activity in a 'self-alienating' way. As the worker's experience of labour is working in capitalist organizations, where the work that is done is felt to be alien to the worker, unsatisfying and tedious, where 'its alien character is obvious from the fact that as soon as no physical or other pressure exists, labour is avoided like the plague' (in Simons, 1994: 62), workers begin to understand all labour as similarly alien. People are at home when they are not working and when they are working they are not at home. Labour becomes only a means to an end, the means to buy their existence, and leisure is then defined as non-labouring time. Work in capitalist organizations turns the unity of people with their activity into its opposite, the alienation of people from the activities they perform:

> activity as passivity, power as weakness, procreation as emasculation, the worker's own physical and spiritual energy, his personal life – for what else is life but activity – as an activity turned against him, independent of him, and not belonging to him. (1994: 62)

The potential to self-create and world create, to develop and express one's freedom through labour in the world, becomes a negative burden, a chore to be avoided.

Further, as well as being alienated structurally and individually, workers are also alienated in their relations with each other. As suggested in the previous section, individuals can only realize their potential to self-create and world create in relations with others. Our self-creation is only realizable as social, cooperative beings. However the dominant relations which capitalism makes available separate people from each other and create antagonistic, competing persons. We are encouraged or compelled to seek personal security against others in an individualized, competitive employment market, and to seek personal development by 'buying into' identities as if they were commodities (see Desmond, Chapter 8 in this volume). This of course includes identities at work, such as those embodied in corporate culture and BPR programmes (see DuGay and Salaman, 1992; Willmott, 1993). Capitalist work organizations encourage us to differentiate ourselves, or rather the product which is us, from our colleagues. Our advancement, our tenuous security, is premised upon our ability to show we are different from and better than our workmates. We 'learn to labour' as separated from our colleagues (Willis, 1977), and the most desired position is where one employs others, that is, where one can treat others as objects to be used or discarded as wanted in order to further one's own individual ends.

Finally, this separation of person from person is mirrored in the separation of person from nature. Just as another person is either a competitor or a commodity, so too nature is conceptualized under capitalism as a threat to be conquered or a resource which is owned. Nature stands opposed from people and people seem distinct from nature (in Simons, 1994: 63; see Fineman, Chapter 11 in this volume). And yet, because they are inescapably materially part of nature, this again represents alienation of themselves. Under capitalism therefore, the dominant relationships people have with the non-human world are antagonistic, narrow and individualistic. Therefore their abilities to self-create and world create are similarly restricted because the relationships that capitalism suggests, demands, and even enshrines in law alienate people from the possibility of purposively creating the world in communal and harmonious relations with nature (Brenkert, 1983). Walton and Gamble (1979: 19) refer to an early article by Marx concerning the law's perversion of the relationship between man and thing in the case of the theft of wood. Here both parties (owner and thief) are subordinated to wood, in as far as they are both represented as functions of wood, rather than as human beings. One is 'the owner of wood' and one is 'the thief of wood'. Therefore, 'lumber as an expression of social relations is placed at the centre of the social relation itself.'

So, through employing these various formulations of alienation, it becomes possible to argue that capitalism itself is an unethical state of affairs because it denies certain human possibilities. Within a capitalist society we are prevented, through the objective structures we create and that create us, from realizing our unique potential to self-create and world create. We are prevented from realizing the possibility of our truly human freedom (Brenkert, 1983). In this sense the flexibility of the concept may be seen as a strength. After all, a narrowly defined version of alienation would seem to lead more readily to the subordination of practice to theory, and the subordination of ethical judgement to supposedly impartial explanation. In other words, it is important that the use of the concept of alienation does not in itself become alienating. Rather than providing easy answers that may prevent us from exploring the complexities of a given situation, the different elements of alienation suggested here may sensitize us, as researchers and as people, to the complex ways that different technologies, relations, subjectivities and structures limit employees' freedom to create themselves and their world.

A humanist Marxist version of alienation thus opens up a rich and flexible alternative critique of the ethics of capitalism and of capitalist organizations, that radically challenges the unidimensional, authoritarian and managerial conceptualizations provided by the official business ethics discourse. Furthermore, the multiplicity of alienations hint at a plurality of possibilities for ethically motivated change and resistance, for the possibility of difference, that far surpasses the tired, and ultimately contradictory, calls for stronger managers to right ethical wrongs. So, if a better world is possible (which is implicit in the possibility of non-alienated labour), then we need to turn to those that Marxism suggests are the agents of such potential – the working class.

Working class

For there to be resistance there must be people to resist, and in Marxist theory the working class are seen as crucial in this regard. Two broad understandings of the role of class in Marxist work may be distinguished. First, the working class may be understood from within scientific Marxism as the subjects of an inevitable future – a classless and non-contradictory society. This society is the true end of human actions, and as the working class are the agents for its development they therefore represent the truth embodied in the present. It is not therefore an ethical choice to identify with the working class, or to attempt to end their oppression; rather it is a scientific and historical necessity, and any science that does not identify with the working class is simply false.

Whilst it might be possible to understand the motives behind this formulation, we prefer to suggest that attempts to identify and challenge the oppression faced by workers are an ethical-political choice, not a 'scientific necessity'. The contingencies of ethics simply cannot be reduced to scientific facts, even if – after Popper, Kuhn, Feyerabend, Lyotard et al. – we could conceive of the latter as a stable ground in the first place. In any case, as we have suggested, there could be no pre-given empirical centrality to the working class if we accept Marx's suggestion that alienated labour is also present in economics, religion, politics and philosophy (McLellan, 1980: 120). However, given the wide definition we insisted upon earlier, this does not rule out distinguishing different forms of alienation within different classes and contexts.

> The propertied class and the class of the proletariat present the same human self-alienation. But the former class finds in this self-alienation its confirmation and its good, its own power: it has in it a semblance of human existence. The class of the proletariat feels annihilated in its self-alienation; it sees in it its own powerlessness and the reality of an inhuman existence. (in McLellan, 1980: 125)

We might therefore suggest that the alienation and oppression of the working class are different from those of the ruling class, and their agents, on the basis of substance and degree rather than presence or absence.

Perhaps more importantly, however, we may differentiate the working class from the middle class in terms of their relation to resistance. Owners of capital and their agents are likely to attempt to maintain existing structures and relations in society because of the material and symbolic benefits they accrue from such structures. Their position in these structures cushions them from the worst effects of alienation, even though it still prevents their freedom in the fullest Marxist sense. The working class have far less of an interest in maintaining the system as the benefits that they accrue from it are not as self-evident:

> the private owner is therefore the conservative side, the proletarian, the destructive side. From the former arises the action of preserving the antithesis, from the latter, that of annihilating it. (in McLellan, 1980: 125–6)

Again, we do not want to read into this statement a determinist position. Marx is identifying trends, not providing guarantees, because being a worker does not necessarily make one a revolutionary, nor does being a member of the bourgeois necessarily make one a reactionary (Simons, 1994: 167). The crucial point here is rather that material existence and experience shape consciousness. Therefore, those that experience 'more' oppression are more likely to resist it, whereas those that experience 'more' benefit are likely to attempt to maintain it.

This materialist conceptualization of knowledge claims is useful in several ways. First, it allows us to suggest that when managers are called upon to re-ethicalize the organization, it must never be forgotten that their role and rewards are founded upon controlling and ultimately ensuring the continual exploitation and oppression of the workforce. As Stephen Fineman documents in Chapter 11, the (supposedly) voluntary nature of the ethical codes and policies that management are encouraged to produce and uphold is in uneasy tension with the formal accountability of such codes for issues of profitability and productivity. These are material contradictions that mere talk about collective ethics policies will not be able to bridge. Secondly, materialism is potentially useful as a counter to idealism, that is to say, the Hegelian notion that abstract trans-historical principles govern the development of consciousness.

> Does it require deep intuition to comprehend that man's ideas, views and conceptions, in one word, man's consciousness, changes with every change in the conditions of his material existence, in his social relations and social life? (Marx in McLellan, 1980: 135–6)

Indeed, a rationalist idealism often seems to provide the basis for the academic re-presentations to which we are opposed. The logic of an argument is conventionally the criteria for its judgement, and emotions, values, ethical commitments and so on are thought to cloud, or even invalidate, the work. In much organizational research, for example, one of the most significant problems is the danger of 'going native', of having *too much* sympathy with those you are studying. Our understanding of materialism challenges this conceptualization of abstract principles – such as those suggested by 'golden rule' ethics – as the basis for knowledge by situating and problematizing academic work itself. It allows us to insist that emotion, commitment and possibly action should be woven into work in a way that requires and encourages more than distanced 'objective' appraisal from either the author or the reader. As Wood puts it:

> There are no universal interests, no cause of humanity in general, no place to stand above or outside the fray. Your actions may be subjectively motivated by impartial benevolence, but their objective social effect is never impartial. The only actions which do not take sides in a class war are actions which are either impotent or irrelevant. (1991: 519)

If materialism means consciousness is conditioned by being, then this serves to open up the issue of the truth or knowledge claims of any arguments. A central insight of materialism – that knowledge is always shaped by perspective (McLellan, 1975) – allows us to self-consciously attempt to re-present the experiences of workers, and not to uncritically reproduce a managerial version of the organization. As standpoint feminists have argued, the issue of perspective also opens up the possibility, or necessity, of writing in a way that is informed and directed by our experiences, ethics, politics, and purposes: that is, to explore ways of producing knowledge that do not claim either to express what someone 'really' meant or to have a privileged insight into the whole truth of a situation. Having said that, however, we do not understand this approach to be either relativist or apolitical: it is – rather a concern not to privilege authoritative knowledges while still insisting on the centrality of political/ethical commitment and the possibility of change (Parker, 1995). Or, as Becker (1967) put it rather more simply, we need to self-consciously decide 'Whose side we are on?'

Of course this does necessarily mean that a decision to explore organizational life predominantly along the axis of class, rather than for example that of gender (see Brewis, Chapter 4 in this volume) or ethnicity, is thus understood as an ethical/political choice itself and not as a self-evident category or problem. In other words, it is possible to be a Marxist but also argue that class is not the only social division that matters. After all, alternative representations of resistance to the structures, processes and subjectivities generated within capitalism are both empirically likely and should be politically welcome if they contribute to (what we deem to be) progressive social change.

Revolution

This section is concerned to explore the most radical conceptualization of resistance within Marxism. Revolution is perhaps the concept most commonly associated with Marxist thought but, ironically, is also often considered to be proof of the irrelevance of Marxist ideas to the modern world (Walton and Gamble, 1979: 217). However, such views are again often based upon a conceptualization of Marxism as a science whose predictions have failed to materialize and, as we have already indicated, this is not a version of Marxism that we favour. Instead we suggest viewing it as an ethical framework which allows us to stress the importance of human agency as resistance to capitalism. Yet, even within the latter formulations there is the possibility that agency might be circumscribed in some rather dogmatic ways. For example, the practice of Marxism might be interpreted as requiring the resistance of the working class to be tightly controlled within specific and predetermined 'revolutionary' boundaries. Effectively this would mean that only certain actions could be considered as revolutionary which implies that many, possibly the majority, of other acts of resistance by oppressed peoples would be deemed to be counter-productive (at best), or counter-revolutionary (at worst). Should resistance be tightly defined and orchestrated, much like a campaign of war, so that specific goals, and the ultimate goal of revolution, are achieved?

Though it might be argued that party constraint is tactically desirable at times, the desire to prescribe what is or is not revolutionary resistance seems to be contradictory in two ways. First, any attempt to know what is or will be revolutionary is confronted by the very nature of revolution itself. Revolutions are by definition a radical departure from the present, not a linear continuation of current trends. Knowing the actions that define the path to the future would effectively rule out that future being revolutionary. Secondly, knowledge of what is and is not revolutionary seems to reproduce similar relations of authority and subordination, and limitations of alternative possibilities, that are critiqued as oppressive within capitalism. Obedience is the role of 'ordinary' party members because: 'In a party one must support everything which helps toward progress, and have no truck with any tedious moral scruples' (Marx and Engels in Brenkert, 1983: 9). In other words, placing boundaries around revolution runs the risk of objectifying it as something other than the means and expression of a search for freedom by the oppressed. Revolution becomes posited as a goal in its own right, as an alienated end that paradoxically requires the subordination of the oppressed at the same time as claiming to be the end of their subordination.

A broader, more open, conceptualization of revolution that considers both the process and the goal might be more useful. One way to develop a richer picture of resistance is to link it to the multiple aspects of oppression suggested by the wide definition of alienation we offered above. In this way, rather than solely seeing resistance in terms of attempts at producing structural change, we may suggest a more complex version of opposition within capitalist organizations (Jermier et al., 1994). First, resistance may be understood according to the effect that it has or is likely to have upon the oppressive structures of capitalist organization. For example, how is management's ability to control and discipline altered by worker resistance? Is management's ability to expropriate profit damaged by resistance? Can workers posit and pursue their own ends more as a result of their resistance? Or, conversely, as some Foucauldians have argued, does their resistance inadvertently strengthen management control? Exploring resistance in this way corresponds to the first element of alienation, where people are unable because of the structures of capitalist organization (which they themselves reproduce) to self-create through their labour.

Another aspect of alienation – workers' relationship to their labour – suggests that resistance may be explored according to the effect it has or is likely to have upon workers' identities and consciousness. This aspect of resistance builds upon the Marxist understanding that people are transformed by their resistance. It is in this sense that Marx writes:

> both for the production on a mass scale of communist consciousness, and for the success of the cause itself, the alteration of men on a mass scale is necessary, an alteration which can only take place in a practical movement, a revolution; this revolution is necessary, therefore, not only because the ruling class cannot be overthrown in any other way, but also because the class overthrowing it can only in a revolution succeed in ridding itself of all the muck of ages and become fitted to found society anew. (in McLellan, 1980: 231)

Thus resistance may be explored in terms of its (possible) effect on the identity of the resistant. They become more aware of their exploited status, and/or of their own abilities to resist further and challenge this exploitation. In addition to exploring resistance in this, somewhat utilitarian, way as a means to the end of possible future resistance, it is also possible to see resistance as simply an end in itself. That suggests that the positing of personal goals and identities in opposition to management goals and organizationally prescribed identities is not only a means to further resistance, but a manifestation of less alienated labour in itself. It is an act of freedom which might admittedly be 'convulsive, half-conscious or conscious' but is aimed 'at recovering their status as human beings' (Engels in Rees, 1994: 77).

Finally, resistance may be explored in terms of its effects upon and opposition to capitalist individualism – people's alienation from each other and from nature. This necessarily involves moving on to say something about the goal of Marxist thought – a new social order.

Socialist society

This final section explores the relationships between the oppressed that might be created through their multiple acts of resistance. Marx actually suggested that socialism was an intermediate stage between capitalist and communist society. Communism was distinguished from socialism on the basis that the former followed a process of the 'withering away' of the state apparatus. Socialism was, in Marxist-Leninist doctrine, the tool to reach communism. Whether this particular teleology is defensible (or likely) is beyond the scope of this chapter, but we use the term 'socialism' here simply because we wish to articulate a more pragmatic alternative to, and critique of, capitalism. In particular, we suggest that notions of 'association' and interdependence in writings on socialist society generate opportunities both to explore the particularity of specific acts of resistance, and to appreciate the ways these particular acts relate to challenges to structural relations of oppression.

In general then, the image and ideal of a socialist society is obviously of great importance to Marxists, as an actual situation that Marxists strive to achieve, but also as a vision, a utopian image or ideal that is drawn upon to fire the imagination, and inspire action.

> Let the ruling classes tremble at a Communistic revolution. The proletarians have nothing to lose but their chains. They have a world to win. WORKING MEN OF ALL COUNTRIES, UNITE!' (Marx and Engels, 1967: 120–1)

This belief in the ethical necessity of the development of a radically new form of social and economic order sets Marxist thought apart from most other critiques of society, politics and self – as many of the other chapters in this volume illustrate. A commitment to the possibility of change in power relations in society allows us to escape from a pessimistic, linear projection of the future as more of the same (see Barker, 1987). If one does not believe in the possibility of radical change, and an understanding of the 'normal' in terms that might lead to these explosive events, it is difficult to see in the routines of oppression and resistance any radical potential. Simply because most resistance does not immediately result in revolution, it is easy enough to make the leap to seeing it as non-revolutionary, as having nothing to do with revolution or radical change and hence being inescapably bounded within contemporary structures. If one, on the contrary, maintains an awareness of the unexpected nature of radical challenges to capitalism then resistance and oppression may be explored not just as petty reactions to management control, or valiant but futile gestures, but as possible steps along a path to revolution. This means that there are no 'special' categories of workers who are defined as likely revolutionaries and that all resistance may be opened up to being explored as potentially radical. To close off the possibility of revolutionary change reifies the present and alienates those who are creating the future.

More specifically, the belief in the possibility of a radically different society, rather than a tepid vision of a new way of reforming or managing the same one, opens up a rich area for the critique of current organizational practice. Practices that may otherwise appear 'normal'and not too oppressive, perhaps only boring, may be represented in a different way. Freed from the need to remain within current managerial or political assumptions, for instance comparing one organization with another similar organization, critique can be informed by a much more open image or vision of what our society and organizations could be like – one which denies that there is no alternative. To put it another way, those practices that are normally taken for granted may be re-presented as not normal, inevitable or necessarily desirable. In a sense then, Marxism (perhaps like feminism) provides an inspirational vision of the future that problematizes the present, challenges everyday activities, and refuses to implicitly validate the everyday.

In addition to radicalizing the re-presentation of oppression and resistance, the image of a future socialist society serves to open up a fundamental aspect of Marxist thought that may be explored in the present – the essentially 'collective' nature of resistance and freedom (Brenkert, 1983).

> The proletarian movement is the self-conscious, independent movement of the immense majority, in the interests of the immense majority. (Marx in McLellan, 1980: 225)

By having as its goal the emancipation of almost everyone, rather than for instance the emancipation of a small group, Marxism privileges ideas of interrelationship, and presents a radical challenge to bourgeois notions of individual freedom and resistance. This is not personal freedom at the expense of others, or personally creative lives in the spaces and the gaps overlooked by overarching oppressive structures. Marx writes that the new society will be

> the complete and conscious return of man conserving all the riches of previous development for man himself as a social, i.e. human being. Communism as completed naturalism is humanism and as completed humanism is naturalism. It is the genuine solution of the antagonism between man and nature and man and man. It is the true solution of the struggle between existence and essence, between individual and species. It is the solution to the riddle of history and knows itself to be this solution. (in Brenkert, 1983: 244)

Rhetoric apart, socialist society may thus be interpreted as presenting the possibility of a new kind of relationship between people, and between people and nature, not based upon antagonistic individual needs, fear, or feelings of powerlessness, or upon obedience and duty. It is an image of inter-relations between free individuals that takes the form of a kind of 'association', where another's difference is not a threat, but a sign of their uniqueness and originality (McLellan, 1980: 246). Under capitalism,

> Grey, all grey, is the sole, the rightful colour of freedom. Every drop of dew on which the sun shines glistens with an inexhaustible play of colours, but the spiritual sun, however many the persons and whatever the object in which it is refracted, must produce only the official colour! (Marx and Engels in Brenkert, 1983: 115)

So, after capitalism, difference will remain but class differences will disappear. Individual differences allow for 'an association, in which the free development of each is the condition for the free development of all'. But 'individual difference' here implies not ethical frameworks which rely on assumptions about individuals making choices – Kantian or utilitarian ethics – but rather Hegelian senses of community as the precondition for meaningful ethical life (MacIntyre, 1971).

This key importance given here to the development of harmonious and supportive relations of interdependence may be used to inform an understanding of contemporary oppression and resistance in organizations. Adding to the discussion of resistance above is the possibility of communal relationships between workers within an organization and between those workers and others. For example, it might be suggested that resistance fosters relations that begin to counter the individualism and competition which are typical of the managerial hierarchy and disciplinary gaze. Of course, resistance might also be engaged in individually which promotes further isolation, or in opposition to colleagues such as the supervisors of work 'teams', but sociability at work could be seen, in and of itself, as an act of resistance to individualizing hierarchical control and the alienation of workers from one another. Interdependence and trust could therefore be explored as both an end and a means of freedom, and this might well begin to include those workers previously categorized as 'managers'. The ideas encapsulated within Marxist conceptualizations of socialist society thus stress the crucial importance of considering the kind of relationships that resistance creates, both in terms of its immediate effects and also in terms of fostering relations that may combine to challenge and resist more effectively the reified oppressive structures of managerial control through new forms of association.

A Marxist formulation of association generates the possibility of interpreting resistance as challenging structures and forces of oppression but without requiring the subordination of difference to this end. Different acts of resistance by different workers for different immediate ends may have multiplicative and combined effects that end up as oppositional to managerial control. By using the idea of association in this way we are stressing the emergence of revolutionary struggle as a combination of localized resistances (see for example Luxemburg in McLellan, 1989: 48; and Barker, 1987). Such a relational view of resistance helps connect a focus upon the uniqueness of specific organizational settings with an appreciation of wider social structures and processes, thus helping to avoid either supposedly apolitical empirical work or abstract alienated theorizing.

To summarize, this section has presented harmonious relations of interdependence between people as the essence of socialist society and hence as the essence of a Marxist ethics. A materialist view of knowledge claims insists on the impossibility of separating ethics from social context, and that context is inescapably communal. Following such an interpretation a fundamental goal of ethical activity is the affirmation of others. 'Our production would be so many mirrors reflecting our nature. What happens so far as I am concerned would also apply to you' (Marx in Simons, 1994: 53). Against the idea that trans-historical 'golden rules' can be chosen by rational individuals, a Marxist ethics works for possible communities as a collective project.

Conclusion

As we suggested at the beginning, we will not be closing this chapter with firm and fixed conclusions because there are enough definitive and totalizing versions of Marxism around already without us adding to them. Our aim was simply to indicate how a Marxist ethics helps us to understand oppression and resistance in non-subordinating ways. An ethical critique of capitalist organizations from a Marxist perspective could begin with the concept of labour – as the potential to self-create and world create – which provides a basis upon which to mount a continual and radical critique of current organizational practices. Further, the concept of self-creation through labour opens up possibilities for exploring resistance itself as an act of creative labour. In other words, resistance is not only a reaction to managerial control but a positing of relations and identities at work. In these terms, a broad notion of alienation is also helpful in sensitizing us to the complex subjective and objective forms which oppression may take, and the multiple possibilities for resistance which follow. This includes not only those acts that challenge structural limits, but also those that free up individual consciousness, that create and maintain dignity, and that create more supportive, less competitive, relations with others. In other words, there might be revolutionary potential in much 'normal' resistance to managerial controls.

A focus upon the working class stresses the materialist basis of Marxist ethics. We argue that knowledge is generated through experience, which justifies our scrutiny of those subject to managerial control and also informs our critique of the self-serving managerialism of much business ethics. It also suggests that our writing is not immune from this material base and should be reflexively informed by an ethical-political engagement which foregrounds our particular interpretations and truth claims. In this sense, the possibility of a socialist society liberates our imagination from the limitations of seeing the future as a necessary continuation of the present in which current organizational practices are deemed to be normal, inevitable or desirable. Ideas of 'association', of community may provide a framework within which to understand multiple and varied acts of localized resistance as not just a narrow issue in one workplace, but rather part of the wider struggle of many oppressed people for freedom.

It needs to be acknowledged, particularly in this volume, that Marxist views of work organizations have been subject to a great deal of critique by proponents of poststructuralism and postmodernism for holding on to a 'grand narrative' (see Letiche, Chapter 6, Willmott, Chapter 5, Munro, Chapter 9, and Brewis, Chapter 4 in this volume): that is to say, for having a view of overarching structural relations of oppression, and the possibility of a revolutionary transformation of these structures at a societal level. Obviously, any critique, of Marxism or otherwise, that leads us toward less oppressive practices is to be welcomed but it is unfortunate that some of those that critique Marxism do not appear to be very committed to the possibility of radical social change. Despite rejecting meta-narrative at a theoretical level, they seem to implicitly accept that capitalism is here to stay. In response we would simply want to insist that the utopian strand of humanist Marxism is worth holding on to, that a vision of the future (however undefined) is a necessary connection between everyday and academic practice. This is not to say that Marxism is immune from such attacks – for its romantic humanist view of people as basically heroic but corrupted by contemporary social and economic arrangements, for example – but rather to hold that we cannot, should not, ignore the power of a Marxist ethical critique of capitalism. For, despite its shortcomings, it is still a form of critique that can be worked with and understood. The crisis of Marxism that is only too apparent in contemporary academic and political terms should not blind us to the value of thinking about the possible, and perhaps of suggesting ways in which the horizon of utopia might come a little closer.

So, in conclusion, we have tried to trace throughout this chapter an interpretation of Marxist ethics that is political and practical, that is useful for understanding resistance and oppression both locally and in connection with the wider structures of capitalism. Ethics in Marxism cannot be 'merely a matter of a different morality . . . of "getting out of one's head" a few "fixed ideas", to make everyone happy and able to enjoy life' (Marx in Brenkert,

1983: 3), but must be a practical political project composed of not only personal and relational elements but also organizational and social forces. It is not a science, either of inevitable historical materialism or of individualizing professional philosophy, but a way of articulating commitment to a new form of community, in organizations and hopefully elsewhere.

> Morality requires a social identity: only then will the moral subject have reason to do what is morally required . . . We will make sense of what we are doing, even of our own existence, because of its place in a larger community. The daunting, indeed impossible, task of creating and justifying one's own existence by oneself can be recognized for the unsustainable delusion that it is. And once we escape from the hegemony of instrumental reason, we can entertain the hope that to begin the task of building such a community is a way – and the only way – of participating in it. (Poole, 1991: 159)

Notes

Thanks to Mihaela Kelemen and Hugh Willmott for their comments on earlier drafts of this chapter.

1 It is worth pointing out that the two authors of this chapter have considerable theoretical differences here which are glossed over for the sake of this account. Edward's faith in terms such as 'creativity', 'agency', 'autonomy' and so on is admired but not entirely shared by Martin. See Martin's concluding chapter in this volume for some further explanations of how this difference might be articulated.[2]

2 In response to Martin, and in the spirit of marking out differences glossed over for the sake of this account (see note 1 above) I do not believe it necessary, as Martin's comments seem to suggest, for us to have a(n uncritical, humanist?) 'faith' in 'creativity', 'agency' or 'autonomy' to be able to use these concepts to order our research and relations with, and representations of, others. Rather I would suggest that there are moral/practical grounds (Seidman, 1994), as distinct from epistemological grounds, for writing, researching and relating to others as if they may legitimately exercise and express 'agency'. To do otherwise it seems to me is to risk reproducing research 'subjects' subordination to our presumed or claimed academic authority and voice: a process that has historically served to pathologize others' expressions and explorations of their agency, and legitimize the further removal of their opportunities to make decisions about their own life and labour (Bauman, 1989, see also Wray-Bliss, 1998).

References

Arendt, H. (1958) *The Human Condition*. Chicago: University of Chicago Press.
Barker, C. (ed.) (1987) *Revolutionary Rehearsals*. London: Bookmarks.
Bauman, Z. (1989) *Modernity and the Holocaust*. Oxford: Polity.
Becker, H. (1967) 'Whose Side are We On?', *Social Problems*, 14.
Brenkert, G. (1983) *Marx's Ethics of Freedom*. London: Routledge and Kegan Paul.
Cowling, M. (1989) 'The Case for Two Marxes Revisited', in M. Cowling and L. Wilde (eds), *Approaches to Marx*. Milton Keynes: Open University Press.
DuGay, P. and Salaman, G. (1992) 'The Cult[ure] of the Customer', *Journal of Management Studies*, 29(5): 615–33.

Jermier, J., Knights, D. and Nord, W. (eds) (1994) *Resistance and Power in Organizations*. London: Routledge.
Kjonstad, B. and Willmott, H. (1995) 'Business Ethics: Restrictive or Empowering?', *Journal of Business Ethics*, 14: 445–64.
MacIntyre, A. (1971) *Marxism and Christianity*. Harmondsworth: Pelican.
Marx, K. (1993) *Grundrisse*. Harmondsworth: Penguin.
Marx, K. and Engels, F. (1967) *The Communist Manifesto*. Harmondsworth: Pelican.
McIlvanney, W. (1990) *The Big Man*. London: Hodder and Stoughton.
McLellan, D. (1975) *Marx*. Glasgow: Fontana.
McLellan, D. (ed.) (1980) *The Thought of Karl Marx*. London: Macmillan.
McLellan, D. (1989) *Marxism after Marx*. London: Macmillan.
Molyneux, J. (1983) 'What is the real Marxist tradition?', *International Socialism*, 20.
Parker, M. (1995) 'Critique in the Name of What? Postmodernism and Critical Approaches to Organisation', *Organisation Studies*, 16(4): 553–64.
Phillips, N. (1991) 'The Sociology of Knowledge: Towards an Existential View of Business Ethics', *Journal of Business Ethics*, 10: 787–95.
Poole, R. (1991) *Morality and Modernity*. London: Routledge.
Rees, J. (1994) 'Engels' Marxism', *International Journal of Socialism*, 65.
Seidman, S. (1994) *Contested Knowledge: Social Theory in the Postmodern Era*. Oxford: Blackwell.
Simons, L. (ed.) (1994) *Karl Marx: Selected Writings*. Cambridge: Hacket.
Walton, P. and Gamble, A. (1979) *From Alienation to Surplus Value*. London: Sheed and Ward.
Willis, P. (1977) *Learning to Labour*. Farnborough: Saxon House.
Willmott, H. (1993) 'Strength is Ignorance, Slavery is Freedom: Managing Culture in Modern Organisations', *Journal of Management Studies*, 30(4): 515–52.
Wood, A. (1991) 'Marx against Morality', in P. Singer (ed.), *A Companion to Ethics*. Oxford: Blackwell.
Wray-Bliss, E. (1998) 'The Ethics and Politics of Representing Workers: An Ethnography of Telephone Banking Clerks'. PhD Thesis. UMIST.

4 Who Do You Think You Are? Feminism, Work, Ethics and Foucault

Joanna Brewis

It is a truism to claim that women are disadvantaged in their working lives. The phenomena of vertical segregation and horizontal segregation are noted even in mainstream texts on the workplace (Mullins, 1996: 160–9). The rigours of women's daily working lives are also well documented – for example, the literature on sexual harassment, or material analysing women's managerial experiences. While there is little room for debate around the existence of gendered disadvantage at work, controversy does, nonetheless, surround the appropriate explanations for, and solutions to, this situation. Leaving aside explanations which are outdated and empirically inaccurate (Parsons and Zales, 1956; Tiger and Fox, 1972), it is still the case that the feminisms of the workplace are in substantial disagreement on these issues. If feminism can be defined as 'an analysis of women's subordination for the purpose of figuring out how to change it' (Gordon cited in Eisenstein, 1984: xii), it is fair to say that these organizational feminisms do not concur on what causes women's disadvantage at work and what ought to be done to resolve it. At their extremes, they share only the objective of rectifying gendered workplace disadvantage.

Therefore, if we accept Gordon's definition of feminism, and the distinction between 'morals' and 'ethics' offered by Anthony, based on Smart's suggestion that ethics is: 'the theory or philosophy which systematizes moral values' (Smart cited in Anthony, Chapter 13 in this volume), we can conceptualize the various workplace feminisms as representing competing theories of ethics. That is to say, they are attempts to regularize a morality of, a 'right' way of doing, thinking and acting in, the organization in terms of gender relations.

Furthermore, it is interesting that Anthony (see also Munro, Chapter 9 in this volume) seeks to distinguish between:

> the task of moral philosophy, of ethics . . . [and] the necessary grasp of moral relationships acquired by men and women going about their business and their lives.

To some extent, the above coheres with Derrida's approach to ethics. Derrida positions ethics on the side of general principles of duty, or laws, as opposed to justice, which he defines as a lived morality, an engagement with specific others in an attempt to honour difference and singularity (Letiche, Chapter 6 in this volume). Bauman (1995) makes a similar distinction which also has some resonance with Foucault's ideas concerning ethics and morality. Foucault (1986a; 1990) is interested in the disjuncture between existing ethical prescriptions and individuals' moral behaviour. He implies that there is a slippage between what we are told we ought to do and what we actually do, morally speaking.

Furthermore, Foucault (1986a) goes on to identify different kinds of social systems in this regard. Code-based moralities (such as those characteristic of Western modernity), he suggests, operate on the basis of centralized authority and a generalized ethical code, which that authority has the power to enforce. Interestingly, Foucault argues that the function carried out by those codes (or power/knowledge regimes) which prevail in Western modernity – that is to say, the internalization by human individuals of what is 'good' and their driving out of what is 'not' – means that contemporary morality is much less reliant on external authority, because modern subjects have become self-policing to a large degree. In contrast, ethics-based moralities (such as those characteristic of Antiquity) require individuals to constitute themselves as moral subjects. That is to say, while 'rudimentary' codes, few in number and less than 'compelling', did exist in such societies, recommending to citizens how they should conceive of and conduct themselves, it was the individual citizen's choice as to how far they complied with these codes (Foucault, 1986b: 361). Moral education, the dissemination of what was good and proper, consisted less of the circulation of hard and fast precepts than of the provision of exercises through which one could work on oneself. For example, Epictetus – a Stoic philosopher – required that one had to be able to regard a beautiful girl or boy without desire (Foucault, 1986b). For those individuals existing within code-based moralities, then, the requirement is to abide by the existing codes or risk sanction, whereas for individuals existing within ethics-based moralities, the requirement is to craft for oneself an ethically satisfactory existence.

Certainly Foucault uses the terms 'ethics' and 'morality' differently than do Derrida or Bauman. However, semantics aside, the distinction between a lived moral experience, and regulations concerning how we ought to behave, is evident across these commentaries.

We come back at this point to the earlier labelling of the various workplace feminisms as theories of ethics (or, using Foucault's terminology, ethical codes or power/knowledge regimes). These feminisms certainly cling more or less firmly to the assumption that, given the decline of 'archaic' belief in a Divine morality, the consequent freedom of human will has to be carefully harnessed so that 'free . . . individuals . . . [can be] prevented from using their freedom to do wrong' (Bauman, 1993: 7; also see Bauman, 1987). The proponents of these feminisms identify gender inequality in organizations as wrong, and recommend particular interventions to eradicate this inequality. They are universalist, legislative and, therefore, modernist in their remit (Bauman, 1993: especially 8–9; 1995, especially 34; and Letiche, Chapter 6 in this volume).

The above having been established, this chapter will, in the first instance, briefly review the various feminist positions on the workplace – those of liberal feminism, Marxist/socialist feminism and radical feminism. This review will attempt to suggest why each of these bodies of knowledge represents a theory of ethics. The chapter then moves to offer an alternative position on gender relations at work, derived from Foucault. A Foucauldian feminism of the workplace, it is argued here, would conceptualize its task very differently in comparison with the more established feminisms. Indeed, this approach could be described as encouraging 'the necessary grasp of moral relationships acquired by men and women going about their business and their lives', as encouraging the conscious living out of moral experience – as opposed to an adherence to a set of ethical prescriptions. It will be suggested in this debate that a Foucauldian organizational feminism is practically more viable, as well as entailing more impact on the gendered inequities of modern organizational life, and towards the end of the chapter this will be explored using empirical material.

Liberal feminism

Liberal feminism has its roots in the Enlightenment belief that the ability to reason is what differentiates human beings from animals, because it enables us to acquire 'autonomous and critical' knowledge about our world so that we can decide for ourselves how best to manage our lives (Goldmann, 1973: 2). Pioneer liberal feminists agreed with this privileging of reason, and the consequent need for the public sphere (where production, government and education take place) to be kept free from irrationality. However, they were angered by the masculinist character of much Enlightenment philosophy – like Kant's claim that women are much less well equipped to reason than men. In opposition to this biologistic ideology of women's natural inequality, such commentators claimed that there were no substantive differences between women and men (Rhode, 1992: 150). Mary Astell and Hannah Woolley (writing in the late seventeenth century: see Kinnaird, 1983) and Mary Wollstonecraft (writing a century later: Wollstonecraft, 1970) agreed that the Enlightenment privileging of reason ought to be understood as meaning that the mind can control and subdue bodily instincts. Consequently, these women suggested that women's capacity to carry and give birth to children has no bearing on their capacity for reason. However, early liberal feminism only demanded equality of access to education. Liberal feminist arguments broadened during the nineteenth century to include demands for equal opportunity for women in the workplace and the political arena as well (Cott, 1990: 45; Humm, 1992).

Liberal feminism, then, has its origins in the understanding that men and women in all significant respects are equals and that this equality should be recognized in the public sphere; it emphasizes the political, educational and workplace rights of the human individual, whether male or female (Jaggar, 1983: 28). In its organizational form, liberal feminism argues that the privileging of reason in the modern workplace has resulted in discrimination against women, owing to the mistaken assumption that women are naturally irrational. Given that equality of workplace opportunity is the central issue for this strand of liberal feminism, it recommends the development of 'long' agendas of equal opportunities in the organization. A long agenda seeks to bring about equal representation for women at every level of the organization – and may include an equal opportunities policy, efforts to alter sexist attitudes at work, skills training for women and flexitime or job share schemes to minimize the problem of the 'home–work interface' for women (Goss, 1994; also see Cockburn, 1991). A short agenda, on the other hand, seeks only to comply with anti-discrimination legislation such as the UK Sex Discrimination Acts of 1975 and 1986. This focus on the long agenda as the only way to govern behaviour so as to rectify gendered disadvantage at work casts liberal feminism firmly in the guise of a theory of ethics, which identifies clearly how members of organizations ought to strive to relate to each other. An alternative critique of the contemporary workplace is provided by Marxist feminism, which this chapter now moves to address.

Marxist feminism

Marxist feminism, like liberal feminism, has its roots in a political philosophy based on the notion that the human condition is rendered unique by one particular feature. However, for Marxism, it is not precisely our rationality which makes us human, but rather the ability that we have to act purposefully upon the world so as to provide for ourselves (Jaggar, 1983; Tong, 1989: 40; Wray-Bliss and Parker, Chapter 3 in this volume). It argues, furthermore, that the specific way in which we seek to organize this activity is the key to explaining the kind of society we inhabit (the key Marxist tenet of historical materialism). Marxist feminism, therefore, assumes that this economic base must be central to analysing the position of women in any particular society – and, in particular, in capitalism, which currently dominates in the West. The task of Marxist feminists, then, is to attempt to connect capitalism with contemporary patriarchy – and to do so in a way which avoids the gender blindness of Marxism *per se* and the ahistorical tendencies of feminism (Barrett, 1980: especially 9; Hartmann, 1981: especially 2; Jaggar, 1983; Eisenstein, 1984: especially xvii; Segal, 1987).

It is the general contention of contemporary Marxist feminists such as Barrett (1980; 1992) and Hartmann (1981; 1992) that patriarchy predates capitalism, but that patriarchy takes a specific form under capitalism. Modern patriarchy and capitalism are seen to represent historically contingent structures; capitalism may support a particular form of patriarchy, but patriarchy is not essentially capitalistic (nor capitalism essentially patriarchal). Marxist feminism also argues that there are irreducible conflicts between patriarchy and capitalism (Hartmann, 1981; Walby, 1986; Eisenstein, 1992; 1993). For example, men acting as men may prefer to keep women at home for the rendering of personal services, whereas men acting as capitalists may prefer to employ women in the labour market for the purpose of generating profit.

More specifically, contemporary Marxist feminist explanations of the position of women in the modern workplace tend to suggest that capitalism is founded on (i) a separation between home and work, and (ii) the existence of a differentiated labour force, capable of performing various tasks within a complex economy (Barrett, 1980). How then does this relate to the positioning of women in the modern capitalist labour market, expected to undertake the bulk of domestic labour, but entering the labour market under certain conditions and in certain ways? Barrett suggests that Marx's 'industrial reserve army' argument is a partially satisfactory explanation, but that the patriarchal ideology which underpins the capitalist division of labour must also be acknowledged in terms of relegating women to domestic labour and/or in terms of the horizontal segregation of the workplace (Barrett, 1980: 157; also see Mitchell, 1971; Eisenstein, 1993: especially 202). Hartmann (1981) also points out that horizontal segregation means that the increasing participation of women in the labour market will not necessarily break down patriarchal arrangements.

Barrett (1980: especially 172) goes on to suggest further interleavings between capitalism and patriarchy in terms of women's oppression at work. She, along with Hartmann (1981), argues that male dominated trade union organization has been powerful in shaping definitions of what constitutes skilled work and that union activity has been centred on building up the bargaining power of 'more skilled' (male) workers. It is suggested that this is because of a fear of women workers representing cheap competition (a fear encouraged by Marx himself), to say nothing of women no longer being available to perform domestic tasks if they are working. This union activity led in particular to demands for a 'family wage' – and the accommodation of these demands by capitalism because of the advantages of having women at home to consume capitalist products and to sustain and reproduce labour power (Hartmann, 1981; also see Foreman cited in Tong, 1989: 45).

Contemporary Marxist feminists suggest that the liberation of women depends on a rejection of patriarchal gender ideology, from which should follow a redistribution of domestic labour, the abolition of workplace segregation and the eradication of women's economic dependence on men (as enabled by their equal participation in paid employment). While Barrett suggests this is not possible under capitalism, she also insists that any movement beyond capitalism be informed by the maxim: 'No women's liberation without socialism; no socialism without women's liberation' (1980: 255; also see Segal, 1987). To achieve this may mean women organizing autonomously from men, although within a leftist alliance. Marxist feminists agree that there are workplace concerns which divide women from men politically, such as maternity leave and sexual harassment, but that other struggles can be fought in tandem, such as the battle against segregation, which serves capitalism as well as patriarchy (Barrett, 1980: 258–9; Hartmann, 1981; Segal, 1987; Eisenstein, 1992: 190).

In conclusion, it seems appropriate to claim that contemporary Marxist feminism is actually socialist (Tong, 1989), because it seeks:

> to abolish the social relations that constitute humans not only as workers and capitalists but also as women and men. (Rubin cited in Jaggar, 1983: 132)

Therefore, it is not interested in explaining women's oppression as solely generated by capitalism. For these theorists, a specific kind of socialism needs to come about, because the eradication of class oppression does not automatically result in the eradication of women's oppression. This established, it is possible to identify Marxist/socialist feminism as a theory of ethics, given its insistence on a particular type of new dawn, on the ethical imperative of a non-patriarchal socialism.

The final workplace feminism to be discussed here is radical feminism, which differs from both liberal and Marxist/socialist feminisms in particular ways.

Radical feminism

Radical feminism differs from the feminisms discussed so far in several respects. First, it is not connected with any wider body of political theory, which Bunch (1992) sees as radical feminism's great strength, because it represents an alternative route to women's emancipation. Radical feminism is also distinguished by its claim that women's oppression is the original oppression and therefore the paradigm for every other form of oppression (Tong, 1989).

For radical feminists, furthermore, the source of women's oppression is biological: the denigration and expropriation of the female body spills over into other areas of social interaction so as to give rise to patriarchy (Jaggar, 1983: 101). Brownmiller suggests that men's physical capacity to force sex on women has been utilized to establish and preserve male power – for example, women being forced into patriarchal marriage to assuage 'fear of an open season of rape' (1975: 16). In a similar vein, Firestone (1971) suggests that female biological reality – the debilitating processes of menstruation, pregnancy and childbirth – renders women vulnerable to and dependent on men within what she calls the 'biological family'. Brownmiller and Firestone, then, argue that negative aspects of female biology are the root of women's oppression. Other radical feminist writers position women as biologically closer to nature, so that they have a positive relationship with the world as nurturers, carers, reproducers. French (cited in Tong, 1989) suggests that feminine traits need to be revalued within society so as to enable social arrangements based on relations of 'pleasure-with' and 'power-to', rather than the oppressive (and masculine) 'power-over'. Daly (1984) argues that women must work to develop their natural 'femaleness', not their femininity, which she sees as a patriarchal trap to render women subservient. Femininity for Daly makes of women 'painted birds'; they are socialized to conceal their womanliness under a carapace of makeup, perfume and elaborate costume, instead of being free to express their essential biological and sexual power, and their natural wisdom.

Further, radical feminism identifies women's special qualities, arguing that women are either different from but equal to, or different from and superior to, men. Solonas (1983: 1) claims that men are naturally deficient 'biological accidents', because the male Y chromosome is an incomplete female X chromosome (see also Dinnerstein cited in Tong, 1989: 100). Radical feminists also emphasize that men consolidate their domination over women through a manipulation of women's consciousness, so that women themselves behave in ways which maintain patriarchy. Millett (1972) argues that male writing is frequently just as prescriptive as it is descriptive. She analyses, in one instance, neo-Freudian psychoanalysis, suggesting that it has used Freud's thesis 'anatomy is destiny' to imply that a woman who refuses to behave in a 'feminine' way courts neurosis in trying to achieve a 'biologically impossible state' (Millett cited in Eisenstein, 1984: 7).

The route towards women's emancipation suggested by radical feminism typically centres around some degree of separatism: women developing their own relationships, roles, activities and organizations, which are populated mainly, if not necessarily exclusively, by other women. Examples of separatism include consciousness raising groups such as the Boston Women's Health Collective, which challenged masculinist medical expertise (McNeil, 1987: 23–4), or political organizing like that undertaken by the UK Greenham Common women. Radical feminist separatism also occurs in the economic sphere, as detailed in French's novel *The Women's Room*. Here, Val tells Mira that, following her daughter's rape:

> 'I belong to all women's groups now. I shop at a feminist market, bank in a women's bank. I've joined a militant feminist organization, and in the future I will work in only that . . . For forty-odd years I've been a member of an oppressed people consorting with the enemy, advancing the enemy's cause. In some places that's called slavery. I'm through with it.' (French, 1993: 477–8)

Here, women are creating their own organizations, which Oerton (1994) suggests tend to be flat in structure and cooperative in ethos, without collaboration with men. This separatism turns on preserving women's (allegedly) special outlook on the world (McNeil, 1987: 47).

However, radical feminism may argue less for separatism than for the total destruction of the patriarchal order – as Solonas does in the *SCUM Manifesto*.[1] Solonas begins by stating:

> Life in this society being, at best, an utter bore and no aspect of society being at all relevant to women, there remains to civic-minded, responsible, thrill-seeking females only to overthrow the government, eliminate the money system, institute complete automation and destroy the male sex. (1983: 1)

Here, she takes a quasi-Marcusian critical theory line that there is no reason to perform drudge-like labour, or indeed to work at all for more than short periods each week, because most of the work that we currently undertake can be automated (1983: 3). Consequently, Solonas suggests that radical feminist SCUM members ought to engage in 'unwork':

> SCUM salesgirls will not charge for merchandise; SCUM telephone operators will not charge for calls; SCUM office and factory workers, in addition to fucking up their work, will secretly destroy equipment. SCUM will unwork at a job until fired, then get a new job to unwork at. (1983: 19)

This 'unwork' forms part of Solonas's vision of the route towards a man-free world – the only scenario in which, for her, women can be emancipated. This is arguably the strongest form of radical feminist argument: that women need to eradicate any traces of masculinity in the world in order to be free.

Radical feminism, then, argues for the development of so-called 'woman-space', in which women can live and work outside the patriarchal control of men. Its insistence that women can only achieve emancipation through separatism or destruction of the patriarchal order allows it to be categorized as a theory of ethics.

To summarize, the three feminisms reviewed so far all rest on particular ethical imperatives, on various prescriptions for interactions between the genders in the workplace (and elsewhere), in order to ensure that morally correct behaviour prevails. The argument which the remainder of this chapter will seek to establish, however, by employing the work of Foucault to sketch out an alternative form of organizational feminism, is that such a feminism can make sense without these prescriptive imperatives.

Foucault and the organizational feminisms

The organizational feminisms analysed in the preceding sections are premised on the understanding that the truth of who we are and how we should, ethically speaking, live is attainable. Theorists within these traditions seek to dismantle what they see as the masculinist 'truths' that we live by on the basis that they are distorting and oppressive; they position themselves as 'marching "toward the [real] truth"' (Foucault, 1988: 112). These feminists assert their right to establish ethical principles in the name of truth, natural justice, progress and ethics, and in the rebuttal of existing systems, which they decry as opposing all of these values (see also Letiche, Chapter 6 in this volume). However, to adopt a Foucauldian perspective means rejecting this opposition between truth and not-truth. Foucault does not inveigh against current knowledge claims, such as those put forward by these feminisms, in the suggestion that they are untrue, but rather asserts that all knowledge is contingent, that there is no ahistorical truth. It is this, in the first instance, which sets his analysis apart from that characteristic of the feminisms analysed earlier. Foucault suggests that, in speaking, writing and thinking about our existence, we have simply generated particular 'grids of intelligibility', ways of making sense of that existence. Foucault's term for these 'grids of intelligibility' is discourses, and he emphasizes that they represent nothing more, and nothing less, than socio-historical interpretations of what it is to be human. Foucauldian analysis is not, however, anti-realist; it simply suggests that the physical objects, human bodies and patterns of behaviour that we see around us do not contain within them an enduring truth which can be attained by human reflection: 'Discourse is not about objects, rather discourse constitutes them' (Foucault cited in Sheridan, 1980: 98). An example is Foucault's (1979) analysis of the discursive construction of 'sex' as a human 'essence'.

Consequently, Foucault also rejects another opposition which is embraced by the feminisms discussed earlier, that of power versus truth/knowledge. Liberal feminists and Marxist/socialist feminists argue that the ideology of biological gender differences leads to an oppressive division of labour, whilst radical feminists suggest that women are naturally different from men, but that this does not mean that they are inferior. These feminisms, then, argue that what is held to be true about women frequently represents a patriarchal distortion of the truth, an ideology produced in line with the interests of the male 'ruling class' – and thus that these 'truths' are actually fundamentally untrue. Consequently, these feminisms aim to isolate the truth about women – whether this is that they are the *same as* and therefore equal to men, or *different from* but equal to or superior to men. Thus these feminisms pronounce that there is a truth of womanhood which needs to be liberated from masculinist distortions.

Foucault, on the other hand, suggests that:

> power relations are not content merely to . . . distort or to limit [knowledge]; power and knowledge are not linked together solely by the play of interests or ideologies; the problem is not therefore of determining how power subjugates knowledge and makes it serve its own ends, or how it imprints its mark on knowledge, imposes on it ideological contents and limits. (Foucault cited in Sheridan, 1980: 132)

He argues that power and knowledge are actually inextricably bound up with each other; that contemporary discourses, masquerading as truths when in fact there is no enduring truth, produce our sense of who we are and how we should live. Thus, for Foucault, knowledge is demonstrably powerful, because it constitutes the ways in which we think of ourselves and behave towards others. Power for Foucault is much more than simply repressive, distorting what we know; instead, it is productive of how we know ourselves. Power here constitutes us as self-aware subjects, able to act on ourselves and on each other. We do not and cannot exist outside power, because power is what allows us to 'know' ourselves and, consequently, to act. Foucault would, therefore, suggest that the established feminisms are themselves power/knowledge regimes, disseminating 'truths' of womanhood which are simply discursive constructions. In attempting to 'identify' and thereby 'free' the 'truth' of womanhood, these feminisms only consolidate the operations of power with regard to individual women (Foucault, 1977: 30). Their arguments regarding the 'true essence' of women mean that these feminisms operate in no way differently from any of the discourses associated with patriarchy, such as the neo-Freudian emphasis on anatomy as destiny (see earlier discussion of Millett in the section 'Radical feminism'). There is, then, a crucial difference between Foucault and established feminist accounts of socialization, because Foucault emphasizes that:

> The individual is not to be conceived of as a sort of elementary nucleus, a primitive atom, a multiple and inert material on which power comes to fasten or against which it happens to strike, and in so doing subdues or crushes individuals . . . [rather] it is already one of the prime effects of power that certain bodies, certain gestures, certain desires, certain discourses, come to be identified and constituted as individuals . . . the individual is an effect of power. (1980: 98)

In other words, for Foucault, there is no human individual outside power/knowledge, no *a priori* truth of wo/manhood distorted by the (patriarchal) operations of the social world.

Another key difference between liberal, Marxist/socialist and radical feminisms of the workplace and Foucault is their conceptualizations of what power actually is. For these feminisms, power is a zero-sum possession: the more power men possess, the less women can wield. Patriarchy (the system which, they claim, currently predominates) is a structure in which all avenues of power, including those in the organization, are in male hands (Millett cited in Eisenstein, 1984: 5). Power here, however, is an entity that could be equally shared; therefore emancipation for women consists of them having the same power as men to determine how organizations, and the wider society, ought to be managed. This ideal state of affairs is, as has already been established, depicted differently by these established feminisms.

Foucault's analysis, however, suggests that power is not a possession, but a relation within which we position ourselves; through our exposure to prevailing contemporary discourses, we come to actively reproduce their tenets in our thoughts and actions (1979: 94). Power operates at the level of each human individual who, in 'knowing' what it is to be 'human', strives to reproduce that 'humanness' in their everyday lives. Thus power operates through us rather than over us:

> [The individual] assumes responsibility for the constraints of power; he [*sic*] makes them play spontaneously upon himself; he inscribes in himself the power relation in which he simultaneously plays both roles; he becomes the principle of his own subjection. (1977: 202–3)

This analysis also means that the power which Foucault sees as constituting us as subjects is not monolithic. Because power/knowledge regimes can only be sustained by the activities of human subjects, because they are in their entirety socio-historical constructs which we reproduce through thinking, being and doing in particular ways, these regimes are always fundamentally unstable, always open to 'rearticulation' (Knights and Vurdubakis, 1994). Power is 'only exercised over free subjects and only in so far as they are free' (Foucault, 1982: 221). Foucault (1977; 1979; 1980; 1982) also maintains that power is fragmented in its operations; that the variety of discourses currently in existence means that the particular way in which an individual formulates their identity is not predictable. We can only surmise that they will construct an identity through locating themselves within certain discourses, and resisting others. For Foucault, power is 'in reality an open, more-or-less coordinated (in the event, no doubt ill coordinated) cluster of relations' (1980: 199). Additionally, Foucault suggests that it is through the operations of current power/knowledge regimes that we are able to resist at all – that it is our construction as active, knowing subjects that makes us able to refuse what we are told is true about ourselves. He suggests, therefore, that wherever there is power, there is resistance: 'It is not that life has been totally integrated into techniques that govern and administer it; it constantly escapes them' (1979: 143). Consequently, Foucauldian analysis is able to unpack the complex character of our relationship with ourselves – the effects of our exposure to a variety of discourses and, equally, of our resistances to them.

For Foucault, resistance is not resistance against all of the power that is wielded over us, so that the end of resistance is freedom from power; rather it is resistance against a specific manifestation of power, a refusal to understand ourselves in a particular way. When we resist the effects of a particular discourse, according to Foucault (1979: 101), we do so from the juncture of another set of discursively constituted understandings. Resistance is always over-determined by its social context; when an individual chooses to resist one set of definitions, to understand themselves in another way, they are entirely bound by the discursive choices available to them. We do not get beyond power to any kind of truth or freedom in resistance, because resistance is a response which in itself is conditioned by power; it carries with it its own limitations and cannot be understood as some kind of liberational force to be harnessed by ethical movements such as feminism (Foucault, 1980; 1988). A germane example for the present discussion would be radical feminism's (re)definition of women as different from men but not inferior to them, which resists many of the prevailing discourses around what it means to be female. However, radical feminism in itself represents a particular discursive construction of what it means to be female and it therefore constitutes (and limits) those who subscribe to it in specific ways. Consequently, even though it can be defined as resistant, the implications of this resistance are not unproblematically positive. For example, for women to understand themselves as essentially different to men is perhaps for them to assume that they naturally possess only certain characteristics and that any other behaviour on their part is unnatural, a product of distorted patriarchal socialization. Consequently, the kind of subject position produced by the resistant discourse of radical feminism can be identified as just as constraining as those produced by 'patriarchal' discourses.

In sum, then, Foucault argues that there is no better truth, no power-free state to which to aspire. He has no notion of the possibility of a better society in terms of the ways in which we live and relate to each other. Foucault's (1991: 79) notion of knowledge being contingent in its entirety means that we have no firm ethical grounds for judging particular practices. The key differences between Foucault and the established feminisms of the workplace having been established, this discussion now moves to review what Foucault has to say regarding ethical practice, regarding the 'right' way to think, feel and behave.

Foucault and ethical practice

What a Foucauldian analysis suggests with regard to ethical practice is very different from the recommendations made by the established feminisms, from their insistence that there is an ethical imperative which we must abide by in order to achieve a morally correct form of behaviour in our gender relations.

Foucault's primary concern is that we modern individuals currently find it difficult to conceive of relating to ourselves in any way except that which we believe to be the 'truth' of what we are. Thus, he argues that our individual projects of identity are relatively devoid of promise; we are so preoccupied with this 'truth' that we do not, indeed cannot, experiment with other ways to be. Foucault suggests that we should work to alter this relationship with ourselves, beginning by rejecting the possibility of any kind of enduring human truth. He implies that, by refusing truth in this way, we will become able to choose from particular discursive constructions, particular ways of being, thinking and doing, understood only as alternative philosophies of life, none more or less 'true' than any other (1986b; 1988). Here again there are echoes of Derrida, whose concept of *epoche* refers to 'the rejection of the *natural attitude*. It is the refusal to take reality for granted or to languish in (a positivist sort of) common sense' (Letiche, Chapter 6 in this volume). It is epoche, claims Derrida, that makes justice possible because it suspends belief in law as authoritative – just as a rejection of the possibility of truth makes ethical practice as Foucault conceives of it possible.

Foucault's notion of ethical practice, then, rests on us beginning to question, criticize and choose ways of thinking about, being and doing ourselves. He posits that it is possible for us to 'separate out, from the contingency that has made us what we are, the possibility of no longer, being, doing or thinking what we are, do or think' (1986b: 46). This is not a standard of ethical behaviour towards which we must strive, as provided by the established workplace feminisms, because there is no recommendation here of how we ought to live in terms of the nature of our behaviour, merely an insistence that we should seek to live in a different way. This different way of living/attitude/ethos frees us from our doomed search for enduring truth and turns on an active and conscious self-fashioning.

Foucault suggests that this 'critical ontology of self' (1986b: 50) may be usefully 'kickstarted' by deliberate participation in 'limit experiences', within which one '[reaches] that point of life which lies as close as possible to the impossibility of living' (Foucault cited in Simons, 1995: 99). A limit experience involves living as dangerously as we can in order to reveal the groundlessness of our beliefs about the constraints around the human condition, to demonstrate to ourselves how our potential has been limited by the internalization of particular discursive constructions (Miller, 1993: 254). By engaging in such experiences, Foucault suggests, we undermine the way in which power/knowledge regimes operate through us. It is this kind of practice which Foucault advocates we build into our lives:

> The critical ontology of ourselves has to be considered as an attitude, an ethos, a philosophical life in which the critique of what we are is at one and the same time the historical analysis of the limits that are imposed on us and an experiment with the possibility of going beyond them. (1986b: 50)

It is also interesting to note that Munro (Chapter 9 in this volume) suggests that we are already at this stage, ethically speaking – that contemporary ethics consists of having the self sit in judgement on the self, of a process of self-formation, rather than a process of conforming to abstract ethical codes, which are external to the self. However, this author is more inclined to agree with Foucault that our 'lived morality' at present consists of a self-policing with regard to internalized rules originating outside us as individuals.

Foucault's perspective, then, bids us focus on individual subjects as the locations in which power is exercised and, therefore, where it should also be questioned and resisted. For Foucault, the criticism which is sometimes levelled at his work, that resisting power at this micro-level cannot change overall structures of power (Fraser, 1989; Hartsock, 1990; Ramazanoglu and Holland, 1993), is misguided – because it distracts us from the importance of resisting power at the level where its effects are felt (Foucault, 1980: 99, 143–4). Furthermore, to conceptualize power as Foucault does allows us to resist, as individuals working against the effects of power in our own lives, in a way that insisting on power as structural (and the corollary of global ethical projects, such as those suggested by the established workplace feminisms) does not.

As suggested earlier, Foucault shies away from offering any kind of recommendation as to how individuals might choose to construct and reconstruct themselves. This has led to critics, including Comay (1986), Habermas (1987) and Purvis and Hunt (1993), alleging that Foucault offers no promise of a better future, and thus no reason for us to engage in the critical ontology of self. This interpretation of Foucault's work suggests that he does not answer the crucial questions 'in the name of what? for the sake of what? to what end?' (Simons, 1995: 59) and, therefore, that he is quietist, even reactionary. Arguably, however, Foucault, unlike the feminist theorists reviewed earlier in this chapter, cannot offer any notion of a better society because, as Gandal points out,

> laying down solutions at the outset or articulating his ethics as a set of principles would pre-empt a task of questioning and of telling new truths, a task he was trying to instigate. (1986: 129)

For Foucault to present a *promesse de bonheur* as existing in some alternative social formation would 'reinstate the forms of power/knowledge [he] set out by opposing' (Knights and Vurdubakis, 1994: 192). Interestingly, Derrida similarly rejects the possibility of providing some conceptualization of what his justice consists of:

> one cannot speak *directly* about justice, thematize or objectivize justice, say 'this is just' and even less 'I am just', without immediately betraying justice. (Derrida cited in Letiche, Chapter 6 in this volume).

Here Derrida appears to be making the same argument as Foucault; he suggests that justice only exists in activity and self-reflexivity, and that to establish what justice might look like is immediately to transform justice into law, code or, in a Foucauldian sense, power/knowledge regime.

Given the above, Foucault insists that we take up and conduct the 'practices of liberation' for ourselves. Otherwise we remain unreflexively subject to the operations of power/knowledge regimes, and therefore unaware of the specific ways in which our relationship with ourselves constrains, not only us ourselves, but also others around us. Foucault (1980: 141–2) also suggests that his conceptualization of power as inescapable is not reactionary; that would mean interpreting power as always oppressive. By way of contrast, we could (should) never want to escape power, because it makes us what we are: self-aware, active human subjects. For Foucault, the point is to become aware of, and seek to change, the ways in which power operates through us, so that we are able to experiment with a wider range of identities.

Furthermore, and importantly, Foucault suggests that the critical ontology of self is motivated by a particular kind of intellectual analysis. Organizational feminists generally suggest that women's experience of the workplace has been marginalized, and ought to be reactivated to provide a more truthful account of organizational life (for example Mills and Tancred, 1992). It is this intellectual privileging of one account over another which Foucault would reject as just as imprisoning as those accounts of organizational life which do not recognize gender differences. He argues that intellectual analysis ought to reveal the relationship between knowledge and power *instead* of generating new truth claims. Thus intellectuals must work in such a way as to *disrupt* prevailing understandings, to suggest that there are other (but not 'truer') ways in which we could understand our existence, to undermine the status of supposedly 'truthful' discourses (Foucault, 1986b: 74; 1988: 36, 124). From a Foucauldian point of view, then, it is not a matter of feminists challenging 'patriarchal' knowledge about the workplace with alternative formulations of what that workplace is like.

Having delineated Foucauldian ethical practice as very different from that set out by the established feminisms of the organization, as well as identifying the kind of intellectual analysis which would impel such practice, this chapter concludes with an analysis of how a Foucauldian feminism of the organization might actually operate.

Foucault, feminism and the organization

A Foucauldian feminist analysis of gender relations in the workplace would focus on the micro-relations of power – how power actually works through the individual (male and) female subjects who populate that particular organizational space to produce the ways that they relate to themselves and, consequently, to each other. The central issue would, arguably, be the way in which these (men and) women understand their 'genderedness'. Questions which might be germane include: how do individual women relate to themselves and others as working women? What are the implications of these identity projects? What other ways of being, doing and thinking womanhood and/or work are available? This kind of approach may seem somewhat disengaged as a mode of ethical practice, in that it requires a sustained degree of self-reflection as opposed to a definite commitment to particular rules of behaviour. However, an analysis of how real working women appear to conceive of themselves, and of what kind of implications this might have for their organizational experience, demonstrates its potential impact. This section of the chapter offers an analysis of this type, using data from research conducted in a university (Smithtown) and a financial services organization (Minerva).[2]

The analysis will focus on a particular section of the data, which contains responses to questions concerning how these women would react to unwanted sexual advances from their male colleagues – and therefore links back to concerns raised by the 'rigours of women's daily working lives' literature (see the introduction). This line of questioning was undertaken to try and tease out precisely how powerful the liberal feminist sexual harassment discourse had been with regard to these female subjects: did they conceive of themselves as helpless victims of predatory males, unable even to identify sexual harassment when it happened to them, let alone put a stop to it – a version of organizational reality which this discourse identifies as the truth?

It seems that the reverse is in fact the case. These women were strongly resistant to this conceptualization of the workplace, stating that they would usually be able to withstand unwanted sexual advances from their male colleagues. For example:

> Like, say, somebody asked me out and I said 'No', I'd think to myself 'Right, that's it. I've said no and that's it.' If they asked me again I'd say, you know, 'Didn't you listen the first time? Can't you get it in your head?' (senior clerk, Minerva)

> Nobody, no matter who they are, puts their hand on me, or gets away with anything. (secretary, Smithtown)

> If someone rang you up from a different department and said 'Would you like to go for a drink at lunchtime?', I'd probably say 'Well, no thanks' because I don't know them, I don't know them from a work relationship point of view. No matter how innocent it may look, it probably might not be . . . if somebody kept doing that all the time . . . I'd probably just turn round and say 'I'd prefer you didn't ask me because, you know, I'm always pretty busy at lunchtimes' or 'I'm always pretty busy in the evenings.' (senior employee relations officer, Minerva)

On the whole, then, these women appear to understand themselves as equipped to deal with any unwanted sexual attention in the workplace. They perceive that, for the most part, their gender does not render them vulnerable to men and suggest that they can be honest with their male colleagues: if these men are behaving inappropriately, these female respondents will have no reservations about making this clear and asking them to stop. Furthermore, their comments also reveal that they are confident that any such behaviour would stop, as a result. For example, a Smithtown secretary suggested that only 'outrageous' or 'over the top' behaviour might be difficult to deal with:

> to some extent verbal, unless it got really outrageous and sort of over the top, verbal [behaviour] you can sort of throw a drink or whatever else, you can deal with, so that's acceptable . . . being in a situation on a one-to-one basis with no one being around with that person when it had got beyond the point of being able to control [their behaviour] would be frightening and intimidating.

These respondents also imply that their belief in themselves as assertive means that they will not tolerate any lesser behaviour in other women. They frequently criticized other women for failing to address harassing behaviour at an early stage. For example, a Minerva employee relations officer said that, if she was faced with the harassment she identified a friend as having endured, she would be much more forceful in dealing with it:

> I would say something, and if it got to the point then that it continued, after I'd said something, then I would say something again . . . I think I'd feel fairly strongly about it.

There is, then, a certain lack of sympathy for those others (only three respondents said that they had experienced sexual harassment themselves) who have been the recipients of harassment. However, this is not only because these women are perceived to have dealt with the harassment in an inadequate way, but also because they are seen to have 'asked for it'. A secretary at Smithtown, in describing the behaviour of a female colleague who had been the target of an attempted sexual assault at the previous year's Christmas party, commented that this colleague seemed to welcome the sexualized attention that she received. Indeed, the woman whom this secretary was talking about also sees herself to be at fault:

> It's me, you see. I get accused of being a flirt and a tease so p'raps it's me . . . I do get meself in [difficult situations] . . . well, I thought I could handle [the Christmas party situation] . . . it taught me a lesson and I thought, you know, in the future just back off before it gets [to that stage]. (female technician, Smithtown)

Furthermore, the female respondents also suggested that they felt themselves to be capable of identifying sexual harassment – that it was simple to differentiate between harassing behaviour and friendly behaviour. For example:

> I think really you can see the *difference*, you can tell, most people can tell you *what the difference* is. (part-time clerk, Minerva, emphasis added)

> [the behaviour of a previous manager] *got to the stage* [of being harassment]. (secretary, Smithtown, emphasis added)

The female respondents at Smithtown and Minerva, then, cast themselves and other women as usually able to identify, confront and stop any kind of unwelcome sexualized behaviour at work. This belief forms part of their identities as women workers and exemplifies how they relate to themselves and others. However, it is important to suggest what the implications of them viewing themselves in this way might be. Certainly their identities are partially constructed in opposition to liberal feminist sexual harassment discourse; they see themselves as having a significant part to play in identifying or controlling the unwanted sexual attention they may receive from male colleagues. Further, this stance would be welcomed by many commentators on the sexual politics of the organization. Roiphe, for example, suggests that discourses such as that surrounding sexual harassment present

> a portrait of the cowering woman, knocked on her back by the barest feather . . . these feminists are promoting the view of women as weak-willed, alabaster bodies, whose virtue must be protected from the cunning encroachments of the outside world. (1994: 67)

Thus in some ways this resistant form of identity may be seen as emancipatory, as morally proper in the sense that it gives women a sense of their own capabilities and strengths. However, as established earlier, it would be misguided to suggest that this resistance is not, at the same time, dangerous in certain ways. In fact, it seems that to understand oneself as on the whole able to cope with unwanted sexualized attention at work, as the Smithtown and Minerva women seem to do, may be to live by the requirement that one continually behaves in this way, always being on guard against possible harassment and dealing with it oneself. In this regard it is interesting to note the description of the behaviour of a male co-worker offered by a senior employee relations officer at Minerva:

> You tend to find as well that the [union representative] . . . makes innuendos all the time. One of the girls was telling me the other day she went down to his office . . . to take some papers, and he said something to her like 'Oh . . . it's a hot day today' and she says 'Oh yeah, I know, it's really [hot]' and he says 'Oh well, get your shirt off then', you know, and she said 'Oh, you know, I got really really very embarrassed by that comment' . . . you just tend to, I mean, I ignore his comments to be quite honest now . . . sometimes he could be quite offensive to you because . . . he goes on, you know, when someone goes on and on and on and you think . . . 'This is [too] much' and you just cut him short, you say 'Oh well, thanks', like that, and he realizes [that he has offended you].

Here, this respondent describes the behaviour of this man as upsetting to her and to other women. Nonetheless, she goes on to imply that she is capable of dealing with it even though he persists: she will 'cut him short' or give some other indication that he has said 'too much'. She apparently sees no need to make an issue of this man's behaviour, or to complain to others about it. The implications of this woman's identity seem to be that she fails to question the behaviour of this man, instead holding herself responsible for withstanding his attentions.

Such comments from the interview data point to the Smithtown and Minerva female respondents not only understanding themselves as having to monitor their behaviour to ensure that they are giving off the appropriate signals to male colleagues. It also seems that they hold themselves responsible for the behaviour of these men – that they believe themselves for the most part able to stop any unwanted sexual attention.[3]

In sum, such a subject position, resistant though it is to a central tenet of sexual harassment discourse, can be identified as just as demanding as understanding oneself to be a victim. It is possible to suggest that this kind of self-image (assertive, independent, strong) results in a particular attitude towards traumatic episodes such as harassment. One has to cope with (i) the harassment itself; (ii) having 'encouraged' this behaviour; and (iii) feeling that it is one's own responsibility to stop the behaviour. For these women, the refusal to understand themselves as victims of harassment therefore confers other restrictions upon them – what Dews refers to as 'the stifling anguish of responsibility' (1984: 84).

Further, it appears that these women understand themselves in ways which might be ethically problematic – in the main because they accept responsibility for any harassment that they might experience, rather than considering the role of the perpetrator. This could be seen to allow harassment to continue to exist in these organizations, because these women seem to have a highly individualized type of identity which does not permit them to see harassment as part of the wider framework of workplace gender relations. That is not to suggest that other subjects may interpret instances of harassment more effectively, or to place all of the responsibility for examining self on to these women, but it is to suggest that their particular subject position is dangerous – and that ethical practice of the kind that Foucault outlines would at least empower these respondents to make more reflexive choices about the ways in which they relate to themselves and to others. It is not appropriate for this discussion to reflect on the ways in which these women might come to see themselves differently, or on what those different identity projects might look like, for this would be to present the kind of *promesse de bonheur* that runs very much against the grain of the Foucauldian ethos. It is sufficient here to present a challenge to existing identity projects, to tell a 'cautionary tale' (Sawicki, 1994) about certain working women's lives, the focus being on the possible harm that they do to themselves and others by settling for one or other way of 'being in the world'.[4] This unsettling form of analysis could, in demonstrating what adherence to certain 'truths' can bring about, conceivably incite others to begin to reflect for themselves on what they understand about themselves as working and gendered subjects and on the ways in which this might be constraining.

This analysis, then, demonstrates in part the kinds of questioning which a Foucauldian feminism of the organization would have us engage in – men and women both. This kind of activity is undeniably accessible in its micro-focus. Unlike the other feminisms described here, there are no grand projects of emancipation envisaged, simply a commitment to considering what it means to think of oneself, and therefore behave, in particular ways. The appeal of Foucauldian feminism as defined here rests not only on this, however, but also on the space that it offers for each individual woman (and man) to engage in a personal struggle against oppressive organizational relationships, as produced by particular power/knowledge regimes. There are no goals to aim for: we are simply given some idea of what might be wrong with the present, and asked to begin to construct our own future. Further, this is a movement which can be carried out alone, or with others[5] – but it is above all a movement which can be seen to address power relations as and where they impact, at the level of the individual subject. For Foucault, the personal is most definitively political. This is not to say that Foucault adds up to some requirement for consciousness raising, to alert women in particular to the ways that gender frameworks operate in their own lives, as radical feminism's interpretation of this slogan suggests. A Foucauldian analysis is premised on the disruption of power/knowledge regimes, not on any notion of enlightenment through greater access to knowledge. It simply instructs that power matters in our own lives, and that we as individual subjects can begin to make a radical difference to the ways in which we live and the experiences that we have. In this, then, it is very much an ethics-based view of morality as opposed to being code-based: Foucault insists that we construct ethical practice on our own terms and in our own ways. Thus his analysis is very different from the claims made by the established organizational feminisms, which suggest that we have to follow certain prescriptions to lead a truly ethical existence.

Notes

1 SCUM stands for Society for Cutting Up Men.

2 See also Brewis (1996).

3 For an example of the possible consequences of an individual holding themselves accountable for others' sexual behaviour see the account given by MacCannell and MacCannell (1993: 208) of a woman who, walking through New York's Central Park on her way home, was raped twice.

4 Taking account of others in one's self-construction is, despite claims to the contrary (see note 5), seen here to be fundamental to Foucault's conceptualization of the critical ontology of self. In this, Foucault echoes Bauman's notion of ethics as a reaction to the 'face of the other' (see Letiche, Chapter 6, and Munro, Chapter 9 in this volume).

5 Foucault departs here from Derrida, who asserts, according to Letiche (Chapter 6 in this volume) that 'in individual and specific interacts, there can be a logic of justice; but in collective existence or "society", there is only the possibility of law.' Foucault does not reject out of hand the possibility of some form of collectivist ethics. His analysis suggests that the critical ontology of self is necessarily embedded in its social context; that individuals could and should negotiate their projects of self with, and with regard to, the others around them. Interestingly, Letiche himself seems to concur with Foucault rather than Derrida on this issue. This apparent difference between Foucault and Derrida means that the criticisms levelled at Foucault's ethics on the basis that they are highly solipsistic (Wolin, 1986; Soper, 1993; see also Munro, Chapter 9 in this volume for a discussion of the problems with solipsistic ethics) are to some extent unfounded (Brewis, 1996). However, Foucault does little to indicate what kinds of communities might arise from the critical ontology of the self. Others are not so reticent: see Haraway's (1990) analysis of cyborg political movements for some idea of what a collective form of Foucauldian ethics might look like.

References

Barrett, M. (1980) *Women's Oppression Today: Problems in Marxist Feminist Analysis*. London: Verso/New Left Books.

Barrett, M. (1992) 'Extract: *Women's Oppression Today: Problems in Marxist Feminist Analysis* [1980]', in M. Humm (ed.), *Feminisms: A Reader*. Hemel Hempstead: Harvester Wheatsheaf, pp. 112–15.

Bauman, Z. (1987) *Legislators and Interpreters: On Modernity, Postmodernity and the Intellectuals*. Cambridge: Polity.

Bauman, Z. (1993) *Postmodern Ethics*. Oxford: Blackwell.

Bauman, Z. (1995) *Life in Fragments: Essays in Postmodern Morality*. Oxford: Blackwell.

Brewis, J. (1996) 'Sex, Work and Sex at Work: A Foucauldian Analysis'. Unpublished PhD thesis, UMIST.

Brody, M. (1983) 'Mary Wollstonecraft: Sexuality and Women's Rights (1759–1797)', in D. Spender (ed.), *Feminist Theorists: Three Centuries of Women's Intellectual Traditions*. London: The Women's Press. pp. 40–59.

Brownmiller, S. (1975) *Against Our Will: Men, Women and Rape*. London: Secker and Warburg.

Bunch, C. (1992) 'Extract: *Not by Degrees: Feminist Theory and Education* [1983]', in M. Humm (ed.), *Feminisms: A Reader*. Hemel Hempstead: Harvester Wheatsheaf. pp. 171–4.

Cockburn, C. (1991) *In the Way of Women: Men's Resistance to Sex Equality in Organizations*. Basingstoke: Macmillan.

Comay, R. (1986) 'Excavating the Repressive Hypothesis: Aporias of Liberation in Foucault', *Telos*, 67: 111–20.

Cott, N. (1990) 'Historical Perspectives: The Equal Rights Amendment Conflict in the 1920s', in M. Hirsch and E.F. Keller (eds), *Conflicts in Feminism*. London: Routledge, Chapman and Hall. pp. 44–59.

Daly, M. (1984) *Gyn/Ecology: The Metaethics of Radical Feminism*. London: Women's Press.

Dews, P. (1984) 'Power and Subjectivity in Foucault', *New Left Review*, 144: 72–95.

Eisenstein, H. (1984) *Contemporary Feminist Thought*. London: Unwin.

Eisenstein, Z. (1992) 'Extract: *The Radical Future of Liberal Feminism* [1981]', in M. Humm (ed.), *Feminisms: A Reader*. Hemel Hempstead: Harvester Wheatsheaf. pp. 185–8.

Eisenstein, Z.R. (1993) *The Radical Future of Liberal Feminism*. Boston: Northeastern University Press.

Firestone, S. (1971) *The Dialectic of Sex: The Case for Feminist Revolution*. London: Cape.

Foucault, M. (1977) *Discipline and Punish: The Birth of the Prison*. London: Allen Lane.

Foucault, M. (1979) *The History of Sexuality. Volume One: An Introduction*. London: Allen Lane.

Foucault, M. (1980) *Power/Knowledge: Selected Interviews and Other Writings 1972–1977*, ed. C. Gordon. Brighton: Harvester.

Foucault, M. (1982) 'The Subject and Power', in H.L. Dreyfus and P. Rabinow (eds), *Michel Foucault: Beyond Structuralism and Hermeneutics*. Brighton: Harvester. pp. 202–26.

Foucault, M. (1986a) *The History of Sexuality. Volume Two: The Use of Pleasure*. Harmondsworth: Penguin.

Foucault, M. (1986b) *The Foucault Reader*, ed. P. Rabinow. Harmondsworth: Penguin.

Foucault, M. (1988) *Michel Foucault, Politics, Philosophy, Culture: Interviews and Other Writings 1977–1984*, ed. L.D. Kritzman. New York: Routledge.

Foucault, M. (1990) *The History of Sexuality. Volume Three: The Care of the Self*. Harmondsworth: Penguin.

Foucault, M. (1991) 'Questions of Method', in G. Burchell, C. Gordon and P. Miller (eds), *The Foucault Effect: Studies in Governmentality*. Brighton: Harvester Wheatsheaf. pp. 73–85.

Fraser, N. (1989) *Unruly Practices: Power, Discourse and Gender in Contemporary Social Theory*. Cambridge: Polity.

French, M. (1993) *The Women's Room*. London: Abacus.

Gandal, K. (1986) 'Michel Foucault: Intellectual Work and Politics', *Telos*, 67: 121–35.

Goldmann, L. (1973) *The Philosophy of the Enlightenment: The Christian Burgess and the Enlightenment*. London: Routledge and Kegan Paul.

Goss, D. (1994) *Principles of Human Resource Management*. London: Routledge.

Habermas, J. (1987) *The Philosophical Discourse of Modernity: Twelve Lectures*. Oxford: Blackwell.

Haraway, D. (1990) 'A Manifesto for Cyborgs: Science, Technology and Socialist

Feminism in the 1980s', in L.J. Nicholson (ed.), *Feminism/Postmodernism*. New York: Routledge. pp. 190–233.
Hartmann, H. (1981) 'The Unhappy Marriage of Marxism and Feminism: Towards a More Progressive Union', in L. Sargent (ed.), *The Unhappy Marriage of Marxism and Feminism: A Debate on Class and Patriarchy*. London: Pluto. pp. 1–41.
Hartmann, H. (1992) 'Extract: *Capitalism, Patriarchy, and Job Segregation by Sex* [1976]', in M. Humm (ed.), *Feminisms: A Reader*. Hemel Hempstead: Harvester Wheatsheaf. pp. 99–104.
Hartsock, N. (1990) 'Foucault on Power: A Theory for Women?', in L.J. Nicholson (ed.), *Feminism/Postmodernism*. New York: Routledge. pp. 157–75.
Humm, M. (1992) 'History of Feminism in Britain and America', in M. Humm (ed.), *Feminisms: A Reader*. Hemel Hempstead: Harvester Wheatsheaf. pp. 1–7.
Jaggar, A.M. (1983) *Feminist Politics and Human Nature*. Brighton: Harvester.
Kinnaird, J.K. (1983) 'Mary Astell: Inspired by Ideas (1668–1731)', in D. Spender (ed.), *Feminist Theorists: Three Centuries of Women's Intellectual Traditions*. London: Women's Press. pp. 28–39.
Knights, D. and Vurdubakis, T. (1994) 'Foucault, Power, Resistance and All That', in J.M. Jermier, D. Knights and W.R. Nord (eds), *Resistance and Power in Organizations*. London: Routledge. pp. 167–98.
MacCannell, D. and MacCannell, J.F. (1993) 'Violence, Power and Pleasure: A Revisionist Reading of Foucault from the Victim's Perspective', in C. Ramazanoglu (ed.), *Up Against Foucault: Explorations of Some Tensions Between Foucault and Feminism*. London: Routledge. pp. 203–38.
McNeil, M. (1987) 'Being Reasonable Feminists', in M. McNeil (ed.), *Gender and Expertise*. London: Free Association Books. pp. 13–45.
Miller, J. (1993) *The Passion of Michel Foucault*. New York: Simon and Schuster.
Millett, K. (1972) *Sexual Politics*. London: Abacus.
Mills, A.J. and Tancred, P. (1992) 'Introduction', in A.J. Mills and P. Tancred (eds), *Gendering Organizational Analysis*. London: Sage. pp. 1–8.
Mitchell, J. (1971) *Woman's Estate*. Harmondsworth: Penguin.
Mullins, L.J. (1996) *Management and Organizational Behaviour*. London: Pitman.
Oerton, S. (1994) 'Sexing the Organization, Eroticizing the Women'. Paper presented to the British Sociological Association Annual Conference, University of Central Lancashire.
Parsons, T. and Zales, R.F. (1956) *Family: Socialization and Interaction Process*. London: Routledge and Kegan Paul.
Purvis, T. and Hunt, A. (1993) 'Discourse, Ideology, Discourse, Ideology, Discourse, Ideology . . .', *British Journal of Sociology*, 44 (3): 473–99.
Ramazanoglu, C. and Holland, J. (1993) 'Women's Sexuality and Men's Appropriation of Desire', in C. Ramazanoglu (ed.), *Up Against Foucault: Explorations of Some Tensions between Foucault and Feminism*. London: Routledge. pp. 239–64.
Rhode, D.L. (1992) 'The Politics of Paradigms: Gender Difference and Gender Disadvantage', in G. Bock and S. James (eds), *Beyond Equality and Difference: Citizenship, Feminist Politics and Female Subjectivity*. London: Routledge. pp. 149–63.
Roiphe, K. (1994) *The Morning After: Sex, Fear and Feminism*. London: Hamish Hamilton.
Sawicki, J. (1994) 'Foucault, Feminism and Questions of Identity', in G. Gutting (ed.), *The Cambridge Companion to Foucault*. Cambridge: Cambridge University Press. pp. 286–313.
Segal, L. (1987) *Is the Future Female? Troubled Thoughts on Contemporary Feminism*. London: Virago.
Sheridan, M. (1980) *Michel Foucault: The Will to Truth*. London: Tavistock.
Simons, J. (1995) *Foucault and the Political*. London: Routledge.

Solonas, V. (1983) *SCUM Manifesto*. AIM/Phoenix.
Soper, K. (1993) 'Productive Contradictions', in C. Ramazanoglu (ed.), *Up Against Foucault: Explorations of Some Tensions between Foucault and Feminism*. London: Routledge. pp. 29–50.
Tiger, L. and Fox, R. (1972) *The Imperial Animal*. London: Secker and Warburg.
Tong, R. (1989) *Feminist Thought: A Comprehensive Introduction*. London: Unwin Hyman.
Walby, S. (1986) *Patriarchy at Work: Patriarchal and Capitalist Relations in Employment*. Cambridge: Polity.
Wolin, R. (1986) 'Foucault's Aesthetic Decisionism', *Telos*, 67: 71–86.
Wollstonecraft, M. (1970) *A Vindication of the Rights of Woman*. Farnborough: Gregg.

5 Towards a New Ethics? The Contributions of Poststructuralism and Posthumanism

Hugh Willmott

> The great issues of ethics – like human rights, social justice, balance between peaceful co-operation and personal self-assertion, synchronization of individual conduct and collective welfare – have lost nothing of their topicality. They only need to be seen, and dealt with, in a novel way. (Bauman, 1993: 4)

Is it ethical?

What is to be made of this question? For me, it invites consideration of whether a particular action, intention or outcome is morally defensible according to some, as yet unspecified but implied, ethical yardstick. Reference to 'ethics' signals a concern to focus attention upon the morality of an action. Such actions include the use of child labour, the dismissal of an individual on the grounds of his or her sexual orientation or ethnic identity, or the copying of another person's work without permission or acknowledgement.

As the question of ethics is raised, a distinctive type of concern is expressed: namely, that some aspect of the world can be, perhaps should be, or even necessarily must be, represented in terms of what is deemed to be 'good' as differentiated from what is considered to be 'evil'. Asking the question 'Is it ethical?' indicates an intent to render a matter accountable by emphasizing or privileging the relevance of moral criteria rather than some other measure, such as feasibility or effectiveness. Consider the issue of plagiarism. Copying or publishing of another person's work without permission or acknowledgement is not difficult to accomplish (is feasible) and it can be effective (so long as it goes undetected) in raising the material and symbolic value of the plagiarist's labour. Introducing the question 'Is plagiarism ethical?' shifts attention *from* an assessment of its efficiency and/or effectiveness *to* an evaluation of whether it is a morally defensible practice. Plagiarism becomes an ethical issue, at least in some contexts, when the debt to others' efforts is considered to be inadequately acknowledged.

In contemporary Western societies, diverse practices, including plagiarism, are routinely represented as (self-evidently) 'unethical'. But how are such claims and concerns warranted? Are certain practices intrinsically ethical or unethical? Do the terms 'ethical' and 'unethical' mirror what is inherently good and evil in the world? Or are such terms simultaneously constitutive of what we understand to be 'good' or 'evil'? The position taken in this chapter, like most of the others in this volume, is that 'good' and 'evil' do not inhere within particular actions. Rather, certain actions are deemed to be morally defensible or repugnant within particular culturally and historically contingent discourses on ethics (see MacIntyre, 1967). Just as one person's terrorist is another person's freedom fighter, what is identified as plagiarism or child labour in one historical or cultural context can be viewed as dutiful respect or as an unexceptional necessity in some other context.[1]

Suppose, for present purposes, that the historical, cultural and contextual contingency of what is deemed to be 'ethical' or 'unethical' is accepted. What ideas, or theoretical resources, might be relevant for developing an approach to ethics which accepts this contingency without embracing a nihilistic attitude of 'anything goes' or 'everything is permitted'? I will suggest that both poststructuralist and posthumanist thinking are of relevance for addressing this question. Such thinking does not provide an immediate 'solution' to problems that, from a conventional or performative standpoint, are deemed to be the most pressing – such as the preoccupation amongst students of business ethics to construct robust ethical codes. Instead, the contribution of poststructuralist and posthumanist thinking resides in unsettling established assumptions and patterns of thought (and action). As the editor of a recent book on business ethics has noted of the valuable contribution of diverse disciplines to the theory and practice of business ethics:

> The separation of economics from politics, sociality, and philosophy leads to an arid pseudoscience or an unworkable political ideology . . . Recent work by Alasdair MacIntyre, Michael Sandel, and Richard Rorty has led to a renewed vigour in political philosophy, which is of the first importance in business ethics. (Freedman, 1991: 5)

Of course, lip-service can be paid to the vital contribution of philosophy and social theory which is subsequently either selectively interpreted or even ignored[2] once its role in establishing some intellectual credibility or fashionableness has been performed. Where a less cynical (more ethical?) attitude towards these resources is favoured, it is possible for them to stimulate reflection that extends beyond the established, narrow confines of business ethics. Instead of assuming the pertinence and legitimacy of established ways of framing questions about (business) ethics, it becomes possible to ask: how is the conventional frame constructed? What is placed within the frame? What is left outside it? Poststructuralist and posthumanist thinking points towards a position in which the contextual embeddedness of ethical discourses is accepted without concluding that this view necessarily renders human actions ethically arbitrary and/or that any ethical anchor for human conduct is impossible. But, to repeat, moving towards this position necessitates a questioning and relinquishing of established ways of thinking about ethics.

This chapter is structured as follows. I begin by positioning poststructuralist thinking in relation to established ways of examining ethics. I do this by surveying a number of different dimensions of the contemporary discourse on ethics: 'descriptive ethics' which aspires to provide an objective account of the content of ethical yardsticks and codes; 'normative ethics' which contributes more directly to debates about the moral defensibility of particular yardsticks; and 'analytical ethics' which addresses questions of how normative ethical assertions are grounded (see Goodpaster, 1995). It is with 'normative ethics' – which is most directly engaged with the process of developing a judgemental standpoint about what is (deemed to be) right and wrong – that this chapter is principally concerned. More specifically, I am interested in considering how the discourse of 'normative ethics', which since the Renaissance has been so strongly wedded to a humanist credo, might be revitalized by paying attention to 'posthumanist' (*not* anti-humanist) and 'poststructuralist' thinking – thinking that is alien to the mainstream humanist and voluntarist conceptions of ethics. More specifically, I explore how this thinking might provide the necessary critical distance to appreciate, critique and move beyond how humanism frames and justifies its discourse of ethics. My discussion of descriptive, normative and analytical ethics is followed by an overview of poststructuralist thinking in relation to structuralism and other related traditions of critical analysis. Readers who are familiar with poststructuralist thinking may prefer to skim or skip the early parts of this section. I then explore how poststructuralist thinking problematizes humanism, including its conception of ethics as a set of universal principles. The limits of humanist discourse on ethics are illustrated through a consideration of issues raised in Ishiguru's novel, *The Remains of the Day*. Taking Max Weber's moral vision of 'the ethical personality' as a sophisticated formulation of a humanist ethic, I show how its limits are exposed through an examination of the lives of two of the novel's central characters, arguing that there is, to borrow Weber's phrase, an elective affinity between the egoism of humanism and the fascism institutionalized in modern organizations.

What is ethics?

'Is it ethical?' In principle, the 'it' in this question may refer to *any* practice. Suppose, for the moment, that the 'it' in the question refers to the sacking of an employee who has an exemplary employment record in all respects but 'just happens' to be black or Jewish. Is it ethical to dismiss a person purely on the grounds of their colour or religion? There are different ways of addressing this question.

Ethics: *descriptive, normative and analytical*

In a social context (e.g. Nazi Germany) where Jews are identified by a dominant group to be unfit to perform certain duties, an observer might well answer this question by saying that, in accordance with the ruling ethical yardstick, the dismissal is unproblematical. This response exemplifies what Goodpaster (1995) terms *descriptive ethics*: the individual offers no personal moral judgement on how Jews are treated. Instead, s/he strives to convey an accurate picture of the ruling yardstick for this treatment. Within the discourse of 'descriptive ethics', discussion is restricted to questions of epistemology and methodology as critical faculties are focused upon the mapping and measuring of ethical yardsticks.[3]

Alternatively, when addressing the same question 'Is it ethical?', it is possible to frame an answer in terms of the ethical yardstick favoured by the commentator. If asked whether the dismissal of Jewish workers is ethical, s/he may express the view, based upon his or her own moral convictions, that it is ethical. Or s/he may challenge its ethics. Whichever view is taken, s/he is not claiming to *describe* what *other people* deem to be ethical or unethical. Instead, s/he is making an ethical judgement about whether the dismissal is ethically right or wrong. In short, s/he is engaging in *normative ethics* (Goodpaster, 1995). When answering the question in this (normative) way, the respondent becomes susceptible to being asked to justify the evaluation of the ethics of dismissing employees on the grounds of their ethnic identity. In justification of their dismissal, it might be claimed that Jews are subhuman or subversive and are therefore unfit or untrustworthy to undertake such duties. This brings us to what Goodpaster (1995) terms *analytical ethics*.

'Analytical ethics' is concerned with the justification of normative ethical claims. In Goodpaster's (1995) formulation, analytical ethics addresses comparatively well-worn questions, such as: 'What are the grounds for normative ethical assertions? Can there be any grounds beyond personal or cultural preference or bias? How are we to interpret moral disagreement and argument (in contrast, say, to disagreement and argument in science or religion or etiquette)?' (1995: 213). Such questions resonate with the concerns of this chapter. For I will argue that by problematizing established structuralist and humanist approaches to posing and answering such questions, poststructuralist and posthumanist thinking contributes to the development of analytical ethics with a *non-specific normative purpose* as it unsettles our comfortable sense of there being authoritative descriptions of ethics and/or ethical norms upon which we can confidently depend.

From a poststructuralist perspective, the very idea of 'descriptive ethics' (see above) is placed in doubt. The coherence of descriptive ethics is challenged on the grounds that it relies upon the assumption that accounts of the world can exist in a relation of externality to what these accounts claim to describe. What ethics 'describes' may conceivably exist prior to and independently of the use of language to identify what is described. However, from a poststructuralist perspective, our knowledge of what is described depends upon the partiality of the language that is used to identify the diverse contents of 'descriptive ethics'. The seemingly self-evident existence of 'descriptive ethics' rests upon the assumption that the factual content of ethics (descriptions of ethics) can be separated from values (ethical judgements). However, as Gouldner has commented, when reflecting upon the claim of social scientists (e.g. Weber) to produce value-free truth,

> The pursuit of 'truth for its own sake' is always a tacit quest for something more than truth, for other values may have been obscured, denied, and perhaps even forbidden . . . In this sense, 'truth for its own sake' is *a crypto-ethic of concealment of other substantive values.* (1973: 65, emphasis added)

As the professed separation of facts from values is doubted and the truth ascribed to descriptions is deconstructed, the production of seemingly neutral statements of others' ethics is suspected to be coloured by normative concerns and judgements. In turn, this awareness highlights the centrality of 'normative ethics'[4] in the production of knowledge, including knowledge of ethical yardsticks. For if 'descriptive ethics' is suspected of harbouring an unacknowledged normative component comprising 'substantive values' other than a commitment to mirror reality, then the category of 'descriptive ethics' collapses into 'normative ethics'. 'Analytical ethics' is likewise understood to be conditioned by 'a tacit quest for something more than truth' (1973: 65) but in a way that can be distinguished from 'normative ethics'. For instead of simply voicing an evaluation or judgement of an issue, it prompts reflection upon the basis of such judgement, yet is not without normative conditions and consequences. More specifically, I will argue that the 'analytical ethics' of poststructuralism has a normative thrust as it challenges the coherence of 'descriptive ethics'. It unsettles any claim that 'descriptive ethics' simply describes 'what is', rather than privileges one way of constituting the sense of the world.

Business ethics

How does this overview of discourses on ethics connect to the theory and practice of management and organization? Consider the contemporary enthusiasm for business ethics and the establishment of ethical codes for corporate employees. In Goodpaster's (1995) terms, these codes fall into the category of 'descriptive ethics'. The ethical codes claim to describe the ethical values of the focal organization as they provide an account of the 'ethical values, beliefs and convictions' of its members (Goodpaster, 1995). Take, for example, the values of SB, a pseudonym for a multinational health care company discussed by Gergen and Whitney:

> We at [SB] will succeed in our competitive aspirations by concentrating our activities around the following values:

> *Performance*
> SB is performance driven. We continuously aim to improve performance in all that we do.
>
> *Customers*
> SB is customer-oriented. We strive to provide products and services of superior value to meet the expectations of our internal and external customers.
>
> *Innovation*
> SB constantly strives to be creative and innovative in all its endeavours . . .
>
> *People*
> SB employees are all partners, working together in the pursuit of the SB mission and strategy . . .
>
> *Integrity*
> SB demands openness and honesty throughout its operations to engender trust, and integrity underscores everything that we do. (1996: 347)

In a world where established, bureaucratic methods of organizational control are increasingly regarded as costly and inflexible, and where shareholders are becoming increasingly sensitive to corporate image and reputation, codes of ethics are intended to buttress other means of improving the prediction and control of employee behaviour – often by encouraging their commitment to the corporate values espoused in the code (see Parker, 1997). As Gergen and Whitney note of the code of ethics developed by SB, it was accompanied by a series of management training workshops attended by participants at which 'the dominant rallying cry' was 'walk the truth' – a phrase which exhorted SB employees to live out the overarching values in the daily performance of their jobs (1996: 345). Codes of ethics seek to establish their authority as an objective 'regime of truth' (Foucault, 1984: 73) as employees are invited to suspend any disbelief they may have in the adequacy of the code's contents as a description of corporate activity.

The context and claim of ethical codes

In common with every other human activity, business dealings depend upon at least a minimal observance of ethical conventions. Without a measure of trust, economic relationships are difficult to form and sustain. Supporting business practice is a raft of moral norms which keeps economic activity afloat. It is this raft which provides a justification for the existence of 'business ethics', whether codified or not, because, 'as a matter of necessity, business practice must rest upon a moral base' (Bowie, 1982: 39). However, it is one thing to acknowledge how economic activity is dependent upon moral conduct if it is not to descend into chaos. It is quite another to use this argument to justify the ethics of business or the specific contents and application of ethical codes. There is also a problem of compliance with codes of ethics. For if competitive advantage for individual employees or firms can be secured by circumventing such codes, especially if competitors are perceived to be complying with these 'rules of engagement', there is a strong incentive to disregard or transgress their requirements. As Arrow (1973: 315, cited in Bowie, 1982: 152) puts it, 'an ethical code may be of value to the running of the system as a whole, it may be of value to all firms if all firms maintain it, and yet it will be to the advantage of any one firm to cheat, in fact the more so, the more other firms are sticking to it.' For example, one health care company (SmithKline Beecham) was charged by the Inspector General of the US Department of Health and Human Services with 'billings for blood tests that were deemed not medically necessary and, in some cases, may not have been ordered by a physician' (reported by Reuters, 10 September 1996 – see http://www.reutersheath.com/news/docs/199609/1990910phb.html). The company agreed to pay the US government $325 million to settle allegations in respect of fraudulent clinical billing involving Medicare and Medicaid claims. A year later SmithKline Beecham was being sued by thirty-seven healthcare insurance companies for allegedly violating federal racketeering laws and overcharging them by hundreds of millions of dollars since 1989, a charge that the company has flatly denied (reported by Reuters citing the *Wall Street Journal* – see http://www.reutersheath.com/news/docs/199708/19970822ina.html).

Contemporary attentiveness to business ethics signals both a greater self-consciousness about the importance of ethics and a degree of anxiety about their robustness. Advocates of ethical codes recognize, albeit implicitly, that the established, capitalist system of economic organization throws up moral problems that it has difficulty in resolving precisely because it is corrosive of relationships that are regulated by morality rather than the cash nexus. As Weber puts it,

> Where the market is allowed to follow its own autonomous tendencies, its participants do not look towards the persons of each other but only toward the commodity; there are no obligations of brotherliness or reverence, and none of those spontaneous human relations that are sustained by personal unions. (1978: 636–7)

The response of the advocates of ethical codes to the insight that capitalism induces firms to 'cheat' is to reassert the importance of establishing and strengthening codes which are understood to fill the moral vacuum identified by Weber, and not to question the ethics of an economic system which stimulates and rewards the violation of moral customs. At the same time, those who suggest that 'business ethics' is a contradiction in terms are deemed to be 'fundamentally mistaken because the very enterprise of business presupposes that participants in business transactions must subscribe to a set of universal moral norms' (Bowie, 1982: 39). It is certainly plausible to argue that most human interaction, including business transactions, relies *inter alia* upon a degree of mutual understanding and trust. But it does not follow that the existence of these so-called 'universal norms' makes the conduct of business ethical. On the contrary, and somewhat perversely, an attentiveness to business ethics potentially exposes (rather than heals) the way in which established norms are, as Weber indicates, exploited and corrupted by the pursuit of business values and priorities. For the message of most business ethics experts seems to be that the individual employee must be sufficiently ethical not to act in ways that are damaging to a firm's operation (e.g. by stealing or its harming its reputation) but not so ethical as to challenge or reject the morality of its basic principles or to harbour deeper and potentially paralysing worries about its 'dehumanizing' effects, as identified by Weber.[5]

The establishment of codes of business ethics is founded upon the calculation that elements of the moral basis of business activity must somehow be appreciated and protected if it is to flourish. Ethics are *instrumentalized* as the value ascribed to the adoption of codes is made conditional upon their contribution to business objectives (note, for example, how the values of SB summarized above are explicitly geared to the successful pursuit of 'competitive aspirations'). This implies that, in principle, the codes will be refined or discarded according to calculations about their continuing contribution to these objectives. It is the calculation that ethics, appropriately formulated, can be good for business which leads apologists for ethical codes, such as Bowie (1982: 153), to argue that pressures to dilute or disregard such codes are 'inconsistent and irrational'. 'Inconsistent' with the preservation and expansion of business activity those pressures to degrade business ethics may be; and 'unfair' (1982: 153) they may be also. But is it irrational, within the context of a system where competitive advantages can be gained by violating ethical conventions, for an individual or a firm to disregard such codes (even or especially when simultaneously encouraging competitors to comply with them)? Instead of regarding such behaviour as 'irrational', it is necessary to acknowledge that this behaviour, often involving a calculated business risk, is unintentionally but relentlessly promoted by the capitalist organization of economic activity, especially where corporate performance is assessed by shareholders in terms of short term share price movements.

Behaviour which weakens business activity by bringing it into disrepute may be addressed by introducing or strengthening ethical codes and/or by lobbying for changes in legislation which can shift the cost–benefit balance of engaging in actions deemed to be unethical (while simultaneously stimulating a market in subterfuge and circumvention). In general, the business community prefers self-regulation because it safeguards a system of internal accountability. Legislation, in contrast, concedes that economic activity is accountable to the polity, and thus potentially opens up the issue of 'economic citizenship' as the regulation of economic activity passes, in principle, to the state where it escapes the direct control of corporations (although in practice the operation of the regulatory apparatus may be substantially funded and shaped by the lobbying and expertise provided by private bodies). It then becomes possible to impose heavy penalties, as in the SmithKline Beecham example, when legal as well as ethical codes are violated.

Ethical codes and the domination of instrumental reason

The instrumentalization of ethical codes is symptomatic of a conventional representation of 'organizations' and 'management' as impersonal instruments which are morally and politically neutral in their formulation and effects. In mainstream textbooks, work organizations are generally characterized as impersonal entities – for example, as 'goal-directed activity systems' (Daft, 1995: 10). The *goals* to which firms are directed may be acknowledged to be value-laden, though they are more usually depicted as shared between diverse stakeholders who cooperate to secure their respective interests. 'Organizations' and 'management' are understood to offer an efficient or effective means of realizing these goals. The latter has an aura of value neutrality but, as MacIntyre has stressed, its logic 'is inseparable from a mode of human existence in which the contrivance of means is in central part the manipulation of human beings into *compliant patterns of behaviour*; and it is by appeal to his own effectiveness in this respect that the manager claims authority in the manipulative mode' (1981: 71, emphasis added). I will return to this issue later in the chapter where I explore the presence of fascism in modern organizations. For the moment, it is relevant to note how the value and priority ascribed to performative criteria are themselves the product of a moral judgement, sometimes characterized as a productivist ethic;[6] and that an effect of commitment or even compliance with the instrumentalization of ethics is the (re)production of a world in which value is practically invested in the treatment of ethics as a means to some other end.

This observation would seem to be particularly apt with respect to codes of ethics, such as the code commended to SB employees. These codes seek to establish 'compliant patterns of behaviour', and are justified in terms of their assumed effectiveness in realizing the 'competitive aspirations' of the company. Codes of ethics invite employees to suspend or defer their personal credos in favour of courses of action, guided by ethical codes, which are deemed to be most effective. Textbooks in which work organizations are presented as technical and value-neutral invite students to read their contents as 'descriptive' rather than 'normative' accounts of their subject matter and, in doing so, to suspend any moral misgivings as well as intellectual disbelief.[7] Codes of conduct and management texts each legitimize a particular kind of closure in respect of the reality of management and organization: a closure, that is, which conflates 'descriptive' with 'normative' ethics. What is arguably a matter of (normative) judgement is presented as a matter of descriptive fact: 'SB is customer-oriented. We strive to provide products and services of superior value to meet the expectations of our internal and external customers . . . integrity underscores everything that we do' (Gergen and Whitney, 1996: 347).

Yet, as poststructuralist thinking would anticipate, there is a recurrent return of repressed dimensions of organizational life. Organizations are irremediably moral orders where ethical as well as performative criteria are widely applied to the assessment of conduct. In practice, issues of fairness and propriety routinely jostle with issues of efficiency and effectiveness (Jackall, 1988; Watson, 1994 and Chapter 12 in this volume); and, indeed, mundane moral considerations about the moral character of individuals and practices have been identified as the very bedrock of communication in all but the most coercive forms of collective action (Roberts, 1984; Anthony, 1986 and Chapter 13 in this volume). More visibly, expressions of recalcitrance (e.g. unsought resignations, withdrawal of labour, whistle-blowing) are an endemic articulation of the impugning or contradiction of the 'normative ethics' of employees, including *their* sense of 'fairness', 'honesty' or 'openness', by the demands of corporate 'descriptive ethics', whether encountered in everyday interactions at work or formalized in codes of conduct.

From this perspective, the kind of 'descriptive ethics' contained in the SB statement is understood to be developed in pursuit of two conflicting objectives. Simultaneously, it is advanced to revitalize, colonize or displace employees' own 'normative ethics' which might challenge or disrupt corporate demands upon them. It seeks to enlist the cooperation of employees by appealing to, and reasserting, the primacy of values such as 'honesty', 'trust' and 'integrity'. But it also seeks to harness and instrumentalize these values in the service of corporate performance improvement. *To the extent* that colonization occurs, the employee's common-sense commitment to certain values – such as producing goods of 'superior value' or 'working together' – is appropriated to increase commitment to the 'competitive aspirations' of the employer. *To the extent* that displacement succeeds, employees act in accordance with the injunctions contained in the statement of corporate ethics. Managerially, the difficulty with such invitations, which extend to associated programmes of employee 're-education' and 'empowerment', is that they assume the existence of autonomous individuals who are capable of choosing their value orientations while, at the same time, demanding a commitment to the corporation which restricts the exercise of this autonomy to following the corporate code (see Willmott, 1986). The idea of the autonomous self who is capable of making such choices is affirmed but is then 'constantly trimmed' (Bauman, 1993: 13). This ambivalence – the tension between the assumption of autonomy and the practice of heteronomy – is productive of a tension that would seem to defy resolution.

Ethics: *'professional' and 'personal'*

What guidance is given by the mainstream business ethics literature to employees who face a conflict between their own sentiments and the demands of their profession or employer? Typically, this literature proceeds from the understanding that 'business ethics begins with the duties associated with *one's role in business*' (Bowie, 1982: 16, emphasis added). By describing the corporate values, such as those contained in the SB statement, codes invite or require an accountability of organizational members to these values. During working hours at least, employees are expected to suspend any 'normative ethics' which might lead them to deviate from the ethics set out in the code of conduct (or face disciplinary action). For example, a person who is committed to 'green' values may object to the exclusion, or minimal inclusion, of such values within a corporate ethical code; but, as an employee, this person is required to behave *as if* the contents of the code were simply 'descriptive' – an 'as if' which, as noted above, poststructuralist thinking challenges as it contends that 'descriptions' are (contextually) constitutive, not (impartially) reflective, of the reality which they claim to represent.

Consider again the SB code. This code makes no direct reference to the personal values of employees. Nonetheless, their values as parents, citizens or consumers are not irrelevant or marginal. Ultimately, the capacity to fulfil the SB values – such as the commitment 'to meet the expectations of our internal and external customers' (Gergen and Whitney, 1996: 347) – depends upon its employees whose allegiance cannot be taken for granted, as the code accompanied by training sessions where employees were urged to 'walk the truth' bears witness. Even if the conversion to 'the truth' of the SB code of ethics extended beyond the duration of the training sessions, there is no guarantee that the voices of other yet-to-be-trained employees would be harmonious or loyal. Their personal values or 'normative ethics' might well be resistant to colonization by the 'descriptive ethics' presented in the code.[8]

At the same time, all but the most illiberal of business ethics commentators pay eloquent lip-service to the view that loyalty does not, or at least should not, require employees to do what an employer demands irrespective of the ends to which their actions are directed.[9] Bowie, for example, recommends that 'One should be loyal; but the object of one's loyalty should be morally appropriate. The virtue of loyalty does not require that one accept blindly the person or cause to which one is loyal' (1982: 14). This caveat is frequently repeated in the textbooks. But there is precious little illumination of how what is deemed to be 'morally appropriate' is to be adduced. The assumption is that the existence of formal codes of ethics will make it most unlikely that employees will be faced with morally testing dilemmas. As a consequence, there is no attempt to address the question of how, for example, an inclination to accept blindly the 'person' or the 'cause' is challenged, or how a clearer vision is to be attained. In effect, ethical codes aspire to eliminate such moral dilemmas. The contents of corporate codes of ethics are expected to provide a substitute for the ethical reasoning and moral struggles of employees. There is an assumption that ethical codes can and should provide the relevant moral guidance. In the following sections, I explore how poststructuralist thinking can contribute to countering the colonization and/or displacement of 'normative ethics' by 'descriptive ethics' and indicate how posthumanism offers an alternative.

What is poststructuralism?

Poststructuralism unsettles claims to provide authoritative descriptions of ethical yardsticks or frameworks. It is concerned to recall what is displaced or 'uncaptured', and yet is simultaneously referenced or constituted, by the use of any such claim or argument. For example, there is an implicit dependence upon some notion of 'evil' when sense is made of what is 'good'. Likewise, an appeal to 'the facts' which are untainted by bias or subjective values routinely displaces recognition of the (moral) move to give special weight to the production of 'facts' and the value choices made in the course of their identification and communication.

Poststructuralist thinking is helpful in re-membering the connectedness of what appear to be antimonies – such as 'good' and 'evil', 'fact' and 'value' or 'self' and 'other'. But, as noted earlier, it does not provide a self-evident basis for resolving the 'problems' of ethics as these have been conventionally formulated. It provides neither an alternative content for ethical codes nor, relatedly, a firm grounding for assessing competing ethical claims. Noting the affinities with other forms of critical thinking, and especially non-dogmatic Marxism (see Wray-Bliss and Parker, Chapter 3 in this volume), Ryan observes how poststructuralism poses a potent challenge to all 'intellectual enterprises that give themselves out to be rational, scientific, axiomatic and self-evident' (1982: 3) – of which the SB code discussed earlier is an example. The 'deconstruction' performed by poststructuralist thinking, he continues,

> teaches one to attend to gestures of exclusion. What is the operation of exclusion in a philosophy that permits one group, or value, or idea to be kept out so that another can be safeguarded internally and turned into a norm? (1982: 3)

In relation to business ethics, poststructuralist analysis explores how its discourse privileges certain kinds of values – such as customer satisfaction or profitable growth – as it excludes, marginalizes or instrumentalizes other values, such as personal or communal well-being. Derridan deconstruction has focused upon the careful teasing out of these tensions and antagonisms within philosophical writings. In contrast, other critical traditions, such as non-dogmatic Marxism, are more interested in the dialectical relationship between critical philosophy and political practice. For these traditions, the answer to questions of the normalization of the values or ideas of a particular group extends beyond the deconstructive critique of 'gestures of exclusion' to the critique of exclusionary practices and institutions. From the latter perspective, the principal value of poststructuralist deconstruction is that it problematizes any tendency for more obviously 'political' projects, which target oppressive practices and institutions, to become forgetful of the precariousness of their own authority as it dis-closes how such authority is founded upon forms of arbitrary, forceful exclusion or repression.

Before poststructuralism

The style of analysis which attracts the label 'poststructuralist' arises from an engagement with, and critique of, structuralist thinking. As Sturrock has observed,

> *anyone who hopes to understand Post-structuralism and its difficult methods requires a grounding in Structuralism*, from which . . . Post-structuralism is a derivation, corrective of certain tendencies within Structuralism but certainly not dismissive of its insights as a whole. (1993: viii–ix, emphasis added)

At the outset, it is relevant to distinguish *positivist* structuralism, as exemplified in the work of Durkheim, from the *conceptual* structuralism developed by diverse social scientists – anthropologists, linguists and political economists – from which poststructuralism has emerged. Briefly, conceptual structuralists reject the (positivist) view that scientific knowledge can directly access and reflect the empirical reality of the world of social structures. In conceptual structuralism, 'structure' is a heuristic for rendering the world intelligible, not a description of the empirical world. The idea of structure is conceived as an invaluable conceptual tool for interpreting and explaining (self-consciously theory-dependent) empirical observations. As a holistic concept, structure allows relations between phenomena (e.g. myths, in Lévi-Strauss's case) to be identified which might otherwise be assumed to exist independently of each other.[10]

In its different guises, structuralism suggests that there are structures governing human behaviour which operate, as it were, behind our backs to shape if not determine our actions. In Durkheim's case, he believed that empirical knowledge of these structures would yield an objective basis for intervening in society to reduce anomie and strengthen normative order (to be discussed below). For Lévi-Strauss, our capacity to change the world is limited by universal structures that will continue to condition human behaviour in any future society, a view that can provide limited insight into the historical specificity of any particular social institution or practice. In Marxian analysis, which also articulates conceptual structuralist thinking, the terms 'capital' and 'labour' are invoked not as descriptions of empirical entities or as universal categories but as interdependent yet asymmetrical elements of a historically distinctive structure of social relations (Ollman, 1976; Marsden, 1996). The idea of 'structure' enables Marx to connect phenomena which otherwise might be assumed (and indeed are commonsensically believed) to exist independently of each other.[11]

In Saussure's *structural linguistics*, language is understood to enable but also to constrain what can be said or communicated. In order to make him/herself understood, each speaker is obliged to adopt a shared structure or grammar of language, comprising the terms or conventions which imbue words with specific meanings.[12] Structural linguistics circles around the relationship between signifiers (e.g. different words) and signifieds (e.g. the meaning associated with words) without addressing the relationship of signifieds to their referents (the reality that words are deemed to describe or represent).[13] The meaning of linguistic signs (that is, words) is understood to be entirely dependent upon the local system of signs from which their meaning is derived. Language is thus analysed as a shifting, self-referential system of differences. From this perspective, 'ethics' has no stable meaning but is contingent upon the system of signs with which it is associated and which serves to differentiate its meaning from other words. As we shall see, Derrida develops and radicalizes this insight as he notes how each term within a given system of differences depends upon a necessary, yet inescapably arbitrary, exclusion of significance that might otherwise be included in it. It is this exclusion which renders the meaning and authority invested in words, such as 'God', 'science', 'ethics' or even 'poststructuralism', inherently unstable and deconstructable, held together only by convention and power or what Foucault has termed power/knowledge.

The diverse varieties of structuralism challenge the coherence of empiricist and atomistic forms of knowledge. In particular, they challenge the autonomy ascribed to individuals, as evident in economic analyses where skills are identified as the possessions of individuals, or in conventional linguistics where words are understood to be neutral means of capturing the phenomena which they are understood to describe. *Structuralism thus offers an antidote to forms of bourgeois humanist analysis in which the autonomy of the individual is assumed and celebrated.* Its thrust has been 'very markedly anti-humanist, which is also to say markedly anti-bourgeois, the bourgeoisie being traditionally seen as the class embodiment of an ill-founded subjectivism' (Sturrock, 1993: 168). Structuralism challenges ideologies of individualism as it stresses how the actions of individuals are shaped and enabled by transpersonal forces.[14]

Poststructuralism and its critics

Saussure's structural linguistics does not extend to the question of how any system of differences is reproduced and transformed through social practices and power relations. However, an awareness of the arbitrariness of the system of differences can prompt questions of how closure – evident in the (precarious and impermanent) identity and continuity of signifiers and signifieds – is routinely accomplished and maintained. In this respect, it is relevant to appreciate how poststructuralism amplifies and radicalizes the limited degree of reflexivity in structuralism. Especially in the work of Derrida, all distinctions, including Saussure's distinction between language and speech, are re-cognized as constructions which necessarily represent the world in particular ways – ways that are non-exhaustive. The reflexive recollection of this process of closure – characterized as a method of deconstruction – addresses how particular knowledge claims depend upon an initial rhetorical and conceptual move which is irremediably arbitrary (e.g. Saussure's appeal to the common-sense, seemingly universal and self-evident distinction between language and speech). This move must be, and is, effectively hidden when, as in structuralist analysis, the attention of the reader is focused upon the claims that the analyst makes rather than the gambit(s) which, as it were, lure(s) the reader into following the author down a particular path. The intent of deconstruction is to expose and disrupt habitual patterns of thought by inducing greater self-consciousness about the presence, operation and partiality of these conventions.

Poststructuralism challenges and departs from the understanding that concepts ('signifiers') mirror what they describe ('referents'). For this reason, it is hazardous if not perverse to ascribe any consistent or fixed meaning to the term 'poststructuralism'! Its meaning or identity is understood to depend not upon what might be deemed essential to forms of analysis or authors (e.g. Derrida, Lyotard, Foucault, Lacan) variously collected within this (declared) genre. Instead, it depends upon how language is deployed to include 'this' and exclude 'that'. The meaning or identity (the 'signified') of any particular term, such as 'poststructuralism', is contingent upon the mobilization of a particular discourse, and not upon some essence to which the concept allegedly makes reference. What comprises 'poststructuralism' (or 'human nature' or 'ethics') is not intrinsic to what it (is deemed to) describe(s). Rather, it is constituted through a discourse that admits certain features as it refuses others (see, Munro, Chapter 9, and Letiche, Chapter 6 in this volume).

Poststructuralist analysis is therefore perhaps best characterized as involving *a commitment to a mood of restlessness* which, as I have already indicated, has significant affinities with, and may usefully complement, other streams of critical thinking which also problematize seemingly authoritative and stable meanings – for example, by locating the (re)production of knowledge within relations of power (see Weiskopf and Willmott, 1997). In poststructuralist analysis, 'poststructuralism' as well as 'self', 'organization', 'society' and, of course, 'ethics' are unstable, contingent concepts whose meaning is shifting and contextually dependent. What may appear through a process of inclusion/exclusion to be authoritative, self-evident and solid is understood and dis-closed to be inherently precarious and contested as forms of closure are repeatedly deconstructed. And to the extent that dis-closure is suspended in order to proceed with analysis, this suspension is acknowledged to be poststructuralism's repressed other which threatens to return, and thus to unsettle the authority vested in its claims.

In defence of poststructuralism

It has been noted that poststructuralist deconstructionism has affinities with, but is by no means identical to, established forms of critique. It is therefore a mistake to regard this non-identity as a threatening opposition rather than as a friendly provocation to appreciate the irredeemable partial and precarious nature of all kinds of knowledge. As Norris has argued: 'the activity of deconstructionism is strictly inconceivable outside the tradition of enlightened rational critique' (1987: 162).

This assessment has not been shared by some leftist critics of poststructuralism for whom the absence of any firm ground is tantamount to nihilism, where any meaning is deemed to be as good as any other. Given the possibility of reading poststructuralism in this way, it is not surprising that commentators committed to, say, a Habermasian formulation of critical social theory – in which analysis aspires to guide and support processes of human emancipation – have been anxious to expose the limits of poststructuralism's coherence and rationality.[15] In a book that has attracted considerable acclaim, Dews, for example, has accused poststructuralism of being 'oriented towards the dismantling of stable conceptions of meaning, subjectivity and identity' (1987: xi).

Dews's account would seem to be consistent with my representation of poststructuralism. But is it? Dews persuasively identifies its key preoccupation; but he also overlooks its positive, normative effects as he deems these to be wholly negative: note his use of the term 'dismantle' rather than 'problematize'. Although not entirely hostile to poststructuralism, which is acknowledged to have exercised an extraordinary influence over intellectual life in the English-speaking world, Dews identifies and assesses its nature and significance very much in the light of the preoccupations and aspirations of Critical Theory.[16] He concludes that the *lack of rational grounds* for justifying its claims 'leads to the collapse of the critical dimension' (1987: 241) in poststructuralist analysis.

Critical Theory assumes that knowledge can be cleansed of ideology as its capacity to repress and oppress is dissolved. In effect, Critical Theory retains the truth of a humanist formulation of the Enlightenment project but seeks to revitalize its emancipatory intent by eliminating the bourgeois spin on humanism. In other words, Critical Theory seeks to substitute a radical concept of freedom for a market-based formulation in which freedom is associated with individuals' capacity to acquire material or cultural capital. This radical humanism assumes that social practices and institutions can be developed which serve to emancipate human beings from forms of distorted, ideological communication. Poststructuralism, in contrast, assumes that a force unacknowledged by Critical Theory, identified by Foucault as power/knowledge, is *necessarily* involved in securing and sustaining the stability of any (privileged) meaning, identity or subjectivity as it is separated and differentiated from some other (e.g. displaced) meaning, identity or subjectivity.

In the post-Enlightenment period, 'truth' can be seen to have become vested in the humanist project; and the identification of human beings as the creations of God has become the discredited other. From this perspective, Critical Theory is insufficiently reflexive about its own immersion in the humanist project. In common with Habermas, poststructuralists like Foucault want to retain 'truth' as a regulative ideal (and indeed would probably challenge the voluntarism implied by 'wants to'). But Foucault stresses the importance of striving to wrest this ideal from established, hegemonic understandings of what counts as truth, including for example, sovereign conceptions of power. When power is understood to be an endemic *condition* as well as a consequence of truth, it is

> not a matter of emancipating truth from every system of power (which would be a chimera, for truth is already power), but of detaching the power of truth from the forms of hegemony, social, economic, and cultural, within which it operates at the present time. (Foucault, 1980: 133)

I take Foucault to be commending greater reflexivity in respect of how the prevailing sense of truth is produced and maintained. Critical reflexivity, Foucault contends, must move away from what, for him, is a particular 'truth politics' which revolves around the (ultimately futile) effort to remove residues of ideology so as to reveal a universal, pristine truth. Seeking to expose and problematize the 'regime of truth' which animates this ill-fated project, Foucault commends an approach that strives to unsettle its hegemonic influence by showing *how* this regime operates to render its sense of truth authoritative and self-evident. Arguably, this is also the morally charged intent of Derridan deconstructionism. As Derrida contends,

> All that a deconstructive point of view tries to show, is that since convention, institutions and consensus are stabilization (sometimes stabilization of great duration, sometimes micro-stabilization), this means that they are stabilizations of something essentially unstable and chaotic . . . Now, this chaos and instability, which is fundamental, founding and irreducible, is at once naturally the worst against which we struggle with laws, rules, conventions, politics and provisional hegemony, but at the same time it is a chance, a chance to change, to destabilize. If there were continual stability, there would be no need for politics, and it is to the extent that stability is not natural, essential or substantial, that politics exists and ethics is possible. (1996: 83, 84)

It is this possibility of 'destabilization' to which deconstructionism points and which it promotes as a way of dis-closing the political and ethical basis of established practices and beliefs. Needless to say, 'a deconstructive point of view' is also a 'stabilization' or 'provisional hegemony'; but in priciple it is one that recalls its precariousness and thereby invites not only a recollection of the politics which serves to stabilize its meaning but a recognition of how closure or stability is an ethical act.

One reaction to the poststructuralist caution or 'admission' that it is hazardous to ascribe any fixed or continuous meaning to any term is to dismiss it on the grounds that it is incoherent, or that its lack of identity or substance renders it practically and politically impotent. Against this interpretation, which represents the glass of poststructuralism as at best 'half-empty', I have argued that it is 'half-full' – that it can make a positive contribution to critical analysis and to moral/political action. It is true that no programme of action springs directly from poststructuralist analysis, in a way that it follows, more or less explicitly, from the contrasting structuralist analyses of Durkheim and Marx. Nonetheless the capacity of poststructuralism to problematize seemingly self-evident categories and oppositions – such as science and common sense, capital and labour, and 'descriptive' and 'normative' ethics – can serve to strengthen rather than undermine the basis upon which the politico-ethical commitments that are productive of 'stabilization' are made. While poststructuralism *may* be invoked to justify a nihilistic standpoint or to support endless prevarication (see Callinicos, 1989), it can also help counter naive or reckless political decisions and adventures. I now elaborate this view.

Poststructuralism and ethics

I have argued that poststructuralist analysis invites us to reflect critically upon assumptions or habits of thought which are unacknowledged or taken for granted such as those incorporated within discourses on 'descriptive' and 'normative' ethics (see earlier). It is for this reason that Derridan poststructuralism best fits the category of 'analytical ethics' (Goodpaster, 1995). Although it does not have a *specific normative purpose*, it does have 'normative' effects. For example, by deconstructing the distinction between 'descriptive' and 'normative' ethics, thereby questioning whether the former can ever be generated through a relationship of externality to what it purports to describe, poststructuralist analysis stresses the normative character of avowedly descriptive ethics.

Contrary to its undeserved reputation for being purely academicist in orientation, Derridan poststructuralism has a deeply moral and political significance. It challenges 'the metaphysics of presence' in which it is assumed, logocentrically, that the reporting of objects is unmediated by the differential play of language engaged by human subjects. This challenge should not be taken as an abandonment of truth, referents, and stable (albeit transient) contexts of meaning or the collapse of any distinction between critical, ethical forms of discourse, including literary criticism, and explicitly fictional work. Certainly, Derridan deconstruction reveals that critical discourse cannot escape a dependence upon conventions which produce their sense. Nonetheless, Derrida expects and requires his claims to be interrogated according to criteria of 'reasoned dialogue and an ethics of open dialogical exchange' (Norris, 1993: 34; Derrida, 1989). In essence, he understands poststructuralism to offer a *more consistently critical* approach to social analysis which, for example, problematizes the residues of bourgeois humanism harboured by Critical Theory.

Poststructuralist analysis involves and invites a letting go of habits of thought and action which have become so established and institutionalized that their authority and good sense appear entirely self-evident. In a way which parallels the capacity of political cartoons or satire to dis-close the limits of a particular version of the truth, the kind of scepticism articulated in Derridan deconstructionism can touch a nerve as it re-members how the other is deferred or repressed, but never completely eradicated, by seemingly authoritative statements and codes. For example, as Bauman (1993) has stressed, a significant contribution of poststructuralist thinking resides in its radical challenge to the claims of ethical codes to nurture morality when, in practice, they can act to weaken it. Such codes are then shown to present parochiality as (Kantian) universality (see Legge, Chapter 7 in this volume) – a move which involves the operation of a totalitarian politics that masquerades as progressive and liberal. Poststructuralist analysis does not claim to offer direct assistance to those who seek to establish some firm or definitive ground for the prescription of ethical conduct as inscribed, for example, in ethical codes. Its contribution dwells in *the subversion of closure* rather than providing an authoritative means of resolving ethical dilemmas.

Posthumanism in poststructuralism

Underlying this position is the understanding that, at the core of human experience, there is an undecidability or openness which renders efforts to achieve stability both necessary and precarious. As noted earlier, for Derrida, institutions are the 'stabilization of something essentially unstable and chaotic', an instability that is 'founding and irreducible'. This understanding runs counter to the humanist view that the autonomous self resides at the centre of human existence, an inner self that is more or less fully realized through a process of self-mastery that is facilitated by the establishment of bourgeois institutions or the development of communication free from power-invested distortions. From a humanist perspective, the social and natural worlds are represented as a separate and malleable other. 'Man' is positioned, as subject, at the centre. Poststructuralism, in contrast, advances a posthumanist understanding of the modern condition in which 'man' is irremediably decentred. The tradition of enlightened rational critique is renewed. But this is advanced not by demanding compliance with ethical codes which are routinely formulated and legitimized by reference to a humanist conception of human existence and behaviour but, instead, by challenging and rejecting the divisive, narcissistic baggage of humanism which, arguably, encourages the opportunistic and materially self-interested behaviour for which ethical codes are commended as a corrective.

Following Derrida, the irremediably decentred quality of human existence means that 'we live and act in infinitude' (1996: 86) where responsibility for the other is not limitable. Drawing a division between 'self' and 'other' is ultimately unsustainable because it depends upon arbitrarily drawn boundaries. 'Undecidability' is inherent in making and applying such divisions and is never overcome by them. Problems of ethics and politics recur because any limit is the product of a political move which is vulnerable to challenge:

> There is politicization and ethicization because undecidability is not simply a moment to be overcome by the occurrence of the decision. Undecidability continues to inhabit the decision and the latter does not close itself off from the former. 1996: 87)

From this it follows that:

> whatever choice I make, I cannot say with a good conscience that I have made a good choice or that I have assumed my responsibilities. Every time I hear someone say that 'I have taken a decision', or 'I have assumed my responsibilities', I am suspicious because if there is responsibility or decision *one cannot determine them as such* or have certainty or good conscience with regard to them. (1996: 86, emphasis added)

Why not? Because, in Weber's (1978) terms, there is always a paradox of consequences. For Derrida, this paradox is not attributed to the substantively irrational outcomes of applying formal rationality. Instead, it is rooted in the infinitude of human existence which makes it likely and perhaps inevitable that any effort to act responsibly towards one party, or with regard to one set of issues, will have some adverse consequences for some other party or other set of issues, if only because of limited time and resources:

> If I conduct myself particularly well with regard to someone, I know that it is to the detriment of an other; of one nation to the detriment of another nation, of one family to the detriment of another family, of my friends to the detriment of other friends or non-friends, etc. This is the infinitude that inscribes itself within responsibility; *otherwise there would be no ethical problems or decisions*. (1996: 86, emphasis added)

The moral to be drawn from this position is not that choices are impossible, arbitrary or contradictory and therefore that any decision is as good as any other decision; but rather that, in Foucault's felicitous phrase, 'everything is dangerous' (1984: 343). For what appears to be unconditionally 'positive' or 'good' is potentially hazardous, if only because a belief in its positivity or goodness can dim the critical imagination and thereby give succour to forms of tyranny in the name of the 'good'.

Humanism is an example of a (political) philosophy which presents itself as unconditionally wholesome and beneficial. A project devised in the Renaissance, humanism has aspired to supply modern societies with 'rules that "will stick" and foundations that "won't shake"' (Bauman, 1993: 9). Embracing an ethos of science and progress, those who founded the humanist project expected that the formulation of humanist principles would be refined, but they were confident that a rational ethical framework based upon a humanist philosophy would gradually but surely be established and adopted. Today, though, humanism is increasingly being problematized by a postmodern sensibility, spearheaded by poststructuralist thinking, which doubts its coherence, feasibility and morality. Instead of being embraced and championed as a key to modern, enlightened processes of personal and social development, humanism is identified as 'a sediment of tribal parochialism of institutional powers that usurp ethical authority' (1993: 14, emphasis added). From a poststructuralist standpoint, humanism is identified as a sacred cow, a cow targeted by Derrida for slaughter because it is seen to impede rather than facilitate the advance of critical reason. That said, the modern attachment to humanism remains strong, with the antihumanist being cast as a contemporary equivalent of the Antichrist, as is evident in the expressions of disbelief and defensiveness aroused when it is questioned. Criticism of humanism rapidly elicits 'name-calling' in the form of charges of relativism and nihilism. The contemporary, modernist faith in humanism is at once revealing and disconcerting, and it is discussed in the following section.

The rise and fall of the humanist project

Renaissance thinkers and later advocates of Enlightenment thought anticipated that society could be set upon a rational basis once the dogmas of tradition and habit had been exposed and removed. Premodern ethics, which privileged the will of the Almighty, were humanized and justified in terms of the welfare of individuals and/or society: the origins of good and evil were no longer sought '*behind* the world' (Nietzsche, 1956: 151, emphasis in the original). Acts deemed to be evil were to be identified and reduced not through devotion, prayer and worship but by developing and applying secular ethical principles and codes – albeit ones derived from a Judaeo-Christian tradition.[17]

The fathers of humanism, such as Erasmus and Pico della Mirandola, had as their founding axiom the understanding that

> man is all-powerful, if his will is strong enough. He can create himself. He can choose to be courageous, honourable, just, rich, influential, or not . . . *Out of his own individual will he can move the earth.* The great individual stands alone; under his feet the earth does not move. (Carroll, 1993: 3, emphasis added)

Begun in the Renaissance, which subsequently represented its pre-history as the Middle Ages or the Dark Ages (Frayling, 1995), the humanist project produced awesome advances in the arts and 'statecraft' as well in the application of science, including the development of productive capacity.[18] Moral standards and discipline were combined with scientific and technological means of transformation advanced by capitalism as an engine of economic development. Among others, Durkheim (1964) believed that modern moral standards could be also supplied by science in a way that would lubricate capitalism and curb its self-destructive excesses. To this end, he attempted to distil an ethical code from the scientific study of the diversity of moral facts:

> Before discovering a summarising formula, the facts must be analysed, their qualities described, their functions determined, their causes sought out; and only by comparing the results of all these special studies shall we be able to extract the common characteristics of all moral rules, *the constitutive properties of the law of ethics*. (1964: 418–19)

Durkheim recognized that the task of establishing 'a positive science of ethics' (1964: 422) presents numerous technical difficulties (1964: 424ff). He nonetheless anticipated that scientific investigation would rapidly develop and mature to the point at which the moral health of a society could be diagnosed by identifying its deviations from the norm for societies of its type (1964: 434–5); and that technical difficulties would eventually be overcome (1964: 433).[19] As a structuralist who believed in the possibility of identifying the existence and connections between the objective aspects of social life (Bottomore and Nisbet, 1978: 565ff), Durkheim never doubted the capacity of social science to replace the speculations of moral philosophers with unambiguous scientific evidence based upon a humanist credo.[20] He anticipated that the scientific-humanist project, with the cult of the human will at its centre, would deliver a less mystified and perplexing, more rational and secure social order.

The scientific-humanist quest for 'the law of ethics' exemplifies 'the moral thought and practice of modernity' which, as Bauman comments, 'was animated by the belief in the possibility of a non-ambivalent, non-aporetic ethical code' (1993: 9).[21] Like engineers who dream of constructing the perfect machine, the architects of ethical codes, including the codes which are intended to regulate business practice, assume that codes are *the* way to ameliorate human conduct; and that, even if it has yet to be achieved, the production of a non-ambivalent, non-aporetic code 'surely waits round the next corner. Or the corner after next' (1993: 9).

However, as Bauman points out, such projects are destined to end in tears. Their neat formality is found wanting in relation to the substantive complexities and ambiguities of practice. Perversely, the intent to strengthen the ethics of practice can have the effect of limiting and undermining the capacity and inclination to appreciate and *wrestle* with ethical issues and dilemmas, and thereby develop and embody 'normative ethics' rather than simply improving their compliance with 'descriptive ethics'. Where mere compliance occurs, there is a *simulation of ethics* as individuals conform to, and thereby contrive to absolve themselves of responsibility for, the 'normative ethics' inscribed in their conduct – on the grounds that they have complied with the 'descriptive ethics' born of scientific humanism.

The limits of scientific humanism

Despite the best efforts of social scientists to identify a 'law of ethics', the humanist project has failed to provide a scientifically based substitute for the moral authority once vested in pre-scientific traditions. As Giddens has observed,

> the reflexivity of modernity actually undermines the certainty of knowledge . . . The integral relation between modernity and radical doubt is an issue which, once exposed to view, is not only disturbing to philosophers but is *existentially troubling* for ordinary individuals. (1991: 21, emphasis in original)

It is indeed paradoxical that humanism, which promised to liberate humankind from subordination to other-worldly forces, has contributed directly to the moral anomie of modern culture which, as Giddens (1997) has put it, 'does not generate a moral or ethical framework of life' but, rather, lives off the declining reserves of premodern values supplemented by postmodern elements, in the guise of religious, feminist and ecological movements that are spreading from its margins. In Marx's words, the modern era, dominated by secular, capitalist values and practices, has the morally corrosive effect of leaving

> no other nexus between man and man than naked self-interest, that callous 'cash payment'. It has drowned the most heavenly ecstasies of religious fervour, of chivalrous enthusiasm, of philistine sentimentalism, *in the icy water of egotistical calculation*. (Marx and Engels, 1967: 82, emphasis added)

The denial of moral absolutes, other than the obligation to be entrepreneurial in the pursuit of the highest 'cash payment', is of course disturbing to humanists, like Durkheim, who aspire to realize a rather loftier, self-determining vision of human possibility and fulfilment. However, as the 500 year love affair with the humanism of modernity becomes jaded, there is a dawning recognition of the seemingly insurmountable problems – social, psychological and ecological – that it has spawned or at least has failed to solve (see Giddens, 1991; 1994). Humanism simply lacks the resources, other than the name-calling of 'nihilism', to counter what are read as the degenerate and dehumanizing tendencies of consumer capitalism. Any continuing belief in a rationally justifiable humanist ethics is unsettled and subverted by a quietly desperate acknowledgement that the humanist emperor has few clothes. This in turn feeds the anxiety that any further revelation of this deficit will speed humanity's secular slide down the slippery slope of relativism into the swamp of barbarism, as has occurred for periods in the ostensibly 'civilized', humanist societies of Western and Central Europe during this century.

The posthumanist vision

In modern societies, the individual human is placed at the centre as others and Nature are rendered subservient to the realization of this vision. The demonstrated capacity of reason to challenge and supplant premodern, sacred ideologies and institutions is accompanied by an institutionalized inflation of the significance and powers of the Cartesian ego, most potently expressed in the cult of the megalomaniacal and dictatorial leader. As moderns, we now find ourselves incarcerated in the prison-house of egoism whose foundations are humanism. Wherever we turn, we find ourselves exposed to risks, uncertainties and threats that, paradoxically, are a product of the modern, post-Enlightenment capacity to deploy disembodied reason continuously to expand and extend human control over natural and social processes (Beck, 1992). The separation of mind and body, advanced and celebrated by the humanist emphasis upon 'becoming what we will' (Carroll, 1993: 3), has contributed to the development of institutions in which the emancipatory impulse to throw off the religious shackles of the Dark Ages has been translated into the mundane deities of contemporary materialism and consumerism. In response, codes of ethics contrive to remoralize the workplace and take care of customers. However, as noted earlier, this instrumentalist response is deeply implicated in the disease it seeks to cure.

When Cartesian humanism is embraced or naturalized, individuals typically 'concentrate on manipulating the external world and measure their living standards by the quantity of material possessions' (Capra, 1982: 421). The world is identified as an alien other which offers itself as a resource for confirming the idea(l) of the autonomous, Cartesian ego. Modern science is not simply inspired by a desire to supplant ignorance with knowledge, but is prompted by 'the overwhelming ambition to conquer Nature and subordinate it to human needs' (Bauman, 1991: 39). In this project, Nature is represented, by the active Cartesian subject, as 'an object itself devoid of purpose and hence waiting to absorb the purpose injected into it by its human masters . . . Denied inherent integrity and meaning, *Nature seems a pliant object of man's liberties*' (1991: 40). Instead of experiencing ourselves as an integral part of Nature, we identify and encounter Nature as apart from us – a representation which legitimizes our manipulation of it – while we become ever more alienated from ourselves as Nature, and the associated capacity to appreciate 'the process of life' (Capra, 1982: 421). While a degree of meaning can be gained from the satisfactions associated with competitive success and the acquisition of wealth, it is fleeting and precarious. The risk and tendency, as noted earlier, is for life to become 'infused with a sense of meaninglessness, futility, and even absurdity that no amount of external success can dispel' (1982: 421).

Our (humanist) impulse is to deploy reason to calculate and control the risks, uncertainties and threats of (hyper) modernity so that our sense of being at the centre of things is secured and sustained. To this end, more systemic, organic and holistic ways of thinking are commended, not least by the gurus of management. However, these generally assume the necessity and viability of a humanist point of departure, as Sampson has observed:

> The concept of the self as integrated, and the valuing of that concept, flow from and participate in the Western world view. *The ego as master in its own household,* seeking to integrate the competing demands it faces and *being successful to the extent that it achieves unified wholeness, has its parallels in theories of governance and of authority within the Western world.* (1989: 15–16, emphasis added)

Sampson then continues, pointing to a posthumanist, poststructuralist alternative:

> *The alternative, more Derridian, view would give us a subject who is multi-dimensional and without centre or hierarchical integration.* It would give us a process and a paradox, but never a beginning or an end . . . In the Derridian logic of the supplement, what something is is thoroughly inhabited by what something also is not.

Here a poststructuralist concept of self, as 'multi-dimensional and without centre', is identified as an alternative to the conventional, Cartesian idea(l) of the autonomous ego which is 'master in its own household'. Instead of assuming a division and an opposition between self and other which promote the urge to objectify and control whatever is perceived to threaten or frustrate the idea(l) of 'unified wholeness', a poststructuralist notion of self conceives of a continuity and interdependence of self and other. In this formulation, the distinction between self and other is understood to be heuristic and paradoxical as it is appreciated how the self is 'inhabited by what [it] is not'.

To clarify this posthumanist position, it may be helpful to compare it with Giddens's humanistic approach to addressing the material perils and moral problems of the modern condition. Giddens commends an approach which relies upon reasoned dialogue based upon (humanistic) values ('values shared by almost everyone'), such as the sanctity of human life and the identification of universal human rights (1994: 20) – values which, he suggests, 'imply ethics of individual and collective responsibility which are able to override divisions of interest' (1994: 20–1). Without denying the potential value and contribution of such dialogue, it is relevant to recall how, as Derrida and Foucault remind us, the ascription of universality or transcendentalism to particular principles or philosophies can be 'dangerous'. For it can enable their adherents to define as alien, unfaithful or subhuman all those who fail to satisfy or subscribe to such requirements. More fundamentally, it is necessary to consider what impedes participation in such dialogue. Universal values are often arrived at 'defensively', having been prompted by 'the collective threats *which humanity has created for itself*', as Giddens acknowledges. Despite this, no connection is made by Giddens between the humanist project and the difficulties and the 'threats' which now present themselves. Nor is a connection made between the modern embrace of an ethic of humanism, including its conception of universal human rights, and the reluctance to engage in dialogue when this is sensed to threaten a curtailment of opportunities to 'become what we will' or to indeed to reaffirm 'what we are' (Carroll, 1993: 3). There is insufficient awareness of how dialogue is obstructed when communication is used to secure a sense of self as a unity or 'master in its own household' in relation to the other – an abstraction which humanist ethics promotes and legitimizes (Willmott, 1994).

The alternative to humanism being commended here is not *anti*-humanist. It does not seek to replace a humanist voluntarism with a structural determinism in which subjects are reduced to effects of processes of interpellation through which identities and interests are ascribed to them (Althusser, 1971). But, equally, it is critical of an anti-poststructuralist humanism in which the reflexive, centred subject is celebrated. The trouble is that binary thinking tends to assume that ideas which are critical of 'humanism' must be 'anti-humanist'. *Anti*-humanism effectively denies the presence and significance of the subject in the reproduction of social structures. *Post*humanism, in contrast, decentres the subject without erasing its key importance and capacity to transform these structures, but not as a unified subject. In Sampson's words, posthumanism gives us 'a subject who is multi-dimensional and without centre or hierarchical integration' (1989:15). It allows that subjects are positioned and constituted within diverse discourses that exist in a relation of tension to each other; and that it is through a process of emotional-rational struggle that a sense of individual and collective self-identity is developed and ethics are practically articulated and rationalized.[22] I now illustrate this understanding by reference to Ishiguru's novel, *The Remains of the Day*.

Understanding ethics: *The Remains of the Day*

Ishiguru's *The Remains of the Day* is set in a large English country house during the period leading up to the Second World War. This setting may seem somewhat remote from the contemporary world and the sphere of business more specifically. However, I will argue that the central themes of this novel do have direct relevance for organization, management and business. It explores strains within modern societies between (i) the liberal, representative notion of citizenship and (ii) the hierarchical, non-representative forms of accountability within corporations which arguably, in the (post)modern world, are becoming the dominant architects of history as they squeeze and displace the vestiges of liberal, representative democracy (Deetz, 1992; Alvesson and Willmott, 1996).

Loyalty and the silencing of voice

Inter alia, it is the institutionalized absence of any opportunity to engage in dialogue or express dissent which Ishiguru addresses through his account of the totalitarian organization of the household and, in particular, the relationship between the master of the house (the owner) and his managers (the butler and the housekeeper). As Rose has observed when commenting upon this novel, Nazism is 'present in microcosm in the organization of the aristocratic household as *a fascist corporation*' (1996: 52, emphasis added) as its employees – principally the butler (Stevens) and the housekeeper – rescind the right to criticize the actions of their employer. On this reading, *The Remains of the Day* is not simply about Lord Darlington's naive representation of fascism as a positive force: '"Look at Germany and Italy, Stevens. See what strong leadership can do if it's allowed to act. None of this universal suffrage nonsense there"' (Ishiguru, 1989: 198–9). The novel is also, and more profoundly, about a fascistic mode of representing the world – a fascism lived and articulated in Stevens's understanding that a condition of providing the most effective service to the state, or to an employer, is a willingness to eschew all criticism.

The household portrayed in *The Remains of the Day* is extreme in its institutionalized silencing of dissent. Yet, there are parallels with the aspiration of the advocates of strong corporate cultures to induce unequivocal loyalty and allegiance in potentially recalcitrant employees (Willmott, 1986). The silencing of dissent is evident in, for example, the treatment of so-called 'whistle-blowers'. Despite a degree of public sympathy and support for those who attempt to voice their concerns about what they consider to be ethically questionable aspects of business practice, not least because of the personal risks and damages they can incur, the vulnerability of whistle-blowers speaks volumes for the value placed upon processes that would render private corporations more publicly accountable.[23] In general, there is not just indifference but hostility from the business community to calls to strengthen such processes. The following assessment is perhaps extreme but is nonetheless indicative of the anxieties which underpin resistance to any extension of even the most minimal notions of citizenship into the sphere of business.[24]

> Some of the enemies of business now encourage an employee to be *disloyal* to the enterprise. They want to create suspicion and disharmony, and pry into the proprietary interests of business. However this is labelled – industrial espionage, whistle blowing, or professional responsibility – it is another tactic for spreading disunity and creating conflict. (Roche, 1971: 141, cited in Bowie, 1982: 141, emphasis added)

The hazards of loyalty for employees are explored in *The Remains of the Day* through the life of Stevens, the butler, who embraces a concept of professionalism which encompasses the belief that good service is contingent upon the deliberate development of an attitude to work that excludes all criticism of the employer:

> it is, in practice, simply *not possible to adopt a critical attitude towards an employer and at the same time provide good service*. It is not simply that one is unlikely to be able to meet the many demands of service at the higher levels while one's attentions are being diverted by such matters . . . a butler who is forever attempting to formulate his own 'strong opinions' on his employer's affairs is bound to lack one quality essential to all good professionals: namely, *loyalty*. (Ishiguru, 1989: 200, emphasis added)

I want to suggest that Stevens's commitment to professionalism, as a means of attaining a *sense* of 'unified wholeness' (Sampson, 1989: 15) which lends meaning and purpose to his life, is indicative of the limitations and dangers of the humanist project. It is a humanist project in so far as Stevens struggles to accomplish a sense of unified wholeness by exemplifying 'professionalism' which requires him to repress or deny other feelings and impulses. Within the restrictions of his social background, Stevens strives to become someone under whose 'feet the earth does not move' (Carroll, 1993: 3). As we shall see, through a life of seemingly selfless dedication to his master, Stevens commits himself to this project only to regret, in the twilight of his years, the denial and repression of dimensions of his experience demanded by his 'professionalism'.

Creating and preserving the ethical personality

Stevens's commitment to professionalism exemplifies Max Weber's (1949) 'humanist' understanding of the construction of a meaningful life – a life guided by norms of the individual's own making, which endow it with dignity, consistency, autonomy and, thus, with moral worth. If it can be shown that Weber's heroic ethic is wanting, then there is a basis for questioning the adequacy of a humanist formulation of ethics. In essence, I will argue that Weber took for granted the legitimacy of a culture of humanism (as compared with, say, Lord Darlington's taken for granted understanding of the merits of fascism) that, with the benefit of hindsight, can now more clearly be seen as less benign than he imagined or hoped.

Contrasting the 'heroic ethic' with 'the ethic of the mean', in which 'man's everyday nature' is taken as 'setting a maximum for the demands which can be made', Weber contends that the 'heroic ethic' 'imposes on men demands of principle to which they are generally *not* able to do justice, except at high points in their lives, but which serve as signposts pointing the way for man's endless *striving*' (1978: 386).[25] Central to this ethic is an active choice of a value orientation – preferably one informed by a knowledge of factual evidence produced by science (to which Weber ascribes value-free findings) that encompasses an anticipation of the likely consequences of making particular choices. Stevens's education excludes him from access to knowledge viewed by Weber as scientific. Nonetheless, he develops a close analysis of the world of service (Stevens's father was also a butler) and, more particularly, what he identifies as the attributes of a 'great butler', whilst also recognizing the difficulties of making such claims (Ishiguru, 1989: 29ff, 113ff):

> There will always be, I realize, those who would claim that any attempt to analyse greatness as I have been doing is quite futile . . . But I believe that we have a duty not to be so defeatist in this matter. It is surely a professional responsibility for all of us to think deeply about these things so that each of us may better strive towards attaining dignity for ourselves. (1989: 44)

It is only by embracing a heroic ethic, Weber contends, that human beings can truly fashion an 'ethical personality' whose life thereby commands a measure of dignity, integrity and autonomy.[26] Stevens's commitment to professionalism is informed by a self-conscious moral effort to give his life meaning and shape. On the basis of his experience of serving in 'the great houses of the country', Stevens forms the opinion that 'the great decisions of the world' are not made in public arenas but, rather, occur 'in the privacy and calm' of the great houses (1989: 115) and are subsequently ratified elsewhere amongst much pomp and ceremony. Working within the great houses was therefore 'the aspiration of [butlers] with professional ambition' for whom 'the question was not simply one of how well one practised one's skills, but *to what end* one did so' (1989: 116). By providing a professional service to one of 'the great gentlemen of our times in whose hands civilization had been entrusted', Stevens understood that he would make 'a small contribution to the creation of a better world' (1989: 116). In this way, he strove to live out his life as a unity and bring it to completion. Stevens's loyalty was not automatically or lightly shown to Lord Darlington but, rather, was '*intelligently* bestowed' (1989: 201) by placing his trust in an employer whom he judged to be wise and honourable. Only then did Stevens feel able to devote his energies unreservedly to the task of providing a professional service.

Professionalism and the heroic ethic of humanism

It might be thought that dedication to the service of a noble, honourable and wise employer is insufficiently elevated to count as a (Weberian) value orientation that endows life with meaning and shape. However, for Weber, no set of values is intrinsically any better than any other. Instead, there is an endless clashing of many competing and irreconcilable value orientations which the individual must choose between as s/he takes a practical "stand in the face of the world" (Weber, 1946: 280). Humanism is equated not with any specific set of values but, rather, with the promotion and celebration of the idea that the individual can and should achieve unified wholeness by making an autonomous, rationally informed choice between competing values. *Any* set of values can provide the individual with a heroic ethic so long as these lift its adherents above the 'ethic of the mean'. There can be little doubt that, in contrast to others who lack any consistent value orientation and are 'at the beck and call of inclination' (Brubaker, 1984: 105), Stevens's life was shaped, even to a fault, by the constancy of his 'relation to certain "values" and "meanings" of life – "values" and "meanings" which were forged into purposes and thereby translated into rational-teleological action' (Weber, 1975: 192, quoted in Brubaker, 1984: 105).

The 'heroic ethic' embraced by Stevens is put to the test when he is instructed by Lord Darlington to dismiss two housemaids because they were Jewish. Would Stevens continue to live out his concept of professionalism by silencing his misgivings about this instruction? Or would he reveal his antipathy, and thereby transgress his sense of purpose and dignity? The background to this instruction is Lord Darlington's dismay at the severity of the reparations imposed upon the German people following the First World War (Ishiguru, 1989: 223). Lord Darlington had been seeking to develop more cordial relations with the Hitler government (1989: 224); and, more recently, had fallen under the influence of a prominent member of Sir Oswald Mosley's Blackshirts. This leads him to tell his butler that 'We cannot have Jews on the staff here at Darlington Hall' (1989: 146). Stevens is personally troubled by this instruction. He can see no good reason to dismiss employees who have given years of excellent service: 'every instinct was opposed to the idea of their dismissal' (1989: 148). Nonetheless, Stevens's commitment to providing his master with a 'first rate' service (1989: 201) leads, or allows, him to set aside his personal misgivings. He also conceals these misgivings from Miss Kenton, the housekeeper. When she questions the instruction by reminding him that the maids have given six years of 'excellent' service and are to be trusted 'absolutely' (1989: 148), Stevens reproaches her for expressing publicly what he had earlier felt 'instinctively' but privately: 'Surely I don't have to remind you that our professional duty is not to our own foibles and sentiments, but to the wishes of our employer' (1989: 149).

Stevens's commitment to his professional role as a butler enables him to rationalize the exclusive channelling of his energies into its 'first rate' execution – a project which demands the utmost emotional restraint so that its reliable delivery would not be 'shaken out by external events, however surprising, alarming or vexing' (1989: 130). Despite his deep feelings of distress at being instructed to dismiss the Jewish housemaids, Stevens has no doubt that 'my duty in this instance was quite clear, and as I saw it, there was nothing to be gained at all in irresponsibly displaying such personal doubts' (1989: 201). In the name of dignity, consistency, autonomy and moral worth, Stevens translates what he personally regards as an ethically contentious issue into the task of executing his employer's instruction in as dignified and 'businesslike a way as possible' (1989: 148). Stevens's decision to execute the instruction, and then to conceal his doubts to Miss Kenton even when she expresses her outrage at the decision, is understood and legitimized by him as an act of individual moral will to avoid an 'irresponsible' display of 'personal doubts'. His habitual denial of sentiments that interfere with his commitment to professionalism spares him the discomfort of dwelling upon his first, private response to his master's instruction. This denial of his feelings saves him the pain of critical reflection upon the value of the 'descriptive ethics' enshrined in the demands of his professional role; and, more fundamentally, it spares him from an interrogation of the virtue of his (humanist) approach to giving shape and meaning to his life. When Miss Kenton asserts that it is simply wrong to dismiss the maids, Stevens firmly dismisses Miss Kenton's efforts to engage him in a discourse of 'normative ethics'. He represents the issue through a discourse of 'descriptive ethics': he considers only how, where and when the maids are to be informed of their dismissal in a way that is consistent with the professional execution of this task.

Reason and the fascism of representation

Later, as he approaches retirement – the remains of his 'day' – Stevens reviews his decision to commit himself to the value orientation of professionalism which, he acknowledges, has limited his sphere of influence and responsibility to the disciplined execution of his master's instructions.

On reflection, Stevens recognizes that his commitment to professionalism led him into the service of a master who was subsequently shown to be 'misguided, even foolish' (1989: 201) in his efforts to befriend and appease the Nazis. With the benefit of hindsight, Stevens acknowledges the flawed judgement of his master but consoles himself by repeating his belief that his loyalty to Lord Darlington was not carelessly or automatically given but carefully and deliberately bestowed. There is nothing undignified or culpable in embracing this value orientation, Stevens reasons, as it was Lord Darlington, not himself, 'who weighed up the evidence and judged it best to proceed as he did, while I simply confined myself, quite properly, to affairs within my own professional realm' (1989: 201). Defining the boundaries of self and the associated limits of responsibility in this way, Stevens also locates his master's fascist sympathies and actions in an 'honourable tradition which could not recognize the evils of Nazism' (Rose, 1996: 53). In justifying his self-imposed exile from active participation in 'the great affairs of today's world' (Ishiguru, 1989: 201), Stevens makes no connection between his decision to devote himself exclusively to the dignified execution of his professional role and his involvement in the reproduction of social structures that limit the possibilities of active citizenship both within the state and within organizations – an involvement which can place a check upon the often well-intentioned but not infrequently misguided or divisive actions of elected and non-elected elites.

Both the power and the limits of disembodied reason are illustrated in Stevens's reasoned commitment to professionalism in the service of honourable, often well-intentioned people who occupy influential roles in organizations and society. The *potency* of this commitment is expressed in the capacity to make an informed decision that lifts the individual above the transient and fickle impulses of 'the ethic of the mean'. Its *limitations* are disclosed when Stevens's impulse to oppose the idea of the maids' dismissal is overruled by his rationally informed and sustained commitment to professionalism. The limitations of reason are shown in his denial of the emotional force of the moral claim which he senses when instructed to dismiss the maids, and his disinclination to share his 'personal doubts' with Miss Kenton.

There is then, a juxtaposition of the respective responses of Stevens and Miss Kenton to receiving an instruction about which they share strong moral misgivings. For Miss Kenton, the sacking of the maids is self-evidently wrong: 'a sin as any sin ever was one' (1989: 149). She also openly expresses her outrage at the impersonal, unfeeling manner in which Stevens communicates his master's instruction – as if they were 'discussing orders for the larder' (1989: 149). She demands of Stevens whether it has occurred to him that to dismiss the maids simply because they are Jewish 'would be simply – *wrong*' (1989: 149, emphasis in original), and declares that she will not work in a house where 'such things can occur' (1989: 149). But she lacks an ethic sufficiently robust or 'heroic' to overcome her fears of confronting Lord Darlington and/or handing in her notice. She is ashamed of her lack of moral courage as she struggles and fails to overcome her fear of translating her 'high principles' (1989: 153) into the practical action of carrying out her threat to hand in her notice. Stevens too has grave misgivings about his master's instruction. But he understands the decision to be unquestionably right. Stevens's firm and thought-out commitment to his professional role ensures that sentiments which threaten to derail his sense of autonomy and dignity do not contaminate his capacity to perform his duties and to rest easily at night. Stevens could justify his collaboration in Lord Darlington's fascism by renewing his belief in the honour and wisdom of his master, a belief which justified his commitment to ensuring that Lord Darlington's instructions were executed without question or delay. Miss Kenton had no comparable ideological or solidaristic basis for numbing her feelings of outrage or for developing the moral courage necessary to overcome her fears of leaving her job. As she later confides to Stevens, had he expressed his own doubts about the decision instead of pretending that he felt no concern, this would have meant a great deal to her. This source of solidarity would, perhaps, have supplied the necessary emotional support for her to act more courageously.

In common with the ethics of Weber and MacIntyre, Stevens embraces 'a morality dominated by the mind' which is inherited from the Enlightenment's 'unquestioning faith in reason' (Mangham, 1995: 199). This dedication required Stevens to stifle his own feelings and suppress invitations to share them.[27] Of course, Stevens does have feelings. Indeed, the effort to develop the temperance, control and courage required to fulfil this vocation demands a Herculean emotional effort to keep errant feelings in check to the point of refusing to acknowledge or share them. Stevens's professional dedication to the service of a great gentleman demanded that he give no hint of his own feelings about the morality of his master's instruction to dismiss the maids – whether supportive or antagonistic – but simply 'inhabit his role to the utmost' (Ishiguru, 1989: 42–3). So, instead of respecting and interrogating his 'instinctual' opposition to the instruction to dismiss the maids, Stevens attends to it as a 'high point' which tests his resolve to act professionally. It is the very strength of his rational-humanist commitment to professional duty that enables him to set aside his 'personal doubts' once the maids had been dismissed.[28] Miss Kenton, in contrast, has no equivalent faith or ideology which allows her to repress her personal revulsion at the decision to dismiss the maids. She later reveals to Stevens how much she had suffered following their dismissal – a suffering which was deepened by what she viewed as her shameful cowardice of failing to tender her resignation for fear of going out into the world and 'finding nobody who knew or cared about me' (1989: 153). This fear could have been alleviated if Stevens had shared his personal doubts about the episode: 'I suffered all the more because I believed I was alone' (1989: 154).

These acts of institutionalized violence, self-inflicted as well as perpetrated upon others, which can easily pass unremarked in everyday life, are justified by Stevens, as noted earlier, in terms of the exercise of the moral will of what Weber, the humanist, would deem to be an ethical personality. By elevating and testing our will, or resolve, to achieve a sense of unified wholeness, we routinely contrive to 'defend our own particular interests, and see only the egoism of the other' (Rose, 1996: 54). In Stevens's case, he defends his 'interest' in the professional value orientation which gave his life meaning by repressing his incongruent feelings and silencing Miss Kenton's efforts to prompt their expression. Whenever there is a challenge to an 'interest' (or, better, I suggest, a perceived threat to a person's sense of 'self-identity'), what Rose (1996) terms 'the fascism of representation' ensures that, instead of using this challenge as a stimulus for reflecting upon the precariousness and moral defensibility of our commitments, the challenge is discounted by interpreting it as an expression of the egoism of the other. Miss Kenton's objections to the treatment of the maids was dismissed as a manifestation of her 'foibles and sentiments' (Ishiguru, 1989: 149) which were considered by Stevens to interfere with the dignified fulfilment of her professional duty to her master.

Doubts about the ethics of our actions are effectively silenced when 'the fascism of representation' reassures us that, despite intuitions or feelings to the contrary, our ethics are sound, beyond reproach. Any challenge to our ethics is the other party's problem, not ours; and the violence inherent in this lack of compassion is rationalized and legitimized as the sovereign exercise of our individual, moral will.

Revisiting the 'heroic ethic' of humanism

Weber's humanist moral vision is not devoid of merit. Its chief virtue resides in the refusal to provide metaphysical sanctity for any particular value orientation – whether proffered by religion or by science.[29] The impossibility of providing an objective justification for any value orientation means that responsibility must be taken for any decision to privilege or disregard particular concerns when choosing between competing value orientations. But, as Weber contends, the nature of this moment of decision is inherently and inescapably supra-rational. The problem is that Weber's vision is compromised by a humanist understanding of the individual: each human being is an atomized, potentially autonomous, being cast adrift from Nature as well as from community.

There is nothing intrinsic to Weber's conception of moral worth and the development of an ethical personality that would encourage or enable a person, such as Stevens, to articulate doubts about others' decisions, such as Lord Darlington's decision to dismiss the maids. Indeed, the reverse is the case since to do so would involve the compromising, if not the disposal, of the commitment to the particular values which endowed Stevens's life with integrity and dignity. Weber's 'heroic ethic' is distinguished not by the process of choice alone but by the capacity of its proponents to adhere to a value commitment in the face of impulses and pressures to depart from it. Only the reasoning powers developed by the atomized individual who 'creates himself' by choosing 'to be courageous, honourable, just . . . or not' (Carroll, 1993: 3) are available to select and pursue his or her chosen value orientation. No consideration is given to the potential significance and contribution of our relation to Nature and community as other resources for framing and revising our choices and commitments.

Of critical importance for the present argument, the moral worth of the individual or the community is *not* evaluated by Weber in terms of the capacity to nurture and sustain a process of critical reflection upon the humanist, Cartesian value orientation(s) to which the individual/community is currently wedded. I accept the impossibility of determining an impartial standpoint for assessing the merits of competing value orientations (here I am in agreement with Weber). Nonetheless, an important condition of nurturing and sustaining an ethical community (as contrasted with Weber's ethical personality) is the kindling of the capacity to reflect critically upon established structuralist and humanist traditions (Pollner, 1987; Willmott, 1994). A condition of this kindling process, which exemplifies the ethical community in action, is the progressive dissolution of the humanist project. For this project, I have argued, inadvertently fosters 'the fascism of representation' (Rose, 1996): an exploiting and controlling orientation to the world which is legitimized by a humanist discourse of ethics that attributes to the exploiters and controllers a valued sense of autonomy, integrity and consistency.

I have drawn attention to an elective affinity between humanism and fascism – at least in so far as humanism propagates, harbours or conceals a 'fascism of representation' in which fascist tendencies within people, organizations and nation-states are normalized as 'honourable' or 'natural'. Conversely, counter-representations which potentially expose their fascism are deemed to be irrational or excessive. Influenced by Rose's (1996) commentary on *The Remains of the Day*, I have argued that humanism contributes to fascism as 'a political culture which we identify as our own' (1996: 54) as it encourages individuals to understand and construct themselves as autonomous beings who can achieve 'unified wholeness' and thereby seemingly ensure that the(ir) 'ground does not shake'. At the same time, I have acknowledged that humanism, as exemplified in Weber's 'heroic ethic', *is* more capable of resisting heterogeneous impulses, including the appeal of diverse forms of fascism, than 'the ethic of the mean'. However, the logocentric ambition of humanism to make people, individually and collectively, 'masters of their own households' renders this project blind to its other.

This blindness is graphically illustrated in *The Remains of the Day*. Stevens exemplifies the heroic ethic of humanism as he strives to make his ego the 'master of its own household'. He is preoccupied with attaining and maintaining sovereignty and control over a tightly defined sphere of operations. Stevens pursues this ethic through a commitment to professionalism which suppresses all thought that might be disruptive of this project. This ethic, he believed, would give his life meaning and direction: 'those of us *who wish to make our mark* must realize that we must best do so by concentrating upon what *is* in our realm; that is to say, by devoting our attention to providing the best possible service to those great gentlemen in whose hands the destiny of civilization truly lies' (Ishiguru, 1989: 199, first emphasis added). The humanist ethic pre-serves the *egoistic* preoccupation with 'making a mark' by acting on the world in ways that secure a confirmation of a value orientation and associated sense of self-identity to which the individual is committed. Even when a rational ethic of responsibility, which pays attention to the secondary and contradictory consequences of the pursuit of a conviction ethic of ultimate ends, serves to check this ambition, the ethic of responsibility remains subordinate to 'making a mark'. In effect, the ethic of responsibility becomes instrumentalized in the anticipation that the humanist project of 'making a mark' will be more perfectly realized and effectively sustained when some of the unintended consequences of pursuing humanism are recognized.

There are parallels here with the humanistic psychology favoured by the management gurus of corporate culturism. Stevens's commitment to professionalism is comparable to the commitment that the advocates of strong corporate cultures wish to instil in employees who, it is hoped, will derive a sense of 'making a mark' (i.e. become 'empowered') by willingly confining their sense of identity and purpose within a narrow value realm that has been defined by and bestowed upon them by corporate managers. Peters and Waterman (1982: 80) naturalize human beings' 'need for self-determination'. Following Becker (1973), they argue that 'the human creature has to oppose itself to the rest of nature'. They note the results of experiments which suggest that 'if people think they have even modest personal control over the destinies, they will persist at tasks' (1982: 80) before, finally, claiming that 'excellent companies' are distinguished by their provision of 'a set of shared values . . . in which practical autonomy takes place routinely' (1982: 323). The lack of accountability of senior managers to other employees thrives on the model of a strong leader in the guise of the CEO coupled to a kind of populism fermented through the establishment of a corporate culture.[30] In this context, an ethic of responsibility is invoked by urging employees to 'make a mark' in ways that are compliant with corporate values.

Concluding remarks: beyond the 'heroic ethic'

The lack of democratic accountability in a corporate context makes it difficult to voice dissent for fear of retribution. It may also stimulate a frustration with abuses of power that are unchecked by processes of accountability. Without denying that the anticipated material and symbolic (e.g. for self-identity) repercussions of challenging the status quo may, as in the experience of Stevens and Miss Kenton, impede or even paralyse forms of individual or collective resistance, I have argued that poststructuralist and posthumanist thinking can open up awareness and debates in ways that can have a non-specific normative purpose. Poststructuralist analysis fosters the understanding that 'the logic of the supplement' unsettles seemingly authoritative claims. It recalls how ethical codes, for example, invariably fail to capture or contain what they seek to control. In this way, poststructuralist thinking can make an indirect but powerful contribution to the discourse of 'normative ethics'(Goodpaster, 1995). There is always an excess which they fail to nail down. Within the corporation, the excess is evident in recalcitrance, including the actions of whistle-blowers who may be indirectly provoked by codes that their employers have breached. In *The Remains of the Day*, Miss Kenton manifests this 'excess' when she recoils at Lord Darlington's instruction to dismiss the maids and contemplates handing in her notice. Stevens's ethic of professionalism also faces a momentary challenge as Lord Darlington instructs him to dismiss the Jewish maids. So, how is this excess to be conceptualized?

Following Levinas, Bauman (1993) conceptualizes the excess as a 'moral impulse' (see ten Bos and Willmott, 1998; and see also several of the other chapters in this book). This impulse, it is claimed, is expressive of a selfless, unreflexive responsibility towards, and care for, others. It is an impulse which, it is argued, 'precedes all engagement with the Other . . . It has therefore no "foundation" – no cause, no determining factor' (1993: 13). It is *perhaps* evident in the immediate response of both Stevens and Miss Kenton to receiving the instruction to dismiss the maids; and, more specifically, by Miss Kenton's insistence that it is 'a sin as any sin ever was one'. According to Bauman, it is an impulse that exists prior to the development of the social self – a social self which emerges through an engagement with others, including an engagement with whatever ethical codes operate, formally or informally, to regulate such relationships because 'there is no self before the moral self, morality being the ultimate, non-determined presence; indeed, an act of creation *ex nihilo*, if there ever was one' (1993: 13)

Bauman (1993: 3) contends that moral action is grounded in a 'non-determined presence' which precedes the construction of social norms. Moral impulses, he argues, 'supply the raw material of sociality and of commitment to others in which all social orders are moulded' (1993: 13) and 'the surrender [of this impulse], if any, occurs on the road leading from the moral to the social self, from being-for to being "merely" with' (1993: 14). These are clearly highly speculative claims that it is difficult to prove or disprove. And since it is impossible to say categorically that the idea of a moral impulse is incorrect, I am unprepared to deny it as a possibility.[31] The notion of an 'ultimate, non-determined presence' is at least helpful in problematizing the humanist idea that human beings create themselves from nothing, and that our fate is wholly or primarily a product of the strength of our will: 'man is all-powerful, if his will is strong enough. He can create himself' (Carroll, 1993: 3). However, the idea of a pre-social 'moral impulse' offers a very fragile basis upon which to construct an alternative ethics to those enshrined in ethical codes.

There is also the worry that debating the idea of a pre-social moral impulse becomes a distraction from the process of nurturing a capacity to respond in ways that approximate the kinds of behaviour ascribed to such an impulse. The principal value of the idea of a 'moral impulse', I suggest, resides in its pointing to the possibility of an 'alterity' which can problematize the grounds of humanist ethics, and not in its direct contribution to an alternative ethics. It is an idea which usefully challenges the conception of individuals as rational choosers, isolated from community and separated from Nature. It can therefore be of value in reminding us of the presence and potential relevance of what is forgotten in formulations of ethics that assume and rely upon the idea of the autonomous, rational individual. In Deetz's words, value debate 'needs to be recovered, but through a recovery of those things feared – the body, the emotions, the feminine, pleasure – suppressed by rationality (in all its forms, not just instrumental)' (1995: 223).

In *The Remains of the Day*, the reactions of Stevens and Miss Kenton to the instruction to dismiss the maids illustrates the role of 'things feared' in mobilizing moral sensibility as well as the role of egoism in inhibiting their translation into practice. Whatever the source of moral sensibility and the engagement of a discourse of ethics there can be little doubt that feelings of community and solidarity with the maids, albeit limited and compromised, fuelled Stevens's personal doubts and ignited Miss Kenton's outrage at their dismissal. However, just as these feelings of community and solidarity indicate a capacity to counter, if not entirely dissolve, egoistic proclivities, the capacity to sustain these feelings in the face of the violence done to them by the maids' dismissal is eclipsed by Stevens's and Miss Kenton's shared, egoistic preoccupation with defending their respective sense of self-identity. Stevens pre-serves his investment in the dutiful execution of his professional role by dismissing as 'personal foibles' the moral force of his own personal doubts about the instruction to dismiss the maids. The sense of self-importance derived from his professional role is undiminished by this event. His loyalty to Lord Darlington is placed above his personal misgivings or any inclination to share them with Miss Kenton. Miss Kenton also discovers that she is unable to shake off her egoistic fear of finding 'nobody who knew or cared about me' (Ishiguru, 1989: 153) as she fails to translate her moral principles into the practical action of leaving Darlington Hall.

The idea of a 'moral impulse' points to an 'alterity' that is displaced by humanist ethics. But, instead of ascribing a positive ethical value to such impulses, it is more plausible to formulate this impulse as a pre-egoic sense of unity-with-the-world in which 'selfishness' and 'selflessness' have no meaning. A posthumanist ethic, I have suggested, is to be founded upon a questioning of the assumption of a division between the human and its other – which may be formulated as 'nature', 'animals' or (misogynistically) as women (see Brewis, Chapter 4 in this volume). As Pepperwell has declared, 'The Post-Human era begins fully when we no longer find it necessary, or possible, to oppose humans and nature' (1995: 165). The poststructuralist implication of this claim is that 'we can never determine the absolute boundary of the human . . . human beings do not exist in the sense in which we ordinarily think of them, that is as separate entities in perpetual conflict with a nature that is *external* to them' (1995: 18). This sense of unity is invariably fractured and denied in the process of self-formation. But it is never lost and, on occasion, can be revived or revealed (Willmott, 1986) in a way that, in common with poststructuralism, has normative effects as it unsettles our comfortable sense of there being authoritative descriptions of ethics and/or ethical norms upon which we can confidently depend. This understanding resonates with Derrida's contention that deconstructionism is 'an openness towards the other' which conceptualizes 'the subject' as a discursive effect of subjectivity:

> The subject is not some meta-linguistic substance or identity, some pure *cogito* of self-presence; it is always inscribed in language. My work does not, therefore, destroy the subject; it simply tries to resituate it. (Derrida, 1984: 125)

Likewise, from this perspective, the opposition or fracture between human nature and Nature is constructed through particular discourses and becomes institutionalized within related practices; it is not ontologically given. It is the primordial ontological continuity which makes it possible to act selflessly. That said, it is unhelpful, I believe, simply to reverse what Bauman (1993) persuasively identifies as a tendency in the Western tradition to assume that selfishness is foundational by ascribing morality to a pre-egoic sense of unity-with-the-world. In making this reversal Bauman seems to depart from his own understanding of the 'inherent and incurable ambivalence' (1993: 15) at the heart of the human condition – an ambivalence which is neither intrinsically good/moral or evil/immoral. Instead of identifying ethical codes as ambivalent phenomena, he understands them to weaken or deaden the moral impulse.[32]

Bauman's basic objection to the codes is that they reflect and reinforce the understanding that the social self produces the moral self, not vice versa. 'It took centuries of power-assisted legal drill and philosophical indoctrination' to accomplish this inversion, argues Bauman (1993: 14). In contrast, I am more willing than Bauman to accept the (pragmatic) value of such codes, so long as they respect and nurture the primacy of the pre-egoic sense of unity-with-the-world, or what Bauman terms 'the moral impulse'. The problem, as Bauman rightly points out, is that they generally deny its presence and stifle its development. They assume anarchy to be the only alternative to the discipline of the code. Bauman comes down firmly on the side of a primordial morality and goodness in claiming that the 'impulse' to act in a responsible, caring manner towards the other precedes the development of the social self. It is more persuasive, and certainly less contentious, I believe, to emphasize the self-lessness of the pre-social self without ascribing 'morality' to its impulses – even though the experience of self-lessness does, arguably, have very considerable moral significance from the standpoint of the social self which, on occasion, it supplants.

For Bauman, the moral impulse is dampened and damaged by the emergence of the social self, including the construction of ethical codes. For him, codes are inherently dangerous – most obviously when they are reified as truths which are used to screen or justify socially unnecessary suffering. *Contra* Bauman, who is perversely blind to their ambivalence and unintended positive consequences, I regard ethical codes as phenomena which, even as they seek to legitimize structures of domination by regulating their reproduction, can simultaneously stimulate a discourse of ethics and an appreciation of the normative basis of social order, including business activity. Their effect *may* be to promote a 'fascism of representation' which, as in the case of Stevens's allegiance to a heroic ethic of professionalism or the royal family's adherence to protocol in the face of unprecedented national grief at the loss of Princess Diana, allows its adherents to deny their own role in pre-serving practices which are productive of unnecessary suffering – such as Lord Darlington's desire to cooperate with the Nazis or to dismiss the maids. But, equally, codes of ethics can provide a basis for subjecting corporate practices to critical scrutiny (e.g. by whistle-blowers); and, more fundamentally, can question whether the values of openness, honesty, trust and integrity are realizable in a corporate context where accountability is invariably top-down, rarely bottom-up. It was Lord Darlington's adherence to a code of gentlemanly conduct which seemingly embodied the values of honesty, trust and integrity that captured Stevens's loyalty and commitment. Stevens's loyalty or 'professionalism' extended to the point of consciously electing to suppress moral impulses that could have prompted him to disclose and criticize its self-serving limits. When Stevens's mundane privileging of the 'fascism of representation' was seriously disturbed by the instruction to dismiss the maids, an opportunity arose to deconstruct the basis of his loyalty. However, he continued to collude in the reproduction of his master's authority, and thereby preserved his own sense of identity and purpose as a 'professional'. Stevens failed to give vent to his moral impulse of revulsion at his master's instruction and thereafter erased its significance from his thoughts. It was Stevens's preoccupation with preserving his (humanist) sense of self-identity, rather than his allegiance to a professional code of ethics *per se*, that impeded the expression of a moral impulse of resistance to his master's instruction.

The value of poststructuralist and posthumanist thinking resides in its capacity to problematize accepted dualisms. For example, it can foster an appreciation of the continuity with Nature in a way that can ease egoistic fears associated with the threats to material and symbolic states that accompany acts of recalcitrance that demand moral courage. Such thinking can inspire, energize and guide a direct yet compassionate questioning of the absence of democratic accountability – as exemplified in the efforts of Lord Darlington, an unelected aristocrat, to forge an alliance with the Nazis and dismiss the Jewish maids, and in the efforts of management gurus to construct 'strong' corporate cultures and ethical codes with which employees either feel compelled to conform or fear to transgress.

Notes

I would like to thank Damian O'Doherty and Martin Parker for their comments on earlier drafts of this chapter.

1 With regard to plagiarism, the managing director of Penguin Italia was reported in the *Times Higher Education Supplement* (3 January 1997: 1) to say that 'Many Italians do not have any sense of copyright'; and another commentator suggested that the acceptability of plagiarism within academia in Italy 'is linked to a feudal system, which places power and practicality over merit and morality', and where 'moral considerations are often secondary to career advancement and financial gain' (1997: 1). Seemingly, in Italy, an 'ethic' of collective silence ensures that few disclosures occur. Despite a degree of acceptance of the view that plagiarism is unethical, there is a strong inclination to accommodate it, if not condone it, as plagiarism of texts, particularly those translated from another language, provides a comparatively undemanding means of establishing and maintaining academic reputations.

2 The writings of only one of the three authors commended by the editor is cited by any of the contributors to the text.

3 This is exemplified in forms of structuralist analysis (to be discussed in a later section) where there is an attempt to map the social world without any direct concern to orient this knowledge to the reflexive process of exploring the contribution of its representations for advancing a sense of purpose and self-understanding.

4 There are parallels here between 'descriptive' and 'normative' ethics and Horkheimer's (1972) essay on the difference between traditional and critical theory. However, while Horkheimer is critical of traditional, bourgeois thought for assuming the ego to be autonomous and thus capable of providing objective descriptions and explanations of the world, he does not problematize the humanist conception of autonomy which is sustained by the contemporary generation of critical theorists, notably Jürgen Habermas. The limits of a humanist ethic are discussed in a later section of this chapter.

5 If the codes are to be honoured, individuals must be selected, trained or developed who are willing to comply with them. If these individuals are not to refuse to participate in business, the nature of their education and development must pose no radical challenge to the ethics of business. To put this another way, either business ethics must relativize ethics so that this radical challenge is given no special privilege; or it must ensure that the view of its basic institutions, such as the market, is more in accord with Bowie's claim that business practice already and necessarily rests upon a moral base than it is with Weber's view that market relations induce their participants to look upon each other as commodities, not as persons, and are therefore inherently corrosive of any moral base.

6 A condition of engaging in 'goal-directed activity' is a preparedness to accomplish closure, albeit temporary, upon the human experience of indeterminacy or openness – what Kundera (1989) characterizes as 'the unbearable lightness of being', a condition which is alleviated only by the weighty burden of commitment to 'this' rather than 'that'. The effects of this impulse to secure closure are morally saturated in the sense that they value 'this' over 'that'. It is relevant to note here that Bauman (1993), following Levinas, conflates the distinction between (i) an impulse which produces a (momentary but frequently repeated) closure and (ii) the *effect* of this closure which is moral in so far as 'this' rather than 'that' is privileged. Bauman refers to the *impulse* that produces closure as 'moral ' whereas I follow Derrida (and Kierkegaard and Weber, for that matter) in referring to this instant as a moment of madness which is moral only in its effects (see Parker, Chapter 14 in this volume). This argument is elaborated in the concluding section of the chapter.

7 Even if their readers forget or dismiss much of their specific, prescriptive, mind-numbingly idealized contents, these texts make a contribution to the formation of corporate functionaries in so far as they equip them with a discourse in which organizational work is deemed to be governed by impersonal imperatives, as exemplified in the SB statement, rather than normative commitments.

8 Reflecting upon the possible tensions between corporate and personal ethics, Gergen and Whitney (1996) note how, in meetings between top managers and human resources representatives, the exclusive focus was upon financial objectives – such as sales growth and improvements in market share. No attention was given to other elements of the code. Gergen and Whitney suggest that this restrictive focus, which is also reflected in annual reports and newspaper coverage, is likely to generate or increase a degree of scepticism amongst employees about the commitment of the company to all the values in the statement. They will be left to ponder questions such as: 'Is the commitment of the company to a set of values *sui generis*, or is it to values as mere implements to profit?' (1996: 351). If the code of ethics is regarded as an instrument for engineering 'compliant patterns of behaviour' (MacIntyre, 1981: 71), to which the company is committed only as a means to this end, it can be anticipated that employees will develop a more instrumental, less

trusting attitude towards the employment relationship. It can be further anticipated that evidence of this attitude will stimulate renewed efforts to include some reference to employee values within the code and/or to find, recruit and train employees whose 'personal' ethics, or the lack of them, render them more responsive to the corporate exhortation to 'walk the truth'.

9 Even those who equate the fiduciary duty of managers with the maximizing of profit acknowledge that managerial actions are practically constrained by ethical custom as well as by legislation (e.g. Friedman, 1988; see also Randels, 1995).

10 For an accessible example of conceptual structuralist analysis, see the Appendix to Castanada (1970).

11 For example, the content and exchange value of individual skills - such as those associated with different sorts of managerial work – are analysed by Marx as a product of the organization and dynamics of this structure, and not simply an expression of the choice or will of particular individuals to acquire, extend or monopolize these skills. In a similar way, Lévi-Strauss, himself indebted to Marx, uses the concept of structure to identify the unacknowledged or unconscious forces which regulate human perception and social existence. However, whereas the focus of Marx's attention was upon the historically distinctive structures of capitalism, Lévi-Strauss's structural anthropology was directed at the 'savage minds' of so-called primitive peoples in an attempt to identify universal structures of thought and behaviour.

12 When analysing the relationship between words and what they describe, a positivist would be inclined to assume that the meaning of any (particular) word is derived from the purpose it serves in identifying the (particular) phenomenon that it describes. In contrast, Saussure understands the meaning of a word (the signified) to be derived entirely from its (shifting) positioning within a structure of signification provided by other words. It is this (arbitrary) structure, Saussure argues, and not anything essential either to what words describe or to their functional value, that accounts for their meaning.

13 As Giddens remarks, 'Saussure evidently wished to claim that the meaning of a word is not the object to which that word might be used to refer, but since he nowhere analyses the nature of reference, this claim remains essentially unelucidated philosophically' (1987: 203).

14 Studies of literature, for example, are shown to have been fixated upon the (bourgeois humanist) belief that the key to analysing a text resides in an interrogation of the life of its author. From a conceptual structuralist standpoint, there are two difficulties with this belief. First, it ascribes the source of whatever is valued in the text to an individual (God-like) creator rather than to the structures which support the nature and content of the writing. Secondly, it fails to appreciate the key role of the (structural) conventions which are deployed by readers and critics to identify authors and to evaluate their work in the process of reading their texts. A bourgeois humanist reading is unaware of how the possibility of a shift in conventions renders the text inexhaustibly open to alternative readings.

15 See, for example, Freundlieb (1989) for an exceptionally clear exposition of the objections to Foucault's 'inconsistency' and 'irrationality' from a Habermasian standpoint.

16 Critical theory assumes the possibility of, and yearns for, what Dews (1987) terms 'an integrated critical standpoint'. Critical Theory contends that such ground(s) are available, or are at least in principle discoverable or deducible, *and that* without the support of these grounds any truth claim is arbitrary. This is the basis of Habermas's communicative ethics. Poststructuralism, in contrast, problematizes this contention as it (repeatedly) 'dismantles' or unsettles the stability of the ground upon which any standpoint, whether it is Critical Theory or its own, is erected. Accepting that all truth claims are theory-dependent, Critical Theory and poststructuralism share the understanding that competing claims about the world cannot be adjudicated by reference to empirical evidence. However, in Habermasian Critical Theory at least,

communication is understood to be underpinned by a 'universal pragmatics' which provides for the possibility, in principle, of resolving disputed claims by reference to the counterfactual existence of a universal and argumentatively attained consensus. Habermasian Critical Theory strives to revive the Enlightenment project by straightening out what is identified as the distorted development of modernization. Poststructuralism, in contrast, views such claims and aspirations as irredeemably flawed. For poststructuralism, the privileging of 'this' as 'truth' necessarily depends upon the suppression of 'that' which, once acknowledged, undermines the authority of 'this' by exposing how its stability is socially organized.

17 In other words, principles based upon the commandments of the Old and New Testaments.

18 The advances have, of course, contributed immensely to its appeal and, relatedly, to its contemporary status as a sacred cow.

19 A parallel can be drawn here between Durkheim's well-meaning yet fundamentally technocratic vision of a society, in which the perfection of normative order is accomplished through the accumulation and application of scientific knowledge, and the aspirations of management scientists – from Taylor to the advocates of TQM and BPR – who ascribe to managers 'The duty of gathering in [the] great mass of traditional knowledge and then recording it, tabulating it and, in many cases, finally reducing it to laws, rules and even mathematical formulae' (Taylor, 1990: 204). In each case, there is an assumption of a structure that can be detected through the application of scientific method. By collecting and analysing information, science would expose deviations from the norm and would thereby provide a basis for determining the application of rules; in turn, this knowledge would provide an authoritative basis for engineering less anomic/inefficient forms of organization. In each case, the vision is underpinned not only by a particular, taken-for-granted view of how social relations could be organized and how science could facilitate this project, but also by a belief in the 'moral duty' of the 'social scientist' (Durkheim) or the 'scientific manager' (Taylor) to use science to produce the facts which would yield 'the constitutive properties of the law of ethics' (Durkheim) or the principles of scientific management (Taylor).

20 'Moralists,' Durkheim writes, 'examine the idea of law, or the ethical idea, not the nature of law and ethics.' He continues: 'They have not arrived at the very simple truth that, as our representations of physical things are derived from these things themselves and express them more or less exactly, so our idea of ethics derives from *the observable manifestation of the rules* that are functioning under our eyes and reproduces this schematically. It follows that *these rules, and not our schematic idea of them, should be the subject-matter of science*, just as actual physical bodies, and not the layman's idea of them, constitute the subject-matter of physics' (23–4, in Giddens, 1972: 89, emphases added).

21 An 'aporetic situation' is defined by Bauman (1993: 8) as one in which there is a contradiction which cannot be overcome. Bauman gives the example of the ascription of autonomy to individuals and the use of codes which runs through modern society. The latter are developed, Bauman argues, in order to ensure that autonomous individuals make the choices which are desired by those who commend the codes either because these individuals identify with values contained in the codes or because they seek to avoid the punishment associated with their violation. The problem is that individual autonomy is demonstrated through rebellion, not conformity. Ascribing autonomy to individuals invites and indeed legitimizes transgression of the codes and, more fundamentally, provokes challenges to their foundations. As Bauman puts it, 'Autonomy of rational individuals and heteronomy of rational management could not do without each other; but they could not cohabit peacefully either. They were locked together for better or worse, bound to clash and struggle without end and with no real prospect of lasting peace' (1993: 7).

22 When revising this chapter for publication, there was an outpouring of grief

following the death of Princess Diana. The strength and breadth of this grief took most commentators by surprise, as it did many interviewed by the media including people who had queued for eleven hours to sign books of remembrance. This unprecedented expression of feeling can be interpreted as a manifestation of emotional-rational struggle by very large numbers of people who identified with and admired not only Diana's beauty and self-effacing charm but her openness and moral courage in sharing her own 'multidimensional' and dislocated life. This was in contrast to the remoteness, stiffness and lack of 'common touch' widely attributed to other members of the royal family, as central pillars of the establishment. Diana's unwillingness, and perhaps incapacity, to present a front of 'unified wholeness' served to highlight the other of the royal family whose silence in the days following her death was interpreted and condemned as a symptom of their emotional stuntedness and inability to appreciate and be responsive to the public mood. However, few commentators have appreciated Diana as a postmodern, poststructuralist icon. Instead of acknowledging and valuing Diana's complex, fragile and fractured makeup, the media have tended to transform her, in death, into a one-dimensional deity – a representation which eschews recognition and appreciation of facets of her life and character (e.g. insecurity, petulance, self-promotion, self-obsession) which were in tension with the saintly image (for an exceptional tribute, see Nicci Gerard, 'The beatification of Diana', the *Observer*, 7 September, 1997: 23–5). Of course, the deification of the dead is not so unusual; but it is especially perverse in Diana's case as it was her vulnerability and multidimensionality that perhaps best explains her appeal to, and the deep sense of loss at her death felt by, diverse groups of people. In the next section, I explore the nature of this struggle through a consideration of Ishiguru's novel, *The Remains of the Day*.

23 To refer back to note 22, Princess Diana can be seen as a whistle-blower on the royal family. Her presence and subsequent confessions drew attention to the stuffiness, remoteness and fascist tendencies of 'The Firm' (as the royal family is not-so-affectionately described by those who liken it to a gang of criminals). Her naive or courageous revelations then provoked a strong counter-attack in an effort to repair the damage and silence the dissenting voice of Diana, the 'loose cannon' who, by design or default, threatened to render a private corporation more publicly accountable.

24 The opinion expressed by James Roche has the merit of directness. It is unvarnished by any concern to sound 'politically correct' or to issue soothing statements about business ethics which give the impression of being attentive to ethical issues whilst devoting the minimum of resources to addressing them.

25 Stevens's heroic effort is to exemplify the virtues (as he sees them) of the professional butler. These parallel the noble endeavours that he ascribes to his master whose exceptional 'moral worth' (Ishiguru, 1989: 114) is deemed to merit Stevens's commitment to providing dutiful service of the highest order.

26 Especially in respect of the emphasis upon integrity, this position is also shared by contemporary communitarians, such as MacIntyre, who argues that 'To ask "What is good for me" is to ask how best I might live out that unity and bring it to completion . . . it is important to emphasize that it is the systematic asking of these two questions and the attempt to answer them in deed as well as in word which provide the moral life with its unity' (1981: 203, cited in Mangham, 1995: 198)

27 Further evidence of Stevens's feelings is presented when Stevens is deeply embarrassed by Miss Kenton as she discovers him reading a romantic novel.

28 The dissonance between his master's instruction and his own instinct was also eased when, having severed his relationship with the Blackshirts, Lord Darlington indicated that 'It was wrong what happened and one would like to recompense them somehow' (Ishiguru, 1989: 151). Only then did Stevens feel that he could communicate his feelings about the dismissal to Miss Kenton without being disloyal to Lord Darlington.

29 This is important because it defies closure of debate about the value of competing value orientations. It offers a principled check upon the (ab)use of reason, in the guise of science, as a supplier of seemingly authoritative justifications for any particular value orientation. For a discussion of the limitations of Weber's conception of science, see Alvesson and Willmott (1996, esp. Chapter 2).

30 As Hitler declared in *Mein Kampf*, 'There is no principle which . . . is as false as that of parliamentarianism' (cited in Lee, 1987: 15), a sentiment that is echoed today in business leaders' rejection of even the most minimal and tokenist forms of worker representation on key decision-making committees.

31 In support of the 'moral impulse' hypothesis, one might point to altruistic acts which, on the face of it, seem minimally clouded or contaminated by rational reference to the requirements of ethical codes or calculations about the penalties to be incurred for their violation: the drowning child is rescued without any thought of what 'ought' to be done or of the risks involved. But, against this, is the argument that bystanders frequently do not react in this way – which suggests that if a moral impulse does exist and is to be expressed, it must also be unhampered by beliefs which impede its expression.

32 Their 'overall effect', Bauman writes, 'is not so much the "universalization of morality", as the silencing of moral impulse and channelling of moral capacities to socially designated targets that may, and do, include moral purposes' (1993: 12). I agree that the universalism ascribed to moral codes is phoney and is inevitably discovered to be particularistic or parochial through a process of practical or theoretical deconstructionism. The former operates to expose its (often naturalized) sectional inspiration; the latter serves to demonstrate its denial of particulars.

References

Alvesson, M. and Willmott, H.C. (1996) *Making Sense of Management: A Critical Introduction*. London: Sage.
Althusser, L. (1971) *Lenin and Philosophy and Other Essays*. London: New Left Books.
Anthony, P. (1986) *The Foundations of Management*. London: Tavistock.
Arrow, K. (1973) 'Social Responsibility and Economic Efficiency', *Public Policy*, 21.
Bauman, Z. (1991) *Modernity and Ambivalence*. Cambridge: Polity.
Bauman, Z. (1993) *Postmodern Ethics*. Oxford: Blackwell.
Beck, U. (1992) *The Risk Society*. London: Sage.
Becker, E. (1973) *The Denial of Death*. New York: Free Press.
Bottomore, T. and Nisbet, R. (1978) 'Structuralism', in T. Bottomore and R. Nisbet (eds) *A History of Sociological Analysis*. London: Heinemann.
Bowie, N. (1982) *Business Ethics*. Englewood Cliffs, NJ: Prentice-Hall.
Brubaker, R. (1984) *The Limits of Rationality*. London: George Allen and Unwin.
Callinicos, A. (1989) *Against Postmodernism: A Marxist Critique*. Cambridge: Polity.
Capra, F. (1982) *The Turning Point: Science, Society and the Rising Culture*. London: Flamingo.
Carroll, J. (1993) *Humanism*. London: Fontana.
Castanada, C. (1970) *The Teachings of Don Juan: A Yaqui Way of Knowledge*. Harmondsworth: Penguin.
Critchley, S.J. (1992) *The Ethics of Deconstruction: Derrida and Levinas*. Oxford: Blackwell.
Daft, R.L. (1995) *Organization Theory and Design*. Cincinnati, OH: South-Western Publishing.
Deetz, S. (1992) *Democracy in an Age of Corporate Colonization*. Albany, NY: State University of New York Press.

Deetz, S. (1995) 'Character, Corporate Responsibility and the Dialogic in the Postmodern Context: A Commentary on Mangham', *Organization*, 2 (2): 217–25.

Derrida, J. (1984) 'Interview with Richard Kearney', in R. Kearney (ed.) *Dialogues with Contemporary Continental Thinkers*. Manchester: Manchester University Press.

Derrida, J. (1989) 'Afterword: Toward an Ethic of Discussion', in *Limited Inc*. Evanston, IL: Northwestern University Press.

Derrida, J. (1996) 'Remarks on Deconstruction and Pragmatism', in C. Mouffe (ed.) *Deconstructionism and Pragmatism*. London: Routledge.

Dews, P. (1987) *Logics of Disintegration*. London: Verso.

Durkheim, E. (1964) *The Division of Labour in Society* (1893). London: Collier-Macmillan.

Foucault, M. (1980) *Power/Knowledge*, ed. C. Gordon. Brighton: Harvester.

Foucault, M. (1984) *The Foucault Reader*, ed. P. Rabinow. Harmondsworth: Penguin.

Frayling, C. (1995) *Strange Landscape: A Journey through the Middle Ages*. Harmondsworth: Penguin.

Freedman, R.E. (ed.) (1991) *Business Ethics: The State of the Art*. Oxford: Oxford University Press.

Freundlieb, D. (1989) 'Rationalism v. Irrationalism? Habermas's Response to Foucault', *Inquiry*, 31: 171–92.

Friedman, M. (1988) 'The Social Responsibility of Business is to Increase its Profits', in T. Donaldson and P.H. Werhane (eds) *Ethical Issues in Business: A Philosophical Approach*. Englewood Cliffs, NJ: Prentice-Hall.

Gergen, K. and Whitney, D. (1996) 'Technologies of Representation in the Global Corporation', in D.M. Boje, R.P. Gephart and T.J. Thatchenkery (eds), *Postmodern Management and Organization Theory*. London: Sage.

Giddens, A. (1972) *Emile Durkheim: Selected Writings*. Cambridge: Cambridge University Press.

Giddens, A. (1987) 'Structuralism, Post-Structuralism and the Production of Culture', in A. Giddens and J.H. Turner (eds), *Social Theory Today*. Cambridge: Polity.

Giddens, A. (1991) *Modernity and Self-Identity*. Cambridge: Polity.

Giddens, A. (1994) *Beyond Left and Right*. Cambridge: Polity.

Giddens, A. (1997) 'Interview', Start the Week, BBC Radio 4, January.

Goodpaster, K.E. (1995) 'Commentary on "MacIntyre and the Manager"', *Organisation*, 2(2): 212–16.

Gouldner, A. (1973) 'The Sociologist as Partisan', in A. Gouldner, *For Sociology: Renewal and Critique*. London: Allen Lane.

Horkheimer, M. (1972) *Critical Theory: Selected Essays*. New York: Herder and Herder.

Ishiguru, K. (1989) *The Remains of the Day*. London: Faber and Faber.

Jackall, J. (1988) *Moral Mazes: The World of Corporate Managers*. Oxford: Oxford University Press.

Kundera, M. (1989) *The Unbearable Lightness of Being*. London: Faber and Faber.

Lee, S.J. (1987) *The European Dictatorships 1918–1945*. London: Routledge.

MacIntyre, A. (1967) *A Short History of Ethics*. London: Routledge.

MacIntyre, A. (1981) *After Virtue*. London: Duckworth.

Mangham, I. (1995) 'MacIntyre and the Manager', *Organization*, 2 (2): 181–204.

Marsden, R. (1996) 'Marx's Method: The 1857 *Introduction* and the 1859 *Preface*'. University of Athabasca, Canada, mimeo.

Marx, K. and Engels, F. (1967) *The Communist Manifesto*. Harmondsworth: Penguin.

Nietzsche, F. (1956) *The Birth of Tragedy and the Genealogy of Morals* (1887). New York: Doubleday.

Norris, C. (1987) *Derrida*. London: Fontana.

Norris, C. (1993) *The Truth About Postmodernism*. Oxford: Basil Blackwell.

Ollman, B. (1976) *Alienation: Marx's Conception of Man in Capitalist Society*, 2nd edn. Cambridge: Cambridge University Press.

Parker, M. (1997) 'Organizations and Citizenship', *Organization*, 4(1): 75–92.
Pepperwell, R. (1995) *The Post-Human Condition*. Oxford: Intellect.
Peters, T. J. and Waterman, R.H. (1982) *In Search of Excellence*. New York: Harper and Row.
Pollner, M. (1987) *Mundane Reason*. Cambridge: Cambridge University Press.
Randels, G.D. (1995) 'Morality and the Manager after MacIntyre: A Response to Mangham', *Organization*, 2(2): 205–11.
Roberts, J. (1984) 'The Moral Character of Management Practice', *Journal of Management Studies*, 21(3): 296–302.
Roche, J.M. (1971) 'The Competitive System, to Work, to Preserve, and to Protect', *Vital Speeches of the Day*, May: 445.
Rose, G. (1996) *Mourning Becomes the Law: Philosophy and Representation*. Cambridge: Cambridge University Press.
Ryan, M. (1982) *Marxism and Deconstruction: A Critical Articulation*. Baltimore: Johns Hopkins University Press.
Sampson, E. E. (1989) 'The Deconstruction of the Self', in J. Shotter and K.J. Gergen (eds), *Texts of Identity*. London: Sage.
Sturrock, J. (1993) *Structuralism*, 2nd edn. London: Fontana.
Taylor, F. (1990) 'General Principles of Management' (1912), in D.S. Pugh (ed.) *Organization Theory*. Penguin: Harmondsworth.
ten Bos, R. and Willmott, H.C. (1998) 'Can Business Ethics be Post-Modernised?', Working Paper, Manchester School of Management: UMIST.
Watson, T.J. (1994) *In Search of Management*. London: Routledge.
Weber, M. (1946) *From Max Weber: Essays in Sociology*, ed. H.H. Gerth and C. Wright Mills. Oxford: Oxford University Press.
Weber, M. (1949) *The Methodology of the Social Sciences*, ed. E.A. Shils and A. Henry. New York: Free Press.
Weber, M. (1975) *Roscher and Knies: The Logical Problems of Historical Economics*. New York: Free Press.
Weber, M. (1978) *Economy and Society* (2 volumes) ed. G. Roth and C. Wittich. Berkeley, CA: University of California Press.
Weiskopf, R. and Willmott, H.C. (1997) 'Turning the Given into a Question: A Critical Discussion of Chia's Organizational Analysis and Deconstructive Practice', *Electronic Journal of Organization Theory*, http://www.mngt, Waikat.ac.nz:80/depts/sm&[/journal/ejrot.htm
Willmott, H.C. (1986) 'Unconscious Sources of Motivation in the Theory of the Subject: An Exploration and Critique of Giddens' Dualistic Models of Action and Personality', *Journal for the Theory of Social Behaviour*, 16(1): 105–22.
Willmott, H.C. (1986) 'Strength is Ignorance; Slavery is Freedom; Managing Culture in Modern Organizations', *Journal of Management Studies*, 30: 515–52.
Willmott, H.C. (1994) 'Bringing Agency (back) into Organizational Analysis', in J. Hassard and M. Parker (eds), *Towards a New Theory of Organization*. London: Routledge. pp. 87–130.

6 Business Ethics: (In-)Justice and (Anti-) Law – Reflections on Derrida, Bauman and Lipovetsky

Hugo Letiche

The word (neologism) *subjectile* is used by Jacques Derrida to denote 'that which lies between the surfaces of the subject and the object' (Thévenin and Derrida, 1986). It is characteristic of Derrida's philosophical method that he tries to make the reader aware of the many, often shifting, meanings which key terms in texts possess, reveal and hide, by using his concepts (words) in a multifaceted and unstable manner (see Willmott, Chapter 5 in this volume, on poststructural thought in general). For instance, in the *subjectile* 'the trajectories of the *objective*, the *subjective*, the *projectile*, of the *interjection*, the *objection*, of *dejection* and *abjection*, etc.' are to be seen (Burgin, 1996: 153–4). Derrida illustrates the *subjectile* as follows:

> with the aid of a match, Artaud opens holes in the paper, and the traces of burning perforation are part of a work in which it is impossible to distinguish between the subject of the representation and the support of this subject, in the *layers* of the material, between that which is above and that which is below, and thus between the subject and its outside, the representation and its other. (Thévenin and Derrida, 1986: 70)

Subjectile, I wish to argue, captures the multiple and complex nature of *justice* which lies somewhere between the surface of the *singular* (self, 'I', consciousness), and that of the *general* (principles, absolutes, laws). I will explore, in this essay, the subjectiles of justice, with use of Derrida's (1992) essay 'Force of Law: The "Mystical Foundation of Authority"'. In this essay, Derrida addresses the possibility of justice: what are the requisite subjectiles of interact which (can) make justice possible? Mere *laws* (statutes, decisions and legal texts), he argues, cannot provide justice; only with *enforcement* does law have any effect at all. And mere *power* (authority, police, and social agency) is certainly not a guarantee of justice. There is a dual danger here, of laws without agency, and of agency without justice. It is one thing to make laws and quite another to enforce them. It is one thing to have (legal, social) power over others and another to strive for justice. The assertion is not merely that laws do not necessarily lead to justice – a rather self-evident and tame claim – but that laws and law making may well make justice impossible.

This (rather radical) claim shows promise of being able to deconstruct the increasingly popular practice within (business) organizations of 'legislating' ethical codes as a (so-called) way of achieving (social) justice. Corporate 'accountability' is supposedly to be attained via 'socially responsible entrepreneurship' (for Douwe Egberts); supported, for instance, by consulting an 'integrity expert' (within a consultancy organization like KPMG) is equipped with an integrity thermometer to test the corporate ethical climate, and advises the client in defining a corporate ethical code of behaviour (Braam and Iding, 1996). Whatever form of justice may be intended,sales can be hiked via ethical entrepreneurship. In this way, Benetton's AIDS campaigns attracted the attention and controversy desired to provide the clothing with 'additional (symbolic) value added', though the company's refusal to contribute to the UK AIDS campaign made it look merely exploitative. American Express's campaign to support the restoration of the Statue of Liberty was attributed with increasing their volume of transactions by 9.4%. Thus, 'corporate responsibility' may just be another form of PR – a way of generating profits via a *simulacrum* of 'a show of social concern'.

In a society wherein the state provides less and less support to the socially weak, and the 'rights' of the poor to shelter, health care, education and/or work have been growing ever weaker, corporate action often seems increasingly appropriate. If the state may not, cannot or will not maintain minimum social standards, corporate action may be (the only) alternative. In the United States, some companies find themselves forced to take action: public services do not provide the levels of transport, hygiene or education the companies require to produce. Companies, then, have to 'care for' their workers to survive. Furthermore, neo-liberal mistrust of the efficiency of any government-provided service may also be leading in Europe to ever increasing forms of corporate 'responsibility'. A prominent first step in this process for most companies (organizations), is the drafting of a corporate ethical code of behaviour. Therein one finds the 'mission' of the company, and rules of behaviour which have been prescribed for (top) management and personnel. What is permitted (integrity) and what is forbidden (corruption), are spelled out. The company clarifies its standards of corporate interaction with its employees and clients, as well as defines its attitude to safety and the environment. Thus, Dow Chemical writes: 'Employees are the basis of our success. We will treat them with respect, we strengthen cooperation in the workplace and stimulate personal freedom and growth. Exceptional achievement will be encouraged and rewarded.'

Obviously such texts sound 'idealistic' and 'vague'; how to actualize or control them is pretty unclear. But I do not want to provide (yet another) critique of corporate ethical codes based on their hyper-real quality by emphasizing how such simulacra belong to the culture of 'zapping' or *tachiyomi* (from the Japanese, meaning the act of reading opportunistically and fragmentarily while on the move; such as in the desultory flipping through of corporate PR reports: Burgin, 1996: 110). My point is a much more frightening one: namely that the effort to achieve justice via corporate ethical codes is, in principle, flawed, and is doomed to produce the very opposite of its espoused goal(s). The code makers may well be purveyors of utterly unneeded, desultory violence, which makes the pursuit of justice more difficult. This assertion will be grounded on my reading of a text by Jacques Derrida, and developed by comparing writings of Zygmunt Bauman and Gilles Lipovetsky's on *devoir* (duty, laws, ethics) in business and organizations.

The aporia of justice's/*Droit*'s (law's) originatory violence

Derrida's (1992) essay is in two parts: the first is grounded in the circumstance of addressing a conference in the United States in English ('C'est ici un devoir, je dois *m'adresser* à vous en anglais': 'It is here an obligation, I must *address* myself to you in English'); and the second takes as its point of departure the reading of Walter Benjamin's essay *Zur Kritik der Gewalt*. Derrida commences with the aporia, that he had been confronted with the *obligation* (*devoir*) of talking about 'deconstruction and the possibility of justice'. It was not his title or 'free' choice. Thus, how can he speak adequately of justice, if he is not, himself, speaking from a free (inter)act of justice? For Derrida, to speak justice requires a performative situation wherein one addresses oneself to the singularity of the other, and/or to oneself, as a unique (an)other. Justice is synonymous with doing justice to the other. An assertion in general of justice – 'this or that is just', 'justice means such and such' – is always unjust. Justice is characterized by attending to singularities; it is situational, circumstantial, and actual. When justice is thematized, it inevitably risks substantialism, i.e. becoming a task, a rule, an obligation. *Devoir* (duty) replaces justice with accountability, obligation, and necessity; i.e. with I 'must', 'should', 'ought to' and 'have to'.

The aporia of Derrida's performative situation, in the text presently under examination, is that his speech (text) was a *devoir*. His problem was how to escape the pitfalls of *devoir,* in order to really be able to speak of justice. If he tried to directly say something about justice, he would defeat his purpose; justice is a relationship and, when reified in positive claims, it betrays itself by becoming authority, obligation, and necessity. Coercive and regulative speech – enforced absolutes and rules – is never justice because such rules lack the relational openness to the other which is crucial to justice. If one speaks about justice, one has more to say about what it is not than what it is:

> one cannot speak *directly* about justice, thematize or objectivize justice, say 'this is just' and even less 'I am just', without immediately betraying justice. (1992: 10)

Laws, or *droit*, on the other hand, have no problems with being stated. Quite the opposite: they have to be communicated and 'enforced' to be what they are supposed to be. Law or *devoir* exists as 'laying down the law', as a rule of action, which demands to be applied. An undefined law is not a law. An open interaction of singularity is not a law. Laws have to be understood. They form a contract. They are meant to be enforced and obeyed. For there to be laws, there has to be a force which is 'authorized' to determine what the laws are and which require compliance. Obviously, authorization can be disputed, but for laws to exist, the principle of authorization has to be met. Derrida's assertion is that justice cannot support any such situation of 'authorization.' Justice cannot 'be laid down'; it is a process of interaction. The chasm between laws and justice threatens to destabilize all efforts to achieve bureaucratized, rule-based, ethics. The 'rules' will be nothing more than a product of the action(s) taken in authorizing them. The power or force needed to authorize the rules becomes their key social signifying characteristic. Thus, the only way for Derrida to make justice possible was to deconstruct his invitation, by revealing how being invited to speak was, in effect, a request to submit to the logic of *devoir*; but he could escape that logic by recasting his speech as open (not predetermined or rule-bound) activity.

Thereby, he demonstrated that *deconstruction*, his radical form of questioning text(s) – in this case questioning his 'invitation' – does, in contradistinction to 'texts of authority', leave potential room for justice. But it is a very uneasy claim:

> I think there is no justice without this experience, however impossible it may be, of aporia. Justice is an experience of the impossible. A will, a desire, a demand for justice whose structure wouldn't be an experience of aporia would have no chance to be what it is, namely, a call for justice . . . How are we to reconcile the act of justice that must always concern singularity, individuals, irreplaceable groups and lives, the other or myself *as* other, in a unique situation with rule, norm, value or the imperative of justice which necessarily have a general form, even if this generality prescribes a singular application in each case? (1992: 16–17)

Deconstruction is to be identified with making the other's language one's own, in so far as one can appropriate and assimilate it; and is a way of discovering the singularity of the other (text, self, situation). The *appropriateness* (*justesse*) of the appropriation determines the possibility of justice: 'this concept of responsibility is inseparable from a whole network of connected concepts (property, intentionality, will, freedom, conscience, consciousness, self-consciousness, subject, self, person, community, decision, and so forth) . . . deconstruction calls for an increase in [this] responsibility' (1992: 20).

In contradistinction, *law* imposes its language on the subject; its injunctions are phrased in a system of regulated and coded prescriptions, which are meant to be applied to any (appropriate) situation. Law is stabilized and statutory, calculable and rule-bound. Justice is unpredictable and 'full of anxiety': what will one discover when one confronts the situation of the other? Justice demands an *epoché,* i.e. a radical form of philosophical questioning,[1] wherein the authority of law(s) is suspended and the question is (re-)posed as to what is 'la relation avec autrui – c'est à dire la justice' ('the relation to others – that is to say, justice') (Levinas quoted in Derrida,

1992: 22). Because Levinas's thought also rotates around the theme of justice in relationship to the other, his thought is often (re-)interpreted in texts dealing with (business) ethics. In Levinas, the other cannot be captured in an abstract *concept of man*, such as one on which a legal system could be based, but is grounded in the practically infinite dis-symmetry of otherness, i.e. in the *equitable honouring of faces* (see Desmond, Chapter 8, and Willmott, Chapter 5 in this volume). Justice, thus, is rooted in the acknowledgement of otherness, which can be revealed by doing justice to the faces of (an)other(ness). Justice in Derrida, following Levinas, is rooted in the 'sanctity' of (the) relationship to (an)other.

Up to now, law has been defined in Derrida's (and my) text in aporia to justice. Law obviously plays a crucial performative (controlling) role in our (modern) society. The modernist political tradition originated, of course, in the destruction of the *ancien régime* and the replacement of hereditary divine rights and privileges by law, supposedly grounded on the rights of man and popular sovereignty. In reality, popular sovereignty has (too) often been confused with the nation (especially in France and the US) and/or has deformed itself on the model of the *terreur* in France into national (revolutionary) dictatorship(s). At best, representative democracy has pursued a modernist agenda of liberty and equality, in defence of the interests of the largest number of persons (citizens). Democratic politics have, in substance, been grounded on the key modernist ideas of progress and rationalization. But the principles of popular sovereignty and of the rights of man, which form the dual supports of democracy, have tended to become impoverished and separated from one another (Touraine, 1992). Popular sovereignty has often been reduced to mere populism, and the rights of man to a one-sided championing of the market economy. Central government has seemingly become an administrative power seen by many as a threat to civil society. Currently, politics appears to limit itself to economic themes such as international competitivity, balance of payments, currency exchange rates and the development (implementation) of new (competitive) technologies. The 'throne' of the *ancien régime* may have been suppressed, but the new princes (the 'law makers') may very well not be much of an improvement. But Derrida focuses more on the conceptual characteristics of *droit* (the law) than on the techno-administrative (bureaucratic) performance of law; thus I will return later, in the second section of this text, to the theme(s) of law and *performativity*.

Law (or *droit*) is not just conceptually difficult to deal with; functionally it encompasses a large (confusing) number of roles too. *Droit* (law) can refer to law makers or enforcers; to the law abiding and fearing as well as the law breaking; to the legal scholar or the professional imposter. Derrida wants to focus on those who make and enforce the laws. Law making, he asserts, is always grounded in an originatory act of violence. For laws to be made, someone has to assert their 'right' to 'lay down the law'. The previous situation of law making (i.e. legitimacy) has to be overthrown and replaced by a new one. Law enforcement is based on (state) violence (which is meant) to conserve obedience to the law(s) already made. The juridical order is based on the state possessing a 'monopoly of violence', i.e. the state has exclusive possession of 'fundamental, founding violence, that is, violence able to justify, legitimate (*begrunden*, "to found") or to transform the relations of law (*rechtsverhaltnisse*, "legal conditions") and so to present itself as having a right to law' (Derrida, 1992: 35). The law makers try to justify their inaugurating of new law(s) on the basis of nature (natural law), progress and/or social ethics.

But at the origin of any new law there is, always, non-law; the state of prior law (or order) must be suspended by a pure performative act of the law maker(s), which is an assertion of a new order (*a-venir*, 'to come'), making it possible for the new law to emerge. While the discourse of the (new) law is almost always one of self-legitimization, performative violence is at the crux of the matter. Prior, legitimate authority has to be suspended (abolished) and replaced by an alternative canon, before a new law is really firmly incorporated. Law making is based upon a radical epoché of the law; it throws society (back) into the state of 'before the law', and into an anxiety born of (radically) indeterminate relationships. Law making is caught in its own iterability; each return to new law making threatens its legitimacy by revealing its originatory performative violence. Maintaining the law, entails seeing to it that the laws that have been made are respected. It also entails institutionalized violence, which protects the legitimacy of the law makers.

The force which maintains and protects the law (no matter what form it takes) Derrida calls the *police*. The police are assumed to be 'figures without limit'; that is to say, 'the police aren't just the police (today more or less than ever), they are there, the faceless figure (*figure sans figure*) of a *Dasein* (being-thrown-into-the-world), coextensive with the *Dasein* of the polis' (1992: 44).[2] In our society, the police have a 'haunting presence everywhere', which (re-) affirms the power of the law makers (the state) to maintain their (its) monopoly on violence. This monopoly enables the legislators to seem credible when they try and determine social relationships to come. Thus, the unmitigated presence of originatory violence is replaced by 'represented' violence (in so-called 'politics'); and the 'represented' violence is, most of the time, forgotten in 'democratic' normalcy. The law makers repeatedly 'forget' the violence, which is the ground of their power. Law making is often replaced by compromise politics; parliamentarianism fosters a 'babbling' which renounces really facing up to circumstances and taking any radical action. Law making passes 'from presence to representation'. The legislator who consciously possesses and exerts violence to realize (his/her) goals is replaced by the politician who is resplendent in the regalia and symbols of legitimacy, but practises 'compromise politics', bargaining power out amongst all claimants (so-called) to 'avoid the worst'. Law making has become 'institutional degeneracy', because consciousness of what law is has been lost. Therefore, 'the police [have] become hallucinatory and spectral, haunting everything; they are everywhere, even there where they are not . . . their presence is not present, any more than any presence is present . . . but the presence of their spectral double knows no boundaries'. Their violence is not physical but spiritual (1992: 45). A system of degenerate law making, (more or less) unable to really make any laws, is linked to a society saturated by a spectral 'police' presence (institutionalized rational, administrative authority). The police (CEOs, techno-experts, controllers and so on), unable to preserve the law (i.e. the legitimacy of the state/organization) with the 'laws' available to them, have *de facto* taken over being law makers. The police no longer only *enforce* the law; they have taken to *producing* it. The unity of legislative and executive power in the state's (organization's) techno-administrative capabilities creates an illegitimate 'police' society.

> Instead of being itself and being contained within democracy, this spirit of the police, this police violence as *spirit* degenerates there. It bears witness in modern democracy to the greatest degeneracy imaginable for violence . . . Why? In absolute monarchy legislative and executive powers are united. In it violence is therefore normal, in keeping with its essence, its idea, its spirit. In democracy, on the other hand, violence is no longer accorded to the spirit of the police. Because of the supposed separation of powers, it is exercised illegitimately, especially when instead of enforcing the law the police make the law . . . In absolute monarchy, police violence, terrible as it may be, proves to be what it is and what it ought to be in its spirit, while the police violence of democracies denies its proper principle, making laws surreptitiously, clandestinely. The consequences or implications are twofold: (1) democracy is a degeneracy of *droit* and of the violence of *droit*; (2) there is not yet any democracy worthy of this name. (1992: 46)

According to Derrida, a relationship to (an)other, without violence, is possible; for instance, in *dialogue* or the 'culture of the heart'. But this takes place, in a reality beyond *droit* (law). For Derrida, in individual and specific interacts there can be a logic of justice; but in collective existence or 'society', there is only the possibility of law. The philosopher or metaphysician can achieve (potential) access to non-violence when action by mutually agreed covenant is a possibility. But the terrain of the sociologist or economist, of politics and management, is that of generalized rules, of *droit*. *Droit* can only respond to the threat(s) of (economic) exploitation, (social) injustice, and 'might-makes-right' by limiting the worst violence with another violence. Beyond law ('beyond all legal systems, and therefore beyond violence') there is the possibility of metaphysical knowledge and action, which may not be 'violent' in the way of *droit* (law), but which may well be 'mythical and violent' (Greek) and/or 'divine violent' (Jewish). That is to say, it might hold to conceptions of 'truth' and 'violence' which transcend *droit*. To summarize, the aporia explored up to now in the domain of *droit* (law) have revealed a conservative violence which can preserve the law at the cost of destroying the principle of law making; and, an activist (form of) law making which can keep the principle of democratic action alive, but only at the cost of (re-)revealing its violent (non-democratic and illegitimate) grounds. Justice (seemingly) belongs to another part of our conceptual universe than law.

Awakening-to-the-face

To pursue the theme of justice versus law but to focus more on ethics in practice, I will pursue the themes of ethics and morality. As many others in this volume have indicated, there is a tension between ethical code and (individual) integrity, transcendental *epoché* (analysis) and perceptual *epoché*, *a priori* philosophy and social constructivism or conventional sociology and postmodernism. In order to address this tension I will explore the texts of, first, Zygmunt Bauman and, in the next section, Gilles Lipovetsky. Both of these social thinkers claim, in their own way, to address postmodernism non-dismissively.[3] Both claim to see important ethical possibilities emerging from the postmodern situation. But they disagree strongly about where a postmodern ethics takes (or ought to be taking) us. They share a more descriptive and, in comparison to Derrida, less conceptually powerful approach – though their discussions circle around the same issues. More than Derrida, Bauman and Lipovetsky focus on social practice. The textual strategy I am following moves, thus, from the conceptual and abstract (deconstruction) to the theoretical but applied (philosophical sociology).

My examination of Zygmunt Bauman's odyssey into ethics begins with his book *Mortality, Immortality* (1992).[4] In this text he compares modernity, which 'deconstructed mortality [which] one cannot overcome, into a series of afflictions [which] one can [overcome]' (1992: 163). The emancipation from necessity – from disease, ignorance, poverty – has served in modernism as a substitute immortality. But this strategy has, supposedly, been *liquidized*, it has lost its former solidity. The project-oriented philosophy of modernism was always focused on a yet to be attained future. But the postmodern mindset, which is replacing the modernist one, focuses on the now; the future is *now*. No (future) moment is thought to be any more real than the present one. Postmodernism is enclosed in an ecstasy of the now; each moment (or non-moment) is immortal. Each moment is just as ephemeral, transient and evanescent as any other. Time in the radical now is unconnected; existence today is in *non-place*. By abolishing time (history), each moment becomes just as important (or unimportant) as any other. The future is just another moment, which will be shoved aside like each and any moment is, to make way for yet another one. Identity can and will be asserted in the culture of now, but as *attention attracting scenarios*. Identity is pursued as theatricality and so Goffman's world of actors without systems has been achieved.[5] Thus, we live an 'endless series of transient moments'. Self-identity may persist as a contest for personal legitimization, but there is 'a collective incapacity to construct life as reality, to take life seriously' (1992: 199). Without *meaning* or *pattern*, doomed to an endless present, humanity, according to Bauman, has lost the dialectic between the present and the future, the real and the ideal, mortality and immortality, which was modernism's way of differentiating between life and death. Life has become permanently attached to death, unable to ever truly realize itself as life.

Bauman asserts that Levinas's *being-for-another* is the only possible way of escaping the meaningless, totally overpowering, grip of the present, and of making one's existence matter: [6]

> *My* responsibility means that the fate of the other depends now on what *I* do. My existence matters, it has consequences, it is more than just another episode . . . I should act as if the alleviation of suffering of every being depended upon my action. Only when dedicated to such an action, my *life* counts . . . my *death*, is no more a senseless, absurd, unjustifiable occurrence . . . Through making myself for-the-other, I make myself for-myself, I pour meaning into my being-in-the-world. (1992: 202)

And,

> a readiness-to-die-for-anOther is the sign of moral awakening from the egoistic somnolence in which life is for most people, most of the time enveloped in Egoism and egotism of quotidianity blurs the moral sense and makes the Other invisible as an object of my responsibility. It takes a shock of which only the Other as the Face, as the command to help and to care, is capable . . . responsibility, not a contractual responsibility, not a responsibility 'from here to there,' 'from worth living' . . . It is a moral world in which the responsibility for anOther goes as far as the readiness to die. It is a cruel, inhuman, and immoral world in which that readiness is called, and required, to be acted on . . . such is the world . . . of the Holocaust, of the Gulag, of the genocide. (1992: 208)

In conclusion,

> No principle or norm can claim to be moral as long as it justifies the death of anOther, let alone the murder of anOther – in the same way as no principle or norm may claim to be moral, if it implies that my responsibility for the Other stops short of the gift of my life. (1992: 210)

Bauman tears apart the two key aspects which are combined in Derrida's concept of justice. Singularity/the now/the immediate/the present is in Bauman alienated from awareness of the other, from difference/face/being. The two contrasting positions – Derrida's singularity *and* being, Bauman's singularity *versus* being; are to be traced back to the different concepts of philosophical analysis (*epoché*) embraced by the two thinkers. *Epoché* is the radical return, in thought, to the key qualities of what is under study. *Epoché* can be a form of stringent empiricism, the return to what is perceptually present; or it can be transcendent, trying to embrace the 'reality' behind the 'real'. Derrida sees *epoché* (in the phenomenological tradition) as the rejection of the *natural attitude*. It is the refusal to take reality for granted or to languish in (a positivist sort of) common sense. It is the demand to see and experience, in an active and mutual relationship between perceiver and perceived. Lived existence, on the *existential* level, is what is studied. Bauman, on the other hand, applies the *epoché transcendentally*. The empirical and immediate level of the perceiver/perceived relationship is transcended and basic principles preceding perceptual experience are (meant to be) discovered. The Derridan phenomenal *epoché* is intended to open perception to *ontic* insight; i.e. to make it possible to perceive how things *are* by focusing on perceptual experience. Bauman's sort of *epoché*, assumes that there is something more than perception, which is more fundamental than immediately lived existence, and which can only be revealed on a depth level (philosophical, transcendent, metaphysical) logically prior to lived experience.

Thus, for Bauman, morality precedes *being*: herein he reverses existentialism's credo that existence precedes essence. For Bauman, essence (morality) precedes existence (ontic activity – perception, identity, and interaction). In Bauman, the self is born not in *opposition* to the other (radically alone and responsible for itself) as in Sartre's existentialism, but out of *union* with the other. Bauman's position restricts the role of individual action – the fundamental significance of otherness precedes the existence of the self. For the existentialists, life (existence) precedes meaning; the self is the first principle of existence. If we assume that existence precedes meaning, we have to assume that the concrete existence assumed by the self can be interpreted to be a matter of *choice*. If meaning/essence precedes existence, what remains of individual freedom? Thus what is at stake in this debate is what degree(s) of freedom we are to attribute to individual existence. The existentialist tradition stresses the self's freedom to assume an identity (even if *absurd*); while transcendental essentialism stresses that determining first principles make the existence of the self possible.

In Bauman responsibility (being-*for*-the-other) makes the 'me' (social role and identity) into an 'I' (self, purposeful being). It bestows uniqueness and identity. The 'I' does not originate in a struggle with the other for liberty and individuality, but via *agape*, spiritual love and charity. Bauman's transcendental logic is not so much a grounding for consciousness (i.e. for what makes perception, cognition, and experience possible) as the basis for the *care* or moral involvement which supposedly underpins the very possibility of identity. Bauman is trying to answer not an epistemological question (i.e. what makes seeing, perceiving, knowing possible), but an ethical one (i.e. what makes the moral self possible). Derrida's self is a phenomenal self, it is what it experiences; whilst Bauman's self is a social-moral self, it is what it is to another. The tradition to which Derrida belongs is epistemologically centred. It identifies the self with the (ontic) ability to see, know, perceive, experience, and questions *how* phenomenal existence occurs. The tradition to which Bauman belongs tries to identify the philosophical (ontological or metaphysical) first principles of humanness. Bauman grounds his observations of social-psychological existence, in an analysis of *being* (the second sort of *epoché*) and not in one of *perceiving*. The first ontic (perceptual and psychological) *epoché* does not count for much for Bauman because he is entirely focused on the second ontological (having to do with being or fundamental logic, and *not* personal, experiential or psychological actuality) *epoché*. But Bauman's *epoché* does have to have some phenomenal role in lived existence; otherwise it could not exert any influence on concrete individual consciousness! Bauman responds to the paradox, of at once rejecting but still being in need of the experiential, paradoxically. He grounds the most basic concept of *life* in the perception of and anxiety for *death*. One knows life in so far as one knows angst for death.[7] But it is only via the overcoming of this angst – by being-for-another – that Bauman's self achieves significance (i.e. the self-perception of being). Thus Bauman has grounded his concept of (fundamental) being in a radical theory of responsibility for another. Hereby being is both social (directed to another) and a *prerequisite* to psychological existence (it underpins self, identity, perception and consciousness).

Bauman pursues these same basic conceptual strategies throughout his ethical work during the 1990s. In *Postmodern Ethics* (1993), he contextualizes his theory and develops his idea of *care*. He argues, at this juncture, that the postmodern condition has opened up ethics as a theme. The modernist culture supported belief in the possibility of a *non-ambivalent, non-aporetic ethical code* (Bauman, 1993: 9). Ethics were, in principle, a generally solvable problem. Correct solutions to social issues/dilemmas were *a priori* possible. Substantively this belief gave the political and intellectual elite's the possibility of prescribing how the 'masses' should behave. *Disbelief* in any such universal ethical code is postmodern. In postmodernism, human morality has been accepted to be ambivalent; mankind cannot be posited to be either essentially 'good' or 'bad'. Nor can moral matters be decided via simple rational procedures; they simply do not fit into any elemental 'means–ends' schemes. In addition, in postmodernism morality is construed to be contradictory because few choices are unambiguously 'good'. Even the choice for the other, if overdone, becomes destructive as it destroys the other's freedom. Nor is morality in postmodernism thought to be universalizable; morality depends on responding to the *moral impulse* and not blindly following any ubiquitous rule(s). Because such a moral impulse cannot be rationally arrived at, it remains the bane of disciplined bureaucratic society. For Bauman the crux of morality is a being-*for*-the-other, which precedes all effort's to be-*with*-the-other. Being-*for*-the-other, thus, is not a social psychological form of activity, for instance a dialogical form of interact(ion).[8] It is a state of *being*, an ethical *a priori* of individual existence.

Bauman's logic is, in essence, *anti-social science*. He is grounding human social identity in a transcendental analysis of being to another. Thus, his assertions neither stand nor fall on the basis of what can be observed, described or studied. Nonetheless, Bauman includes very rich sociological observation(s) in his writing. For instance, he stresses that the unpredictability and irrationality of the hyper-industrialized postmodern society forces humanity to accept uncertainty, paradox, contradiction and unpredictability. And he underscores that enlarged ambiguity increases the (social) space that moral persons have to make choices. In modernism, Bauman argues, the belief in an all-encompassing rationality made individual choice very difficult. Ethics were conceived of as problems demanding social collective and political answers. But the more modern society tried to legislate welfare, order and justice, the more disorder, messiness and unpredictability emerged. The more techno-administrative power was developed, the less clear became the guidance as to how to make use of it. The effort to banish ambiguity only served to create more of it. The more engrossed mankind became with creating a purely rational social order, the clearer it became that the effort was counter-productive. The efforts to legislate social relationships, to determine cultural values and to control natural phenomena have all broken down. All of them proved to produce as much disorder, unpredictability and chaos as order.

Bauman has long centred his analysis of contemporary society on this idea of the paradox within rationality; the will to control reality is, in his eyes, irrational, and practically flawed. The more obsessive the process of rationalization became, the more it led to ever more extreme forms of *risk society*, with ever increased unforeseen social and technological dangers.[9] According to Bauman, modernism collapsed from the paradoxes in its own programme. Instead of producing safe and secure order, it has generated more and more dangerous forms of unpredictability. Society has become ever less under control, rather than more so. Contingency and ambiguity cannot be banished; they can better be accepted. Thus, instead of abolishing individual choice in shared order as it tried to do, modernism reinstated personal (moral) choice at the very centre of existence. Ethical choice, for Bauman, takes the form of a social psychologization of the philosophy of Levinas. This produces a repersonalized morality of intimacy, grounded in human impulses and emotions. Morality is conceived to be based in the logic of *irreplaceable* selves in *asymmetrical* relations:

> Attitude before the relations, one-sidedness, not reciprocity; a relation that cannot be reversed; these are the indispensable, defining traits of a moral stance. 'In the relation to the Face, what is affirmed is asymmetry; in the beginning, it does matter who the Other is in relation to me – that is his business.' This sentence of Levinas can be read as a definition of the Face: Face is encountered if, and only if, my relation to the Other is *programmatically* non-symmetrical; that is, not dependent on the other's past, present, anticipated or hoped-for *reciprocation*. And morality is the encounter with the Other as face. Moral stance begets an essentially unequal relationship; this inequality, non-equity, this not-asking-for-reciprocation, this disinterest in mutuality, this indifference to the 'balancing up' of gains or rewards – in short, this organically 'unbalanced' and hence non-reversible character of 'I versus the Other' relationship is what makes the encounter a moral event. (Bauman, 1993: 48–9)

Morality is not rational or calculable; it is not rule-bound. Morality produces responsibility manifest in the care of being-*for*-the-other. Laws, the legislating or codifying of morality, are (ethically) counter-productive. Morality is thoroughly personal; it occurs in an abandonment of one's own freedom, a state of absolute anomie. As in Derrida, the split between justice (morality) and law is absolute. In fact, according to Bauman, law makers and police fear morality because it is for them unpredictable and uncontrollable. The question of law, for Bauman, rotates around the politics of otherness – the position of the other in the polis. Bauman begins to explore this theme, which will increasingly dominate his thought, by asking himself who is the *stranger* and what happens to him/her. The dilemma of the stranger is that s/he confronts the community with their *not-knowing-how-to-go-on*. What sort of *mis-meeting* will result from an encounter without certain, shared, social-cognitive structures? Contemporary urban life constantly generates social indeterminacy and emotional uncertainty because humanity is incessantly confronted with 'strangers'. For Bauman the haunting question (which he quotes repeatedly in his writings from Cornelius Castoriadis) is: 'Can the existence of the other [stranger] as such, place *me* in danger? . . . It can, under one condition: that in the deepest recesses of one's egocentric fortress a voice softly but tirelessly repeats "our walls are made of plastic, our acropolis of paper-mache"' (1993: 237). Postmodern community has, in Bauman's eyes, few defences against such doubts. Bauman is convinced that postmodern humanity wanders about, as so many nomads, vagabonds or tourists, lacking in traditional community and susceptible to anxiety. He does not believe that postmodernists can group together to exchange their local, immediate experiences. He believes that postmodern community is fraudulent, because it is based on an assumed shared (social and cultural) condition, instead of on an *a priori* assumption of *responsibility*.

In *Life in Fragments* (1995), Bauman focuses on the conflict between ethics and morality. *Ethics* is described as laws, 'truths' set down by a modernist authority which are intended to be followed; and *morality* is defined in the perspective of the individual's relationship to another, involving an identity determining response to *difference*. Thus, despite the differences between Derrida and Bauman, both distinguish in a rather similar way between two levels of action: one centring on routinized and depersonalized *control* and the other on an autonomous identity, constituting process of (radical) responsibility. For both writers, *ethics* is a code of law(s) which prescribe(s) correct behaviour. Bauman sees ethics as an effort of humanity to avoid chaos, a 'primal state . . . marked by fluidity, formlessness, indetermination, indifferentiation, total confusion' (1995: 12). Because human beings cannot endure chaos – they are unable to encounter the abyss – a continuous 'cover-up operation' is put into place. 'A thin film of order' is kept over the chaos – an illusion of stability and familiarity is maintained to hide pure immanence. 'Human order is never forced to admit that it can draw on nothing but itself to explain either its presence or its limitations' (1995: 15). Postmodernism is out to 'stand up straight and confront chaos'. Modernism ascribed order to providence, human reason and progress; it rejected 'pure arbitrariness' and remained committed to the principle of some form of order and meaning.

> Modernity was, and had to be, the *Age of Ethics* – it would not be modernity otherwise. Just as the law preceded all order, ethics must precede all morality. *Morality* was a product of ethics; ethical principles were the means of production; ethical

> philosophy was the technology, and ethical preaching was the pragmatics of moral industry; good was its planned yield, evil its waste or sub-standard produce. (1995: 34)

Modernity may have been the age of ethics, but Bauman hopes that post-modernity will be the age of morality. Ethics was a regime of dominators and dominated. Ethical legislation tried to force the dominated to account for their lives in terms set for them by their dominators. It fostered a rule-governed logic of fear and not one of fellowship or love. Following the rules replaced real morality (see Willmott, Chapter 5 in this volume). 'Ethical correctness' can be made socially necessary, but it is for the most part a thoughtless and conformist, insensitive and indifferent attitude. Morality demands real involvement in the other which Bauman rephrases, again based on Levinas, as:

> the shock of hearing the inaudible call for assistance, which the vulnerability and weakness of the Other, revealed in the nakedness of the face, issues without speaking; the shock so over-powering that it renders ridiculously insignificant all those rational considerations which bask in self-importance in the world of conventions and contractual obligations. The birth of the moral person is the self-command: s/he is my responsibility, and my responsibility alone . . . 'At the moment I am responsible for the Other, I am unique. I am unique in so far as I am irreplaceable, in so far as I am chosen to respond.' (1995: 60)

The other, being for the other as the face, is crucial to morality; and an anathema to ethics. Modernity tried to achieve solid and stable identity; morality demands flux, openness and the acceptance of the other as a problem. In morality one is not sure what to do; ethics is an escape from that uncertainty.

According to Bauman, the crucial danger of postmodern existence is that the person will not engage him/herself with the other but will remain a stroller, vagabond, tourist, and *flaneur*. All the uncertainty, chaos, impermanence could stop one from ever becoming emotionally involved, whereby one never really meets another or can accept responsibility for the other. The morality of social existence can, as with the *flaneur*, be reduced to a purely aesthetic (perceptual) relationship wherein one observes and sees, but never engages or feels. Modernity shifted responsibility to supra-individual rules and agencies, and left the other to the bureaucratic rule of nobody. Postmodernity could render human relations so fragmentary and fleeting that (almost) nothing can happen. Postmodernism has a disturbing tendency to emphasize the fleeting and to ignore the substantive. It is a troubling trend of our times that all eyes are on the personal ethics (financial, social, and sexual) of 'important persons', but almost no-one debates the morality of the actions, policies, worlds that they create and implement! But, between modernity's deadening order and regimentation, and postmodernity's experiential consumerism and uncertainty, Bauman has no problem in choosing. Postmodernity produces an 'autonomous, morally self-sustained and self-governed, therefore often unruly, unwieldy and awkward' personality, which can discover morality (1995: 287). Postmodernism may degenerate into ersatz community or techno-cruelty or withdraw into a world of simulacra, but the discovery of face always remains a possibility. Modernist legitimization of an orderly, accident-free, deviation-free society destroyed the very possibility of any such discovery. Ethics belongs to the modern dream of total order, to the universe of rational domination and political mastery run wild. Only a social order, grounded in fear and humiliation, which blocks all spontaneous being-with-the-other, can keep such *terreur* in place. But in all societies, the largest group of persons will try to maintain their (seemingly) stable identities; real encounters with another threaten the self with uncertainty, lack of clarity and the unknown. Meeting another melts all that is solid, and forces us to know that the centre of our beliefs may not hold. The (an)Other breaks the spell of normalcy. If the group wants to keep its identity, it cannot accept such boundary breaking interventions. Thus for Bauman, diversity and difference form our hope of morality, but also pose the threat of renewed Holocaust (see Munro, Chapter 9, and Desmond, Chapter 8 in this volume).

Ethics: the face of the self

If I agreed with Bauman, there would be no real need for a third reflection. The next step, I suppose, would then have to be to apply Bauman's ideas to practice. But I do not agree. I think Bauman is cheating intellectually. He grounds his position (and him*self;* and, in effect, all self) in the transcendental possibility posed by the encounter with another; but continues, nonetheless, to write apparently empirical descriptions of society. If Bauman wants to abandon social science, and embrace transcendental theory (metaphysics) as his realm of discourse, that is well and good. But he makes use of his ability, as a sociologist to observe social change, to legitimize his metaphysical assertions to his reader. I find the non-empirical goals of his use of sociology, methodologically very troubling. His goal is not to observe society, but to move the reader in the direction of his transcendental assumption(s). His discourse is not perceptual or phenomenal; he is not talking about things we can all (reasonably claim to be able to) see. Bauman's books are a statement of belief; what he *sees* is transcendent belief. He has collapsed the difference between practical theology and sociology. Of course, there is the rebuttal that, actually, postmodernism has done this for him. Postmodernism has been plagued by criticism of its supposed nominalist or nihilist character (see for example Anthony, Chapter 13 in this volume); but Bauman, in effect, reverses the direction of the debate. His postmodernism destroys the modernist differentiation between empirical social science and metaphysical/transcendent reflection, giving free reign to *belief.*

While I willingly approach the issue(s) of justice and laws with (Derrida's) sceptical epistemology, I do want to stay within the parameters of a discourse which claims to report on (potentially) shared phenomenal themes. My refusal to accept Bauman's textual strategy has led me to Lipovetsky. I knew that Bauman began his *Postmodern Ethics* with a rather strong attack on Gilles Lipovetsky's interpretation of postmodernism's import for ethics; thus I supposed Lipovetsky might just offer the desired alternative.

> Lipovetsky . . . suggests that we have finally entered the epoch of *l'après-devoir*, a post-deontic epoch, where our conduct has been freed from the last vestiges of oppressive 'infinite duties', 'commandments' and 'absolute obligations'. In our times the idea of self-sacrifice has been delegitimized; people are not goaded or willing to stretch themselves to attain moral ideals and guard moral values . . . yesterday's idealists have become pragmatic. The most universal of our slogans is 'No excess!' Ours is the era of unadulterated individualism and the search for the good life, limited solely by the demand for tolerance (when coupled to self-celebratory and scruple-free individualism, tolerance may only express itself as indifference). The 'after-duty' era can admit of only a most vestigial, 'minimalist' morality; a totally new situation according to Lipovetsky – and he counsels us to applaud its advent and rejoice in the freedom it has brought in its wake. Lipovetsky . . . commits the . . . errors of representing the *topic* of investigation as an investigative *resource*; that which should be *explained* as that which *explains*. To describe prevalent behaviour does not mean making a moral statement . . . If Lipovetsky's description is correct and we are facing today a social life absolved from moral worries . . . the sociologist's task is to find out how it has come about that moral regulation has been 'decommissioned' from the arsenal of weapons once deployed in society's self-reproductive struggles. If sociologists happen to belong to the critical current in social thought, their task will not stop at that point either. They would refuse to accept that something is right simply for being there. (Bauman, 1993: 2–3)

Lipovetsky's work is composed of three books. The first, *The Era of the Void* (1983), focuses on the social psychology of the postmodern consumer society. The theme is accurately specified in the book's subtitle: *Essays on Contemporary Individualism.* Nowhere does Lipovetsky place himself outside the phenomena he is describing. The revolutionary individualism which is overwhelming modernist practice is changing the pattern of social interaction. Communication is not motivated by any external (transcendent) truth outside, above and beyond the text. Communication, including his own, exists to communicate. The speaker speaks to speak, the writer writes to write. The text is totally desubstantialized because the narcissistic pleasure of expression has become a goal unto itself. This pleasure may have its problems (the indifference of desubstantialization, the anomie of deterritorization), but it has its advantages (no totalitarianism, a 'cool' tolerant relationship to the other) as well.

Lipovetsky's map of postmodern society contains three signposts: narcissism, the consumer society and *personalization*. His subthemes are seduction, desertification, holism and the humoresque. *Seduction* is the term he uses for the replacement of coercion by communication. Material production and the (re)production of society are no longer achievable by the mere use of force (authority). There are as many people employed in so-called service occupations, *seducers*, as there are 'producers'. And the public (now called 'clients') all want to be individually seduced. Massification has been rejected as authority's appeal has had to be personalized. Everyone from the politician to the police, from corporate communication to the boss, has been 'humanized'. Mere domination does not get (enough) results; the individual has to be emotionally appealed to (seduced) so s/he will play the role wished of her/him. The radical individualization of the appeal reveals the lack of common norms, goals and identity. There's nothing abstract or general left on the 'human level'. Significance is local, specific, and instantaneous. There's been a loss of shared reality. The individual ego is now in a 'soft isolation', atomized and alone. The 'social' has lost its significance. Commitment floats, meaning follows pleasure. Fundamental autonomy produces indifferent solitude. A laxist, relaxed culture supports few convictions and no social mobilization. The person is most often uninterested and uninvolved – threatened more by a loss of reality and depression than by violence and subjugation. This psychologized way of life is characterized by withdrawal into the self and the 'pleasures' of immediate hedonistic existence. Its social universe is desertized; there's only empty space where in modernism there were shared values, common causes and moral absolutes. The relationship of the person to his/her psyche and body has overwhelmed all other considerations.

Accompanying the neutralization or banalization of the social, there is the hyper-investment in the private. One lives in autoabsorption, autoconsciousness and the autoseduction of desire. This is, of course, narcissism.[10] Lipovetsky claims that an anthropological mutation is taking place, wherein a new stage of individualism is achieved. The self has become the individual's central preoccupation, resulting in self-analysis or the psychologization of consciousness becoming the dominant cultural form. But the self, without a social world, isolated from others, has little or no ability to discover itself. The self alone is nothing. The self without the mirror of others, has no identity. Thus, paradoxically, the more the self is centred entirely on itself, the less identity and the more incertitude it meets. Social roles lose their substance (who would one play them for?); the capacity to be expressive deteriorates (to whom would one express oneself?). Intersubjectivity becomes, more and more, a mere struggle for the signs (symbols) of 'winning', 'success', 'status'.

For Lipovetsky the 'new' postmodern person is a product of the paradox of modernism; Modernism was *creative* as *negation*. Traditional unfreedom(s), restrictive cultural and expressive norms, the social economic status quo, all fell to modernism's dynamism. Modernism was the *tradition of the new*, but the unbridled pursuit of the new was doomed, eventually, to exhaust itself. In the process, the disciplinary, authoritarian, puritan, (petit) bourgeois society was dismantled, and replaced by an individualist, hedonistic, mass consumption society. Capitalism was legitimized as the economic system wherein the self – defined as the individual's 'free' consumption choices – could prevail. The shared and collective was devalorized; the individual, unique and 'new' was valorized. But a purely *personalized* existence, wherein identity depends on individual consumption choices of objects and experiences, is dominated by ambiguity and indetermination. How does the self choose, when there are no aesthetic criteria, social norms, analytic rules, left to guide one? The options and choices augment ceaselessly, producing a supermarket existence: one just takes a bit of this and a bit of that.

Postmodernism produces a convivial, humoresque society wherein it is normal 'to keep smiling'. According to Lipovetsky the carnivalesque culture of the Middle Ages put control temporarily in abeyance in order to fiercely reassert it. Thus the profane (a donkey) would be led into church, but later the church's enormous power over society was reimposed. In the eighteenth and nineteenth centuries, laughter was identified with the ridiculing of authority and was generally mistrusted. The farce of the nineteenth century was, in effect, an attack on those in power. Humour was used to show the weakness of the other, and to attack (and hopefully to hurt) the other. In the humour of Charlie Chaplin, or the Marx Brothers, one can see an attack on authority and the powerful anger that traditionally underpinned humour. After all, humanity once laughed at the burning of cats. But in our society, passionate group involvement and rebellious aggression have all disappeared and hence humour has been devitalized. It has become mere nonsense. Woody Allen's humour is about him*self.* Humour is no longer social protest (or rebellion) but a reflexive form of (mild) pleasure. Allen makes his self the centre of his universe to such a ridiculous level that it becomes impossible to really take his self very seriously. Thus the self of the other has become an object of humour and bemused absurdity.

Lipovetsky closes *The Era of the Void* with a comparison of holistic, modern and postmodern society. In traditional or *holistic* society, the significance of interactions between people is all-important. In holism there is no differentiation between sectors of activity (economy and recreation), the person and their group (the individual and his/her family), the living and the dead (oneself and one's ancestors). Thus if one's friend becomes richer (material goods) than oneself, there is something wrong which has to be corrected. Friends are supposed to be alike, and to share equally. In holistic society there is no economy, apart from the personal and social relations. Personal things – respect, honour and prestige – count, not the possession of objects. The rule of total reciprocity applies to all contact. Interaction has to be mutually acceptable: if not, violence will be used to reassert the balance. Obviously, in capitalism, no rule of total reciprocity applies to the setting of wages, prices or working conditions. Total reciprocity subsumes the individual to the group. No one can excel, no self can be differentiated at a cost to another. This is a social order without history, enclosed in a permanent present. In this lifeworld, existence is not meant to change. Order, defined as total mutuality, is the absolute truth. Anything which tries to destroy that order is to be met (destroyed) by violence. In contemporary (human resources) literature one sees holism returning as a suggested cultural norm which lessens alienation, compartmentalization and absurdity (for a critique see Legge, Chapter 7 in this volume). Such writers do not seem to have adequately understood the limited position holism ascribes to the self. Holism might put an end to the social and material exploitation which is typical of Taylorism; but it would also destroy individualization as we know it.

Modernism has replaced the iron law of reciprocity with the rule of law (power of the state) and with the legitimization of private property. In holism, violence befits whoever feels that his/her reciprocity of relationships – i.e. I am just as rich, happy, creative as the other – has been destabilized. In modernism, the state takes possession of violence. Social differentiation, history and change, get a chance. The autonomous individual appears; the person no longer exists in so far as the norm(s) of the group permit, but groups exist in so far as persons choose to let them exist. The overwhelming power of the group norm in holistic society is replaced by the might of the rich, strong and determined. But individuals lose the right to impose social order with violence. The state, which is in the hands of the powerful, sanctions and rewards behaviour.

Modernism is rapidly losing out to *postmodernism* wherein autocontrol replaces the authority of the state. The self is less and less involved in others as consumer society replaces scarcity with welfare. Hyper-absorption in the self leaves little energy to involve oneself in comparisons with the existence of the other. The state is seen as a costly, inefficient organization which individual self-interest needs less and less. A 'cool culture' results from individuals pursuing their private self, distanced from everyone else, enjoying the welfare of the consumer society. Identity collapses and emotional emptiness endangers this culture; but it has no will for totalitarianism or *terreur*. Thus, Lipovetsky has done exactly what Bauman was afraid he'd do; he's written a purely descriptive book which makes no appeal to transcendent knowing (*epoché*) whatsoever, in its characterization of contemporary social action.

In the first half of his second book *The Empire of the Ephemeral* (1987), Lipovetsky abandons a purely descriptive form of writing and traces the rise of modernism (and its succession by postmodernism) as part and parcel of the history of fashion. But in the second half of the book, he reverts to the descriptive mode, in order to examine the workings of culture, business and communication in current society. Fashion, Lipovetsky asserts, developed parallel to, and from the same sources as, liberal democracy. Fashion's loss of momentum in the second half of the twentieth century parallels the decline of the state and of liberal democracy. What fashion and liberal democracy share in common is *the ideology of the new*. Traditional culture has always abhorred the new. In the Middle Ages one had to defend innovation by denying its very existence and claiming that whatever one had done was merely a repetition of classical Greek or Roman models. Tradition was 'truth' and newness heresy. But in the mid nineteenth century, individualization took off as a cultural phenomenon in Western Europe. Instead of wanting to possess what had always been 'right' or 'valued', people wanted the 'newest' or something 'original'. To some degree, this was a reaction to increased welfare. Traders and industrialists could now afford the goods and services which had been previously reserved for the cultural elite. That elite, supposedly, tried to protect its position, by staying one step ahead of the emergent merchant (capitalist) class. Only in 1793 (in France) were the people granted the right to dress as they pleased, rather than being required to display their social position in more or less prescribed clothing. Thus the ability to individualize one's appearance via dress is, historically speaking, a rather recent matter. Traditionally clothing was made to order; it was not until 1857–8 that couturier fashion first appeared. The mass production of everyday clothing started earlier (1820).

But fashion required a paradoxical balance of individuality and massification. The audience for high fashion has to be drawn from a cultural elite, which is on the lookout for something new, special, and unique to wear. Such an elite has to have embraced, at least in appearances, the non-conservative values of change, creativity and innovation. On the other hand they have to accept that the couturier creates fashion; i.e. that they will be dressed as the couturiers determine. In order to adjust the power balance, tilting it towards the elite, fashion shows were created, wherein the couturiers display their models and the customers *chose* which models were successful. Hereby the customer retained a sense of control in a process which is really determined by the fashion industry. The actual production of the clothing took place in industrial circumstances, which were no better than what happened in any other factory. The appearance of the fashion house was individualistic, artistic and elitist; and the circumstance of production was downtrodden, exploitative and repressive. Fashion, thus, is based on the total alienation of the logic of display (marketing) from the logic of production (labour). Fashion quickly became a token of social superiority – an important way to manifest 'taste', being 'in the know' and individual self-worth. But fashion is a very steep slope. The ideology of the 'new' progressively destabilized the social order; fashion did not stay reserved for a small elite but spread through the whole society. At first fashion was reserved to the very rich but, between the world wars, it expanded to include the middle class. After the Second World War it was even more democratized as *prêt à porter* came on the market, only to be followed by couturier jeans. On the one hand fashion was a way for the wearer to assert her/his individuality; and on the other it was a way for the fashion houses to make money by determining what was fashionable. In the stride between individuality and control, the former won and fashion collapsed into a sort of nominalist chaos ('fashion is whatever I say it is') during the 1970s.

Early on, in the history of fashion, the differences in models and possibilities of attire were pretty well restricted. For instance, Paris remained for long the centre of the world for women's dress design. There may have been innovation and individual customer choice; but there were a restricted number of 'models', and at any one time a single norm for what was 'fashionable'. Democracy worked on the basis of the same principles. Elections, based on limited suffrage, were held to choose political leaders who arranged matters '*en petit comité*'. In theory individuality reigned; but in reality small groups of persons defined the intellectual, political, artistic, fashionable practice(s) of the day. These small innovative elites had an enormous influence. The populace looked to them to define new novelties and fresh styles. Today, cultural leadership (in so far as it still exists) is spread very widely about; and no-one knows for sure where to look. The modernist system was formally democratic and open, but actually it was dominated by the centres of action. Contemporary cultural production is diffuse and fairly flat in its organization. The effect is that almost nothing new gets broadly communicated or widely accepted and change has become increasingly rare. The dynamism of the modern system has been sacrificed to achieve broader participation. Individuals look less to their surroundings for innovative models of action and are themselves. Since most persons never have been very creative, the rate of change has ground to a near halt. The old system still functions in the development and implementation of new technologies; wherein a few decision-makers and a small number of innovators have (nearly) all the strings in their hands. But the fashion system has fallen into disrepair: in the clothing industry, in most forms of intellectual activity, and in politics as well as in the arts. The contemporary individual seems to pursue an essentially isolated and conservative strategy; s/he tries not to be overwhelmed or bullied by (fashion) experts. Autoabsorption and uninvolvement in the new currently predominate. The social code points to a negotiated peace with one's surroundings, which provides for one's welfare and peace of mind. This is not a strategy for change, but a self-defensive attitude to 'remain oneself' and to stay whatever one already 'is'.

Paradoxically, while the norms of fashion have captured the whole economy – the *ephemeralness* of short product life-cycles, the *seduction* of marketing and client-centredness and the *marginal differentiation* of the so-called 'new and improved product' – the fashion system has actually broken down. We live in a society of total fashion, wherein the citizenry defend themselves as best they can against fashion's power. The reaction against fashion takes the form of: trusting only what one sees, sticking to what one has done oneself and knows well, and refusing to adopt the norm of the other as one's own. 'Performance' and 'quality' have become catchwords; permanence and reliability are driving (transient, catchy, playful) fashion out of the marketplace. The emotive and symbolic needs, which are met by fashion, are threatened with being neglected. The emotional, ironic and fantastic have lost out to performativity. People are not willing to pay for the poeticized and ludic. The supermarket society of hyper-choice does not want originality but wants predictability and a circumstance which leaves individual existence unthreatened. The individual does not accept violent infringements of his/her space: the power of propaganda has weakened, coercive rhetoric is unacceptable. The media provide us with lots of little events, but with no interiority. High speed perception – a constant stream of images with no dead time – float past, never analysed or assimilated in any depth. Lipovetsky describes a chewing-gum culture wherein a sceptical populace easily accepts and rejects, changes its mind quickly and treats representation (text, film, and ideas) as objects of consumption. The culture is pragmatic, centred on the immediate existence of the self, and not utopic. There is a strong love of order; chaos is abhorred. Consumerist individualism, the so-called autonomy of the self, can only sustain itself in a highly ordered society wherein the individual exists with a minimum of direct support and cooperation. The worst irony, of the individualist society of the self, is that it lends itself to epidemics of mimicking; there is so much surface and so little depth that everyone ends up imitating the same ideas, actions, poses.

In his third book, *The Twilight of Duty* (1992), Lipovetsky explores ethics in the new individualized era. A shift in consciousness has occurred. During high modernism, what Lipovetsky calls a *first degree of perception* prevailed. Everyone saw, and acknowledged, more or less, the same things. There was *one* shared reality, which remained under the control of the various political, cultural and economic elites or centres. But as modernism advanced, and variation in individual perception was more and more emphasized, most persons evolved into the *second degree of perception.* The person became more aware of his/her story – of telling her/his version of what 'is'. Most texts remained outwardly directed – descriptions of a world supposedly 'out there' – but the speaker has become increasingly aware of his/her role as the storyteller. Perceptionalism, the story is a text *chosen* by the speaker, has been gaining ground. Currently we are confronted by a *third degree of perception.* The speaker makes use of his/her text, almost as a form of abstract art, to communicate states of emotion and tones of feeling. The effort to render 'a single, shared reality' in text is falling by the wayside. Communication is increasingly becoming pure individual sentiment – a mirror of personal disposition and spirit. Expression advertises the self; expresses individual pleasure(s); decries subjugation; claims new areas for emotional development.

The Twilight of Duty explores the ethical universe of the postmodern world of a third degree of perception. The analysis is based on the principles of periodization, which Lipovetsky has developed in his oeuvre. The secularized liberal universe has replaced the Christian metaphysical universe, though fundamentally it has retained the same authoritarian mindset. Thus 'the collective or social good', as well as 'the individual's duties to state family and work', were prioritized far above 'individual pleasure', 'satisfaction' or 'experience'. The Christian God may have been replaced by secular 'musts' but these 'musts' were just as absolute and demanding as God had ever been. Eventually, the modernist movement, and its consumer economy, chiselled away at the disciplinary, anti-individual culture. Instead of the *moral interdict* of bourgeois society (keep the untrustworthy self under control), and the *work interdict* of Taylorism (do not take initiative; follow instructions), a culture championing desire, innovation and flexibility developed. The idea emerged that the individual *will* could successfully lead to social order; the self could be an appropriate source of order.

Bauman, in the modernist tradition, saw the self unto itself as ethically inadequate and in need (via transcendence of another) of achieving an ethical identity; whereas Lipovetsky sees, as postmodernist, the contemporary self as a (potentially) self-sufficient source of ethical action (compare this with Foucault's notions of caring for self in Brewis, Chapter 4 in this volume). For Lipovetsky, just as the *principle of chaos* reveals how myriads of seemingly atomized elements really possess order, individualist postmodern society possesses an ethical logic and identity. Not imposed ethical commandments, nor ethical text dished out as so much corporate cosmetics, but the actual structure of postmodern psychologized interaction provides the postmodern bedrock of ethical behaviour. Though modernism rejected religion as the key institution which determines ethics and replaced it with a human rational ground it still tried to regulate ethics within an absolutist frame of reference. Thus the 'rights of man', 'the social contract' or 'the social sciences' remained last judges of right and wrong. Modernism never really trusted the individual self to be the final arbiter of ethical action. Supposedly, the self would reveal itself egoistic, irresponsible and prone to excess. Only existence for the other (i.e. something outside the self) could, supposedly, be ethical. Ethics was equated with the sacrifice of the self to the collective good. Lipovetsky's argument is that pursuit of self, the love of self and not abnegation of self, is an adequate postmodern route to ethical action. The new Jerusalem of mass consumption, the body, self and comfort is anything but lax. It imposes its own ethics. Its ambition is not to control everything but to make the *culture of happiness* workable. Thus in many situations, there is now more law and justice and not less. Psychological violence (racism, discrimination, stalking), sexual violence (rape in marriage, sexual harassment), workplace violence (requiring people to work dangerously, browbeating, disregard for individual integrity) have all been legislated against. People are more atomized and more materialist, and the relationship to 'things' (brand names, luxury, and tangible goods) has strengthened and the relationship to 'others' (social causes, political idealism, artistic/intellectual movements) has weakened. Information is valued for its commercial use-value; complex theory and 'deeper' analysis are devalued. Attention is for concrete physical existence – the immediate and phenomenally actual.

The preconditions of consumerist well-being are demanding; the quality of production (work and consumption) has to be high for pleasure to be achieved. The postmodern person consumes his/her own life with the same critical gaze as the goods s/he selects. The postmodernism society is characterized by self-organized rational hedonism. The green movement is a typical product of the period: it critically examines the prerequisites for the most pleasurable experiencing of the physical and economic environment (see Fineman, Chapter 11 in this volume). This is an exacting form of consumerism. Individuals apply the same attitude to themselves. The physical, aesthetic, intellectual demands that individuals put on themselves, are enormous. Responsibility is to oneself and the self demands enthusiasm, commitment and achievement. The culture of 'zero faults', 'total quality' and 'bench marking' is demanding. The maximum valorization of the self pushes the individual to top accomplishments. Hedonistic autonomy sets far higher standards of excellence than did bureaucratic control. But within postmodern hedonism, suffering is intolerable. The self is supposed to take care of itself by intelligently managing its actions. Pain, disaster and calamity have no place. Bad fate is reacted to sentimentally – as if it does not really belong to the order of things.

Lipovetsky examines, in particular, two traditional conservative values: family and work. Under modernism both were 'duties'. The person was expected to sacrifice him/herself to raise a family and to be productive (i.e. work). Paradoxically, family and work have been readopted as postmodern values. Individualized society has left the family as virtually the only place where joy, pleasure and success can be shared. Having a family is seen not as an obligation but as fulfilment; it has become an affirmation of individuality. Likewise, work is no longer thought of as a mindless Taylorist prison, but as a chance for achievement and fulfilment. Via corporate culture, the self can (supposedly) find identity, involvement and purpose (see Legge, Chapter 7 in this volume). Work is no longer where one is exploited, but where one achieves social integration and develops one's identity. The postmodern self is potentially much more radically committed to work than was the modernist one. However, only if genuine identity and real self-development are possible will the 'advantages' of the postmodern identity be tapped.

In an economic climate which champions winning just to win, power for power's sake and the cult of success, the chance is great that companies will hypocritically adopt the rhetoric of engagement, in the hope that they can (once again) manipulate their employees to achieve a bit more profit (see Willmott, Chapter 5 in this volume). Ethicism, the false aping of ethical rhetoric, is a real danger. Reified ethics – all the ideas encoded, no actions undertaken – is a major danger. Experts will be hired to write ethical codes for major organizations; this is not a bottom-up liberating of the self in the work situation, but a perverse exercise in public relations which is designed to fool one's personnel and the public. Real self-engagement makes excellence, flexibility and innovation possible. But 'empowerment' is the prerequisite to self-commitment. How many top managers really want the best possible results from their personnel if they have to abandon their power positions to get it? How many companies prefer excellence to hierarchy, flexibility to managerial privilege, innovation to status and authority? Corporate results with committed personnel are superior to the results of disinterested alienated work, delivered via modernist systems of control. But the politics of the self may be too democratic for the corporate powers that be! Another, probably even more difficult problem is that the development of identity and excellence in the workplace may only be an option in the capitalist post-industrial society, for the well-educated and creative 'happy few'.

The seventh and concluding chapter of *The Twilight of Duty* is on 'The Marriage of Ethics and Business' (Lipovetsky, 1992). Obviously, it is difficult to incorporate the extremes of the *third level of discourse* (grounded in the third degree of perception) into any organization. Traditional (bureaucratic) organization will break down if the personnel just keep creating the text ('story', 'situation') of their choice. The self may become so all-encompassing that it loses contact with the 'world', and hence collapses into meaningless babble or falls into depression. But it is much more likely that the postmodern self will seek out opportunities for identity formation as a negotiated process of interaction. Self will seek responsibility and opportunities for self-realization. But most organizations are of the *second type* and are rule-driven as well as inclined to regulate themselves. Contrastingly, *organizations of the third type* try to be pleasurable, i.e. to be places of learning, challenge, creativity and achievement. Employers are mostly committed to organizations of the second type, but have to adapt to management of the third type to succeed. In the workplace, the employers need commitment and creativity. To succeed, the employees' self will have to be recognized and engaged. But to reach the employees' self, the employers will have to include the personnel in an ongoing process of negotiating their statute of employment – negotiating what the personnel do, how, why and with what incentives.

But it is much easier for employers to initiate ethical audits and codes of good conduct than to really address the self in the workplace. Pretended dialogue may seem a lot safer than real dialogue. Employers may want to set down the law. Companies may claim that 'our people are our most important resource', but that does not necessarily mean that those companies want to reckon with their employees' needs or desires. Corporate policy may state that 'when corporate values are not congruent with employee values, high motivation is impossible', but that does not ensure that top management is interested in the values of its personnel. Ethics can be a tool of management – a rhetoric to be used to get employees to do exactly what management wants them to do. Ethics is, then, a simulacrum of dialogue, and a counterfeit of interaction. Ethics as a management trick tries to convince the workforce that it is ethically imperative to do what management wants done. If management's goals are not met for whatever reason(s), the workforce is supposed to feel guilty. This is a much more powerful way of getting things done than merely ordering people about. Instead of using middle management to control worker action, workers control themselves. Obviously, the trick is in convincing the workforce to internalize the management directives. It is attractive for management to shift responsibility from itself to its employees. If things go wrong, it is no longer perceived to be a result of mismanagement but is seen as a result of insufficient ethical congruity. It will be cheaper to get employees to buy into what they are supposed to do and thereby to reduce the costs of (middle) management. Real postmodern management, which is grounded in *self*-development in a flexible proactive organization, requires that management spend time (resources) attending to employee needs and points of view. Ethics, as a two-way interaction, supports and furthers real individuality.

Top-down ethical rhetoric, as part and parcel of 'corporate communication', enacts a mere simulacrum of the self. Ethics can be (mis-)used as an attempt to rearm managers who have lost power and prestige through business process re-engineering, downscaling, automatization or standardization of business. Managers can grasp ethics as a manipulative rhetoric to improve short term results. But they can also learn new negotiating skills, wherein they really take on the challenge of seeking moral congruence and self-development, within a more flexible and creative organization. The industrialization of the office, of course, has moved from the secretarial/administrative level, via middle management, towards more senior aspects of decision-making (expert systems, management information systems and decision support systems). Via new wave or other ethics texts, managers can try to (re-) assert their significance. However, real autoregulation creates an organization which is not 'in control' but is creatively under way. Most business ethics is mere simulacra – an effort to sell an image to increase profit without interfering with the decision-making practices or with the patterns of interaction. Many managers do not want to share authority. Ethics is then merely part and parcel of having an up-to-date 'look'. If one substitutes responsibility for obedience, one creates a work organization radically different from (post-) Taylorism. Shared ideas replace authority; humiliation (as a form of influence) is banned from the workplace. But hired manipulators – business ethics consultants who can create the image of participation while avoiding the substance – seem the order of the day. Real motivated involvement would generate flexibility, create a strong identification of a workforce with the organization, and marshal maximum involvement.

Would such a flat, open, networked organization compete successfully in the current economy of hyper-performativity, within the framework of capitalist relationships? For Lipovetsky the modernist rationale is already bankrupt. Rationalized, bureaucratic organizations, which are out to tell their members what they ought to do, just are not, in his opinion, very effective. Such organizations are unable to motivate the contemporary person, who is hedonistic, self-preoccupied, searching for identity, and profoundly consumerist. But Lipovetsky's trust in organization of the third level sounds optimistic. A revanchism of modernist power remains possible. Instead of championing flexibility and innovation, management can focus on cost cutting, control of the work situation, and heightened predictability. Via outsourcing and virtual organization, management can make personnel more economically dependent. Such a workforce either meets management's (its customer's) demands (quality and price) or it goes hungry. An ethics of shared values and a developing self are interesting enough for persons committed to live/work/create together; but when is this in our society really the case?

(In-)justice and (anti-)law

My reading of the title: 'Injustice and Law; Justice and Anti-law'. Derrida's text made it possible for me to pose the contradiction between law and justice. Ethical rules have been opposed to responding to another; morality has been opposed to (business) ethical codes. If we assume that justice is radically situational and cannot be captured in laws, then it is evidently radically linked to direct person-to-person reactions. But are these reactions to be understood via Bauman's transcendental *epoché* (i.e. a transcendent insight into humanness) or via Lipovetsky's phenomenal *epoché* (i.e. social empirical observation of contemporary culture)? The problem is still: *how can one know justice?*

Notes

1 *Epoché* is an ancient Greek term meaning 'suspension of beliefs', in modern philosophy (phenomenology) it is used to indicate a radical questioning of the beliefs upon which an idea (or point of view) is based. Different versions of *epoché* will be discussed in this chapter.

2 Heidegger's concept of *Dasein* stresses that humanity is always in the world; that human existence can only be perceived as involved, engaged, as a part of the world. We have no living (existential) access to anything 'purely human' detached from circumstance and transcending activity. No (transcendent, metaphysical) *being* is logically prior, or provides ethical certainty, to direct lived action (see Munro, Chapter 9 in this volume).

3 I accept that the postmodern society of radical time and space compression (Harvey, 1990) has deeply altered the management researcher's potential strategies of investigation (Baudrillard, 1983; Letiche, 1996), yet I suggest that many differing approaches to the arisen crisis in knowing remain possible (Letiche, 1995).

4 I have not chosen, like others in this volume, to take Bauman's prior work, such as *Modernity and the Holocaust*, into account; because, though it is certainly focused on social ethics, it does not refer to the postmodern, post-Fordist, post-industrial society with which I am concerned. The comparisons I wish to make with Derrida and Lipovetsky have directed me to the latter, more comparable, work of Bauman.

5 Goffman's sociology of the *presentation of the self* was criticized because it seemed to imply a dramaturgy of social interaction (an existence of *roles* and *role-playing*) without social economic structures of causality. The social psychology of postmodern *hyper-reality*, existence enclosed in the now, seems to remarkably resemble Goffman's universe.

6 Levinas's existential philosophy of social responsibility is a key source to much contemporary ethical thought. Derrida's deconstruction, and Bauman's/Lipovetsky's applied thought, all refer at moments to it. Because I am not committed to framing (business) ethics as he does (see below), I have chosen to let Levinas play a secondary role here, as a figure others comment on (but see Desmond, Chapter 8, and Willmott, Chapter 5 in this volume for some commentary on Levinas).

7 This is, of course, an intellectual move pioneered in contemporary thought by Heidegger (again, see Munro, Chapter 9 in this volume).

8 Thus, there's little or no link to Karl Weick's process-oriented, social psychology of organizing.

9 Ulrich Beck has developed this theme in a strongly empirical manner.

10 Lipovetsky wrote his essay *Narcisse ou la stratégie du vide* (reprinted in *L'ère du vide*) in part in response to Christopher Lasch's *The Culture of Narcissism* (1979) even before Lasch's book was translated (in 1980) into French.

References

Baudrillard, Jean (1983) *Les strategies fatales.* Paris: Grasset.

Bauman, Zygmunt (1992) *Mortality, Immortality and Other Life Strategies.* Stanford, CA: Stanford University Press.

Bauman, Zygmunt (1993) *Postmodern Ethics.* Oxford: Blackwell.

Bauman, Zygmunt (1995) *Life in Fragments.* Oxford: Blackwell.

Beck, Ulrich (1992) *Risk Society*. London: Sage.

Braam, Stella and Iding, Wim (1996) 'De Zorgzame Markt', De *Groene Amsterdamer*, 120 (51/52): 24–5.

Burgin, Victor (1996) *In/Different Spaces.* Berkeley, CA: University of California Press.

Derrida, Jacques (1992) 'Force of Law: The "Mystical Foundation of Authority"', in D. Cornell, M. Resenfeld and D.G. Carlson (eds), *Deconstruction and the Possibility of Justice.* New York: Routledge. pp. 3–67.

Harvey, David (1990) *The Condition of Postmodernity*. Oxford: Blackwell.

Lasch, Christopher (1979) *The Culture of Narcissism*. New York: Warner.

Letiche, Hugo (1995) 'Researching Organization by Implosion and Fatality', *Studies in Cultures, Organizations and Societies*, 1(1): 107–26.

Letiche, Hugo (1996) 'Postmodernism Goes Practical', in Steve Linstead, Robert Grafton Small and Paul Jeffcutt (eds), *Understanding Management.* London: Sage. pp. 193–211.

Lipovetsky, Gilles (1983) *L'ère du vide.* Paris: Gallimard.

Lipovetsky, Gilles (1987) *L'empire de l'ephemere.* Paris: Gallimard.

Lipovetsky, Gilles (1992) *Le crepuscule du devoir.* Paris: Gallimard.

Thévenin, Paul and Derrida, Jacques (1986) *Antonin Artaud – Dessins et portraits.* Paris: Gallimard.

Touraine, Alain (1992) *Critique de la modernité.* Paris: Fayard.

Part 2: PRACTICES

7 Is HRM Ethical? Can HRM be Ethical?

Karen Legge

The last two decades in UK society have been marked by the extent to which socio-politico-economic issues have been cast in moral terms. Proponents of the enterprise culture – a heady cocktail of such ingredients as the free market, private enterprise, rugged entrepreneurial individualism, consumer sovereignty – have tended to present it, not just in terms of a personal preference or as a legitimate option, but as a morally correct way to counter the 'evils' of the 'British disease'. In the eyes of the Conservative government and their supporters there was 'no other alternative', if a cure was to be effected, than a strong dose of monetarism and market competition, never mind if the side effects of high interest rates, a strong pound and resultant recession and unemployment threatened to kill the patient. Such medicine was seen as the *right* way to combat the evils of low productivity, high inflation and poor competitiveness stemming from a parasitical, overblown public sector and indulgent corporatism, where monopoly unions conspired with monopoly suppliers to produce poor quality, high priced goods and services for the force feeding of captive, downtrodden consumers at massive cost to the disgruntled taxpayer (Young, 1990: 353). That patron saint of the enterprise culture, Margaret Thatcher, a self-declared 'conviction' politician, prone to quoting both the tenets of Methodism and the nineteenth century reconstruction of the words of St Francis, saw the matter clearly:

> I am in politics because of the conflict between good and evil, and I believe that in the end good will triumph. (The *Daily Telegraph*, 18 September 1984)

Thus were the virtues of individualism and the Protestant work ethic united in the pursuit of the economics of sound housekeeping. After all if 'there was no such thing as society', but only individuals and families, this made sense. Self-reliant, hard working individuals would survive and, if through age or sickness they were unable to support themselves, their virtuously accumulated savings and their families could step in. With rising consumer expectations and demographic change it was wrong to prop up a welfare state that encouraged dependency and passivity: rather the public sector monies tied up in nationalized industries and direct tax revenues should be ploughed back to where they could do most good – in the hands of enterprising free individuals exercising free choices in free markets.

If the outcome in the late 1980s was a culture celebrating 'loadsa money', equally there were voices that spoke with increasing strength and conviction of the evils of a society with an increasing divide between the 'haves' and 'have nots', of a 'no-hope' generation of young people in the deprived inner cities, of crass materialism and of the need to recognize the collective obligations of society (Gilmour, 1993). Importantly, though, even the critics of the enterprise culture, by the 1990s, were couching their moral message in terms that appeared to have accepted at least the means, if not the ends, of the enterprise culture. In 'New Labour' in particular, the message of managerialism – the effective generation of resources – is as evident as in the messages of the Conservatives and of big business.

It is against this background that we can pose questions about the ethics of human resource management in the UK, and perhaps elsewhere. For, in many ways, human resource management itself encompasses values dominant both in the enterprise culture and in the 'one-nation', communitarian social vision that questions the former's Darwinian materialism. For as is now a commonplace, HRM is represented (and there is nothing outside the text) in contrasting ways. It has been depicted as embodying the values of the American Dream, of rugged individualism, hard work and achievement (Guest, 1990b) and likened to a journey to some promised land (Dunn, 1990). But it has also been depicted as a 'wolf in sheep's clothing' (Keenoy, 1990a) and as a case of 'the emperor's new clothes' (Armstrong, 1987). As Keenoy (1990b) has pointed out, the very words 'human resource management' contain a 'brilliant ambiguity': we can simultaneously refer to both human *resource management* and *human resource* management. In the first case we have what has been termed the 'hard' model of HRM, reflecting a 'utilitarian instrumentalism' (Storey, 1987; Hendry and Pettigrew, 1990). In essence this model of HRM, in emphasizing the importance of the close integration of human resource policies, systems and activities with business strategy, regards employees as a headcount resource to be managed in exactly the same rational, impersonal way as any other resource, i.e. to be exploited for maximal return. In contrast, *human resource* management asserts a 'soft', 'developmental humanism' model of HRM, seeing employees as valued assets, a source of competitive advantage through their commitment, adaptability and high quality (of skills, performance and so on). Rather than exploitation and cost minimization, the watchwords in such a model are investment and value added. But – to take a deconstructive reading of this text – this opposition does not imply either/or but *both. Human resource* management *à la* the 'soft' model is only viable if the organization is seen to be economically successful or 'hard', if it constructs an identity of effective human *resource management*. Hence in the downturn in air traffic consequent on the Gulf War and recession in the early 1990s, BA's 'text' of organizational life could contain a *resource management* discourse – the cost cutting programmes winningly entitled 'Sprint' and 'Gap Closure' – that enabled the *human resource* discourse of the 'Advice and Support Centre signal[ling] the extent of BA's concern for its people in tough times' (Höpfl et al., 1992: 29). This may be presented as the world of 'tough love'. And here we have a problem. The judgement one might make on the ethicality of HRM would depend on which model was being adhered to – quite apart from which ethical theory one applied. The question becomes more complex, though, if in a sense both models are being employed, and if at different time periods or with different groups of employees.

In this chapter I want to do three things in considering the ethics of HRM. First, I want briefly to outline some evidence of the 1980s and 1990s as to the extent to which these different models of HRM have been implemented. Secondly, I want to assess the ethicality of HRM practices from the standpoint of some well-known theories of business ethics. Thirdly, I want to query whether the management of people at work can ever be truly ethical in a capitalist system, where at the very least, in Marxist terms, HRM exists to assist in the realization of surplus value through obscuring the commodity status of labour or, in Weberian terms, to mediate the tensions between instrumental and substantive rationality.

The experience of HRM

So, what does the practice of HRM look like? It might be useful just to summarize some of the conclusions I drew in a recent book from analysing the published empirical data on HRM implementation in the late 1980s and early 1990s (Legge, 1995). I recognize that some of these conclusions may be a bit dated now and I will indicate where I think so. As a starting point, I took David Guest's (1987) well-known 'soft' model of HRM and looked for evidence of the extent to which HRM policies and practices achieved integration with business strategy and internal consistency, commitment, flexibility and quality. This is a bit old-fashioned. Today the done thing (Purcell, 1996a; Guest, 1996; Huselid, 1995; Wood, 1995; 1996) seems to be to consider HRM in terms of best practice 'high performance work practices' (Huselid, 1995) or 'high commitment management' (Wood, 1995; 1996; Wood and Albanese, 1995). Admittedly these reflect the values of Guest's (1987) normative model, and have been summarized by Purcell (1996a: 4) as comprising:

- careful recruitment and selection (with emphasis on traits and competency)
- extensive use of systems of communication
- teamworking with flexible job design
- emphasis on training and learning
- involvement in decision-making with responsibility
- performance appraisal with tight links to contingent pay.

Huselid found some evidence that such 'high performance work practices' are associated with positive outcomes, such as (low) employee turnover and (higher) productivity and short and long term measures of corporate financial performance. Similarly Guest and Hoque (1994) found that, on greenfield sites, using above the median level of HRM practices, when combined with a strategic HRM approach, appeared to result in superior HRM outcomes (commitment, employee quality, aspects of flexibility) if not superior productivity or product quality.

One may, of course, be sceptical about the direction of causality in such cross-sectional studies. One may question the universal appropriateness of such policies if cost effectiveness, as a route to market share and profitability, is the goal. One may even wonder if the outcomes are a one-off effect of a change process – a sort of Hawthorne effect. Certainly John Purcell (1996a) has these doubts. But, it is possible that if such policies are applied in the spirit of mutuality then this interpretation of the findings might be right.

My analysis of the research findings of the 1980s and early 1990s presents a more downbeat view. In brief, as far as the treatment of people at work was concerned, I found the following.

First, there have been some increases in numerical flexibility (that is, an organization's capacity to adjust labour inputs to fluctuations in demand and output requirements via the use of non-standard contracts). In the 1980s and early 1990s these largely reflected sectoral changes in the private sector and government policy in the public sector and, although significant, were not extensive. Further, at least in the private sector, use of part-timers, temporary labour from private agencies, freelancers, seasonal workers, appeared a continuation of established practice rather than any new consciously thought-out strategic initiative.

However, today evidence is emerging that organizations are now strategically rethinking their employment policies. In particular the search for competitive advantage has led to attempts not only to analyse what is the organization's core competency but to identify the key human resources that create this competency. This, in turn, refocuses attention on defining who are the core employees of the organization and who are peripheral to its achievement of its core competency. While the former are coopted, as permanent staff on highly rewarding contracts, the peripheral employees, engaged on non-core competency tasks, are increasingly becoming a contingent workforce on non-standard contracts (fixed-term, temporary, zero-hours, etc.). In particular, Purcell (1996b) has identified an increasing use of more radical forms of numerical flexibility, the development of a 'contingent' workforce – not only through outsourcing of peripheral activities (cleaning, catering, security, etc.) but also through what he terms 'insourcing', the use of manpower agencies, not just to supply temps, but to supply and manage wide sections of the workforce.

Secondly, there has also been some increase in functional flexibility (that is, an organization's capacity to deploy employees between activities and tasks to match changing workloads, production methods or technology).

However, these appear to have more to do with job enlargement, where management were seeking a reduction of porosity, an intensification of effort and a reassertion of managerial prerogative rather than any widespread multi-skilling. As for financial flexibility – performance related pay – there are queries as to its degree of implementation and effectiveness.

Thirdly, where a flexible response to product market competition is most readily and obviously seen is in widely reported cases of delayering and downsizing. This has resulted from the contraction of the manufacturing base in the early 1980s, from the impact of privatization and of 'market disciplines' and regulatory control, not to mention cash limits, on erstwhile public sector industries and services, and partly from IT, but also from the deregulation and merger-inspired rationalization of financial services in the 1990s. This has gone hand-in-hand with increased temporal flexibility (zero-hours), and a reported increase in managerial working hours for those lucky enough to hang on to employment (Vielba, 1995).

Fourthly, turning to team building and employee empowerment and involvement – yes, there is evidence that all three are formally taking place, especially the latter. What in practice these mean depends very much on the prevailing organizational culture and market environment (Marchington et al., 1994). Certainly the messianic accounts by managerialist writers and the positive experiences reported by employees (on TV), for example at Rover, may be juxtaposed against the more critical accounts of writers in the labour process tradition who, in place of the 'tripod of success' of 'flexibility, quality and teamwork', identify a 'tripod of subjugation' of 'management-by-stress', 'management-through-blame' and 'management-through-compliance' (cf. Wickens, 1987; 1995; Garrahan and Stewart, 1992; Delbridge and Turnbull, 1992). You pays your money and takes your pick.

Fifthly, there is evidence too of cultural management programmes – such as the oft-cited programmes at BA – designed to secure employee commitment to the values embodied in the company mission statement, notably to quality, whether in product or customer service. Whether such programmes secure attitudinal commitment or, in the context of continuingly high residual unemployment and job insecurity, generate what has been termed 'resigned behavioural compliance' (Ogbonna and Wilkinson, 1990), is a matter of debate. As Ron Todd said in 1983, 'we've got 3 million on the dole, and another 23 million scared to death.' Either way, it is extremely difficult to demonstrate a link between commitment or behavioural compliance and performance.

Finally, there is evidence of the internal contradictions of HRM: there are tensions (paradoxically) between commitment and flexibility, individualism and teamworking, personal empowerment and the pressures for standardization and control embodied in a range of HRM associated and interrelated initiatives such as TQM, JIT, customer sovereignty and corporate cultural management.

What we have here, I guess, are all the tensions expressed in the distinction already made between the 'soft' 'developmental humanism' and 'hard' 'utilitarian instrumentalism' models of HRM. Or, put somewhat differently, are we seeing, as Sisson (1994) suggests (Table 7.1), how the soft rhetoric of the 'HRM organization' may be used to meet the reality of the hard face of managerial prerogative in the service of capitalism and competitive advantage and in the iron grip of the market?

TABLE 7.1 *Sisson's model of rhetoric and reality in HRM*

Rhetoric	Reality
Customer first	Market forces supreme
Total quality management	Doing more with less
Lean production	Mean production
Flexibility	Management 'can do' what it wants
Core and periphery	Reducing the organization's commitments
Devolution/delayering	Reducing the number of middle managers
Downsizing/right-sizing	Redundancy
New working patterns	Part-time instead of full-time jobs
Empowerment	Making someone else take the risk and responsibility
Training and development	Manipulation
Employability	No employment security
Recognizing contribution of the individual	Undermining the trade union and collective bargaining
Teamworking	Reducing the individual's discretion

Taking it all together, what are the implications of these findings for the recipients of HRM? My best guess is that if you are a knowledge worker with highly demanded and scarce skills, life may be good – empowerment, high rewards and some element of job security (if at the cost of a workaholic lifestyle). For the bulk of the workforce, though, things are not so rosy. Not only are part-time and fixed-term contract jobs growing at the expense of full-time, permanent jobs, but all jobs are increasingly insecure. Further, there is indisputable evidence that labour intensification is increasing all round (see Legge, 1988; Metcalf, 1988; 1989; Nolan and Marginson, 1990; Guest, 1990a; Edwards and Whitston, 1991). So, can HRM be said to be ethical? Before I can begin to answer this question, it is necessary to consider the nature of business ethics.

The nature of business ethics

Business ethics is about reflection on the nature and place of morality in business (for some general discussions of business ethics, see Beauchamp and Bowie, 1988; Donaldson, 1989; Donaldson and Werhane, 1993; de George, 1990). As this implies a limitation to profit-seeking organizations, I prefer to think in terms of organizational ethics. Key concepts when we think in terms of organizational ethics might include right, obligation, justice, fairness, good, virtue, responsibility, trust and so on. Such concepts are implicit in any evaluation of our socio-economic order. Just as capitalism highlights such 'goods' as freedom, autonomy, efficiency and sees 'justice' in terms of equality of opportunity, so the Marxist critique would point to the injustice of exploitation, alienation and the protection of the interests of the few at the expense of social justice for the many (see Wray-Bliss and Parker, Chapter 3 in this volume). If capitalism rests on the premise that a transaction is fair if both parties to it engaged without coercion and with adequate and appropriate knowledge of relevant aspects of the transaction, Marxism would question this assumed lack of coercion and equality of knowledge in a social system of structural inequalities. All organizations and markets rest on an assumption of some level of trust, but we sometimes forget the extent to which our assumptions about the management of employment relationships have ethical foundations. The concepts that I have mentioned are embedded in four normative ethical theories in terms of which we can evaluate HRM policies and practices. These divide into basically deontological theories (that is, those that emphasize the rules and principles that should guide actions) and teleological theories (that is, those that evaluate all actions in terms of whether they achieve a desired end state or purpose). The deontological theories addressed here are those of Kant and Rawls, and the teleological theories those of utilitarianism and Aristotelian – or human nature – ethics.

Deontological theories maintain that the concept of duty is, in some respects, independent of the concept of good and that some actions are right or wrong for reasons other than their consequences. Kantian ethics fall into this category. Kant argues that what makes an action right or wrong is not the sum of its consequences but the fact that it conforms to moral law. Moral laws of duty demand that people act not only in accordance with duty but for the sake of duty. It is not good enough to perform a morally correct action, because this could stem from self-interested motives that have nothing to do with morality. Rather an action is moral if it conforms to moral law that is based not in intuition, conscience or utility, but in pure reason. We can determine moral law by analysing the nature of reason itself and what it means to be a rational being. Reason has three major characteristics: consistency (hence moral actions must not contradict one another); universality (because reason is the same for all, what is rational for me is rational for everyone else); and *a priori* derivation (it is not based on experience – hence the morality of an action does not depend on its consequences). A person acts morally if the sole motive for an action is the recognition of moral duty based on a valid rule. Kant develops this notion into a fundamental moral law that he characterizes as the 'categorical imperative' – 'categorical' because it is absolutely binding and 'imperative' because it gives instructions about how one must act. For an action to be moral it must (a) be amenable to being made consistently universal ('I ought never to act except in such a way that I can also will that my maxim should become a universal law'); (b) respect rational beings as ends in themselves, never solely as means to the ends of others; (c) stem from, and respect, the autonomy of rational beings. This fundamental moral principle states the form moral actions have and provides the criteria against which we can test whether an action or injunction containing substantive content ('pay people fairly', 'treat people equally'), a second-order principle, is moral.

Another form of deontological theorizing focuses less on the rules that might identify what is 'good' in society and organizations and more on what is right (i.e. the just distribution of the 'good'). Much of this theorizing centres around trying to establish universal principles of a just society on the basis of what might be called 'social contracts through experiments'. If we could imagine a situation of no laws, social conventions or political state, what principles might reasonable people agree on that might guarantee social order and stability while at the same time placing the fewest constraints on individual freedoms? Locke's ideas about 'natural rights' and Nozick's 'entitlement theory of justice' would both be examples of the enduring nature of this approach, stretching over 300 years.

However, the contractarian theories of justice highlighted here are those involving stakeholder/Rawlsian analysis, as these are becoming particularly popular in discussions of business ethics. (Tom Sorell in Chapter 2 discusses stakeholder theory in more detail than I have space for here.) Popular versions of stakeholder theory (e.g. Evan and Freeman, 1988) assert that organizations have stakeholders, that is, groups and individuals who potentially benefit from or are harmed by an organization's actions. Stakeholders of an organization might comprise, for example, not just shareholders (owners), but management, other employees, customers, suppliers and the local community. The stakes of each group are reciprocal, since each can affect the others in terms of harms and benefits as well as rights and duties. Acknowledging this principle of reciprocity, two principles have been derived:

- The organization should be managed for the benefit of its stakeholders: its customers, suppliers, owners, employees and local communities. The rights of these groups must be ensured and, further, the groups must participate, in some sense, in decisions that substantially affect their welfare.
- Management bears a fiduciary relationship to stakeholders and to the organization as an abstract entity. It must act in the interests of the stakeholders as their agent, and it must act in the interests of the organization to ensure the survival of the firm, safeguarding the long term stakes of each group.

'Participating in decisions that substantially affect their welfare' has resonances of Rawls's 'egalitarian theory of justice'. Rawls (1971) argues that we should look for a conception of justice that nullifies the accidents of natural endowment and the contingencies of social circumstances as counters in the quest for political and economic advantage. His approach is very much Kantian in that he attempts to derive principles of distributive justice that should be acceptable to all rational people and, hence, universal. In order to find such principles, Rawls suggests we perform a thought experiment. Suppose all people are behind a 'veil of ignorance', where we know we are rational beings and that we value our own good, but we do not know if we are male or female, rich or poor, talented or untalented, able-bodied or suffering disability, white or black – and so on. What principles would we call just or fair if we did not know what place we would have in society (read 'organization')? In such circumstances, Rawls argues, people would agree two principles of justice:

- Each person is to have an equal right to the most extensive basic liberty compatible with similar liberty for others.
- Social and economic inequalities are to be arranged so that they are both (a) reasonably expected to be to everyone's advantage and (b) attached to positions and offices open to all.

Turning to the teleological theories we find, in sharp contrast to a deontological position, utilitarianism. Utilitarianism, as I've said, adopts a teleological approach to ethics and claims that the morality of actions is to be judged by their consequences. An action is moral if, when compared with any alternative action, it produces, or tends to produce, the greatest amount of good (or the least possible balance of bad consequences) for the greatest number of people directly or indirectly affected by that action. The 'good' may be variously conceptualized as 'pleasure' (hedonistic utilitarianism), 'happiness' (eudaimonistic utilitarianism) or all 'intrinsically valuable' human goods (ideal utilitarianism). The maximization of the good calls for efficiency. It also allows that people might be treated as a means to an end, if the end is the maximization of the good (or minimization of the bad) for the greatest number.

Although, at first sight, utilitarianism appears a relatively straightforward theory, it contains a major paradox, that is implicit in Bauman's (1989) discussion of morality and the Holocaust. Bauman argues that the Holocaust challenges the Durkheimian view that morality can be explained in terms of the social institutions that give it a binding force. Instead, he suggests, we might base our morality on Levinas's (1982) view that 'being with others', the most essential aspect of human existence, means responsibility for those others, in that our subjectivities are interwoven. Conversely, if we divorce ourselves from others by replacing proximity with a physical, social or psychological distance, responsibility breaks down and fellow human subjects may be transformed into objects different from ourselves for whom we feel no responsibility. Hence the Jews, isolated from their German neighbours, first by acts of definition, then by dismissals of employees and expropriation of business firms, then by concentration, then by exploitation of labour and starvation measures, physically, socially and psychologically could be translated into a different category than the human 'other' and 'evicted from the realm of moral responsibility' (Bauman, 1989: 191). Those institutions of modernity – an instrumental technical rationality embodied in bureaucracy – enable physical, social and psychological distance. In other words, I do not have to experience the consequences of my action if a minute division of labour and the length of the chain of acts mediate between the initiation of a policy and its ultimate tangible effects. I am only part of the chain in which my moral responsibility is to apply my technical expertise in the way that my superordinates, legitimized by their superior technical expertise, direct me. In other words, in a bureaucracy,

> actors serve as mere agents of knowledge . . . their personal responsibility rests entirely in representing knowledge properly, that is in doing things according to 'the state of the art', to the best of what extant knowledge can offer. For those who do not possess the know-how, responsible action means following the advice of experts. In the process personal responsibility dissolves in the abstract authority of technical know-how. (1989: 196)

Loyalty to the organization, expressed in loyalty to a hierarchical authority resting on expertise, becomes the guiding ethics of organization.

This is where utilitarianism presents us with a paradox. Its teleological nature points us towards examining the consequences of any action and, in theory at least, this should alert us to our responsibility for the other. But utilitarianism also embodies an instrumental rationality in its call for efficiency, the very form of rationality that facilitates the removal of people from the realm of moral responsibility. The difficulties this poses are considered later in this chapter and in Steve Fineman's discussion of the invisibility of ecological ethics issues outside the boundary of managers' organizationally defined moral parameters (Chapter 11 in this volume).

Finally, we have Aristotelian ethics, which are teleological in the sense that they consider that ethics should be based on the achievement of a desirable end state, in this case the achievement of human beings' inherent potentialities. Human beings have the purpose to actualize their mental, moral and social potential. Humans are not individualistic but must be understood as part of a broader social community, in which fulfilling one's potential involves developing wisdom, generosity and self-restraint, all of which help to make one a good member of the community.

Now obviously there are some difficulties with all these theories. It is often said that deontologists covertly appeal to utilitarian consequences in order to demonstrate the rightness of actions, particularly when there is a clash of moral rules. Perhaps more importantly, as discussed by Sorell in this book (Chapter 2), Kantian ethics suffer from the 'alienation problem' – that by the very stern and dogmatic standards they impose, they can be dismissed out of hand by practitioners as being 'too far removed from business to be any good' (see also Stark's 1993 critique; and Parker, Chapter 14 in this volume). Stakeholder analysis has the problem of short versus long term justice and the dangers of pseudo-participation. Rawls's second principle can be attacked as being too strong (as long as equal opportunities exist, why should rewards have to take account of producing benefit for the least advantaged groups in society?) or too weak (in that it would allow the very, very rich to get very much richer as long as the very, very poor got only a little less poor). Apart from the paradox I've already raised, utilitarianism has to cope with the problem of lack of knowledge of all consequences, of weighing together different kinds of good and evil and of the issue of unjust consequences. Aristotelian ethics face the criticism that it is difficult to demonstrate the assumption that human beings do have specific inherent potentialities and that these are the same for all human beings. Further, some might question the assumption that humans are basically good.

But leaving these on one side, we may take the central tenets of each theory and evaluate HRM policies and practices in their light. For the purposes of this discussion, I see the central tenets, very much simplified, as follows:

Kantian ethics Treat people with respect and as ends in their own right, not solely as means to others' ends. Any moral rule (such as 'A fair day's work for a fair day's pay') must be capable of being consistently universalized, must respect the dignity of persons, and must be acceptable to rational beings. Any action performed out of self-interest is not moral.

Stakeholder/Rawlsian ethics The good must be distributed with mutual consultation and so that no organizational stakeholders are complete losers while others are clear winners. Management must place a priority on the long term interests of stakeholders and the survival of the organization.

Utilitarianism The greatest good to the greatest number allows people to be treated as means to ends, if it is to the advantage of the majority. Actions should be judged in terms of their consequences.

Aristotelian ethics Create an organization in which each individual can achieve some form of self-actualization that contributes to social harmony.

The ethics of HRM policy and practice

How ethical is HRM? As I've suggested, this very much depends on the theory of ethics you adopt. The Kantian deontological position at first sight resonates with the values embedded in 'soft' model HRM. For a start, it is consistent with HRM's emphasis on individualism and responsible autonomy. Take Walton's (1985) classic statement of mutuality in HRM:

> The new HRM model is composed of policies that promote mutuality – mutual goals, mutual influence, mutual respect, mutual rewards, mutual responsibility.

This also asserts respect for human beings and is consistent with the idea of responsible autonomy for rational beings. In theory it could be universalized. However, there is a potential problem. Walton (1985) goes on to say

> The theory is that policies of mutuality will elicit commitment, which in turn will yield both better economic performance and greater human development.

Even in this most 'utopian' model (Purcell, 1996a: 130), treating people with respect is justified in terms of 'better economic performance' and hence, in part, people are being used as means to an end, violating a basic principle of Kantian ethics. However, it might be argued that all is not lost. According to some commentators (Beauchamp and Bowie, 1988: 38), Kant does not prohibit the use of persons categorically and without qualification. He argues only that we must not treat another person exclusively as a means to our own ends. Or, as MacIntyre (1981) puts it, to treat someone else as an end is to offer them a rational argument for acting in a particular way and, assuming their rationality, to leave it to them to evaluate the argument and to decide on a course of action. To treat someone as a means, by contrast, is to seek to make that person do something to further one's own purposes by exerting manipulative influence. Hence, what must be avoided is to disregard someone's personhood by exploiting or otherwise using them without regard to their own interests, needs and conscientious concerns. If 'soft' model HRM genuinely promotes 'greater human development' for *all* employees, it could be argued that, if so implemented, it would pass muster in terms of the deontologists.

The problem is, how often does this occur? If we follow the core–periphery ideas about organizational design and the employment contract, for example, can we be sure that employees on non-standard contracts are being treated with equal regard as those in the core? Possibly, when terms and conditions are equalized pro rata and the non-standard contract is freely chosen (as in Hunter et al.'s 1993 'supply side' factors, referring to people who actually seek part-time in preference to full-time work). However, much anecdotal evidence would suggest this is not the case. Some time ago, when I was considering this issue, there was a report in The *Independent* (5 March 1996: 6), 'School-Leavers' Pay Down 20%'. Reporting a study by the Low Pay Unit on data from the careers service and Job Centres in Greater Manchester, it was claimed that nearly half the sixteen-year-olds who leave school are paid less than £1.50 per hour and that their average wage has dropped in real terms by one-fifth in five years. However, the anecdote that caught my eye was the story of a sixteen-year-old who was paid £30 for a forty-hour week in a garage. When he inquired about compensation for losing the top of a finger at work, apparently he was told that he was a 'subcontractor'. So, this may be one of David Guest's (1995: 125) 'black hole' firms, rather than an adherent to 'soft' model HRM, but note the HRM-type language of the flexible firm. The author of the report, Gabrielle Cox, is reported as saying: 'It is bad enough for adult workers to face exploitation, but a society which allows its young people to be treated in this way must question its sense of values.'

But, another difficulty remains. For an action to be moral it must be consistently universalized. But what happens if there is a clash between the actions that two second-order moral rules command? What if 'I must respect the interests of my employees' clashes with 'I must respect the interests of my shareholders'? Either we must construct a maxim of our action in such a way that allows for the exception needed in the resolution of conflicting interests, or we must decide which course of action takes priority in terms of *prima facie* obligations. The problem with the latter, as hinted earlier, is that in prioritizing *prima facie* obligations we tend to resort to evaluating consequences (if in terms of respect for people) and hence are incorporating utilitarian reasoning.

The deontologist's notion that, for a rule (and consequent action) to be moral, it must be capable of being consistently universalized, may be acceptable if a 'best practice' (Purcell, 1996a) model of HRM is adopted, such as 'high performance work practices' or 'high commitment management'. Indeed Wood explicitly states: 'The implication of this research is that high commitment management is universally applicable' (1995: 57). However, if integration with business strategy points to a contingent rather than absolutist approach (Legge, 1987; Purcell, 1996a) the universalization of any moral rule (respect for the employee, from which might derive injunctions about employee development and training, job security, fair rewards and so on) becomes suspect both in theory and in practice. The contradictions embedded in HRM are illustrative of the Kantian dilemma that second-order moral rules can clash and that resolution can often only be achieved by a back-door admission of utilitarianism.

So, in terms of Kantian deontological ethics there is question mark over HRM. It works well if respect for the individual is universally and consistently applied as a moral good irrespective of consequences; not so, if otherwise. By these injunctions empowerment, for example, must genuinely be about increasing employees' autonomy, choices and development as a good in itself, not, as Sisson (1994: 15) has it, 'making someone else take the risk and responsibility', or, as Kaler (1996) puts it, 'what is happening is that management is being relieved of some of its "responsibilities of command" by employees converting them into "responsibilities of subordination".' Certainly the so-called 'empowerment paradox' (Gandz and Bird, 1996), whereby empowerment is used to disempower people through their cooptation into a group that represses dissent, would be highly unethical from the Kantian standpoint. While 'soft' model HRM, on the most generous interpretation, may just qualify as ethical from the deontologist standpoint, 'hard' model HRM, which treats the human resource as something to be used like any other factor in production (or, in Marxist terms, to be 'exploited'), is definitely immoral.

Happily, utilitarianism sends a far more reassuring message. Irrespective of what downsizing and labour intensification imply for the respect for individuals as ends in themselves, utilitarianism is the route to justifying such activities. It is perfectly ethical to use people as means to an end, if this is for the greatest good of the majority. Leaving aside the practical difficulty of quantifying different forms of goodness (and evil), here is the moral justification for choosing whatever strategies would appear to deliver competitive advantage. The argument would be that competitive advantage ensures organizational survival, and organizational survival protects employees' jobs, quite apart from maintaining employment in suppliers, satisfying consumer needs and so on. Hence, using people to achieve competitive advantage is quite alright as long as it does deliver positive consequences to the majority of stakeholders. So 'tough love' in all its forms is morally justifiable: employees may be compelled to work harder and more flexibly for 'their own good' and they may be made redundant for the greater good. Injustices, in terms of *prima facie* obligations (for example, to 'do as you would be done by'), are justified if the consequences of such actions are to the benefit of the majority. And it could well be argued that such a logic has prevailed in the years of the enterprise culture and the advent of HRM in all its forms in the UK. The standard of living of the majority in employment in the UK has increased markedly over the last twenty years. Even in the depths of recession in manufacturing industry in the early 1980s, with high levels of inflation and inexorably rising unemployment, real earnings for the majority in work rose steadily. With falling unemployment in the mid to late 1980s, combined with rising house prices but otherwise fairly low inflation, the experience of the majority *was* of 'feeling good' with 'loadsa money' – the upside, some might say, of the enterprise culture (or downside, depending on your ethical position). That this diminished in the 1990s was because not only did the real standard of living of those in employment remain static or marginally decline (pay increases below the rate of inflation, negative equity), but employees who had been and always saw themselves as part of the benefiting majority (white collar and managerial employees in large bureaucracies) now became victims of downsizing, delayering, labour intensification and other manifestations of 'tough love'. But such actions, as far as utilitarianism is concerned, are perfectly ethical if the balance of good consequences outweighs the negative. The problems technically of making such an assessment, as already suggested, are enormous. But, very loosely speaking, if as a result of such actions the majority remain in employment; if that employment is more secure and capable of generating enhanced benefit to its recipients than if the action had not been taken; if only a minority suffer; and if their suffering does not outweigh the benefits to the majority; then the action is ethical.

But what of this minority? If a Kantian deontologist would not accept their fate, those adopting a contractarian deontological position and engaging in stakeholder/Rawlsian analysis would also raise critical questions. Stakeholder analysis, asserting the Kantian principle that stakeholders should be treated with respect and not just as means to an end, would be concerned that some employees might lose out in order that the interests of other stakeholders are not ignored. Thus, if you accept Garrahan and Stewart's (1992) and Delbridge and Turnbull's (1992) critical accounts of JIT and TQM, employees are called upon to experience a measure of labour intensification in the interests of customers (enhanced quality and customer responsiveness) and shareholders (greater competitive advantage leading ultimately to capital growth and/or profit). However, by this logic, shareholders may be required to forgo the maximum amount of dividend payment, in the interests of investment in job-creating new plant and in long term development activities such as training. In practice, though, management are provided with a loophole, through their obligation to act 'to ensure the survival of the organization, safeguarding the long term stakes of each group'. Almost any action (redundancy, wage-cutting, freezing of recruitment and training expenditure, seeking cheaper suppliers, cutting dividends) could be justified in terms of the long term survival of the organization, irrespective of the damage to the present incumbents of the stakeholder positions. All that is required for the action to be moral is that the groups involved must participate in decisions that affect their welfare. And here we are back to the Marxist criticism of capitalist 'free' transactions, that structural inequalities do not allow an equal participation in such decision-making. How meaningful is employee consent to decisions that adversely affect them, if they perceive little choice ('3 million unemployed, 23 million scared to death', to echo Ron Todd again) or if, via HRM-type cultural management, their awareness of their real interests is obscured (cf. Lukes, 1974)? Further, stakeholder analysis, in its very commitment to safeguarding 'the long term stakes of each group', affords little protection to individual members of each group in the face of present (possibly adverse) action in the interests of organizational survival. I, as a shareholder, might have to forgo dividends in order that the organization can invest for future survival and profitability, for the good of future shareholders. Hence shareholders as a *group* are not damaged, even if I as an individual shareholder (who might walk under a bus tomorrow) have lost out.

Rawls's ethical stance might be seen as pointing to the golden mean of 'do as you would be done by': certainly such a maxim would seem consistent with the implications of the 'veil of ignorance' and the idea that inequalities should only be tolerated if reasonably expected to be to everyone's (including the least advantaged's) benefit. Is the core–periphery distinction, or performance related pay, or any other form of differentiation, to which differential benefits are attached, clearly to everyone's advantage? Certainly a case can be made that all organization rests on differentiation and if Marx argued 'from each according to his ability, to each according to his need', the Taylor-inspired Lenin proposed 'from each according to his ability, to each according to his work'. Concepts of fairness may accord too with differential benefits for differentiated work. The importance of fairness in relation to satisfaction and motivation and, hence, contribution may be argued. The problem is the quantitative issue. How much extra should be given to scarce skills, high levels of contribution, even if it is recognized that such differentiation benefits all? Certainly, in the UK, Cedric Brown's vast salary increase at British Gas, at a time when showroom staff were confronting at best real pay cuts and at worse redundancy, could hardly be said to be ethical in terms of Rawlsian principles (particularly given the declining levels of performance of British Gas *vis-à-vis* its range of stakeholders, on virtually every performance measure you would care to take). Is it ethical to justify high levels of pay and job security for core staff on the grounds that they are crucial to the achievement of competitive advantage and organizational survival, when paying very low wages to staff in the periphery, by arguing that the core staff in the long term are guaranteeing the jobs of the staff in the periphery and someone must subsidize their wages, in the long term interests of all?

Finally, there is Aristotelian ethics, which argues that what is ethical is that which enables the full development of human beings' inherent potentialities. This seems to resonate with many of the human relations inspired initiatives of the 1960s and 1970s – let alone HRM – whether socio-technical systems analysis, OD, QWL, you name it. Lately ideas about the 'learning organization' seem consistent with this ethical standpoint. Surely then at least the aspirations of 'soft' 'mutuality' models of HRM would appear ethical from this standpoint? In theory, perhaps, 'yes', but let's look at the problems.

If I am working in a low-skill occupation in the service sector, say, on a non-standard zero-hours contract, how much of my potentiality as a person is being developed (let alone how many of my supposedly Maslowian hierarchy of needs are being satisfied)? If management convinces me that I am developing social skills and gaining satisfaction through my standard formulaic interactions with the customer (establishing social harmony with my fellow person through defusing aggro in the checkout queue, providing a 'service'), to what extent am I really developing my inherent potentialities to achieve my true fulfilment as a person? Or to what extent is management, through intensive 'cultural management', manipulating meaning for me, so that I act as a means to achieve management's purpose? Suppose, in contrast, I am a professional person with highly valued core competency skills in an organization that encourages me to develop them to the full, if in their own interests rather than in mine. Can I achieve the fullest development of such potentialities without using others or, in the context of scarce resources, colliding with similar professionals bent on a similar pursuit? But, even if the tensions between competition and cooperation, individualism and teamwork can be mediated, from MacIntyre's (1981) standpoint, another problem remains.

In today's organizations, even if one has a highly challenging and potentially developmental job, and is part of the organization's core competency staff, the common complaint is of heightened pressure through increasingly demanding and shifting targets in the context of diminishing resources, and this results in labour intensification. To survive, many develop workaholic lifestyles before collapsing into 'burnout'. This, in itself, reflects three interrelated processes that inhibit the development of our full potentiality as people. First, in organizations, we tend to engage with each other not as a whole person, but in terms of our organizational role and, in highly differentiated organizations, this can present only a tiny portion of our full selves. Secondly, the exigencies of these roles may require us to engage in inauthentic behaviour, both manipulating others and allowing others to manipulate us (Jackall, 1988). As MacIntyre (1981: 107) states – and he is not alone – 'the most effective manager is the best actor'. Thirdly, a workaholic lifestyle may prevent the development of ourselves in family and community roles that could allow a fuller expression of ourselves as a person. Hence the present maxim 'No one on their deathbed has said "I wish I spent more time at the office"; many have said "I wish I'd spent more time with my family".' MacIntyre argues that, as a result, in modern organizations and societies, we stand no chance of enacting the Aristotelian ideal, as role fragmentation, inauthenticity and an unbalanced development of potentiality deprive us of the opportunity of developing a substantial integrated narrative of our lives and, hence, of rendering our lives meaningful to ourselves and to the community as a whole.

Can HRM be ethical?

I take this hypothetical question to have two meanings. First, given our present economic order, is it likely that an ethical form of HRM will be enacted? And 'ethical' in what sense? Secondly, what might an ethical form of HRM look like in the real, rather than the utopian, world?

In answering the first question, I start from the position, mentioned in the introduction, that several commentators beside myself (e.g. Keenoy and Anthony, 1992) have characterized HRM as the rhetoric of the new right, of the enterprise culture. This is not surprising given its trumpeting of the virtues of individualism, its somewhat anti-collectivist stance, and its identification as an instrument to achieve competitive advantage in an increasingly deregulated, global and consumer-oriented economy. So it is not unreasonable to see HRM as essentially wedded to the values of capitalism. (It must be remembered that the famous 'caring' fathers of personnel management, the Cadburys, the Rowntrees and Lever Brothers, had been quick to see – and I quote Cadbury – 'that business efficiency and the welfare of employees are but different sides of the same problem'.) If capitalism is, or has the potential to be, viewed as ethical, then HRM similarly has a good chance. If not, it is difficult to imagine how an ethical system of managing people at work can emerge from an essentially unethical economic order.

Now it is not hard to make a case, in theory, for the ethicality of capitalism. If we go back to Adam Smith's *Wealth of Nations* we can see that his concerns were primarily ethical and the economic system he devised was the means to achieve a more moral and just social order (Bassiry and Jones, 1993). Briefly, the *Wealth of Nations* sought to critique the evils of mercantilism, an economic system geared to maximizing the power of the nation-state relative to other nation-states through the pursuit of self-sufficiency (i.e. autarky). In its quest for self-sufficiency, the mercantilist political economy required a high degree of administrative centralization, and colonial possessions to provide raw materials as well as markets for finished goods. It was, therefore, consistent with non-democratic political institutions and non-competitive (i.e. monopolistic) economic structures. Mercantilism benefited producers and vested interests at the expense of consumers who were forced to pay inflated prices for domestically produced goods which were shielded from foreign competition by protectionist mechanisms.

Smith's model of 'pure' capitalism, of *laissez-faire* and free market competition, was developed as a more moral alternative to mercantilism. Smith proposed a production system organized in the consumer's interests (expressed as demand) which would be compatible with a democratic political system oriented to maximizing the welfare of the citizen as a political consumer. Bassiry and Jones summarized this well:

> Smith's paradigm shifted the institutional emphasis from centralized to decentralized structures, from authoritarianism to representative democracy, from monopoly to competitive markets, from autarky to international interdependence through a spatially expanding division of labor, and from product appropriation of the societal surplus to consumer sovereignty. (1993: 622–3)

And here we have virtues that would be identified as such from either a Kantian or a utilitarian position. From a Kantian position, capitalism appears ethical as it assumes each person is an autonomous, rational individual, who therefore should be free to make his or her own choices, providing they are compatible with like freedom for all. Further, from a utilitarian point of view, capitalism is moral (according to Smith at least) in that it promotes efficiency and social good. Each person, in pursuing his/her own good, indirectly and unknowingly also promotes the public interest. With this happy combination of individual freedom and productive efficiency, it is hardly surprising then that the end of the Cold War might be interpreted as the triumph of the good guys, representing democratic capitalism over the baddies promoting totalitarian socialism. Indeed, the 'end of history' (Fukuyama, 1991)? If this position is accepted, capitalism is ethical and provides an ethical underpinning for its servant, HRM.

But there's another view, summarized in my youth by the motto from a politically correct cracker: 'Show me a caring capitalist and I'll show you a vegetarian shark.' Now, it is unnecessary to resurrect the old Marxist critiques of the evils of capitalism – exploitation of workers, ripping off their surplus value, the reserve army of labour, alienation, gross inequalities and so on (see Wray-Bliss and Parker, Chapter 3 in this volume). Liberals have made a fair attempt to answer these objections in ways we all know well. Nor do I want to consider the ecological downsides of capitalism (which are well covered by Steve Fineman in Chapter 11), because many of these problems are the fruit of industrialism and bureaucratic rationality, rather than of capitalism *per se*. The point is, though, that Smith himself saw potential problems with capitalism, many of them stemming from the massive concentration of economic resources into the hands of a small minority of firms – these days, global players. Pure capitalism argues that individual free choice (about what to buy, what business to engage in, how much to offer for a commodity or service, at what price to sell your labour) rests on fair transactions. And, as stated earlier, a transaction is fair only if both parties engage in it freely (without coercion) and if both parties have adequate and appropriate knowledge of the relevant aspects of the transaction. And here there is a problem. It is acceptable from a utilitarian perspective to condone many employees being used as a means to the end of greater economic prosperity, particularly if they participate as consumers in that prosperity. But to what extent are the transactions involved truly fair? Can a potential employee today refuse to accept a non-standard contract if the alternative is no other contract and diminishing state benefits? Do any of us have any genuine free choice about refusing the enhanced workloads that accompany delayering, downsizing and resource cuts unless we 'choose' early retirement or a very alternative lifestyle? Our 'free' choice may be diminished further if a management programme of cultural change has persuaded us that labour intensification is really a form of empowerment. Are our choices as consumers fully informed when large firms have access to the media and resources for information acquisition and manipulation denied the ordinary consumer? And what would Aristotelian ethics have to say about the crass materialism embodied in the present hegemony of consumption over production-related values and activities? How do we reconcile Aristotle's view of human potentiality with that implicit in Britain's most popular tabloid, The *Sun*?

Conclusion

So where do we go from here? It would be very convenient if we had overwhelming evidence that Walton's 'soft' mutuality model of HRM – that scores well in terms of deontological and Aristotelian ethics – delivered universally the holy grail of competitive advantage. Unfortunately, this is not the case, for reasons I've touched on earlier. At best, in my view, such a model may be implemented by organizations in knowledge-based industries seeking high value added, but even then the motive is likely to reflect self-interest and see employees as a means to an end. This, of course, is perfectly acceptable in terms of utilitarianism. The majority of employees can enjoy the benefits of softish HRM at the core and in the first periphery, and a quite reasonable justification can be given for the rightness of actions that result in unfortunate consequences for the minority. This is probably the most ethical HRM we can hope for in the world as it is presently ordered, and this is fine as long as these unfortunate consequences touch only a minority. But when most of us are on non-standard, temporary, fixed-term contracts, facing high employment insecurity and ever increasing labour intensification, the fact that a minority have salaries like telephone numbers becomes unacceptable. Utilitarianism obviously only provides a moral justification if actions taken in its name *do* produce benefits for the majority that outweigh the costs to the minority. As already discussed, the ethics of stakeholder analysis, while looking persuasive at first sight, contain potential escape clauses that can render them little more than well-meaning rhetoric in practice. (Hence, no doubt, their appeal to well-meaning politicians.) The recognition of the customer's stake is certainly in tune with the ideas of flexibility and responsiveness that underlie most models of HRM. Perhaps it is helpful too in according employees a dual identity. 'You may not like what is happening to you as an employee, but you'll appreciate the outcomes as a customer.' Finally, Rawlsian ethics, though formally Kantian in its attempt to derive *a priori* principles of distributive justice that are acceptable to all rational persons, in practice, comes over as a form of utilitarianism. Keeley's (1978) well-intentioned adaptation of Rawlsian principles – that an organization's worth should be judged by the extent to which it minimizes the proportion of its employees who regret their involvement with the organization – appears both utopian and at odds with the spirit of the times: 'On yer bike' being a more likely reaction to the demoralized or disillusioned. Sadly, in a world of intensified competition and scarce resources, it seems inevitable that, as employees are used as a means to an end, there will be some that lose out. For these people 'soft' model HRM may be an irrelevancy, while 'hard' model HRM is likely to be an uncomfortable experience.

In spite of my caveats, though, perhaps the most hopeful and practical way forward is to look constructively at the positive messages that can be derived from utilitarianism and from Bauman's interpretation of Levinas. In other words, in our actions towards all organizational stakeholders, we should accept the moral obligation to fully consider the consequences of our actions, particularly towards those that appear to bear the costs rather than the benefits, and to resist the exclusionary and sometimes exploitative dictates of an instrumental, technical rationality. The values of a Judaeo-Christian tradition – not a million miles away from Rawlsian ethics or even Aristotelianism – that 'I am my brother's keeper' and 'Do as you would be done by', under a utilitarian gloss may be offered not, in the Kantian sense, as duties to be enacted for their own sake, but as sound business principles for the building of long term, mutually beneficial relational contracts (Kay, 1993) or, in a language I prefer, the building of reciprocal high trust (Fox, 1974).

Note

This chapter is based on the Alec Rodger Memorial Lecture, of the same title, that I delivered on 26 September 1996 at Birkbeck College, University of London.

References

Armstrong, M. (1987) 'Human Resource Management: A Case of the Emperor's New Clothes?', *Personnel Management*, 19(8): 30–5.

Bassiry, G.R. and Jones, M. (1993) 'Adam Smith and the Ethics of Contemporary Capitalism', *Journal of Business Ethics*, 12: 621–7.

Bauman, Z. (1989) *Modernity and the Holocaust*. Cambridge: Polity.
Beauchamp, T.L. and Bowie, N.E. (1988) *Ethical Theory and Business*, 3rd edn. Englewood Cliffs, NJ: Prentice-Hall.
de George, R.T. (1990) *Business Ethics*, 3rd edn. New York: Macmillan.
Delbridge, R. and Turnbull, P. (1992) 'Human Resource Maximization: The Management of Labour under Just-in-Time Manufacturing Systems', in P. Blyton and P. Turnbull (eds), *Reassessing Human Resource Management*. London: Sage, pp. 56–73.
Donaldson, J. (1989) *Key Issues in Business Ethics*. London: Academic Press.
Donaldson, T. and Werhane, P.H. (eds) (1993) *Ethical Issues in Business: A Philosophical Approach*, 4th edn. Englewood Cliffs, NJ: Prentice-Hall.
Dunn, S. (1990) 'Root Metaphor in the Old and New Industrial Relations', *British Journal of Industrial Relations*, 28(1): 1–31.
Edwards, P.K. and Whitston, C. (1991) 'Workers Are Working Harder: Effort and Shopfloor Relations in the 1980s', *British Journal of Industrial Relations,* 29(4): 393–601.
Evan, W.M. and Freeman, R.E. (1988) 'A Stakeholder Theory of the Modern Corporation: Kantian Capitalism', in T. Beauchamp and N. Bowie, (eds), *Ethical Theory and Business*, 3rd edn. Englewood Cliffs, NJ: Prentice-Hall. pp. 97–106.
Fox, A. (1974) *Beyond Contract: Work, Power and Trust Relations*. London: Faber and Faber.
Fukuyama, F. (1991) *The End of History and the Last Man*. New York: Harper and Row.
Gandz, J. and Bird, F.G. (1996) 'The Ethics of Empowerment', *Journal of Business Ethics*, 15: 383–92.
Garrahan, P. and Stewart, P. (1992) *The Nissan Enigma: Flexibility at Work in a Local Economy*. London: Mansell.
Gilmour, I. (1993) *Dancing with Dogma: Britain under Thatcherism*. London: Pocket Books.
Guest, D.E. (1987) 'Human Resource Management and Industrial Relations', *Journal of Management Studies*, 24(5): 503–21.
Guest, D.E. (1990a) 'Have British Workers Been Working Harder in Thatcher's Britain? A Re-consideration of the Concept of Effort', *British Journal of Industrial Relations*, 28(3): 293–312.
Guest, D.E. (1990b) 'Human Resource Management and the American Dream', *Journal of Management Studies*, 27(4): 378–97.
Guest, D.E. (1995) 'Human Resource Management, Industrial Relations and Trade Unions', in J. Storey (ed.), *Human Resource Management: A Critical Text*. London: Routledge.
Guest, D.E. (1996) 'Human Resource Management, Fit and Performance'. Paper presented to the ESRC Seminar Series on Contribution of HR Strategy to Business Performance, Cranfield, 1 February.
Guest, D.E. and Hoque, K. (1994) 'The Good, the Bad and the Ugly: Human Resource Management in New Non-Union Establishments', *Human Resource Management Journal*, 5(1): 1–14.
Hendry, C. and Pettigrew, A. (1990) 'Human Resource Management: An Agenda for the 1990s', *International Journal of Human Resource Management*, 1(1): 17–44.
Höpfl, H.J., Smith, S. and Spencer, S. (1992) 'Values and Valuations: Corporate Culture and Job Cuts', *Personnel Review*, 21(1): 24–38.
Hunter, L., McGregor, A., MacInnes, J. and Sproull, A. (1993) 'The "Flexible Firm": Strategy and Segmentation', *British Journal of Industrial Relations*, 31(3): 383–407.
Huselid, M. (1995) 'The Impact of Human Resource Management Practices on Turnover, Productivity and Corporate Financial Performance', *Academy of Management Journal*, 38(3): 635–72.
Jackall, R. (1988) *Moral Mazes: The World of Corporate Managers*. New York: Oxford University Press.

Kaler, J. (1996) 'Does Empowerment Empower?'. Paper presented at the Centre for Organizational and Professional Ethics, Institute of Education, University of London, Workshop on Ethics and Empowerment, September 1996.

Kay, J. (1993) *Foundations of Corporate Success: How Business Strategies Add Value.* Oxford: Oxford University Press.

Keeley, M. (1978) 'A Social-Justice Approach to Organizational Evaluation', *Administrative Science Quarterly*, 23: 272–92.

Keenoy, T. (1990a) 'HRM: A Case of the Wolf in Sheep's Clothing', *Personnel Review*, 19(2): 3–9.

Keenoy, T. (1990b) 'HRM: Rhetoric, Reality and Contradiction', *International Journal of Human Resource Management*, 1(3): 363–84.

Keenoy, T. and Anthony, P. (1992) 'HRM: Metaphor, Meaning and Morality', in P. Blyton and P. Turnbull (eds.), *Reassessing Human Resource Management*. London: Sage. pp. 233–55.

Legge, K. (1987) 'Human Resource Management – A Critical Analysis', in J. Storey (ed.), *New Perspectives on Human Resource Management*. London: Routledge. pp. 19–40.

Legge, K. (1988) *Personnel Management in Recession and Recovery: A Comparative Analysis of What the Surveys Say. Personnel Review*, 17(2): (monograph issue).

Legge, K. (1995) *Human Resource Management: Rhetorics and Realities.* Basingstoke: Macmillan.

Levinas, E. (1982) *Ethics and Infinity: Conversations with Philippa Nemo*, trans. R.A. Cohen. Pittsburgh: Duquesne University Press.

Lukes, S. (1974) *Power: A Radical View*. London: Macmillan.

MacIntyre, A. (1981) *After Virtue: A Study on Moral Theory*. London: Duckworth.

Marchington, M., Wilkinson, A., Ackers, P. and Goodman, J. (1994) 'Understanding the Meaning of Participation: Views from the Workplace', *Human Relations*, 47(8): 867–94.

Metcalf, D. (1988) *Trade Unions and Economic Performance: The British Evidence*. Discussion Paper 320, LSE Centre for Labour Economies, London.

Metcalf, D. (1989) 'Water Notes Dry Up: The Impact of Donovan Reform Proposals and Thatcherism at Work on Labour Productivity in British Manufacturing Industry', *British Journal of Industrial Relations*, 27(1): 1–31.

Nolan, P. and Marginson, P. (1990) 'Skating on Thin Ice? David Metcalf on Trade Unions and Productivity', *British Journal of Industrial Relations*, 18(2): 225–47.

Ogbonna, E. and Wilkinson, B. (1990) 'Corporate Strategy and Corporate Culture: The View from the Checkout', *Personnel Review*, 19(1): 9–15.

Purcell, J. (1996a) 'Human Resource Bundles of Best Practice: A Utopian Cul-de-Sac?' Paper presented to the ESRC Seminar Series on Contribution of HR Strategy to Business Performance, Cranfield, 1 February.

Purcell, J. (1996b) 'Contingent Workers and Human Resource Strategy: Rediscovering the Core-Periphery Dimension', *The Journal of Professional Human Resource Management*, 5: 16–23.

Rawls, J. (1971) *A Theory of Justice.* Cambridge, MA: Harvard University Press.

Sisson, K. (1994) 'Personnel Management: Paradigms, Practice and Prospects', in K. Sisson (ed.), *Personnel Management*, 2nd edn. Oxford: Blackwell. pp. 3–50.

Stark, A. (1993) 'What's Wrong with Business Ethics?', *Harvard Business Review*, 71(1): 38–48.

Storey, J. (1987) Developments in the Management of Human Resources: An Interim Report. Warwick Papers in Industrial Relations 17, IRRU, School of Industrial and Business Studies, University of Warwick, November.

Vielba, C.A. (1995) 'Managers' Working Hours'. Paper presented to the British Academy of Management Annual Conference, Sheffield University Management School, 11–13 September.

Walton, R.E. (1985) 'Towards a Strategy of Eliciting Employee Commitment Based

on Policies of Mutuality', in R.E. Walton and P.R. Lawrence (eds), *Human Resource Management, Trends and Challenges*. Boston: Harvard Business School Press. pp. 35–65.
Wickens, P. (1987) *The Road to Nissan*. London: Macmillan.
Wickens, P. (1995) *The Ascendant Organization*. London: Macmillan.
Wood, S. (1995) 'The Four Pillars of HRM: Are They Connected?', *Human Resource Management Journal*, 5(5): 48–58.
Wood, S. (1996) 'High Commitment Management and Payment Systems', *Journal of Management Studies*, 33(1): 53–78.
Wood, S. and Albanese, M.T. (1995) 'Can We Speak of High Commitment Management on the Shop Floor?', *Journal of Management Studies*, 32(2): 215–47.
Young, H. (1990) *One of Us*. London: Macmillan.

8 Marketing and Moral Indifference

John Desmond

Either marketers have been notoriously unsuccessful at raising trade to a more moral level or they have achieved this but have failed to market this startling truth to the general public. On this score they are damned either way: in the first instance by turpitude, in the second by ineptitude. It certainly is true that the public perception of marketing scarcely fits the fact that morality has been a prime concern for marketing academics from the inception of the subject. Henry Assael, a distinguished writer on consumer affairs, routinely reminds his readers that the advertising and sales professions are ranked last in public surveys of professional workers: 'All marketers are portrayed as hawkers, con artists and cheats' (1995: 99–100). In his view this portrayal places the integrity of all marketers into question and is a characterization that the discipline of marketing cannot afford.

Given the fact that the academic discipline of marketing set sail with high ethical hopes, it is scarcely surprising that marketers are concerned to see that ship founder on the rock of public opinion. What went wrong? As we shall see, this question has been asked quite often in the (rather short) history of the academic study of the subject. On occasion those who have sought to answer this question have come up with solutions which have had the unintended effect of creating further problems for the subject. Each 'solution' has led to a new strand of marketing theory and as a result the subject is fragmented into a number of quite different approaches: 'social' marketing, 'green' marketing, 'activist' marketing, 'relationship' marketing, 'postmodern' marketing, to name a few. Because of this diversity it is probably more accurate to talk of *marketings* than of a unified academic discipline. In my view such differences may be traced to the very beginnings of the subject, so that one can never really say that marketing had a unity of purpose, particularly with respect to morality. However it is possible to discover what J.K. Galbraith (1967) described as a 'conventional wisdom' in marketing, a loose formation of 'in-groups' sometimes referred to by scurrilous outsiders as the Church of Marketing, with the editor of the *Journal of Marketing* at its head.

This chapter focuses on the issue of adiaphorization – the production of moral neutrality – with respect to the marketing process; consequently there is no more than a passing reference to adiaphorization and consumer identity, a subject which has been the topic of some recent debate.[1] The first part of the chapter sketches the background to the current diversity in the subject to give a feel for the differences and the consequences which some 'solutions' – for example 'social marketing' – may have had for marketing practice. The main arguments in the chapter are dealt with under the heading of 'Marketing: an adiaphoric subject?', which considers whether the marketing process produces moral subjects or moral objects. This line of argument is informed by Zygmunt Bauman's (1993; 1995) work and is an extension of Hugo Letiche's discussion of Bauman in Chapter 6 in this volume. By *adiaphoric* Bauman means that the subject of such processes is rendered morally indifferent or neutral, beyond morality. The discussion of marketing morality draws upon the processes of *socialization* and *socialty* (Bauman, 1993) in relation to modern and postmodern forms of adiaphorization.

These processes are centred around V.W. Turner's concepts of societas and communitas, or structure and counter-structure, two mutually opposite conditions which Bauman links to moments in modern and postmodern accounts of adiaphorization. *Societas* relates to processes of socialization which seek to codify, classify and regulate social space into a hierarchical stable pattern. In moral terms, the process of societas removes the face of the moral subject (renders the subject morally neutral) through processes of objectification, distance and dissembly. The notion of societas will be used to explore the marketing process, the mundane act of deriving marketing objectives from corporate objectives, formulating marketing strategies based on the '4 Ps' and then implementing these. This process alone is unique to modern marketing. It will be argued that the marketing process is a technology which renders its subjects adiaphoric. On the other hand the major new development of 'relationship' marketing seeks to overcome the 'distancing' effects of traditional marketing by building on notions of trust through the exchange of promises. It is argued that relationship marketing may just as easily be explained as an extension of the codification of space. On the other hand the concept of *communitas* may provide a better explanation of relationship marketing. Whether or not relationship marketing is an extension of societas or an irruption of communitas, either way the moral subject remains in an adiaphoric state.

Marketing: a moral subject?

One can trace a concern with morality to the very beginnings of modern marketing thought. It must be stated that most academic accounts of the developments of marketing thought are selective, focusing on the USA. Jones and Monieson (1990) trace the academic roots of the subject of marketing to the late nineteenth century to two economic schools of thought at the University of Wisconsin and at Harvard. The Wisconsin group, many of whom were German educated, headed a 'reformist' movement which spearheaded the development of the American Economic Association as a protest against (British) *laissez-faire* economics. A major focus of interest was in agricultural marketing where one strand of research explored the role of intermediaries in the dairy industry. The economists worked closely with the state of Wisconsin to investigate claims that small farmers and customers were losing out to a cartel.[2] While the economists at Wisconsin worked closely with the state, those at Harvard, who were also influenced by the German historical school, developed a more managerialist orientation in setting up the first business school in the USA. It was here that the 'discipline' of marketing formed around the development of 'marketing science' – an inductive research programme calculated to yield general principles of marketing and a 'case' approach to teaching.

From a moral perspective, marketing was informed then by two positions: a reformist position which maintains that marketers should work in the overall interests of society by aiding the state regulation of the marketplace (Wisconsin); and a *laissez-faire* view (Harvard) that one should entrust morality to the actions of individuals who, by 'freely' (of regulation) pursuing their rational self-interests, would thereby set in motion the 'hidden hand' of the marketplace and thus ensure the best possibility for moral action. From an ethical point of view this latter position represents a form of ethical egoism. For many writers on ethics this could be regarded as a 'strong' position to argue from in that it is based on the recognition that the individual acts in her best interests (not desires) and seems to employ the idea of objective value (Graham, 1990: 26).

If one now teleports to the marketing academy of the 1960s it is possible to see that the academic subject of marketing has taken the Harvard view as its own. Marketers are not portrayed as 'referees' seeking to ensure fair play between sellers and buyers. The formalization of the marketing concept may be traced to McKitterick (1957) who places the remit on firms to be 'skilful in conceiving and then making the business do what suits the interests of the customer'. The guru Theodore Levitt's bluff, no-nonsense pragmatism sums up the marketing approach as an extension of *laissez-faire* in contending that marketing is not a 'do-gooder' treatise, but a 'tough minded explanation, outline and example of how to serve yourself by serving the customer better' (1962: 8). To 'sell' has connotations of selling into bondage, of betraying one's colleagues, even one's country; its image is tainted with larceny or more likely the selling of an imperfect bill of goods. By marketing, or serving the needs of the customer, one is working pragmatically in one's own self-interest. This did not mean that the concern for regulation of marketing activities had gone away. Far from it: in the USA a web of legislation was woven around marketing activities. However state intervention in the regulation of marketing has not been uniform. In the USA this reached a peak during the 1970s; there then was a period of progressive disengagement from regulation, with a move under the Reagan administration to self-regulation; more recently there has been a move back towards engagement under the Bush and Clinton administrations.[3]

The 1960s seems to be the time when marketing briefly came into its own and when marketing fragmented. Marketing came into its own as there seemed to be a greater recognition among major companies that understanding and responding to the needs of customers might help create a competitive edge. The fragmentation of the academic subject of marketing happened at around the same time and for similar reasons: as a response to growing protests about materialist values; a concern that in practice marketing did not so much serve needs as frame them; and also in response to a range of environmental concerns. In the USA public consciousness was raised by a number of high profile academic and social commentators. Milton and Rose Friedman (1979) mention J.K. Galbraith (1958; 1967), who argued for the *revised sequence*, so named because he argued that needs were moulded to the interests of production and not the other way round; Vance Packard, whose stories highlighted the attempts of marketers to manipulate the market via strategies of 'subliminal' perception and 'planned obsolescence'; Ralph Nader, who sought to demonstrate that contemporary car design was inherently dangerous for consumers and thereby spearheaded the rebirth of the consumer movement; and Rachel Carson, whose book *Silent Spring* raised environmental concerns. All of these works, added to the general broth of discontent reflected in a diverse range of social movements, resulted in what seemed to be a wholesale rejection of materialist values. For example Gartner and Riessman (1974) noted that in one year only 8% of Harvard graduates opted for business careers.

From the above, it appears that from critics' points of view marketers worked in the interest of producers and not of consumers. Consumers relied on whistle-blowers from outside the marketing discipline to provide a focus for their concerns and were themselves 'reduced' to using their market power by means of selective boycotts (Smith, 1990). Increasingly government resorted to the exercise of condign power via regulation and legislation (with Galbraith playing the role of theorist and political adviser). The social viruses of 'entitlements' and 'rights' provoked a rush to litigation and legislation, leaving most of the spadework of 'practical' marketing ethics to be performed in Senate committee rooms and in the courts and via other mechanisms such as consumer boycotts. Contemporary consumer society was thus not the sole creation of marketers; its other parent was embodied in the counter-cultural claim for equal status and consumer rights.

From a moral point of view one of the most important attacks on marketing concerned J.K. Galbraith and Herbert Marcuse's (quite unrelated) texts which highlighted marketing's role as acting primarily in the interests of production, and in particular as creating 'false needs' through advertising. The notion of the creation of false needs has been tackled by other 'critical' theorists (see for example William Leiss, 1976; Jean Baudrillard, 1988) and found to be wanting (for example, can one really separate out 'psychological' needs from 'physiological' needs?). The whole issue of the creation of false needs quietly slipped off the critical agenda following 'poststructuralist' questioning of the value of 'ruling ideas' in perpetuating 'false consciousness'. However, the moral questions remain. Can we buy our way to happiness? How can we talk of the satisfaction of needs if the offer precedes demand? If commodities buy their own prospective customers? If wants themselves are industrial products? If needs are not rational but rather the hysterical symptoms of desire?

During the 1960s marketing academics reacted in a variety of ways to the barrage of criticism. Some denied that marketing had much to do with the problem (Stidsen and Schutte, 1972). Others agreed that there was a problem and focused on the marketing concept. Of this latter group one point of focus was on marketing practitioners' failure to implement the marketing concept (Drucker, 1969; Kotler and Levy, 1969). Phillip Kotler made much of the theoretical running at this stage, arguing with Sidney Levy (1969) that in a 'post-industrial' age the marketing concept should be applied also to non-business organizations. Extending this line of argument, Kotler and Zaltman (1971) advocated 'full-blown' social marketing, the application of marketing technology to social issues such as drug abuse and health care. Kotler (1972a) developed the generic concept of marketing, the idea that marketing principles could be applied to any organization and to any of that organization's stakeholders. By reorienting the marketing concept to recognize societal needs it was argued that marketing could recover its worth to society. Kotler's (1972b) second paper of the year recognized the value of one such stakeholder; the consumer movement. In an attempt at *rapprochement* he argued that consumerism was good for marketing. He also advised companies which made 'pleasing' goods (which satisfied desires and not long term interests, for example cigarettes) that they should remodel their perspective away from the satisfaction of consumer desire and towards the satisfaction of long run consumer welfare (a plea which seems to suggest that many 'practitioners' had either not heard of McKitterick's marketing concept or had decided to turn a deaf ear to it).

The various critiques of marketing and marketers' responses to these gave birth to a number of different approaches to marketing, among them social marketing and green marketing (Arnold and Fisher, 1996). But what has been the legacy of the 1960s? Arnold and Fisher (1996) suggest that despite this diversity the fundamental marketing approach is still business marketing. I would agree with them – to an extent. However I also tend to agree with Hirschman (1983) that Kotler won the day so far as the extended marketing concept was concerned. The discourse of social marketing has now insinuated itself into a whole host of 'social' spheres: charity, religion, education have all succumbed to the marketing of ethics. The direction taken by social marketing has been quite different to that envisaged by Berry (1971) who argued that the satisfaction of the needs of customers should be seen to be only one factor to consider within the social system. It seems that what has triumphed here is marketing technology, the straightforward application of marketing tools to areas of social concern. Laczniak et al. were prescient in noting that while the notion of social marketing was fascinating, it could open a Pandora's box, releasing ethical and social problems reflecting concerns of those outside the discourse of marketing:

> For example is it in the best interests of society for politicians increasingly to rely upon individuals skilled in advertising and marketing to tailor their campaigns? Is it proper that marketing research methods are used to determine which issues appeal to various constituencies and how these often conflicting views can be optimally incorporated into the party platform without alienating many voters? Is it beneficial that image studies shape the candidates' external appearance? – that copywriters and public relations people stage appealing TV speeches and appearances for the candidates? – that politicians are sold like soap? (1979: 32)

The next section focuses on marketing technology and on attempts to overcome the shortcomings of this by relationship marketing.

Marketing: an adiaphoric subject?

The aim of this section is to consider the morality of the marketing process with respect to whether or not this is adiaphoric. Other contributors to this volume have indicated that theoretically this might indeed be the case. For example in Chapter 12 Tony Watson discusses 'David's dilemma' where one of the group of managers who were discussing organizational morality said:

> *David*: You could have a death camp operating with a clear morality where all the guards trusted each other, were open and honest with each other, treated each other fairly and, well, would that be moral?

In the wake of 'developments' in Bosnia-Herzegovina we know that such things can happen, that neighbour can fall upon neighbour with ferocity. But how can this happen?

As discussed in several other chapters in this volume, Zygmunt Bauman (1988; 1993; 1995) offers a convincing explanation of how such an effect may occur by means of the creation of moral distance. Even though we may be physically proximate to the other, we objectify them by effacing their moral 'face'. In brief, he argues that the spontaneous recognition of the face of the other demanded by moral behaviour poses a threat to the structured monotony and predictability of organization and its instrumental or procedural criteria for evaluation. The removal of action beyond moral limits frequently involves mediation of action: actors rarely need to see the consequences of their actions, whether this is upstream, for example child slave labour in the production of textiles, or downstream, the massive quantities of waste and pollution generated by the organization. These others are rendered as being adiaphoric, morally neutral or indifferent. Once the face of the other has been 'effaced', employees are freed from moral responsibility to focus on the technical (purpose centred or procedural) aspects of the 'job at hand'. The moral drive of the employee is redirected away from the other (which is now an object) towards others in the organization.

This former description is an example of what Bauman (1993; 1995) refers to as the spacing of societas: social organization. In *Modernity and the Holocaust* (1989) he discusses the means by which processes of socialization render the moral subject adiaphoric. These are now dealt with singly with respect to the role of marketing in creating adiaphoric subjects.

Stretch the distance between the action and its consequences

Bauman is not the only author to express concern about the effects of distance on the human moral capacity. Marshal McLuhan and Quentin Fiore (1988) noted that:

> It is obviously true that most bomber pilots are no better and no worse than other men. The majority of them, given a can of petrol and told to pour it over a child of three and ignite it, would probably disobey the order. Yet put that decent man in an aeroplane a few hundred feet above a village and he will, without compunction, drop high explosives and napalm and inflict appalling pain and injury on men, women and children.

Like bomber pilots, it is rare for organizational actors to be faced directly with the consequences of their actions. More importantly, Bauman argues, even if they were, they would hardly conceive of them as the consequences of their deeds. This is because most actors within organizations are cast in an 'agentic' state and are likely to perceive their own job as being small and insignificant when compared with other jobs. This results in what Hannah Arendt called 'rule by Nobody'. This tendency is reinforced by the exemplar of bounded rationality (Simon, 1976), by means of which theorists classify organizational decision making into a hierarchically ordered means–end chain in terms of organizational goals and values. Goals and values cascade down the organization such that the means developed at the highest level become ends for those at the next level and so on. Thus the 'problem' is divided into a series of 'subproblems' which become the responsibility of groups whose objectives have been established and whose task is to devise strategies to attain these objectives. It is scarcely surprising that such a process effects a 'distance' between the employee and the other. This line of argument is based on the (large) assumption that people in organizations do actually plan in this way.

A second distancing effect is created as the result of the cognitive definition of the problem space. Simon (1976) notes that most organizational problems are ill-defined, yet they tend to be framed by means of an organizational discourse which foregrounds rational instrumental and technical considerations, the 'practical realities' of day-to-day survival in the corporate jungle, licking the competition and serving the customer well. Just as Eichman became obsessed with the logistical details of timetabling trains for the 'final solution', so the modern-day marketer may become absorbed into the mundane detail of the job at hand. As Stephen Fineman points out in Chapter 11 in this book, the discourse of managers in modern organizations is saturated with rationality, hierarchy, patriarchal power and win–lose situations:

> Their realities are firmly embedded in a web of short and medium term actions which are rewarded according to their contribution to the production of goods and services.

In marketing, the separation of ends from means is further exacerbated as projects frequently involve specialists working for different organizations. A given project may thus include marketers from the 'client' who split the project into a research phase where a marketing research agency becomes involved; a brand development phase when brand specialists become involved with representatives from other functions within the client organization; and finally a media phase when PR, advertising or direct marketing agencies may be utilized to draw up a communications plan. For each organization the 'problem' will be framed in different ways, different 'solutions' will be called for and the morality of action will be regulated by different codes of conduct.

One could argue that ethics has already been accounted for within the complex web of corporate, professional and regulatory codes which weave themselves around the project. It is definitely true that within the last thirty years there has been a veritable explosion of 'voluntary' regulatory activity. For example Chonko (1995: 126) states that by 1979 approximately 75% of all companies had ethical codes. Stevens (1994) states that the most important aspect of such codes is that they are messages through which corporations hope to shape employee behaviour. However there is little research evidence to suggest that this actually is the case; authors despairingly report on the intransigence of marketing practitioners who seem to be almost code-proof. This does not stop academics from continuing to exhort their flock to observe what codes there are and to recommend that new codes are devised to regulate the industry. Related to this issue is the discussion of the success with which US and (to a lesser extent) European agencies have regulated the advertising industry.[4] The existence of codes for regulating the moral behaviour of marketers might provide a crumb of comfort but for the fact that their exercise frequently results in a focus on technical interpretations of the code – 'the letter of the law' rather than on the moral face of the other. Chonko (1995: 101) says that the mere existence of a code has little effect on ethical behaviour. He feels that marketing codes in particular involve major problems. First, they are often viewed as public relations documents and consequently many managers may be sceptical of their 'operational value' to the corporation. Secondly, they are often vague since they can hardly be exhaustive given the variety of ethical problems that a manager might encounter. Finally, Chonko argues that many codes are not enforced, offering the example of the AMA (American Marketing Association) code which is written at the back of their membership card.

Some would argue that as government's ability to make and enforce law has declined, so the 'hidden hand' of the market has been restored to its rightful place in regulating the moral impulse. They might point to the establishment of the Marine Stewardship Council (MSC), established by a major multinational food company and the World Wildlife Fund (WWF) Roy Gerrans (1996) described the establishment of the MSC in February 1996 as:

> an independent body that certifies retail fish with a logo that indicates the fish was caught from fisheries certified as sustainable and well managed. By buying only fish caught with environmentally friendly gear or in areas where fish stocks are healthy, consumers can encourage industrial fleets to change their indiscriminate fishing practices.

Prior to the launch of the code, both WWF and the company conducted a detailed feasibility study involving consultations with fishing industry experts, scientists, regulators and other environmentalists. The MSC seems to be the outcome of a pragmatic alliance between environmentalists and a company, both of which were concerned to maintain the ultimate survival of a central resource, as a response to continued over-fishing, the inability of supranational agencies to adequately legislate for this and the failure of national governments to adequately police the situation. It is too early to attempt to judge the effectiveness of the MSC code. However it is possible to consider the forms of justification for it. Andrew Crane (1997) discusses the decision processes involved in a similar venue where the company (described as ABC) sought to develop a code for regulating sustainable forestry.

> According to respondents this strategy is principally driven by changes in the marketing environment; it is believed that it has become increasingly important for ABC to remain credible and responsible in the eyes of the public compared to their competitors but at the same time, as one respondent put it, to avoid risking 'putting our heads above the parapet' which may incite unwanted or inappropriate attention from outside bodies.

Crane's findings are strikingly similar to those of Stephen Fineman in Chapter 11 in this volume. ABC executives were at ease discussing 'green' issues within the familiar organizational context of cost savings and other commercial justifications. Environmental concerns were framed in terms of economic priorities: 'If it's not making sense economically, then it is probably not making sense environmentally.' Despite their linkage in an original environmental strategy document, managers at ABC tended to separate ethical and environmental issues. At its most extreme, managers avoided linking ethics with environmental issues, and steered well clear of 'ethically contestable' notions such as sustainability, biodiversity and ecocentrism. Crane reports that:

> In general then, executives at ABC involved in the process of environmental marketing act to de-moralise the environment in order to secure organizational endorsement for their activities. (1997: 10)

While the MSC initiative is surely to be welcomed as promising the means for ensuring the sustainable management of world fishing stocks, in the light of the 'ABC' study there must be some concern that it could ultimately revert to a case of 'business as usual'.

When one speaks of cognitive 'distance' one can refer to the situation where two people are physically proximate but cognitively separate, that is, they are strangers to one another. However corporate contexts usually ensure that the cognitively separated parties are also physically distant from one another. Physical distance makes it much more difficult for an interested observer to discern what is going on. Organizations such as the Body Shop and Ben 'n' Jerry's, for example, have been riding high on a wave of public goodwill in the wake of their highly publicized ethical approach to business. These claims are based on a complex chain of activities many of which relate to helping communities which live in remote regions of the world. Too often such claims have been passed unedited by media correspondents and even academics. It is worth noting that several of the claims made have been actively contested (cf. Entine, 1995; 1996a; 1996b; Hanson, 1995). For example Entine takes a swipe at the fashionable 'ethics in business' movement in which he claims 'good intentions' have become the new standard of corporate ethics. But who is the 'interested observer' to believe? The company? Entine? The journalist? As it becomes increasingly clear that what facts exist are mediated and that one cannot escape such mediation, the suspicion grows that these are underdetermined by the values of the mediators: the company's interest in preserving its good image; the critic's interest in preserving his or her version of events; the news values of the journalists, editors, and publishers. Taken to its extreme this pushes close to Baudrillard's (1988) notion of hyper-reality – a state of affairs where every explanation could simultaneously be true.

From the above discussion it should be apparent that the organizational space is codified from top to bottom. Despite this, marketing academics tend to lament the fact that for marketing practitioners – usually advertisers – moral behaviour is not codified enough. Pratt and James (1994) argued for stricter adherence to deontological principles, arguing that a de-emphasis on these would lead to a *laissez-faire* approach to ethical issues. More recently Nantel and Weeks (1996) have argued that a deontological approach would improve the ethical quality of marketing decisions.

Marketing also creates a distance between the product and those who produced it by drawing a veil over the origins of products. Products are not simply functional assortments, they are badged with identities by means of advertising. Product identities fulfil a double role: they provide an image which the consumer identifies with (the brand image) and they disrupt the connection between the product and the circumstances relating to its production. For example we don't believe that butter is produced by happy dancing cows, but perhaps there is a part of us which wants to tolerate the fiction. The alternative is to live with the disturbing knowledge that we depend on the mass exploitation of animals for our momentary enjoyment.

Such ads are intentionally humorous; the precise intent is that they are not to be taken seriously, nor is anyone who is silly enough to point out that they might be misleading (we are complicit in the ads' construction, we already know they are misleading). In any case, in the age where one can't believe it's *not* butter, who is to know whether or not cows are involved? If we are not sure, can we be bothered to find out? The purchase situation itself is an act of spacing. The ambience of the supermarket, together with the image of the product and our own purchase intentions, propel us downstream towards the act of consumption. Jean Baudrillard (1968) points out that the paradox of consumption is that we participate in the mass market but we feel that we purchase as individuals. In the supermarket we are confronted with a sea of produce which we want to enjoy; it is tempting to think – 'okay so this company reputedly has a bad human rights record but how can I a mere individual influence this? In any case what will my friends think if I *don't* buy X?'

Exempt some others from the class of potential objects for moral conduct: remove the face

As part of the discussion on 'distance', reference was made to the reframing of the moral subject as a technical not a moral 'problem'. The reframing of the moral subject has a direct bearing on Bauman's second statement which relates to the 'removal of the face'. The moral subject has been subjected to means–end analysis, parcelled out as a set of problems to be solved, framed within organizational discourse in relation to short term goals of competitive advantage and customer satisfaction. In 'effacing the face' the subject becomes a moral object, excluded from the class of 'beings' and therefore capable of evaluation in terms of technical or instrumental value. This is a device used to move sensate creatures to the status of object. The Cartesian separation of knowing human mind from body, the sacred from the profane, brackets all of those things without minds into the status of an object; thus the animal kingdom and the natural world are already objects. The human self is destroyed as the totality of the moral subject is reduced to a collection of parts or attributes. The actual removal of the face in marketing takes place at a number of levels. Principally this involves a denial of the moral capacity of the other. In marketing terms this involves the veiling of products' origins. However it also takes place in terms of the construction of the target market, the targeting of a particular group by means of mass marketing or segmentation. The key factor here is that the individual in the target group is no longer regarded as a moral agent, but as someone to whom something must be done (i.e. as a target for the marketing mix). This process is indifferent to whether the target is someone who is identified as an object for the purposes of selling insurance, promoting a 'no smoking' campaign, or 'ethnic cleansing' for that matter. The key point is that *someone else* decides that it is in the person's or society's best interests to sell them insurance, or the no smoking campaign, or ethnic cleansing; the person's own moral capacity is silenced, although their active participation may be sought in promoting the 'campaign' itself.

Whatever the goal may be, the marketer has exempted this group of persons from the realm of moral agency and responsibility. For example in campaigns for slimming products, targets are displaced from their own moral agency; the aim of the campaign (to lose weight) is presented as the only right thing to do. Frequently the path to the removal of the face is paved with good intentions. In a rare example of an academic seeking to legislate for good practice, Krohn and Milner (1989) accuses condom manufacturers of negligent homicide in failing to aggressively market condoms to gays. However, in Krohn's piece, 'gays' emerge as an isolated objective category, fragmented in terms of key variables such as political orientation, religion, lifestyle, rendered passive and adiaphoric as a function of the application of the marketing method. The morality of Krohn's argument is injected into the discourse from outside where Krohn and Milner place themselves at the centre of a panopticon, setting themselves up as arbiters of what is 'rationally' good. The danger of such moralizing becomes quickly apparent.

Dissemble the other human objects of action into aggregates of functionally specific traits, held separate so that the occasion for reassembling the face does not arise

Commentators have noted how in the early days of modern marketing, the consumer (usually a woman) was herself 'consumed' by the male gaze. This is also the case for the 'target' markets discussed in the last section. The target market is not usually known to the marketer as a group of people; usually this consists of a group of variables, organized in terms of social class, demography, lifestyle, frequency of use or some other category, as in Krohn and Milner's (1989) treatment of gays. Once the marketer has obtained a database of marketing characteristics and 'cleaned' it (made sure that it is accurate), this may then be offered for sale to other interested parties, who no doubt will use the list as the basis for some form of 'personalized' approach to address the targeted individuals. For many companies this is what passes for 'relationship marketing', something which will be discussed in more detail below.

The components are combined into a newly reconstituted whole

They acquire a new face via marketing

While Bauman does not mention these I think that they are important in explaining the role which marketing plays in the cognitive organization of space. The final process of marketing concerns the momentary reassembling of a face, the 'product' which is being sold. When products first appear they do not 'mean' anything. In providing a meaning for a product marketers draw on referent systems which are relatively stable cultural stocks of knowledge that already have a meaning for the consumer. For example Judith Williamson (1978) showed how two perfume products, Chanel No. 5 and Babe, drew on the 'celebrity' referent system by associating the products with two well-known celebrities, Catherine Deneuve (cool, sophisticated) and Margot Hemingway (a 'tomboy'). One can see examples of this today, with perfumes associated with 'super-models'. The idea is that the consumer identifies with the face in the ad (which recalls the ego-ideal) and desires the product because it promises to close the gap between her feelings of fragmentation and the perfect image offered by the 'mirror' of the ad. It is important to note that the celebrity in the referent system is not a person but a series of signifiers. In the following passage Rein et al. discuss how Olivia Newton-John was repackaged to signify 'energy' and 'pace':

> The transformation of Newton-John was not some mysterious force propelled by luck or fluke. It was the state of the art in the techniques of the Pygmalion Principle. The fitness craze of the 80s had created an opportunity for a performer to symbolize the energy and pace of a new social trend. So Newton-John was transformed to meet the market fulfilment strategy devised by her producer. Not unlike the development of Federal Express or large breasted turkeys, Newton-John was changed and fitted to a newly developing market. (1987: 194)

The role of advertisements is thus to create a meaning for a product (initially by means of the plundering of referent systems) which is meaningful to the target consumer. In so doing the person, ONJ, is sucked out, leaving the cadaver of the celebrity in her stead. As Judith Williamson (1978) points out, the new faces or brand identities which are created as a result of this process subsequently begin to radiate their own meaning. It is not trite to say that over the past forty years major brand identities have been more stable and 'trustworthy' than many social institutions. People grow up with brands; they convey a sense of value to those who purchase them and manufacturers tamper with them at their peril. One need only be reminded of the 'New Coke' fiasco to illustrate this point. The belief that consumption is an individual (private) activity coupled with the power of brands and the satisfaction and sense of identity which these are seen to offer to consumers presents a major difficulty to campaigners. For example in 1997 I attended a public meeting where activists urged attendees to boycott Nescafé. The response from many people was outrage: 'how dare they tell us what to do, it's my decision, I have always drunk Nescafé and so do my friends.' One could just as easily extend this argument to the recent 'McLibel' case. While the reputation of McDonald's has suffered in the view of 'informed opinion' (who either read the 'quality' press or felt that it was their duty to watch a tedious television reconstruction of the case), one wonders whether the total effect of all of this has been anything more than marginal so far as McDonald's core business is concerned.

Relationship marketing: closing the distance?

In the above discussion one of the major criticisms of the marketing process was in terms of the creation of distance. However many marketers may retort angrily that marketing has moved on from there. From the introductory discussion of marketing this could scarcely fail to be true as there are many different approaches to the subject. However those who advocate the relationship marketing approach say that it is not just another line of theory but forms the basis of a new marketing paradigm. The remainder of this chapter discusses the moral implications of a relationship marketing approach.

The elimination of distance was a primary concern of those who sought to develop the new 'paradigm' of relationship marketing. Christian Grönroos (1996), a major contributor to the 'Nordic' school of thought, provided the keynote address for the first on-line 'relationship marketing' conference. Grönroos's main point of attack was the '4 Ps', the marketing mix, which he argued is oversimplified and is bound to set marketing off track because it is competition and production oriented. He argued that rather than being in the consumer's interests (i.e. somebody *for whom* something is done) the implicit approach of the '4 Ps' is that it implies that the customer is somebody *to whom* something is done. Basically he suggests that this approach has distanced marketers from the marketing concept and that, as a result, marketing has become the province of specialists. Specialization of marketing has resulted in a double alienation (1996: 4). First, this has had the effect of alienating the rest of the organization from marketing. Because of this alienation it is difficult, if not impossible, for marketing to become the truly integrative function that it should be. Secondly, the specialists organized within the marketing department may become alienated from customers, because managing the marketing mix means relying on mass marketing. Customers become numbers for the marketing specialists, whose actions therefore typically are based on surface information obtained from market research reports and market share statistics. Frequently such marketers act without ever having encountered a real customer.

Grönroos's concerns echo many of those which have been expressed earlier in this chapter with respect to the creation of *distance* by marketing processes. He suggests that these contradictions could be resolved by means of a 'new paradigm', a dynamic and fluid relationship marketing approach, which alone can counter the strait-jacket of the clinical, transactions-based, mass market approach of the '4 Ps'. According to Grönroos the aim of relationship marketing is to establish, maintain and enhance relationships with customers and other partners, at a profit, so that the objectives of the parties are met. This is achieved by the mutual exchange and fulfilment of promises. Such promises are usually, but not exclusively, long term. The establishment of a relationship can be divided into two parts: to attract the customer and to build the relationship with that customer so that the economic goals of that relationship can be achieved. This shifts the ground towards the 'part-time' marketer (the recognition that within organizations, many non-marketing specialists are actually practising marketing functions). Internal marketing is needed to gain the support of these people. Both internally and externally, relationships are to be regulated by means of the exchange of promises, towards the establishment of trust, through the formation of relationships and dialogue with both internal and external customers. While the ultimate objective is to build a loyal customer base, there is no doubt that this refocusing of marketing to emphasize qualities of connectedness, dialogue and trust represents an attempt to *uplift* the process of marketing. Grönroos employs a strong religious rhetoric to advance his cause.

At first glance relationship marketing looks like a promising development towards a more moral approach to marketing. In focusing on dialogue, on the establishment of trust which must contain some aspect of vulnerability and uncertainty, he seems to be offering to reconnect the marketer to the moral subject. But how is this to be achieved? A relationship marketing approach seems to be a million miles away from the automaton described below:

> The flight attendant's smile is like her makeup; it is on her, not of her. The rules about how to feel and how to express feelings are set by management, with the goal of producing passenger contentment. Company manuals give detailed instructions on how to provide a 'sincere' and 'unaffected' facial expression, how to seem 'vivacious but not effervescent'. Emotional labourers are required to take the arts of emotional management and control that characterize the intimate relations of family and friends . . . and package them according to the 'feeling rules' laid down by the organization. (Ferguson, 1984: 53)

The above seems to be a perfect example of a rule guided 'cognitive' organization of space which is quite different to the ethos of relationship marketing. For example it does not square well with Gummesson's (1988: 15) insistence that front line staff should not be curbed with 'unnecessary and stifling regulations' but should be allowed freedom of action. This seems much more in line with the following description:

> An airline cabin attendant . . . must create a believable performance of friendliness towards passengers to effectively sell the company's product. The more management can do to get the employee to genuinely embrace the appropriate posture, the better the performance and the more business interests are served. (Biggart, 1988: 170)

However neither Grönroos nor Gummesson go into much detail about *how* the employee's freedom of action can be consistent with the aims of the organization. Grönroos talks of the implementation of a form of virtuous circle that, via internal marketing, will ascertain and serve the needs of internal customers, reduce waste, ensure that operations will work more efficiently and that quality will improve as fewer mistakes will be made. Overall everyone will be happier because a win–win situation will be created which will benefit the whole brotherhood of the workplace and in turn the final customer. Talk of internal marketing and the creation of 'win–win' situations puts one in mind of a TQM programme. Gummesson (1988) offers a link in suggesting that all employees have a role to play in marketing the organization 'as bearers of a desired company culture that would provide a focus for the business and its customers'. It seems clear to me that both authors were influenced by the writings of Deal and Kennedy (1982) and Peters and Waterman (1982).

Relationship marketing: extension of the code?

Gideon Kunda (1992) explored the effect which such 'strong' cultures can have on the workforce. He discusses Etzioni's (1961) distinction between a traditional utilitarian form of control, the use of economic power to elicit compliance with rules and regulations, and normative control, which involves controlling the 'underlying experiences, thoughts and feelings that gauge their actions'. Under normative control, membership is founded not on a traditional economic transaction but on an experiential transaction, one in which symbolic rewards are exchanged for a moral orientation to the organization. In this transaction a member role is fashioned and imposed that includes not only behavioural rules but articulated guidelines for experience. Generally normative control is built into the structure of bureaucracy as a form of internalization of the rules and an identification with the goals of the company. This places heavy claims on the self of the employee as domains of the self once considered private became the legitimate domain of bureaucratic control structures. Kunda (1992) quotes William Whyte who said that the 'organization man' was 'imprisoned in brotherhood': the soulful corporation demands the workers' soul – or at least his identity.

> The member role is 'incorporated', based on strong identification, an inextricable connection to the company with little 'demarcation'. It involves the 'whole person' and is based on powerful emotional ties expressed in 'zeal' or at least in 'enthusiasm'. (1992: 91)

It is therefore possible to read relationship marketing as an attempt to 'engineer' culture. This is not via some crude exercise of power but by working on the culture. As the boss of 'Tech' said to Kunda: 'The idea is to educate them without [them] knowing it. Have religion and not know how they ever got it' (1992: 5). The resulting effect on the (full-time) workers at Tech seemed to have badly backfired:

> If the attempt to engineer culture and accomplish normative control is aimed at defining members' selves for them, this very attempt undermines its own assumptions. The engineers of culture see the ideal member as driven by strong beliefs and intense emotions, authentic experiences of loyalty, commitment and the experience of work. Yet they seem to produce members who internalize ambiguity, who have

> made the metaphor a centerpiece of their sense of self, who question the authenticity of all beliefs and emotions and who find irony in its various forms, the dominant mode of everyday existence. (1992: 216)

Kunda talks of normative control as a form of socialization, as the internalization by employees of the 'rules' of the organization.

Grönroos (1996) and Murphy et al. (1996) impute a central role to promise keeping and trust in the development of marketing relationships. To what extent can one argue that trust is based on a system of rules? The definition of trust used in relationship marketing is based on Rotter (1967) where: 'trust is a generalized expectancy held by an individual that the word of another can be relied upon.' Within this context trust is built gradually as the net result of successful reciprocal arrangements between parties. Reciprocity is thus one of the key dividing lines between a transactions-based marketing approach and a relationship marketing approach; the success of relationship marketing depends on the successful exchange of promises between parties.

Now Bauman (1993: 57) makes the point that no business transaction would be possible without *some* form of trust in a partner's readiness to keep his word or act on his promise. However, he differentiates this from a moral approach, by noting that it assumes that calculation precedes morality. Instead he insists that a stance does not wait to be moral until it has been reciprocated; the duty of one party is not the other party's right. In any case he notes that even this oblique connection between transaction and morality is questionable. The 'moral' position of each party is further questioned as:

> pernickety legal regulations and threats of stern penalties envelop the conduct of the parties to the extent of making their moral postures all but invisible and above all irrelevant, while making the breach of promise a 'bad business' in a quite tangible, calculable sense.

Bauman argues that reciprocity stems ultimately from an explicitly selfish standpoint, the relationship (contract) is entered into for one's own well-being. Attention is focused away from the person to the task in hand, the exchange of a service for a sum of money. There is nothing personal in the 'relationship'; the partners are not persons but legal constructs. The reciprocal duty of one partner to another is thus ultimately enforceable; 'duty' has an extrinsic meaning but no intrinsic one; partners are seen as means to an end (my well-being) rather than as ends in themselves.

From the above a view is built up of relationship marketing as an attempt to engineer culture through normative control, the internalization of rules; reciprocity on which the relationship is based is also underpinned by rule structures. It would not be unreasonable to suggest that relationship marketing is an extension of the social organization of space. What of the effects on external customers? Writing years before store loyalty cards, Dwyer et al. (1987) cite frequent flyer programmes, book clubs, church and professional memberships as examples of consumer relationships. It now becomes clear that in practice, one way of defining the 'loyal customer base' which is its object is as a technological base, a database, which in the aggregate constitutes a range of databases.

Relationship marketing: socialty?

To use Bauman's (1993) terms, another way of trying to understand relationship marketing is as return to socialty, the powerful expression of control which can be expressed by the crowd. In this respect relationship marketing may be construed as a direct appeal to socialty, the spirit of the 'crowd', a levelling down, a turning away from socialization, a tearing up of rulebooks, freeing the worker from the chains of bureaucracy, the substitution of an equally constraining but quite different order, the discharge that is achieved by the notion 'we are all one, we fight the just fight, we are all in this together'. The emotional discharge of the crowd produces a rush of energy releasing feelings of togetherness, of oneness and connection that the dry rulebooks of cognitive spacing could never have hoped to achieve. But where is the 'freedom of action' that Gummesson (1988) talks about? The implication of Gummesson's statement is the freedom to *be yourself*. But how can you 'be yourself' when you are part of a crowd? As Bauman (1993) notes, in socialty the self merges into the crowd.

There is something not quite right about Kunda's (1992) discussion of 'Tech'. For example he found that part-time workers emerged from the process more or less unscathed as they had 'minimal selves': they were perceived to be peripheral to the company. So how can organizational boundaries be breached? How can those on the periphery be motivated (or un-demotivated)? Biggart (1988) provides a fascinating account of network DSOs (direct selling organizations; in the UK these used to be called pyramid selling organizations). In the USA network DSOs employed 5% of the total workforce in 1988. In many ways these organizations epitomize the 'part-time marketer' ideal. Biggart (1988) says that they are based on a value rationality (belief in a goal such as 'duty', 'honour', 'the pursuit of beauty') not on economic rationality. As Biggart (1988) notes, almost everything is different about a network DSO. Most employees are women; they have virtually flat structures:

> Distributors see themselves as part of a community sharing common beliefs. Because bureaucratic controls are weak or non existent in DSO's moral controls may serve the important function of mediating competitive relations between distributors.

The moral engine of the network DSO is not hard to find: look at Amway (American Way), at United Sciences of America (United Sciences Inc.). The motivations are religious and patriotic. In the USA people feel bound to the organizations because they value entrepreneurship and the transformative power of products. The crucial aspect of the membership role is that it is more than a job (1988: 108). The people who join are motivated by a sense that they are in control, that they are part of a family or a community. This is no small thing. When approached by MCI to prospect for customers, Amway brought in 800,000, more than Sears and Amex together.

Network DSOs share some things in common with current trends in relationship marketing. Take for example the approach to strangers (customers). Bauman (1993) notes that the stranger is a difficult category of person to deal with, neither friend nor enemy. The bureaucrat deals with strangers through perfecting the arts of 'mis-meeting' – a series of rules for engagement, which help to regulate social distance. The relationship marketing concept seeks to dissolve such boundaries. For example in *Beyond Smiling,* Adelman et al. (1994) talk of the role of the marketer in providing social support which relates directly to the interpersonal context as a means of *going beyond* previously defined acceptable limits for managing interactions with strangers. The authors quote the example of an estate agent who might find day care for the children of a couple during a house move; or who 'assures [an] embarrassed couple that petty bickering is often the outcome of a stressful move'; or who 'introduces newcomers to friends'. The authors go on to discuss the role that service providers (such as hairdressers, bartenders) play as 'quasi-therapeutic' providers.

Bauman, however, is (rightly) suspicious of such therapeutic concerns:

> The cult is no more than a psychological (illusory and anxiety generating) compensation for the loneliness that inevitably envelops the aesthetically oriented subjects of desire; and it is, moreover, self-defeating, as the consequence-proof interpersonality reduced to 'pure relationships' can generate little intimacy and sustains no trustworthy bridges over the sandpit of estrangement. As Christopher Lasch noted a decade and a half ago, 'The cult of personal relations . . . conceals a thoroughgoing disenchantment with personal relations, just as the cult of sensuality implies a repudiation of sensuality in all but its most primitive forms.' (1995: 100)

One can hence view relationship marketing from three standpoints: as a genuinely more moral approach to marketing; as the progressive extension of the code into the last vestiges of free space; or as resurgence of socialty. While not ruling out the former altogether, it is possible to detect instances of both the latter tendencies, neither of which hold out much hope for a more moral approach to marketing.

In any case do people *want* 'relationships'? Murphy et al. (1996) discuss this issue. In their view, if relationship marketing is to fulfil its promise then it must satisfy three conditions: it must be free from coercion between the parties in an exchange; the relationship must be 'genuine' and not a pretence; and finally ethical relationship marketing should possess three distinct virtues – trust, commitment and diligence. Lack of coercion is a key concern. Murphy et al. (1996: 27) insist that to be ethical and true to its philosophy, relationship marketing must be voluntary. The authors ask the question:

> Do large assemblers in industries such as aerospace, automotive and electrical products give their suppliers a choice? This is an ethical question. Similarly, with consumers in the financial services area – what if they prefer to remain with a short-term transactional approach? There is very little evidence that customers want to enter into long-term partnerships and alliances with suppliers.

This question has surfaced on the ELMAR marketing newsgroup, with contributors suggesting that some consumers do not actually want a close relationship.

Concluding thoughts

The core of this chapter focused on the marketing process and the codification of space. In seeking to consider marketing morality the point of departure was Hugo Letiche's discussion of Derrida and Bauman in Chapter 6 in this volume, specifically the distinction which these authors effect between modernist attempts to codify morality and the postmodern condition which Bauman describes as offering the possibility of being able to stand up to chaos (the ambivalent nature of all moral situations). To briefly recapitulate the central themes, both authors differentiate between justice/morality and law/ethics (see also Willmott, Chapter 5 this volume). For Derrida justice is located in deconstruction, the ability to comprehend the language used by the other; to Bauman the recognition of the other as a face is the primary precondition for morality. Each author suggests that institutional developments such as the law and ethical codes are attempts to regulate moral space; as such they act to distance moral actors from the other as singularity (Derrida) or as the face of moral responsibility.

Issues related to the creation of distance were explored with reference to the process of *adiaphorization*, the rendering of the moral subject as some thing which is morally neutral. The traditional marketing process can be described as a process of adiaphorization and this is consistent with Letiche's argument. It is important to say that while this may ring true for many larger business organizations (and for many large social marketing organizations) it is not universal across all organizations, many of which tend to 'muddle through'. Ironically it is through the adoption of a more professional marketing approach that the process becomes adiaphoric. Where I would depart from Letiche is in suggesting that new developments in marketing, such as relationship marketing, represent attempts to *go beyond* the social codification of space in an attempt to solicit the employee's investment of self in the enterprise. This can be described either as an extension of the code into what had previously been regarded as the private space of the self or as an expression of socialty. Either way the outcome for morality is not promising as moral distance is created by cognitive or aesthetic criteria.

Notes

I would like to acknowledge the help of Matthew Higgins, Nikos Tzokas, Andrew Crane and Gavin Jack.

1 This topic has also been addressed by Bauman (1988; 1991; 1993; 1995) and more recently by Tester (1997). In my view there is an explicit link between marketing practices and the evolution of the postmodern identities described by these authors. For example one may talk of marketing processes acting (in concert with others) to disembed identity from previously established contexts for identity formation. Bauman's use of the *mining* analogy is useful here. To Leiss et al. (1990) the establishment of a market economy involves a process of unravelling and recombination, not only of specific things, habitual routines and norms, but also of the integument holding them together, their sense of collective identity. The new consumer society represented a form of freedom – freedom not just to buy the latest commodity but also freedom from the stifling constraints of preordained identities. In the postmodern environment identity is not so much about construction as the avoidance of being pinned down. Notions of 'strolling' and 'play' are positively encouraged in the newer managed marketing environments which have a distinctly 'carnivalesque' tone; shopping malls, leisure parks, interpretive centres, computer games, even the World Wide Web. This 'playfulness' encouraged by these formats echoes Bauman's discussion of socialty.

2 This pragmatic response provides echoes of the earlier movement by the Rochdale Pioneers (subsequently to become the basis for the UK cooperative movement) in seeking to redress inequities in food distribution by providing good measure for what was paid and by ensuring that food was not adulterated (for example by tainting flour with salt and corn with sand).

3 The period of engagement lasted from the late nineteenth century to the end of the 1970s. Recognizing the potential limitations of the market, anti-trust legislation embodied in the Sherman Act was passed in 1890. The creation of the Food and Drug Administration (FDA) in 1906 and the Federal Trade Commission (FTC) in 1914, initiated the state regulation of brands and the monitoring of 'deceptive' advertising. The Wheeler–Lea Amendment to the Federal Trade Commission Act passed in 1938 enlarged the powers of the FTC to prosecute unfair and deceptive trade practices, in particular advertising. During the 1960s the Kennedy administration introduced a number of measures. Bauer and Greyser (1967) refer to President Kennedy's attempt in 1963 to establish the rights of consumers to be informed, to choose, to have safe products, to be heard. Consumer 'rights' referred to include the true interest cost of a loan; the true cost per standard unit of competing brands (unit pricing); the basic ingredients in a product (ingredient labelling); the nutritional quality of foods (nutritional labelling); the freshness of products (open dating); and the prices of gasoline (sign posting rather than pump posting). President Johnson also made a 'consumer message' in 1966 which raised interest in these affairs. Major legislation in the late 1960s included laws relating to consumer protection in the USA: the Labeling Act (1966); the Child Protection Action (1966, amended 1969); the Traffic Safety Act (1966); the Flammable Fabrics Act (1967); the Wholesale Meat Act (1968); the Consumer Credit Protection Act (1968); the Wholesale Poultry Products Act (1968); the Radiation Control for Health and Safety Act (1969).

In 1960, in the US, no state had a consumer affairs office; by 1970 thirty-three did and by 1973 all fifty did. In 1970 the ten most common complaints received were in respect of automobiles, advertising, appliances, credit, non-delivery of merchandise, home improvements, franchise dealers, warranties, guarantees and sales tactics. (Source: Office for Consumer Affairs, State Consumer Action, Summary 71 (Washington DC), US Government Printing Office).

Two important agencies were established in the 1970s: the Consumer Product Safety Commission (CPSC) was empowered to set product safety standards, and the Environmental Protection Agency (EPA) was established to set controls on industry emissions, toxic wastes and car pollution. However during the 1980s the Reagan administration pursued a strong neo-liberal agenda which promoted industry self-regulation. During that period most agencies suffered severe reductions in their budgets, resulting in major cutbacks at the FTC (regulation of advertising) and the EPA. This was followed by a further period of engagement with Bush and Clinton extending agency powers once more (Friedman and Friedman, 1979; Assael, 1995).

4 Stevens (1994: 64) notes that most studies of the use of corporate ethical codes consist of content analyses and fail to discuss or explore how codes are communicated or the extent to which they are used. Stevens's findings support those of Fritzche (1991) and Jones (1991) in reporting that situational ethics is the overwhelming preference for US managers. Further support is provided by Pratt and James (1994) who considered the usefulness of codes for regulating ethical behaviour by advertising practitioners. Respondents were presented with four scenarios: gift giving to a potential client; lying about an update on an account; finally seeking confidential information. Results indicated that practitioners tended to adopt a relativist view (with only 10% endorsing the deontological perspective). Pratt and James however urged that strict adherence to deontological principles could help draw a clear boundary between good and bad practice for practitioners.

References

Adelman, Mara B., Ahuvia, Aaron and Goodwin, Cathy (1994) 'Beyond Smiling: Social Support and Service Quality,' in Roland T. Rust, and Richard L. Oliver (eds), pp. 139–73. *Service Quality: New Directions in Theory and Practice*. London: Sage.

Arnold, Mark J. and Fisher, James E. (1996) 'Counterculture, Criticisms and Crisis: Assessing the Effects of the Sixties on Marketing Thought', *Journal of Macromarketing*, Spring: 118–132.

Assael, Henry (1995) *Consumer Behaviour and Marketing Action*, 5th edn. Cincinnati: South-Western College.

Baudrillard, J. (1968) 'The System of Objects', in Mark Poster (ed.), *Jean Baudrillard: Selected Writings*. Cambridge University Press, 1988.

Baudrillard, J. (1988) 'Consumer Society', in Mark Poster (ed.), *Jean Baudrillard: Selected Writings*. Cambridge University Press, 1988.

Bauer, Raymond A. and Greyser, Stephen A. (1967) The Dialogue that Never Happens. *Harvard Business Review*, November/December: 2, 3, 4, 6, 8, 10, 12, 186, 187.

Bauman, Zygmunt (1988) *Freedom*. Minneapolis, MN: Universtity of Minnesota Press.

Bauman, Zygmunt (1989) *Modernity and the Holocaust*. Cambridge: Polity.

Bauman, Zygmunt (1991) *Modernity and Ambivalence*. Ithaca, NY: Cornell University Press.

Bauman, Zygmunt (1993) *Postmodern Ethics*. Oxford: Blackwell.

Bauman, Zygmunt (1995) *Life in Fragments*. Oxford: Blackwell.

Biggart, Nicole (1988) *Charismatic Capitalism: Direct Selling Organisations in America*. Chicago, IL: University of Chicago Press.

Chonko, Lawrence B. (1995) *Ethical Decision Making in Marketing*. Thousand Oaks, CA: Sage.

Crane, Andrew (1997) 'The Dynamics of Marketing Ethical Products: A Cultural Perspective', *Journal of Marketing Management.*
Deal, Terrence E. and Kennedy, Allan A. (1982) *Corporate Cultures*. Reading, MA: Addison-Wesley.
Drucker, Peter (1969) 'The Shame of Marketing', *Marketing/Communications*, 297 (August): 60–4.
Dwyer, F. Robert, Schurr, Paul H. and Oh, Sejo (1987) 'Developing Buyer–Seller Relationships', *Journal of Marketing*, 51 (April): 11–27.
Entine, Jon (1995) 'Blowing the Whistle on Meaningless Good Intentions', *Chicago Tribune*, 20 June 1996, Section 1.
Entine, Jon (1996a) 'Let Them Eat Brazil Nuts: The "Rainforest Harvest" and Other Myths of Green Marketing', *Dollars and Sense*, March/April: 30–5.
Entine, Jon (1996b) 'A Social and Environmental Audit of The Body Shop, July 1996'. Presented to Joint session of Symposium on Corporate Identity and Marketing Education Group Conference, 8 July, University of Strathclyde, Glasgow, Scotland.
Etzioni, Amitai (1961) *A Comparative Analysis of Complex Organizations*. New York: Free Press.
Ferguson, K. (1984) *The Feminist Case against Bureaucracy*. Philadelphia: Temple University Press.
Friedman, Milton and Friedman, Rose (1979) *Free To Choose.* Harmondsworth: Pelican.
Fritzche, D.J. (1991) 'A Model of Decision Making Incorporating Ethical Values', *Journal of Business Ethics*, 10: 841–52.
Galbraith, John Kenneth (1958) *The Affluent Society*. Harmondsworth: Pelican.
Galbraith, John Kenneth (1967) *The New Industrial State*. Harmondsworth: Pelican.
Gartner, Alan and Riessman, Frank (1974) *The Consumer Society and the Service Vanguard.* New York and London: Harper & Row.
Gerrans, Roy (1996) 'WWF forms Marine Stewardship Council'. http://www.srbnet.org/discussion/hypermail/0146.html, 2 May.
Graham, Gordon (1990) *Living the Good Life: An Introduction to Moral Philosophy*. New York: Paragon.
Grönroos, Christian (1996) 'From Marketing Mix to Relationship Marketing: Towards a Paradigm Shift in Marketing'. Keynote paper. MCB University Press: http:www.mcb.co.uk.
Gummesson, Evert (1988) 'Marketing Organisation in Service Businesses: The Role of the Part-Time Marketer'. Presented at the conference on *Current Issues in Services Research*, Dorset Institute, Poole, 24–25 November.
Hanson, Kirk (1995) 'Think! Act! Change!!: Kirk Hanson Social Report: The Body Shop International Social Evaluation 1995'. http://www-gsb.stanford.edu/khanson.html.
Hirschman, Elizabeth C. (1983) 'Aesthetics, Ideologies and the Limits of the Marketing Concept', *Journal of Marketing*, 47 (Summer): 45–55.
Jones, D. G. Brian and Monieson, David D. (1994) 'Early Developments in the Philosophy of Marketing Thought', *Journal of Marketing,* 54 (January): 102–13.
Kotler, Philip (1972a) 'A Generic Concept of Marketing', *Journal of Marketing*, 36 (April): 46–54.
Kotler, Philip (1972b) 'What Consumerism Means for Marketers', *Harvard Business Review*, May–June: 48–57.
Kotler, Philip and Levy, Sidney J. (1969) 'Broadening the Concept of Marketing', *Journal of Marketing*, 33 (January): 10–15.
Kotler, Philip and Zaltman, Gerald (1971) 'Social Marketing: An Approach to Planned Social Change', *Journal of Marketing*, 35: 3–12.
Krohn, Franklin B. and Milner, Laura M. (1989) 'The AIDS Crisis: Unethical Marketing Leads to Negligent Homicide', *Journal of Business Ethics*, 8: 773–80.

Kunda, Gideon (1992) *Engineering Culture: Control and Commitment in a High-Tech Corporation.* Philadelphia: Temple University Press.
Laczniak, Gene R., Lusch, Robert F. and Murphy, Patrick R. (1979) 'Social Marketing: Its Ethical Dimensions', *Journal of Marketing*, 43 (Spring): 29–36.
Leiss, William (1976) *The Limits of Satisfaction.* Toronto: University of Toronto Press.
Leiss, William, Kline, Stephen and Jhally, Sut (1990) *Social Communication in Advertising: Persons, Products and Images of Well-Being*. London: Routledge.
Levitt, Theodore (1962) *Innovation in Marketing*. London: Macmillan.
McKitterick, J.B. (1957) 'What is the Marketing Concept?', in F. Bass (ed.), *The Frontiers of Marketing Thought in Action*. Chicago, IL: American Marketing Association. pp. 71–82.
McLuhan, Marshall and Fiore, Quentin (1988) *Laws of Media: The New Science*. Toronto: University of Toronto Press.
Murphy, Patrick, E., Wood, Graham and Laczniak, Gewe, R. (1996) 'Relationship Marketing = Ethical Marketing', ESOMAR Publication Series, vol. 204, Research Methodologies for Marketing, November, pp. 21–40.
Nantel, Jacques and Weeks, William A. (1996) 'Marketing Ethics: Is There More to It than a Utilitarian Approach?', *European Journal of Marketing*, 30(5): 9–20.
Peters, Thomas J. and Waterman, Robert H. Jr. (1982) *In Search of Excellence*. New York: Harper & Row.
Pratt, C.B. and James, E.L. (1994) 'Advertising Ethics: "A Contextual Response Based on Classical Advertising Theory"', *Journal of Business Ethics*, 13(6): 455–69.
Rein, I.J., Kotler, P. and Stoller, M. (1987) *High Visibility*. London: Heinemann.
Rotter, J.B. (1967) 'A New Scale for the Management of Trust', *Journal of Personality*, 35: 651–5.
Simon, Herbert A. (1976) *Administrative Behavior*, 3rd edn. New York: Free Press.
Smith, N. Craig (1990) *Morality and the Market: Consumer Pressure for Corporate Accountability*. London, New York: Routledge.
Stevens, Betsy (1994) 'An Analysis of Corporate Ethical Code Studies: Where Do We Go From Here?', *Journal of Business Ethics*, 13: 63–9.
Stidsen, Bert and Schutte, Thomas F. (1972) 'Marketing as a Communication System: The Marketing Concept Revisited', *Journal of Marketing*, 36, October.
Tester, Keith (1997) *Moral Culture*. London: Sage.
Williamson, Judith (1978) *Decoding Advertisements.* New York: Marion Boyars.

9 Ethics and Accounting: the Dual Technologies of Self

Rolland Munro

> Being itself, interpreted as an idea, brings with it a relation to the prototypical, the exemplary, the ought. As being itself becomes fixated as idea, it strives to make good the resulting degradation of being. But by now this is possible only if something is set *above* being, something that being never is yet always *ought* to be. (Heidegger, 1959: 197)

To think about ethics is to take aim at the heart of the present; and the present, for Euro-American societies, is self. As mirror to the soul, ethical discourse confronts self with questions of a continuous 'election'. Are you *sure* you are a member of the group of humans? How can you be certain that these responses are really yours? Could you think *that* for a moment and still feel human, still feel you? Are your desires not more those of the green-eyed monster, someone who is hurt, revengeful, or envious? Or finding yourself *lacking* the passions of jealousy and rage, how can you be sure you are not some cold, calculating sociopath?

I over-generalize. These questions caricature the Euro-American as ultra-reflective, whereas people often 'just go along with' something and 'see where it leads'.[1] Yet there is little doubt that we often feel beset with having to make decisions about ourselves, in a somewhat endless process of working out who we are. So perhaps our questions, and the troubles they carry, usually appear in a more particular and specific form. Am I really enjoying this course on ethics? Do I really want to become an accountant? Am I right to feel hurt? Should I retaliate? Is this an opportunity to get the record straight? Shall I say what I know? And there are other questions to do with our working in organizations. Will I get away with failing to turn up for a meeting? Can I afford to miss another deadline? Can I go on sacrificing my family life for work?

What is this ethics which sets itself up so normatively – and yet so insinuates its questions upon oneself? As John Roberts (1991) has framed the matter: we 'account for the self, to the self'. This is the point on which a contemporary ethics seems to insist: that each of us holds ourselves in judgement, by ourselves. It is not to be left to others to judge – as they will! But is this not a curious form of election that leaves so many rulings to the court of self? In more usual forms, such as the election of a leader, or election to a party, others seem to decide the matter. So there is an odd sort of circularity in this seeking out of evidence – either for or against. How *would* we know? How could we even begin to see 'outside' ourselves? Worse. What if ethics itself is no longer 'outside' self, but has become entirely integral to the very formation of self?

In what follows I suggest how 'the ought' has become split in contemporary society. On the one hand there is our entrapment in the *play of self*, an ethics that carries the minimum moral force of an opinion. And on the other, there is our emplacement today in *language games* like accounting, whose 'procedural fairness' becomes binding on a community by virtue of its prior adoption of their rules. My purpose in stressing this division is less to provide a contrast, all too readily assumed, between ethics and accounting. The aim is rather to stress the complicity that arises out of a subjectivity that becomes so exaggerated as to demand the emplacement of self within technologies of control like accounting – no matter how arbitrary or immoral these 'objectivities' turn out to be.

Ethical imperatives

The essence is its *exercise*. Traditionally, ethics is less about ideals to which we aspire, and much more about the 'regimen' in which we go about conducting ourselves in the world: trying this here; avoiding doing that there, at least for now. Inevitably we reflect upon what has happened and this sometimes leads to the appearance of moral laws, such as the Ten Commandments. Of course. But it is clearly a mistake to go on to think of ethics as reducible to a logical set of rules about how we *should* conduct ourselves; to treat ethics, as Kant does, as a list of categorical imperatives is to engage in an 'abstract universality' (Hegel, 1952: 89) that confuses ethics with morality.[2]

Although some philosophers will insist on treating it so, ethics cannot be abstracted from everyday life into a philosophy of will. But neither should ethics be considered a human science, a discourse of empiricism whose practical observations on people's customs and habits would leave us free, at will, to amend our own conduct. To begin to ask, as Kant did at the formation of the Enlightenment, 'What is Man?' is certainly to urge an anthropological study, as Foucault (1984) suggests. Yet Kant's point is hardly just to urge a study of the practices of the *other*. In contrast, it is to begin to restage the world in a particular way.

Compare, for example, the earlier doctrine of Protagoras that 'man is the measure of all things' (see also Willmott, Chapter 5 in this volume). Of course both positions centre 'man', but they do so in very different ways. In the Greek doctrine, man looked *out* onto the world, and valued things accordingly. In Kant's move, the flow turns the world the other way round. The question 'What is Man?' turns scrutiny *in* on itself. To understand how radical this shift is, we might begin by imagining the Enlightenment as a film audience who no longer go to see Superman, but pay to see Clark Kent movies . . . about an obscure muscleman who disappears into a phone box, reappears dressed in all the glamour of his business suit and glasses and then thrills the audience for the rest of the film by working in an office asking introspective questions. The plot, of course, is already in Hamlet, but today there is a further twist. In an age where we appear to star in our own movies, the question 'What is Man?' seems absurdly general and the answers given by Hamlet in his most famous soliloquy no longer apply. Instead, the question of identity is considered to be a matter of personal choice: you are who you wanna be.

At the time of Kant, however, it was still a novel question and forms a critical break in the post-Newtonian quest for knowledge.[3] Rather than continue to privilege an undefined humankind as *the* standard against which judgements can be made – 'China is very big' and 'Norfolk is very flat' – judgement is being turned by humans back upon themselves. Conduct moves from being seamlessly included in descriptions of how the world 'is' and becomes fractured by the normative interrogation over which *decision* we 'should' make.

The turn inwards is to what Kant calls 'the moral law within'. This is not just, as most commentators have assumed, a move that entails a greater scrutiny of self. It is more that the nature of knowledge is being changed *in order to facilitate* this continual 'scission' of self. The call is no longer a simple injunction: 'Lead the good life!'[4] For it is exactly the classical equation of the 'good life' being the 'examined life' that is disrupted. An equation of the good life with the examined life is stable only when the examining flows outward – questioning the life, not self. It cannot survive the double doubt that is entailed when the self 'examining the life' is undercut by questions that put in doubt the very identity of the would-be examiner. Epistemological doubt looks to be triumphing over ethics. Not that it is time to worry yet.

At the time of the Enlightenment, there were certainties to hand in the form of Kant's (1949a) 'imperatives of duty'. These were to be derived from the one 'categorical imperative':

> Act only according to that maxim by which you can at the same time will that it should become a universal law. (1949a: 80)

In one stroke, Kant slips between the endless arguments over consequences which seek to justify evil acts and the binding custom of community which may perpetuate pain, sorrow and genocide. To be moral, for Kant, is not to follow the law of the herd, or to seek out consequences in order to justify and excuse. It is to do only what one would *will* everyone else to do. Thus, his universal imperative of duty is expressed as follows:

> Act as though the maxim of your action were by your will to become a universal law of nature. (1949a: 80)

Kant believes he has uncovered the rock on which his new epistemological ethics is to be built. Perhaps. But the implications are vast. No longer is knowledge to serve for its own sake. Now knowledge is to be harnessed to *serve* this inward looking ethics.

This is the turn. And it is to see the human – the culmination of the evolution of the species – as specially charged with bringing this teleology of 'accounting for the self to the self' to fruition. The 'practical imperative' is the following:

> Act so you treat humanity, whether in your own person or in that of another, always as an end and never as a means only. (1949a: 87)

These are the principles which he imagines should guide people's conduct. In contrast to 'things', which have only a relative worth as means, rational beings are designated 'persons', because their nature indicates that they are 'ends in themselves' (see also Legge, Chapter 7 in this volume).[5]

The change is fundamental. The change is to begin to ask what *needs* to be changed, so that the world can be made a better place, with less suffering and more happiness. It is as if all the threads that make up life, labour and love are to be redrawn through the eye of a needle. Thus the power of Kant's question is not so much that it asked 'What is Man?', but rather that the question itself asks 'What is moral?' Which, when turned upon self, is not one question, but an endless barrage of further questions. Here is the conundrum. As fast as ethics becomes a matter of *producing* self, it has also become centrally implicated in its own *consumption*. One is always – perversely – making oneself confront the very self that one is making.

In the rest of this chapter, I will try to undo some of this vicious circularity – a conception of ethics that pits self against itself. I will suggest that what is wrong with the analytic tradition is not only that it 'individuates' pitting itself against society. The problem is that a Kantian ethics individuates in a way that encourages us to split knowledge between the primary task of conducting a surveillance of the 'core' self and the secondary matter of knowing others in terms of their 'needs'. But, before developing this theme of decision-making and 'ethical distance', we need to say something about accounting.

Antipathy

Accountancy and ethics appear in a distinct antipathy to each other. The standoff is usually reciprocal. If ethics professors seem too buried in the reverie of armchair examples (cf. Howell, 1997: 8) to ever consider accounting practice, it is also the case that accounting practitioners see their procedures and reports as lying outside the domain of ethics (see also Sorell, Chapter 2, and Parker, Chapter 14 in this volume). The various practices by which financial data are collected, collated and considered are presented as concerned only with 'matters of fact'. Accountancy re-presents itself, variously, as 'technical', 'neutral', and 'value-free'.

This neutrality view, which remains in general circulation,[6] has come under increasing attack. The nub of criticisms against it is that accounting numbers do not simply appear by virtue of their collection and collation; they are *socially constructed*, often creatively so. For example, many critical researchers attribute financial reporting's importance in society to the large number of ways in which accountants are able to bias and manipulate the numbers. In this respect, a series of influential studies, such as Berry et al. (1985), demonstrated, among other matters, the extent to which a 'flexibility' over choice of accountancy procedures was complicit in the closure of UK coal pits. Other studies followed suit, expressing outrage at how arbitrarily defined profit criteria could be used to close so many factories and ruin people's lives. For many, financial accounting has come to represent the destruction of particular working communities. Indeed, the effects of accounting on *organizational* practice are often argued to be insidious more generally. Across all manner of institutions, from the hospital to the school, an increased reliance on accounting numbers is seen to be eroding values across all walks of life, undermining, for example, relations of trust (Armstrong, 1987; Neu, 1991) and feelings of community. Tony Tinker (1988) has suggested that much of the problem of accounting lies in the way in which a marginalist economics has colonized our notions of efficiency. This is undoubtedly so, but there are other matters which affect everyday social practices.

Euro-American concepts of time, which divide up an unknown future from a recordable past, can be likened to driving a car using only the rear-view mirror. But the problem is deeper than that of drawing lines across chronological time, between the future as fantasy and the past as real. For example, the idea of being able to report only on the past synchronizes 'accounts' (the explanations and reasons which we offer each other) with attempts to report historically accurate data. Rather than ask 'what next?', post-war internal reporting practices have tended to direct inquiry backwards into histories of 'what happened?' If this looking 'in' the past for objective explanations – especially when that past has just been constructed – has increasingly appeared futile, then it is little wonder senior managers are adopting a more 'macho' attitude in which reasons for not meeting budgets become dismissed as 'excuses' (Munro, 1995).

Such arguments might be expected to put paid to the neutrality view, which they do – at least among informed views within the academy! Yet the same arguments might have been expected to prove fatal to stories about the rising importance of accounting in society. Unexpectedly, the opposite has occurred. Far from Euro-Americans abandoning the pretence of so-called neutral technologies, and returning to a revitalized ethics which puts people first, accounting has been accorded ever greater status.

Collusion

Accounting, especially within the UK, has become even more central to business and government. In recent years, accountancy has penetrated much of the organizing and the running of the hospital, the school, local government and the civil service. Far from the exposure of accounting as 'socially constructed' leading to its demise, accounting has become revitalized. Ironically, it has become a *socializing* force.

Accounting is now represented as being productive in entirely new ways. As well as enabling 'action at a distance' (Robson, 1992), it is assumed to bring 'discipline' and 'order' to areas like the health service, previously branded (tautologically) as chaotic from its *lack* of accounting procedures and as open to abuse from the push of powerful interests associated with 'medicine'. As McSweeney (1996) captures the difference, the general shift is one of public organizations moving from managers using 'management accounting' (as a support service) to a new hegemony of 'management *by* accounting'. The main legacy from the Thatcher years may come less from her Victorian values, and more from the serendipity of her consort being Dennis Thatcher, someone with an unblinking reliance on running businesses through balance sheets.

In what I have called elsewhere the *centrality* view, accounting has come to be seen not only as disinterested, but as 'offering' objectivity. Two effects can be considered to have been working together here. First, in response to a note of relativism inherent in many understandings about 'social construction', objectivity's time-honoured link with matters of truth has been spirited away. Accounting, like the Mercator system for mapping the globe, or the alphabetic system for writing, is increasingly viewed as a technology of representation, whose main attribute is the social agreement that has sedimented around it over its use. Secondly, an appreciation of accounting being *socially constructing* as well as socially constructed has led to accounting practices, particularly under the influence of the new right, being *invested* with values.

Accounting's objectivity is thus no longer drawn from its spurious connection with the past, but becomes accredited with new qualities, such as 'procedural fairness'. Power, drawing on Porter (1991), captures this vital turn in representation:

> the quantification which enables certain calculative procedures, is legitimized by an objectivity which has less to do with the truth or realism of any metaphysical variety and more to do with an anonymous procedural fairness (1992: 487).

There is more to accounting than its acting as an arbitrary system of scoring. The point is 'everyone faces the same rules on equal terms' (1992: 488). So accounting is even seen as 'democratic' (1992: 487). It is further held to make people more accountable – especially to the customer and shareholder – and this idea is at its most worrying when practices like audit deliver 'our own values', like clarity, back to us (Strathern, 1997).

Accounting is now represented as a 'good thing'. In what follows, I explore a notion of ethics which takes seriously this idea of procedural fairness. For example, procedural fairness implies that there might be organizational spaces that are free from any other ethical involvement. This contrasts with the more radical assumption, implicit in the critical accounting view, that there is no space free of an ethical involvement. Before discussing the 'collapse' of the subject, sufficient to make such a deification of accounting possible, some discussion of the idea of ethical distance is required.

Ethical distance

As other chapters in this book have suggested, Zygmunt Bauman's (1991) analysis of the Holocaust helps explicate a long standing complicity between administrative procedures and analytical ethics. For Bauman, the Holocaust should not be dismissed as an inexplicable, never-to-be-repeated, one-off event. On the contrary, all the conditions of its possibility are already to be found in *social* matters, like well-developed administrative procedures.

Bauman's thesis that the social is the root of evil is somewhat shocking. One problem of social groupings is clearly the creation of categories, such as 'them' and 'us', which inevitably lead to the exclusion of the 'other'. This, of course, is exactly where, against the binds of custom and community, Kant's imperatives would be expected to work. The ethical hero would never do anything that he would not, universally, will others to do. Yet this does not mean evil can be avoided. For in ways that Kant has not anticipated, the effects of the social are to 'emplace' self in ways that will precisely effect evil. But this is to jump ahead.

Bauman's analysis proceeds in terms of effacement, rather than simple exclusion. Consider the Jews. All you are asked to do is compile a list of people in your area who have a Jewish mother or father. Surely there can be no real harm in making such a list and, indeed, there may be possible benefits. Perhaps someone *might* misuse such a list, but this cannot be your fault. The evil lies in the other person and is in their misuse of the list; it is not possible for you to envisage all the consequences of making such a list. Nor would it be possible, or desirable, for you to seek to control the actions of others. What others do is surely up to them?

Consider now the people before you. They are reluctant to get on a train that has been arranged for their travel. Perhaps they are worried about where the train is going and what might happen to them at its destination? But this is not your concern. Yes it is possible that evil persons may try to harm those on the train when they arrive; but, equally, evil people could also try to harm them here and now. And although some people say it is because they are *jews*[7] that they are going on the train, you do not know this for sure. All you have is a list of names, there is nothing in writing about their religion. Your responsibility is surely only to ensure that this list of names matches the list of those who are being put on the train. It is not, again, your part to contest the always contestable reasons why people are grouped together like this, or hypothesize about what others might wish to do in another place, another time. The important thing is to ensure that the whole matter is conducted smoothly so that there is no mistake and so that the next train can run on time.

Then turn to the prisoners. You do not know who brought them here. Or what crimes they may have committed. But surely the fact that they are here is evidence enough? It is not for you to question trial judges. Or believe the prisoners, when they say there was no trial. Of course they protest their innocence, as you lead them to the death chambers. Don't all criminals, especially if they face the consequences of their actions? And if they are so innocent, why now so cowed, so accepting of their fate?

Bauman's idea is that a lack of *response-ability* (see also Latimer, 1998) in society comes from an 'effacement of the face'. Administrative procedures give far more than roles to act out. First, most obviously, procedures give us 'reasons' and 'obligations' that pervert a prior sense of duty. Secondly, responsibility is divided up into different roles in ways that seem to diminish specific attribution.[8] Thirdly, wherever there is a division of labour, the likelihood that each may not know of the other's actions is made all the more probable. Overall, then, procedures not only help us close our eyes to the consequences of our actions, they 'efface' the other. By circumscribing our sense of self to the duties and obligations of a role, they help reduce the other to a knowledge about their needs. In that there is a series of events between act and outcome, an *ethical distance* is created between our actions and our knowledge of their impact on others. In these ways, the 'rationality', on which Kant relies, is made contrary to 'ethicality'.

Ethical distance is the by-product of administrative systems which divide up space in ways that delimit responsibility over what has been made 'near', and free up responsibility from those who have been made 'far'. Thus a concern to make trains run on time can help us to treat people as 'in the way'. Even if you, the reader, feel that it could never have been you who collected the names, is it not possible to see how law-abiding persons might have assisted in helping the right people go on board the right train? (See Willmott's discussion in Chapter 5 in this volume of Stevens's attitude to fascism, for example.) Assuring their victims that, yes, this is certainly the train that corresponds to their name? Or even if you, like Schindler, begin to guess something of the horror, why be so reckless as to reveal your resistance or revulsion to the whole thing? Might you not help more by appearing to 'go along' with it, giving only the names of the old and the already dying, or concealing the young, the brilliant, or the most important?

Bauman's argument, then, is precisely that it is modernity's continuing creation of 'ethical distance' that makes possible the reduction of persons to 'things'. The reduction of persons to things is what facilitates the use of people as means instead of as ends, the very process deplored by Kant's practical imperative, discussed earlier. And yet, it is precisely this creation of ethical distance which makes possible Kant's ethical decision-making. It is important to see that without this condition of 'ethical distance', Kant's project of treating people as 'ends in themselves' would collapse under the infinite number of decisions that would have to be made. The ethical self would founder under the sheer weight of knowledge which it would be necessary to gather, and assess, prior to making each decision.

Complicity

It is the technologies of modernity, such as accounting and its procedures, that make ethical decision-making, *à la* Kant, possible and, for society, durable. Unfortunately, Bauman overlooks this aporia. Instead of pursuing a complicity between deontological ethics and the present failure to 'see' the *consequences* of our acts, Bauman retreats to a primeval myth that serves to fabricate the notion of a 'pure' contact between humans.[9] Response-ability, for him, is to experience *directly* the face of the other. As I now argue (though for different reasons than Letiche, Chapter 6 in this volume), this solution to ethical distance is mistaken. The danger of this myth is its insistence on a separation between humans and technology, social and material. This keeps open a fissure through which technology can be scapegoated whenever things go wrong: on the one side are the humans who are fundamentally 'good' and on the other there is technology which, by increasing ethical distance, becomes fundamentally 'bad'.

These matters are perhaps relevant if we go on to explore a not unusual pretence of a senior manager using the accounting numbers *as* the bosses. 'I'm sorry,' says your manager, 'but we've got to let you go. There is just not enough revenue to support your job.' So perhaps this is one of the occasions in which we might think a reference to the pathetic fallacy would be helpful? We could call the manager's bluff and remind them that it is *them,* not the numbers, who is making the decision. But in so far as this is obvious to the manager, this would likely take us nowhere. We would get an odd look, an agreement that 'Yes, it is *me* that is making the decision' swiftly followed by the point: 'but the numbers leave me with no choice.'[10]

The pathetic fallacy, as I understand it, is the attribution of agency to things; as if institutions or governments had intentions. If so, Mrs Thatcher got it right when she dismissed the idea of society. There is no such thing as society, she is quoted as saying, only individuals (and, she added, families). Silverman (1970) used much the same line when dismissing the notion of systems from organization theory. But it is important to see how *convenient* this separation of humans from technology has become. We blame a proliferation of knives and guns for murders, calling for these dangers to be removed. Or we lay the blame on 'monsters', like Hitler or Frederick West, content that the inhuman will be demonized and locked up before they can do further harm.

Yet, as Althusser (1971) asks, why are we forever lining up behind two sides of an 'antagonism'? Surely, rather than pitch technology against society, the point is to see the different possibilities that lie within various forms of prosthesis. As Prince Philip suggested, in his attempt to forestall the outlawing of guns after Dunblane, a cricket bat can be used to murder. Just so, but this is to overlook how the extensions offered are markedly different. The prosthesis available through a gun over, say, a cricket bat is a difference in the speed, certainty and scale of slaughter. It is as if the scope of technology itself has become so vast that it threatens to overcome a human scale of choice. Such an analysis necessarily calls for ever greater ethical heroics – as witnessed in much of the whistle-blowing literature – to combat the might of technology; a point we will return to below. But this is not the only way forward. Rather than insist, ever more stridently, on an increased responsibility for humans to be ethical, we might begin to understand how ethics works as a technology.

Obviation

Bauman's analysis demonstrates a startling complicity of mundane administrative procedures with everyday human conduct. In his analysis of modernity, people and technology move hand in hand. The machinery produces a systematic effacement of consequences and, in so doing, creates 'ethical distance'. In explaining the creation of distance and spaces of 'unseeing', he helps bring out why more recent administrative procedures, from HRM to TQM, can rightly be called 'technologies of control' (see Legge, Chapter 7 in this volume, for example).

As will now be discussed, much of the workings of society are *excluded* from the machinations of bookkeeping. Owing to the property rights which pertain to them, accountants mainly focus on goods which can be traded and seem 'blind' to the consequences of decisions on other matters. Thus many 'social goods' are excluded altogether. As David Cooper has pointed out: 'Clean air, trust, social harmony, community health and safety do not have market prices. Without a price, their worth tends to be devalued' (1988: 183; for an illustration see Fineman, Chapter 11 in this volume). And while labour *is* traded, it is unusual for property rights over it to be accumulated. The effect is that, unlike other investments, labour is seldom shown as an asset; more typically it is represented as a cost. It is as if financial capital is to be nurtured, but human effort discarded. Or more pointedly, financial risk is rewarded, but the dangers in which people put themselves – of ending up on the scrapheap – are left unrepresented and, hence, appear ignorable.

The main problem here is that a 'procedural fairness' is never fair. There is a pervasive bias in what is sometimes called 'due process', but might be better addressed by what Roy Wagner calls 'obviation'. Obviation is a recursive processual form that is manifested:

> as a series of substitutional metaphors that constitute the plot of a myth (or the form of the ritual), in a dialectical movement that closes when it returns to its beginning point. (1986: xi, quoted by Strathern, 1991: 79)

The effect is to make some matters 'obvious', while others are 'obviated' by being reduced to a taken-for-granted background. For example, socio-legal arrangements for reporting make some matters 'obvious', such as the need to report to shareholders as the 'owners of capital', while other matters, such as employees devoting their lives to an organization, become excluded from view. In this way, attempts to develop a 'human resource accounting', by expanding the transactions base of financial bookkeeping away from its recording of the trading prices of goods, usually founder on the rites and rituals that help preserve the Euro-American fetish for private property.

Equally, in as much as researchers tend to follow suit, these arrangements can often bias the direction of studies about other absences in disclosure, such as the afore-mentioned 'social goods'. For example, David Cooper goes on to question the taken-for-granted nature of Freedman and Jaggi's (1986: 194) contention that 'the main objective of disclosure requirements is to enable investors to make better judgments'. As Cooper goes on to remark:

> What would investors make decisions about that would make corporate pollution information of any relevance? What is the nature of a society where the stock market would be the focus (the dependent variable) for statements about corporate social responsibility behaviors regarding pollution? (1988: 184)

Cooper's analysis here is of interest, particularly since he is stressing, for reasons of justice, the importance of *countervailing* technologies. For Cooper, rather than try to improve corporate accountability through an even greater expansion of accounting disclosure, an (obvious) direction from a European perspective is to strengthen the powers of regulating bodies, such as the courts, or the state.

I am in agreement with Cooper over the importance of institutions but add that the gain is better understood in terms of what Jean-François Lyotard calls a 'multiplicity of justices', each one of which is 'defined in relation to the rules specific to each [language] game' (see Parker, Chapter 14 in this volume). But this alone is not enough. In so far as accounting and the law become complicit, as in the examples above, they form a hegemony of due process. In this case, the existence of many technologies is insufficient to ensure multiple justices. There also has to be:

> a justice 'of multiplicity . . . [which] authorizes the "violence" that accompanies the work of the imagination,' while prohibiting the 'terror' by which a game, a prescriptive system, attempts to impose itself upon the others, to set itself up as the dominant game, thus reducing multiplicity to silence. (Weber, 1985: 102)

One terror today is the ascendancy of accounting: a deification in which the 'procedural fairness' it offers begins to silence what was previously 'obvious' to us as common sense.

This said, it is important to see that another terror may have already taken place. This is our *prior* emplacement within the even more taken-for-granted regime of ethical decision-making. In contrast to Cooper, I suggest that the compelling question is whether, by a process of obviation, we have made it obvious that accounting, the law and the like, are technologies of control, but take a Kantian ethics so much for granted that we forget that it, too, is a technology.[11]

The collapse of the subject

None of this is to suggest that ethics has remained a 'singular justice'. Other matters are afoot. When Kant abandons the world of sense, turning ethics *inwards* on what he calls 'my invisible self', it is no longer an exercise, a regimen that disciplines the body towards leading the good life. In the hands of Kant, ethics becomes instead the ultimate humanist project. And, from this moment on, humanism defines itself primarily by its concern over the realm of 'self-consciousness' as central to conduct.[12] Self-consciousness, for Kant, becomes imagined as a 'conning tower', watching over one's extensions into the world.

> Has not every even fairly honest man sometimes found that he desists from an otherwise harmless lie which would extricate him from a vexing affair or which would even be useful to a beloved and deserving friend simply in order not to have to contemn himself *secretly in his own eyes*? (Kant, 1949b: 194, emphasis added)

This version of self-surveillance, while not yet integrated into Foucault's panopticonism, involves having a conscience from which self must, centrally, direct and survey all we do and say beforehand *in a series of decisions*.

The consequent difficulties for Kant's ethics are twofold. First, Kant is relying upon a Western metaphysics[13] that treats thought as originating *inside* an individual human being, in self-conscious forms such as 'intentions' and 'beliefs', or in unconscious forms such as 'desires' and 'motives'. Secondly, this humanism insists on reason as the ability to think through these things *beforehand*. Thus, it seeks to normalize the 'cells' of thought in ways that are counter, as already indicated, to a more everyday conduct geared to 'go along with' what is happening and 'see where it leads'. But there is a fundamental problem with an analytic tradition that demands that knowledge should come *ahead* of the fact. How could we know what to do, or even know what to know, before we have done something? Further, in making self the final court, the 'singular justice', a decision-making ethics sets up an idea of knowledge *as if* we are 'singular' and act alone, when we do not. This imagined 'aloneness' keeps us busy with a multitude of 'decisions' about who we are – whether we like broccoli or peas – but also makes it necessary to think through the morals of giving fifty pence to the street people instead of to Oxfam; and to make decisions about who we would like to see elected as President of the United States; and who will win the World Cup.

Here is the catch. Self is not only constructed, as Kant anticipated, by a questioning that is preoccupied with self as moral; it creates a self that seems imminently ready to *implode* through its own scrutiny. The joker in the pack is knowledge. To gain knowledge, it is now widely accepted that we need to take up different perspectives and 'positions', many of which appear to be contradictory to the other. But the effect of taking up multiple positions is to destroy the valency of a single self. We can never get sufficient knowledge of self in place *fast enough* to prevent the destabilizing of self that is inherent in the search for (self)knowledge.[14] Yet I do not argue that Kantian ethics has collapsed entirely. For the problem is not that self is nothing; the difficulty is how to understand this perceived multiplicity. In a Kantian ethics, self is not only expected to shadow self. All along the watchtower, the view changes with different knowledges and the 'centre cannot hold'. The result is a massive loss of confidence in subjectivity and an enhanced need for 'objectivity'. Self becomes a shadow of its former, more literal self. The result is a different phenomenology of self: self appears to self as something in which there can be no certainty, no core, no centre, no authenticity. However, as will be discussed, self continues to have its place, even if in order to do so, it is variously 'emplaced'.

Refusing and using the future

During their long reign in UK government, Conservative ministers constantly refused to answer any hypothetical questions. It was like finding oneself pushed on board the train of Britain, but without anyone being prepared to reveal its destination. Likewise, before coming to power, Labour was not about to say what they would do about taxes. This was also deemed to be a hypothetical question! In the context of the preceding discussion on Bauman, I find this creation of distance through time startling. Tomorrow, and the day after tomorrow, belongs to a future in which anything could happen. Of course, in the careful logic of David Hume, the philosophy of the new politicians is correct. There is an infinite gap in reasoning about tomorrow from today; the idea that the future will resemble the past is always fraught with induction. Thus, armed with their undeniable understanding of the limits of deduction, today's manager of the country manages only for today. Tomorrow is not something today's incumbent feels responsible for.

Yet an interest in this 'distancing' of the future is made even more compelling by a comparison with the procedures of moral philosophers. This is because the questioning used in ethical debate, particularly by those who seek a more pragmatic bent than is entailed by Kant's categorical imperatives, is hypothetical in form. Utilitarians, for example, are concerned to evade the 'moral law' proscription against any evil act by applying the rule of the 'greatest good for the greatest number'. Indeed, the line of questioning is often elaborately hypothetical. For instance, what would you do if you were captured by the enemy and if you had a secret that would lead to the loss of many lives if revealed? Please also assume that you have a capsule on you that, if taken, will cause instant death and imagine that you have no family, friends, or relations, etc.[15]

Hypothetical questions, of course, are often traps for the unwary, as a young woman found out after she had agreed to have sex with an old man in exchange for a million pounds. 'Well,' he said brightly as they got off the bus together at his stop, 'having cleared up what sort of person you are, all we are doing now is haggling about the price.' The joke, as a joke, may be tasteless as well as politically incorrect, but the point is not so whimsical. For this is the way that many ethical categories work; if you are in the category for a million pounds, then you're also in for a penny. I will return to the importance of this particular point in a moment, but first I want to clarify differences in the accountability system in which politicians and most managers in business organizations, at the time of writing, are answerable.

While so-called historical accounting numbers were used to calculate profit as if it had been made in the past, accounting numbers are now used more typically for marking out responsibilities for producing the *future*. Specifically, the main board agree a five- and ten-year plan that does little more than distribute a series of numbers over the annual budget periods for the next ten calendar years. This set of figures is then disaggregated into several further sets of numbers, each of which is then allocated to a senior line manager as a personal responsibility. The process of disaggregation is repeated at all stages down the line until each operating manager has been given a profit budget spread over the next ten years for which he or she is responsible.

Following a long discussion in the behavioural accounting literature in the 1960s, the tendency in budget setting came to invert the order of this process, from a top-down imposition of budgets into a bottom-up process of participation. 'Emplacement' is then viewed as a matter of making one's own destiny: once you set your 'own' target, the responsibility for meeting that budget figure belongs to you. Despite coercion often being used to force the budget figures up (whenever aggregate figures fell short of expectations at board level), this notion of people 'owning' the budget has remained. It is important here to draw attention to the 'disciplining' features that stem from this ownership of budgets. For example, when your boss sits there waiting for an explanation as to why you have missed the budget by say £10 million, there's no use turning to your boss, patting their knee and reminding them that the budget figure is just a number that you (but more likely she or he) dreamt up over a year ago.

More recently, in line with the practices of highly successful companies like Johnson and Johnson (Munro, 1997b), the fashion has been to invite 'bids' from operating divisions and then distribute resources accordingly with whoever has offered to make the highest budgeted profit figures. The coercion is more hidden, since it works through 'voluntary' bids. But, of course, the *need* to make a bid is much enhanced. For example if, as an operating manager, your bid is seen as low, then your department may be starved of the very funds that could have made your initial bid possible. To underbid, therefore, is to court disaster; better to overbid and start finding out exactly what it is that you have to do to influence the future. The point about 'emplacement' is that one's participation is always constrained by being caught in ever larger networks of power. Once the idea is abroad that accounting numbers offer a 'procedural fairness', this helps sustain the notion of larger, more compelling contracts in which the 'needs' of shareholders, customers and auditors all begin to dwarf the importance and relevance of your own employment contract. Note, then, how, within this process, people are no longer seen to be some core self, a good old boy whose ill-luck is to have been given a hopeless patch. People are treated in extension. Self is your arrival at a number, on the due date (see also Hoskin, 1996).

This is the point of the earlier story of the old man's proposition. Regardless of whether you miss your budget by a penny or a million pounds, you are open to being called a failure. So, as an operating manager, you had better make that number. And the 'justice' of the system is surely undeniable? Against understandings which let the whim of senior managers run riot, accounting is offering its procedural fairness. Yet this is no longer a concept of fairness that treats everyone the same, or that insists on like cases being treated alike. Instead, it is a circulation of verdicts that allows winners to be winners and losers to lose quickly. Yes, if you can't bid high to gain resources and protect the jobs of your staff, you should give way – and fast – to someone who can.

Sewing technology back into self

According to Hegel (1952: 107–9), the right of individuals to be subjectively destined to freedom is fulfilled when they belong to an actual ethical order. This is because a conviction of their freedom finds its truth in such an objective order, and it is in an ethical order that they are actually in possession of their own essence or their own universality. Hegel argues against the elevation of morals over ethics as follows:

> In an *ethical* community, it is easy to say what man must do, what are the duties he has to fulfil in order to be virtuous: he has simply to follow the well-known and explicit rules of his own situation. Rectitude is the general character which may be demanded of him by law or custom. But from the standpoint of *morality*, rectitude often seems to be something comparatively inferior, something beyond which still higher demands must be made on oneself and others, because the craving to be something special is not satisfied with what is absolute and universal; it finds consciousness of peculiarity only in what is exceptional.

Hegel rejects self as the standpoint of morality, seeing it for the chimera that it is. As he says, when the ethical substantial order has obtained its right, 'the self-will of the individual has vanished together with his private conscience which had claimed independence and opposed itself to ethical substance.'

The point here is not to conflate ethics with community, any more than I would confuse morality with society – which is Parkin's (1985) critique of Durkheim (see also Howell, 1997: 7–8). It is to press Hegel's point about duty in an ethical community being about 'following the well-known and explicit rules *of his own situation*'. Yet, in as much as we never quite know what the rules are, I take ethics to be more about a *mutuality* of conduct within a group. Members work out 'permissions', being careful not to disadvantage another member and taking care not to 'cross' a previous alliance. The point is that ethics is not about making moral decisions *per se*, but rather about working through *situated* relations. I would exactly, for this reason, resist ideas that conduct can be determined by an 'ethical code', such as is published by many professions and organizations today (see Willmott, Chapter 5 in this volume).

In contrast to this emphasis on ethics as mutuality, I take morality to be about the doing of things deemed to be good or evil. So how is it that matters of mutuality can come to be overlooked, even outside the conditions of modernity analysed by Bauman? Marilyn Strathern answers this question, in part, by developing Harrison's (1993) argument that collective ideologies can make people 'morally deaf'. In a most provoking analysis, Strathern (1997) suggests how an *exaggeration* of relations (i.e. asymmetries in mutualities) can lead people to amoral or immoral acts. For example, a wife might be prevailed upon by her kin, through a male or female line, to bring her husband into an open space in which he can be killed by those who seek revenge from an earlier killing. Persons only feel free from belonging to one ethical community (and the bind of custom), by falling prey to an 'exaggeration' of relations by another.

In these terms, a Kantian form of ethics may appear as no more than an exaggeration of relations. Yet far from this exaggeration privileging moral decision-making, *à la* Kant, it is far more likely to privilege its own internal administrative machinery, intended to 'manage' the many facets of self we experience. The effect then would be for the concern for self to instigate its 'own' ethical community, a sense of duty to self that makes us ethically deaf to our duties to others who are near and (should be) dear. If this is so, it may be that it is the very 'right' of the individual to be moral that can lead someone on to commit immoral acts. To be sure this administration of self is not the same as the machinations of modernity that concern Bauman, but in so far as procedures of self help to make the 'invisible self' visible to self, it is no less real.

All this seems problematic enough, but there is more. This is the point at which we can begin to see that it is this same internal machinery that is also making these selves visible and available to others. The question I am opening up, therefore, is not only whether an incitement of self-will appears at the very moment in which we are most caught in a procedural fairness. My concern is that this incitement to be oneself – to go for it – further entraps one in a procedural fairness that is morally deaf.

Discussion

In contrast to freedoms of self assumed by a philosophy of will, the theme of this chapter is that self is 'emplaced' by technology. Or, as Sam Weber (1995) might frame it: self is 'set up' to be 'up-set'. In terms of clarifying the 'set-up', I have explored how a Kantian ethics constructed a decision-making self as master of the world of its own making (and then denied that presence in writing). Kant's ethics is a mythology that creates the world as matters of choice, rather than fact. Then, in terms of explicating the 'up-set', I went on to suggest how accounting came to act as a complement to the knowledge 'needs' of this decision-making self. Indeed, far from accounting erasing ethics, as is popularly assumed, accounting intensifies and *expands* the space of ethical decision-making. This is where self is 'set up' *as if* it could be the final court. But this is only half the story. For in drawing attention to a subsequent 'collapse' of self, I also drew attention to how ethics came to be displaced, in turn, by this complementary technology. The outcome is that the centrality of the decision-making self has itself been 'up-set' in ways that make the 'subjectivity' of self – as flimsy – the main reason for relying more and more on accounting's 'procedural fairness'. The play of self must be subordinate to the rules of the game.

So where now? We should not, it seems, underestimate the capacity of the new technologies to create an ever greater incitement for humans to be vigilant and good – and then exploit these capacities. Equally, it seems vain to suggest we (should) counter the 'monsters' of technology by continued recourse to a humanist ethics. Even if power corrupts, there seems little alternative to creating, in the image of Superman, Batman, Robocop and the Terminator, ethical cyborgs, such as ever increasing numbers of ombudsmen, and watchdog posts, such as the Director of Fair Trading.

This said, we shall go on expecting ethics to resuscitate the 'collapse of the subject', at least in preference to believing that 'only a god could save us'. But perhaps some of this called-for vigilance could be better directed at asking why we have the ethics we do. Self-reflection is not enough. As Marilyn Strathern has decisively remarked, reflexivity never disembedded anyone. If the journey 'outwards' to knowledge is often an endless and unfruitful information gathering, the journey 'inwards' to self simply deepens the embeddedness of consciousness in its decisionist framework.[16]

There is an alternative. Instead of dividing humans off from technology, our ethical impulse could insist on their *inseparability*. Persons appear to cast off their prosthetics at a moment's notice, but this overlooks the condition of possibility for such obviation. Obviation, as has been discussed, is made possible by extension through the prosthetics of another technology. We move, as I have discussed elsewhere, not 'out' from a core self, taking in various materials and devices; and then back 'in' by discarding these materials (Strathern, 1991; Munro, 1996). Instead, we are always in extension. Just as there never is an unmediated 'response' to a face, so too there is no 'core' self. Albeit our form sometimes take on the 'figure' of magnification, and at other times take on that of diminishment, we move nonetheless from one form of extension to another. This is to say that any disposal of persona, role, image or 'projection' is made possible only by means of a simultaneous incorporation of other materials and devices.

As I do not want to abandon notions of self altogether, I do not see any alternative to revitalizing ethics. Even if it can be argued that it is a Kantian construct of self as acting alone – the individual – that helps us ignore the very moments when evil is perpetuated, it is also the individual who is expected to find in herself the good Samaritan. But all this is difficult because the seduction of a humanist ethics is precisely in its making *self* central.[17] What we never like to do, it seems, is recognize our own shifting monstrosity as we move, back and forth, between a technology of ethical decision-making and a technology of procedural fairness. Or from a technology of community, *à la* Hegel, to a technology of will, what Weber (1995) discusses as 'the will to will'.

In-conclusion

Far from accounting eliminating ethics, as some fear, the story can be told differently. The rise in a 'need' for objectivity may be less tied to the rise of science and more precisely traced through a movement from Kant's 'inflation of self' to its present-day 'collapse' in the face of the 'needs' constructed for the shareholder, for the customer, and for the auditor. Self cannot manage its own surveillance and look outward at the same time. Yet the problem is not just the impossible demands a decision-making ethics makes on self. For, by decision-making reducing the other to a calculable set of needs, modernity's creation of ethical distance also rescues much of this particular dilemma. It is more that the very nature of knowledge – once invested in serving the ethical self – changes in ways that bring about its collapse. While information merely circulates to leave us unchanged, *knowledge* can only be acquired by adopting different positions and perspectives and it is this multiplicity, augmented today by a cultural relativism, that turns self into a chimera of shifting shadows. So that knowledge, then, must eventually desert self as too flimsy, too corrupt. Yet the story does not end there. For if knowledge is no longer to serve self, as Kant imagined, what then should it serve?

The answer, it seems, is a procedural fairness, such as is now offered by accounting. Far from eliminating ethics, it is accounting that is making ethics, with all its technology of decisions and choices, durable. Yet, once a 'procedural fairness' is in place, knowledge no longer matters in quite the same way. It is the *carriers* of knowledge that are to serve; and in ways that fix self to the circuits of information and help keep these in place (Munro, in press). This raises Heidegger's (1977) arguments about technology and 'emplacement' and the complexities of understanding a 'set-up' (Weber, 1995) which emplaces us within a *dual* arrangement of technologies of self. For it appears that neither ethics nor accounting can carry society alone.

Each of us must align ourselves with the numbers and, simultaneously, make a presentation of self *as* ethical. As I understand it, in a process of *double* obviation, we try to have things both ways. One moment we cut a figure of ourselves as 'ethical', forgetting due process. The next moment we insist on the figures of accounting and the like in an appeal 'not to shift the goal-posts'.[18]

The issue, I suggest, is one of understanding self as *always* extended by technology. We are always 'in' technology. We move back and forth between one 'set-up' and the other. This is the point about technology; there is no exit. Indeed, extension is all that we are ever 'in'. Even when we retreat to self and go 'in', all we may be doing, perhaps, is shifting to other, perhaps older and more familiar, forms of extension, such as meditation. For once language is recognized for what it is – an ancient and highly integrated technology in which thought and expression move together – rather than being seen merely as a dulled echo of self-consciousness, then it turns out that forms of self that are *minus technology* are a null set.[19]

Given this 'emplacement' of self within the circuits of information, there is little point in trying to shift the burden of ethical responsibility from the solipsistic world of one's mind to a mimetic response to another's face, as Bauman would have it. Or arguing for a switch to a more dialogical ethics of 'I' and 'thou', as espoused by Martin Buber. What is important to see is that these are not options as long as we (and how can we not?) continue a decisionist image of self making its ethical choices. And yet we should not despair, but rather seek to weaken this sense of weakness. For example, it is possible to recognize that a decisionist ethics which presses our questions inwards to the infinite realm of the 'invisible self' also has the unintended consequence of reducing self to voice – the soundbox of presence. So it is hardly surprising when I ask myself what I am doing for the world, that – in the face of Bosnia or Ireland – I seem to be doing so little. In this interpellated state, we are not only clearly helpless; we are also condemning ourselves to an unwitting impotence. In hailing others with voice alone, we effectively stand back calling on others to act.

To the extent that we are already 'emplaced', the sort of ethics we have is hardly a matter of personal choice. If this is so, the called-for vigilance over moral acts might pay attention to the different ways in which philosophers have constructed ethics as a technology of self. For example, we might examine how much a surveillance inherent in ethical decision-making has framed the dressage of 'face' (see also Goffman, 1955). Or we might begin to ask how it is that accountability is no longer 'outside', a matter of duty and obligation, or of good conduct in a dialogue between the 'I' and 'thou', but has become a matter, as well, of our endlessly having to render 'decision-making' transparent. And ask, too, how this transparency has become associated with devices, like minutes of meetings, that place decisions on permanent record. These questions may help us understand how the seductions of a philosophy of will has led, circuitously through ethics, to a procedural fairness that enshrines today's demand for the 'will to will'.

Notes

1 The definitive text here on methods and procedures of everyday life is Harold Garfinkel's (1967) study of jurors. Garfinkel's findings suggest that persons do not abandon their habitual rules for making social judgements when they become jurors. Rather, when offered new rules for making decisions, they 'just go along with' these, as a modification, to 'see where it leads'. To Garfinkel, this opens up the possibility that, 'in everyday situations', the person 'defines *retrospectively* the decisions that have been made' (1967: 113–14, emphasis added). His emphasis, that the *outcome comes before the decision*, contrasts with the 'usual emphasis in studies of decision making' where persons are supposed 'to know beforehand the conditions under which they will elect any one of a set of alternative courses of action, and that they correct their previous elections on the way through the action as additional information turns up' (1967: 113).

2 In Signe Howell's (1997: 2) view, 'there are few useful definitions of morals, morality or ethics', but she does draw attention to Edel and Edel's (1959: 7) distinction between 'ethics narrow', which pushes to the fore the idea of *obligation* or *duty*, and 'ethics wide', which assumes that moralities are part of the whole field of human endeavour. The latter is about 'values' which Edel and Edel see as 'far too broad, far too promiscuous'.

3 Kant's (1949b: 259) division is between 'the unbounded magnitude' of the 'starry heavens above' and the 'true infinity' that 'begins from my invisible self'. Since there were earlier links between the life course and the course of the stars, differences between this version of the subject/object divide and Kant's require further comment. One version of the Renaissance is a rediscovery of Greek thought and values; thus Michelangelo's statue of David embodies the optimism encapsulated in the doctrine 'man is the measure of all things'. However, the break between the Enlightenment and the Renaissance (see also Foucault, 1970) is not formed merely by Kant's division making an elision of the lifeworld, and its heroes. The break comes as much from his having made impossible any link between the 'starry heavens above' and the 'invisible self', for these are ruled quite differently. In proportion to the celestial order being ruled by gravity, Kant's (1949b: 259) ambition is to find the 'moral law within' that will make 'a life independent of all animality and even of the whole world of sense'.

4 Ahead of Kant, David Hume has already thrown the spanner in the works by pointing to the epistemological gap between habit and reason (see also Anthony, Chapter 13 in this volume). Thus a new question has appeared, one in which we will always be left asking: 'How do we *know* how to lead the good life?' Not surely just from mere custom or habit! In the Age of Reason there has to be more.

5 To know the categorical imperative, then, is to seem to be in possession of firm principles by which each can judge our acts. Once in possession of the categories, it seems possible to engage in a deferral over questions about the destiny of mankind, or where we are going as a society. But this deferral is only possible by an intensification in each of us asking questions about *what I am doing*. It is for Kant (1949b: 259) to ask questions about the nature of the *teleos,* what he calls 'the moral law'; and, having solved this, to leave to each to decide 'the purposive destination assigned to my existence by this law'. Thus, it is no longer possible to see knowledge as an end in itself, a matter of aesthetics, curiosity, or learning. It is more a matter of seeing knowledge, instrumentally, as beginning to serve a higher purpose: the formation of the good self, which for Kant is identical to the formation of the good will.

6 A condition of possibility for the neutrality view is a culturally received wisdom that sees facts and values as distinct. While the fact/value divide is attributed to David Hume, this traditional reading owes much to Kant. Recent scholarship, rather than see Hume's philosophy culminating in his famous 'logical gaps', such as the 'is' and the 'ought', puts a stress on his view that man is a 'social animal'.

7 Lyotard (1990) uses the term 'jews' to cover any discriminated group subject to

genocide or other atrocities, including events in Bosnia. Bauman's analysis is intended to be generally applicable and, as people seek to clean up their own backyard of impurities, 'cleansing' operations extend into academic life. For example, it is sad and ironic to think of how sociology, having survived attempts to eradicate the Marxists during the Thatcher years, is now conducting its own purge of postmodernists.

8 This property, when used carefully, can have positive effects. For example, the division of keys to banks vaults, or code numbers to computer files, between two or three different officers can look like examples of a lack of trust, but such devices have the benefit of protecting people by *reducing* suspicion.

9 In Bauman's view, violence is made possible by an 'effacement' of the other's face. As we have seen, effacement is made normal and mundane, either by categories that exclude persons from the group of humans, or by devices that obscure from view the consequences of one's acts. Thus, moving back to a mythical, pre-technological age Bauman seeks to recover a *proximity* that withdraws us from the dangers of technology. Drawing on the existential philosopher Emmanuel Levinas, Bauman insists on the ethical impulse as stemming solely from an 'unmediated' response (see Letiche, Chapter 6, and Willmott, Chapter 5 in this volume).

10 You could go on a bit here. For example, you could say: 'So it's the *numbers* then that are making the decision.' To which they could only agree, because that's what they said in the first place. Any further move by you to go on and insist that they were committing the pathetic fallacy would likely produce frustration at your inability to understand (more proof of how lucky they are to be getting rid of you) and an assurance that the manager is taking 'full responsibility for the decision'.

11 This obviation allows a decision-making ethics to insinuate itself as a 'singular justice', one that 'sees to it that singularity itself is respected in its irreducible multiplicity' (Weber, 1985: 102). While this has desirable aspects, it allows *ethics* to set itself up unquestioningly as the 'set-up' (cf. Weber, 1995). My concern, then, is less with a complicity between technologies, such as accounting, the law, and the legisature. These pale before the collusion that becomes *necessary* between a 'subjective' ethics, centred on self, and 'objective' reporting systems, which seek consensual material for scoring their games.

12 Conscience might be regarded as a kind of sieve of experience that tempers our worst excesses. But in Kant's emphasis on self-consciousness, the focus is on a *knowing* self, one in which reason can prevent outbreaks of animal behaviour beforehand. In contrast to his feelings of annihilation when he contemplates the 'starry heavens above', Kant suggests how the 'moral law within me . . . infinitely raises my worth as that of an intelligence by my personality, in which the moral law reveals a life independent of all animality' (1949b: 259). Where self-consciousness is equated with reason and unconsciousness is equated with animal behaviour, humanism is prefigured in terms of a 'consciousness-raising' programme; which, through education and the like, expects results in the form of an elimination of greed, envy, malice and lust.

13 Anita Jacobson-Widding defines conscience as 'an inner sense of individual responsibility for what one does to other people' (1997: 50). As she adds: 'This notion, in turn, presupposes the idea of the individual as a single, moral unit, with an autonomous psychic structure. Such a view of the person is, according to Geertz, "a rather peculiar idea within the context of world cultures".' She expresses the view of many anthropologists when she goes on to add that 'socio-centric conceptions of personhood seem to dominate in non-Western cultures'. One purpose of the present chapter is to help illuminate the extent to which the philosophy of Kant, with others, has helped formulate ethics into a technology of self (see also Foucault, 1988).

14 Lyotard, in conversation with Thebaud, remarks that a 'philosophy of the will cannot be passed, as such, for a political philosophy. It does not work' (1985: 90). Weber comments that it does not work 'because, in a way, it works too well – goes too fast' (1985: 101). Thebaud dismisses a philosophy of will as American, which is both accurate and odd, given its Kantian and Nietzschean roots. Lyotard's reply that it is

a 'politics of capital' is nearer the mark, but only once the collusion of analytical ethics and financial reporting practices are appreciated. It is the *combination* of the will to will and modern accounting practices that makes a philosophy of will seem American in origin (Munro, 1997b).

15 It is worth making reference here to Rae Langton's (1992) paper on letters between Kant and Maria von Herbert. Briefly, von Herbert has, belatedly, followed Kant's advice in his books over always telling the truth to the terrible detriment of her life, and she is now writing to him to request that he rethink his proscription over suicide. In his unthinking refusal and belittling comments, it is difficult to see Kant as other than insular, shabby and chauvinist in this affair.

16 The fact/value division is prefigured by a subject/object divide. Decisions taken in proximity to consciousness as the seat of values are also based on facts gathered from the world where they have been objectively assessed. My analysis echoes aspects of Heidegger's (1959) discussion on 'Being and the Ought'. Since Kant had situated in nature what Heidegger calls 'beings', Kant opposed the categorical imperative to nature, while seeing both as determined by reason and as reason. Yet as the priority passed to 'beings' in the nineteenth century, the ought was endangered in its role as standard and criterion. Heidegger continues: 'The ought was compelled to bolster up its claim by seeking its ground in itself. The moral claim had to present its own justification. Obligation, the ought, could emanate only from something which in itself raised a moral claim, which had an intrinsic *value,* which was itself a *value*.' (1959: 198). With value being its own value, it is not only the fact/value division that is made complete, it is the subject/object division which is re-emphasized. In the next few paragraphs Heidegger is at his most scathing, suggesting that, with the 'being of values', a 'maximum of confusion and uprootedness was achieved'. As he points out, however, even Nietzsche remained entangled within this perspective.

17 The humanist assumption that agency is *primed* by consciousness, what Derrida (1982) critiques as 'presence', should therefore not be confused, as Latour (1993) does, with the tendency by Euro-Americans to *attribute* agency solely to other humans. Both positions play down the importance of the object world, but they do so for very different reasons. For example, Heidegger (1959; 1962) has systematically deconstructed Western metaphysics as rooted in epistemologies that insist on a subject/object divide, while asymmetries over agency attribution suggest 'accountability' conventions that are deeply embedded with retributive systems of justice.

18 The story that the 'numbers do not work' is a mystical one, and each time this news is 'broken' afresh to one of its victims, it should be delivered by the 'good' person who can doublespeak the ethical care. Procedural fairness walks hand in hand with those incorruptibles who are incontrovertibly held to be looking after the larger good.

19 An examination of any specific 'incorporation' would entail, for example, not only greater recognition of the enabling aspects of technology, but a considerable expansion in particular materials and devices to be included in the sociology of accounts (see Munro, 1997a).

References

Althusser, L. (1971) 'Ideology and Ideological State Apparatuses', in *Lenin and Philosophy and Other Essays*. London: New Left Books. pp. 121–86.

Armstrong, P. (1987) 'The Rise of Accounting Controls in British Capitalist Enterprises', *Accounting, Organizations and Society,* 11: 415–36.

Bauman, Z. (1991) 'The Social Manipulation of Morality: Moralizing Actors, Adiophorizing Action', *Theory, Culture and Society*, 8(1): 137–51.

Berry, A.J., Capps, T., Cooper, D., Ferguson, P., Hopper, T. and Lowe, R.A. (1985) 'Management Control in an Area of the NCB: Rationales of Accounting Practices in a Public Enterprise', *Accounting, Organization and Society*, 10: 3–28.

Cooper, D.J. (1988) 'A Social Analysis of Corporate Pollution Disclosures: A Comment', *Advances in Public Interest Accounting*, 2: 179–86.

Derrida, J. (1982) *Margins of Philosophy*, trans. A. Bass. Hemel Hempstead: Harvester.

Edel, M. and Edel, A. (1959) *Anthropology and Ethics*. Springfield, IL: Charles C. Thomas.

Foucault, M. (1970) *The Order of Things: An Archaeology of the Human Sciences.* London: Tavistock.

Foucault, M. (1984) 'What is Enlightenment?' in P. Rabinow (ed.) *The Foucault Reader*. Harmondsworth: Penguin.

Foucault, M. (1988) 'Technologies of the Self', in H.M. Luther, G. Huck and P.H. Hutton (eds), *Technologies of the Self.* London: Tavistock. pp. 16–49.

Freedman, M. and Jaggi, B. (1986) 'An Analysis of the Impact of Corporate Pollution Disclosures Included in Annual Financial Statements on Investors' Decisions', in B. Merino and T. Tinker (eds), *Advances in Public Interest Accounting*, Vol. 1. Greenwich, CT: JAI Press. pp. 193–212.

Garfinkel, H. (1967) *Studies in Ethnomethodology*. Englewood Cliffs, NJ: Prentice-Hall.

Goffman, F. (1955) 'On Face Work: An Analysis of Ritual Elements in Social Interaction', *Psychiatry*, 18: 213–31.

Harrison, S. (1993) *The Mask of War: Violence, Ritual, and the Self in Melanesia.* Manchester: Manchester University Press.

Heidegger, M. (1959) *An Introduction to Metaphysics*, trans. R Mannheim. New Haven, CT: Yale University Press.

Heidegger, M. (1962) *Being and Time,* trans. J. McQuarrie and E. Robinson. London: SCM Press.

Heidegger, M. (1977) *The Question Concerning Technology and Other Essays*, trans. W. Lovitt. New York: Harper and Row

Hegel, G.W.F. (1952) *The Philosophy of Right* (1821), trans. T.M. Knox. Clarendon Press: Oxford.

Hoskin, K. (1996) 'The "Awful Idea of Accountability": Inscribing People into the Measurement of Objects', in R. Munro and J. Mouritsen (eds) *Accountability: Power, Ethos and the Technologies of Managing.* London: Thomson.

Howell, S. (1997) 'Introduction', in S. Howell (ed.), *The Ethnography of Moralities.* London: Routledge. pp. 1–22.

Jacobson-Widding, A. (1997) '"I Lied, I Farted, I Stole . . .": Dignity and Morality in African Discourses on Personhood', in S. Howell (ed.), *The Ethnography of Moralities*. London: Routledge. pp. 48–73.

Kant, I. (1949a) *The Foundations of the Metaphysics of Morals* (1785), in *The Philosophy of Immanuel Kant*, iv, trans. L.W. Beck. Chicago: University of Chicago Press.

Kant, I. (1949b) *Critique of Practical Reason and Other Writings in Moral Philosophy* (1788), in *The Philosophy of Immanuel Kant*, iv, trans. L.W. Beck. Chicago: University of Chicago Press.

Langton, R. (1992) 'Duty and Desolation', *Philosophy*, 67.

Latimer, J. (1998) 'The Dark at the Bottom of the Stair: Participation and Performance of Older People in Hospital', *Medical Anthropology Quarterly*.

Latour, B. (1993) *We Have Never Been Modern*, trans. C. Porter. London: Harvester.

Lyotard, J.-F. (1990) *Heidegger and the Jews*, trans. A. Michel and M. Roberts. Minneapolis, MN: University of Minnesota Press.

Lyotard, J.-F. and Thebaud, J.-L. (1985) *Just Gaming*. Minneapolis, MN: University of Minnesota Press.

McSweeney (1996) 'The Arrival of an Accountability', in R. Munro and J. Mouritsen (eds), *Accountability: Power, Ethos and the Technologies of Managing.* London: International Thomson.

Munro, R. (1995) 'Governing the New Province of Quality: Autonomy, Accounting and the Dissemination of Accountability', in H. Willmott and A. Wilkinson (eds), *Making Quality Critical.* London: Routledge. pp. 127–55.

Munro, R. (1996) 'The Consumption View of Self: Extension, Exchange and Identity', in S. Edgell, K. Hetherington and A. Warde (eds) *Consumption Matters: The Production and Experience of Consumption.* Sociological Review Monograph. Oxford: Blackwell. pp. 248–73.

Munro, R. (1997a) 'Power, Conduct and Accountability: Re-distributing Discretion and the Technologies of Managing'. *Proceedings of the 5th Interdisciplinary Perspectives on Accounting.* Manchester: University of Manchester. pp. 4.2.2–10.

Munro, R. (1997b) 'After Reality: Rubbing the Talk Up Against the Numbers'. *Proceedings of the AOS Conference on Accounting, Time and Space,* ed. H.K. Rasmussen, Copenhagen Business School. Vol. 2, pp. 509–38.

Munro, R. (in press) 'After Knowledge: The Language of Information', in S. Linstead and R. Weston (eds), *The Language of Organization.* London: Sage.

Neu, D., (1991) 'Trust, Contracting and the Prospectus Process', *Accounting, Organizations and Society*, 16: 243–56.

Parkin, D. (1985) 'Introduction', in D. Parkin (ed.) *The Anthropology of Evil.* Oxford: Blackwell.

Power, M. (1992) 'After Calculation? Reflections on *Critique of Economic Reason* by Andre Gorz', *Accounting, Organizations and Society,* 17: 477–99.

Porter, T. M. (1991) 'Objectivity as Standardization: The Rhetoric of Impersonality in Measurement, Statistics and Cost–Benefit Analysis', *Annals of Scholarship*, 8.

Roberts, J. (1991) 'The Possibilities of Accountability', *Accounting, Organizations and Society,* 16: 355–68.

Robson, K. (1992) 'Accounting Numbers as "Inscription": Action at a Distance and the Development of Accounting', *Accounting, Organizations and Society,* 17: 685–708.

Silverman, D. (1970) *Theory of Organizations.* London: Heinemann.

Strathern, M. (1991) *Partial Connections.* Maryland: Rowman & Little.

Strathern, M. (1997) '"Improving Ratings": Audit in the British University System', *European Review*, 5(3): 305–21.

Tinker, T. (1988) 'Waiving Goodbye to the TWA Bus: "Paper Prophets" and the Sraffian Critique of Marginalism', *Advances in Public Interest Accounting*, 2: 121–41.

Wagner, R. (1986) *Symbols That Stand for Themselves*. Chicago: University of Chicago Press.

Weber, S. (1985) 'Afterword', In J.-F. Lyotard and J.-L. Thebaud (eds), *Just Gaming*. Minneapolis, MN: University of Minnesota Press.

Weber, S. (1995) *Mass Mediauras: Form, Technics, Media*. Stanford, CA: Stanford University Press.

10 Governance and Regulation: an Institutionalist Approach to Ethics and Organizations

Glenn Morgan

The dominant approach to business ethics has been shaped by its attempt to confront and challenge a particular view of organizations and management. Where it is assumed that there are certain invariant relationships between 'objective characteristics' of the business world – for example between technology and structure or between efficiency, output and economic performance – a technicist view of how organizations work is the inevitable outcome. As Alvesson and Willmott state:

> Representing management as a predominantly technical activity creates an illusion of neutrality. Management theory is sanitized and management practice is seemingly distanced from the structures of power and interest that, inescapably, are a condition and consequence of its emergence and development. (1996: 12)

In this technicist view, there is an expectation that 'scientific', positive knowledge can be generated which can offer management prescribed ways of acting in particular contexts; these prescriptions constitute a rational response to contingent circumstances.

What the discourse of business ethics tries to insert into the contingency theory view of management and organizations is the idea that there is a moral and ethical dimension to the management decision-making process. This can be achieved in two ways. First, it can be argued that even within the contingency framework, 'strategic choices' are exercised by management; that is, there is a 'loose coupling' between organization structures, economic environments and performance outcomes. As a result, alternative strategies can be followed with varying outcomes. Therefore, moral and ethical issues can be placed into the basic contingency framework without necessarily endangering organizational survival. This leads to the second approach which is to argue that there are potentially positive performance outcomes to including moral and ethical issues. Thus such arguments are usually accompanied by the claim that ethical business makes for good business practice because in the short term, if properly marketed, it brings valuable publicity and new customers, as well as improved motivation and morale amongst the workforce. Moreover, in the long term, it places ethical organizations ahead of others in what is expected to be an inevitable 'moralization' of business as customers, governments and workers increasingly recognize the necessity for ethical input to business decisions. In these arguments, organizations are essentially technical constructions; issues of ethics and morality have to be inserted from outside. The question for the proponents of business ethics is therefore primarily how to get managers to listen to and take seriously their arguments about the need for a moral dimension in decision-making. Within the space so constructed, it is then possible to debate philosophical questions about the appropriate means for deciding moral questions, for example Kantianism or utilitarianism or other more recent theories such as that of Rawls (see the discussions in Sorell, Chapter 2, and Legge, Chapter 7 in this volume).

For most researchers who identify themselves with a 'critical approach to organizations' (leaving aside for the moment the many different variants of this approach), this view of business ethics is frustratingly narrow. Indeed, one response to the whole 'business ethics' field is simply to reject it as a non-issue. This approach can be caricatured in the following way. If organizations are social rather than technical constructions and their conditions of production and reproduction emerge out of processes of social conflict and power relations, then there is little point in debating their ethics. Cooperating in debates couched in the framework of business ethics is simply colluding in the maintenance of an unequal system. It is treating the symptom, the moral dilemma and not the cause, which is the structure of society itself. Clearly such a view does not exempt its proponents from issues of morality and ethics 'in the long term' since it implies a society which can be governed in a 'just' way, free from these dilemmas, though the reality is that very little attention is paid to the economic and social structure of such a 'just' society in comparison with the critique of capitalism (or patriarchy). This negative approach to the field of business ethics has led to its sidelining within the ranks of those committed to a critical view of organizations (as can be instanced by the uniqueness of this particular volume). Whilst there is no shortage of analyses of power, conflict, class, gender and race in organizations, it is rare that analysts make explicit their own moral position, rather than leaving it implicit within the critique which they have mounted (though see Alvesson and Willmott, 1996 which does try to make the link explicitly).

What sorts of interventions can be made into the field of business ethics from a critical point of view? In this chapter, I argue that the first step in such a process of intervention must necessarily be the recognition that organizations cannot be conceived in technicist, amoral terms. On the contrary, organizations are arenas within which moral debates and arguments are central; there is a great amount of 'common-sense' moralizing that occurs all the time within organizations. To treat organizations as a technical sphere where ethical codes must be introduced from the outside is to ignore the inherently moral nature of organizations and management. The second point in my argument is that when we examine organizations across time and across different locations, we can observe that the result is a complex variety of structures and forms which reflect how different groups have resolved moral dilemmas. From these two points, I conclude that the creation of a separate sphere or discourse of 'business ethics' is doomed to self-destruction if it does not seriously link to the constitution of organizations as social and moral institutions. In effect, we need a much more nuanced appreciation of organizations as moral arenas – whether that is derived from the sort of ethnographic fieldwork illustrated in the contributions by Watson (Chapter 12) and Fineman (Chapter 11) to this volume, or the more historical and comparative approach advocated in this chapter, or indeed in the more aggressively anti-modernist tone that Burrell employs to illustrate the nature of (and need for) 'retro-organization theory' (1997: 52). As Anthony states in his contribution to this book (Chapter 13):

> We should postpone the promulgation of advice for the improvement of managerial morals while we engage more effectively in the study of their practice . . . [which will show] that managers are in fact constantly engaged in a political process that requires the exercise of moral judgement.

The question can however be justifiably asked as to where does this sort of 'descriptive' commentary on ethics take us? What judgements are we finally making about the nature of morality and ethics? Have we simply reproduced the variety of the organizational world within our text so that whilst this may claim to be superior (judged from the point of view of 'completeness') to the one-sided accounts of the technicists, it provides no means of discriminating between the various 'local moralities'? It is therefore an ultimately futile activity from the point of view of ethics (if not from the point of view of a sociological account of organizations and their functioning). In the conclusion to the chapter, I tentatively argue that the institutionalist approach does lead to particular moral positions as can be seen when the discussion is linked to Bauman's notion of postmodern ethics.

Institutionalist theory and social values

Organizations and the fields within which they compete, cooperate and are regulated are governed by particular rules of action. These rules of action can be conceived of as ways in which social values and ethical choices are institutionalized, i.e. become the conditions for the production and reproduction of social order within particular contexts. Central to many of these systems of rules are issues concerned with the nature of property and how property can be bought and sold on markets. What is it morally acceptable to buy and sell and on what terms? What rights are granted to property owners, in particular over other human beings (both as direct subordination within the labour force, and indirectly in terms of the impact of economic activities on the wider social context)? What rights do citizens and communities have which override market considerations? Resolutions of these issues vary across time and across different societies. In an era when the 'end of history' has been proclaimed and the victory of capitalism celebrated, it is crucial to provide a corrective account. Issues of property and the market lie at the heart of many debates which arise within business ethics and yet there is a lack of recognition of the historical and comparative variation in forms of property and markets and what this means in terms of the values and moral codes which have been constructed in particular contexts.

In order to develop my argument, I draw heavily on institutionalist theories of organizations. Institutionalist theory has enjoyed a revival within the social sciences over the last decade. It is not the intention here to provide an evaluation of the different groupings within institutionalism, economic and sociological, old and new (see the reviews by Ingham, 1996a and 1996b, for an evaluation and assessment of some of the different strands; also the collection by Smelser and Swedberg, 1994); nor is it my intention to provide an account of the epistemological and ontological status of institutionalism. Within this chapter, I use this as a perspective which offers a way of looking at the world; in doing so, I also explicitly make links to other theoretical traditions in the belief that this is useful to stimulating ideas at this early stage in the development of these debates.

The essential element in institutionalism of concern here is the way in which it reveals that economic relations are embedded in social institutions. There have to be rules which ensure that certain activities can be conducted and legally defended in the event of disputes. These rules define the legal subjects which can own and dispose of properties and the terms on which such dispositions can be made. Ownership of property does not confer absolute rights. It is constructed in a social setting which defines what is acceptable and what is not. Ingham refers to this as the 'widely accepted Durkheimian proposition that markets require a "moral" – that is normative – infrastructure that specifies the procedural and substantive rules of exchange' (Ingham, 1996a: 270; see also North, 1990; 1991).

Fligstein (1996) distinguishes four aspects to the institutionalization of rules concerning property, markets and how these work. These four aspects are described as follows:

> *Property rights* 'are social relations that define who has claims on the profits of firms'.
> *Governance structures* 'refer to the general rules in society that define relations of competition, cooperation and market specific definitions of how firms should be organized'.
> *Conceptions of control* 'refer to understandings that structure perceptions of how a market works and that allow actors to interpret their world and act to control situations'.
> *Rules of exchange* 'define who can transact with whom and the conditions under which transactions are carried out' (1996: 658).

In the next section I wish to take each of these aspects in turn and suggest that, by examining them in detail, it becomes possible to identify the range of ethical positions which have become embedded in organizations and markets. Rather than taking for granted the dominance of certain principles, particularly those of private property and markets, it can be seen that debates about the nature of property, ethics and values have been endemic in industrial societies and societies in transition to industrialization. In this respect, the institutionalist approach 'relativizes' existing institutions but it particularly undermines the notion of certain natural and dominant economic relations expressed in terms of private property and markets.

Property rights

Fligstein tends to assume a certain definition of property rights – one in which rights of ownership give the individual the right to a share in 'profit'. However, property rights and the benefits accruing from them are historically and comparatively much more variable than the ideal type of alienable individual capitalist property which seems to underpin Fligstein's model. The key variation revolves around the distinction between forms of collective ownership and forms of private ownership. The idea that property and resources can be collectively owned is historically the norm; it is individual ownership which is the exception, taking the *longue durée* view. Collective ownership has taken many forms, being embedded in different social entities such as families, local communities, religious and voluntary bodies. The idea of collective ownership has a different meaning and significance depending on where and when one is considering. Property is vested in the group as a whole rather than the individuals who make up the group. In many collectivities, individuals who leave the group give up all rights to the benefits of ownership; in others, they may receive some form of compensation for doing so but this compensation will be less than their share calculated on a purely arithmetical basis.

In historical and comparative terms, one of the key issues is the degree to which the collectivity itself relates to ownership in an active or a passive manner. Where the collectivity is weakly conscious of its own shared identity and the benefits of collective ownership, its interest in or capacity to defend that ownership will be reduced. On the other hand, where the collectivity has a high sense of shared interests, it will be more active in the defence of collective property rights. Clearly certain forms of collective ownership are exclusionary; they define insiders and outsiders and restrict benefits accordingly. On the other hand, it is possible to define collective ownership in ways which are inclusionary, that is to say, they extend to a wide group of the population.

The variability of private and collective ownership is not just a historical issue. It is a vividly contemporary aspect of current arguments in Western industrialized societies. The ease with which the privatization of public utilities has occurred in Britain indicates the degree to which the salience and significance of certain forms of collective ownership as a set of social values declined in the post-war period. Equally, however, the sensitivity of the Conservative government in the 1980s and 1990s to charges of privatizing the National Health Service indicates that a sense of collective ownership can be sustained. These issues are also reflected elsewhere. A major part of the financial institutions of Britain have traditionally been mutually owned (see Hopkins, 1995 for a historical analysis). Over the last few years, more of these institutions (building societies and life insurance companies) have sought to move over to private ownership. Although opposition has been weak (owing to the financial incentives to individual members to approve this switch), the virtues of 'mutuality' have been reaffirmed by those institutions which have decided not to convert to PLC status. Whilst this trumpeting of 'mutualism' has a strong commercial logic (in terms of differentiating themselves from the PLCs), it nevertheless contributes to a reawakening of interest and understanding of the implications of different forms of ownership.

From a comparative perspective, it could be argued that the dominance of private property ideology in Britain and the USA still remains the exception rather than the rule. Looking more widely at institutions in Europe, Africa, Latin America and Asia, collective ownership through the state (local and national), voluntary groups and the family remains strong. The point is that in spite of nearly two centuries of capitalist industrialization in the West, private, individual ownership is not inevitably triumphant. It becomes so the more powerful certain specific institutions become. For example, the more dependent industrializing societies become on outside capital for funding infrastructure developments as well as commercial investments, the more they become dependent on Western capital markets and institutions such as the World Bank and the International Monetary Fund (see e.g. McMichael, 1996). All of these institutions tend to make capital provision conditional on 'structural adjustment' which generally means a reduction of state expenditure on welfare and education and the privatization of most state infrastructure (see Wade, 1996 for a discussion of how the World Bank works to reproduce liberal free market ideology in the face of contradictory evidence; also Pauley, 1994 on the normative role of the IMF). Private ownership only becomes dominant under particular circumstances where the forces defending collective ownership have become weakened. The decline of state socialism in Eastern and Central Europe is not 'the end of history'; rather (as the experience of these societies itself reveals) new forms of property are emerging there, embodying new forms of collective and private property rights (see e.g. Stark, 1996; Whitley et al., 1996).

All modern societies continue to possess forms of collective as well as private ownership; where the boundaries between the two should be drawn is open to debate. In the UK, the debate has been dominated by those seeking to push privatization further. The defence of collective ownership has withered along with its forms. The time is ripe therefore for debating the ethics of forms of ownership in a more overt way and rediscovering what the point of these collective forms of ownership was in the first place. Mutual ownership of financial institutions, educational and welfare institutions, public utilities is still strongly embedded in many European societies as well as surviving, even if in a beleaguered state, in Britain. Their survival (and in some cases, extension) represents an achievement which reflects the strength of the collective groups supporting them. In conclusion, an institutionalist approach encourages the search for these alternative forms of property rights, their original purposes, and their social supporters. This can provide a significant contribution to the critical analysis of organizations and ethics.

Governance structures

Fligstein refers to these in terms of the general rules in society that define relations of competition, cooperation and market specific definitions of how firms should be organized. From a wider institutionalist perspective, this raises a number of issues.

First, modern societies are characterized by forms of regulation which place limits on how firms can be managed (see Ogus, 1994 for a general treatment). There are regulations which specify the sorts of people who can be directors, the sorts of capital required, the forms of disclosure and auditing which are required of public companies. There are also regulations about the sorts of goods which can be produced, how they can be produced, how they can be sold and advertised. The last twenty years has seen a massive rise in the number of groups lobbying for new forms of regulation, ranging from professional consumer bodies to environmental groups such as Greenpeace and Friends of the Earth (see also Desmond, Chapter 8 in this volume). The politics of regulatory structures and regulatory change are complex and shaped by many factors. Nevertheless, there is, in these arguments and debates, a strong ethical content. What rights do consumers have to information, redress and complaint? How should environmental considerations be included in the control and monitoring of firms? Critical organization theory has not been much concerned with how systems of rules and regulation for the governance of organizations have been constructed. This has meant that demands for deregulation, which are frequently merely ways of demanding greater freedom for individual property owners to make decisions about the allocation of resources without reference to collective values and interests, have been relatively unchallenged. The regulation of private property has traditionally been one of the main means by which those with less economic power in a society have been able to exert a collective influence over the market. Indeed, even where collective ownership has been given up to the forces of privatization, there has been debate and discussion about how the privatized utilities should be regulated so that they do not act against the public interest. Institutionalist arguments highlight that organizations exist within a regulatory framework and the construction of that framework is based upon certain ethical choices. As groups develop collective identities and voices, they become able to articulate both new and old ethical principles in terms of how organizations should be regulated for the collective good (see the experiences of regulation and deregulation in European financial services as described in Morgan and Knights, 1997; also Boyer and Drache, 1996).

Secondly, institutionalist theory can contribute to debates about corporate governance itself. In Britain, there are a number of aspects to this debate. At a limited level, there have been questions concerning who should be represented on boards of directors and what should be the role of non-executives. At a broader level, there is the issue of the capital markets and how these operate to discipline and control managers and firms. In the USA and Britain, rapid turnover in the capital markets based on short term returns creates a finance driven model of performance. In other countries, governance structures are such as to link together interests in a more long term framework. This derives from long term relationships and networks between banks and firms of varying size and specialism. Over the last twenty years, as these different models have come into competition with each other on world markets, there has been considerable debate about how reforms should occur – whether societies should move towards the Anglo-American model or more towards what Albert (1993) terms the 'Rhineland' model of cooperative capitalism. As authors such as Hutton (1995) have shown, these debates are not simply about technical models of economic development. They depend on views about the role of collective cooperation in the economy. In these terms, they raise ethical questions about how organizations should be structured internally and externally.

Collective cooperation occurs in all forms of capitalism. In some industries, it is often taken for granted. For example, Campbell et al. (1991) in their studies of governance in the USA indicate that certain industries such as agriculture and defence cannot work properly without the state assisting in the creation of forms of cooperation to limit and control production as well as to set the rules of the market. The contrast in the 1980s between the level of support for the coal mining industry in Britain and that provided to agriculture through the European Community's farming subsidies is an example of how ethical and political judgements are made to decide when cooperation and support is a 'good thing' and when it is unacceptable. Cooperation may also be institutionalized as a result of long standing social networks in which individuals and groups agree to work together to achieve common objectives. As experience in Japan, Germany and other countries indicates, forms of cooperation between organizations (as well as within them) can create the conditions for innovation and success which are difficult to achieve in more competitive environments (see some of the studies in Whitley and Kristensen, 1996). As has already been mentioned, cooperation can be based on exclusionary tactics; thus the creation of monopolies and cartels can be seen as a form of cooperation but one which has detrimental effects on those outside the power centres. Therefore, the nature of cooperation itself, and who and why groups are advantaged by it, needs opening up for analysis. Cooperation as a form of governance raises questions about the ethical basis of this form of social action. It is not simply an economic response to particular problems but also a social and value-based approach to organizations and economic life.

In conclusion, it is possible to identify how organizations are governed and regulated in particular social contexts. These processes of governance and regulation imply particular sets of ethical values and norms. By uncovering what these are and contrasting them with those which shape other contexts, it is possible to raise questions about alternatives and therefore to contribute to a public policy debate about the nature of organizations. Governance structures are institutionalized as a result of conflicts and negotiations between groups within societies. In this process, there are different values and ethics being debated. Critical organization theory can participate in these arguments and show which interests are gaining from particular decisions. It can raise perspectives on different ethics which can be taken into account, broadening the debate to include consumer interests, environmental interests and other groups struggling to participate in the arguments.

Conceptions of control

In Fligstein's approach this refers to understandings that structure perceptions of how a market works and that allow actors to interpret their world and act to control situations. In his analysis, this mainly concerns the way in which owners and managers perceive the context for corporate and market control. In a wider institutionalist perspective, this raises broad issues about the way in which social groups within and between organizations are structured, and their expectations about their role in the broader social context. For example, Kristensen (in Whitley and Kristensen, 1996) has argued that social groups develop perceptions of their own social honour – in other words, what they are worth within the wider scheme of things. These are expectations about what is their due within the organizational setting, which in turn is reinforced by conceptions of citizenship and responsibility in the political arena. These expectations about social honour, status and responsibility stand in an uneasy and uncertain relationship to market settings. They can be reinforced by strategic action within political and economic contexts or they can be undermined. In some contexts, for example, workers may be able to enforce their concepts of honour because of the strategic, collective power which they exercise within the workplace. In other words, they utilize their market power to reinforce their social status. Skilled workers have traditionally maintained their status differentials through concentrating their industrial power into craft unions which have restricted competition for jobs, thereby creating stronger bargaining powers for their members. On the other hand, skilled workers have also traditionally led movements for wider rights for trade unions and workers. Their own sense of honour and status has been both a means of distinguishing themselves from others and the power basis from which they have been able to build wider alliances. The ethics of these movements therefore needs careful analysis depending on the context.

In some contexts, ideas of citizenship and responsibility may provide for the creation of wider coalitions of interest which reinforce through legal channels certain rights within the workplace that workers by themselves are not powerful enough to achieve. For example, the campaign to achieve the Factory Acts and the restriction of the working day in Britain in the 1840s was seen by Marx as resulting from the coalition of middle class reformers as well as working class radicals. In the Scandinavian countries, the creation of coalitions of interests across the working class, the farmers and the salaried middle class was crucial to the creation of egalitarian welfare state systems in which rights to work, retraining and high levels of income support at times of unemployment or illness were embodied (Esping-Andersen, 1990). By contrast, in Britain, these cross-class coalitions have tended to be temporary and middle class support for working class aspirations has died out quickly once status and earnings differentials have been threatened.

In these contexts, the idea of control implies creating a space within the dynamics of a market economy whereby certain rights and duties are placed above the criteria of economics. The institutionalist approach sees this as endemic to modern capitalist societies. There are always groups aiming for political recognition and to establish their own status demands. Feminism and movements for equal opportunity of gender and ethnicity constitute ethical challenges to taken-for-granted structures of organizations (though see Brewis, Chapter 4 in this volume for a more critical approach to issues of gender). These struggles open up opportunities for critical organization theory to engage with debates by identifying the nature of the ethical issues involved and the implications of taking certain positions.

Rules of exchange

According to Fligstein, rules of exchange define who can transact with whom and the conditions under which transactions are carried out. From a broader institutionalist perspective, this raises the whole question of what it is that can be traded and sold on the marketplace. What is the legitimate extent of commodification? (See Ritzer, 1996 for the argument about the extension of market relations.) Once again, all modern societies contain restrictions on what can and cannot be traded. Some societies either formally or informally allow market trade in body parts and blood (Titmuss, 1971); in other societies, these are embedded in collective 'gift' relationships where the donor receives merely status or honour from the process and the thought of payment or a market in such donations would be considered an affront to collective values. The whole area of health services raises similar ethical distinctions between different societies. In the USA, it is generally accepted that access to medical services is dependent on private savings through insurance schemes. Safety net procedures for the elderly and the poor are structured in ways which mean that many fall through the net and are effectively denied access to adequate facilities. Attempts to change this situation, such as Clinton's health care plan in his first administration, lead to major conflicts with entrenched interest groups. Other countries consider access to health care a right of citizenship not dependent on individual ability to pay. Even where rights to treatment are based on citizenship rather than the ability to pay, rules of exchange may be created as in the quasi-market for health services in the UK. Thus, notional budgets can be allocated to purchasers, and providers have to compete for business. The result is that health service care is subjected to a certain logic of the market, creating different tiers of 'consumers' depending on who is purchasing on their behalf. Some purchasers (GP fundholders) in effect exercise power to gain privileged access to providers on behalf of their clients. Providers on the other hand are subjected to budgetary constraints and financial targets which may lead to the closure of certain provision as a result purely of these financial factors rather than any assessment of the needs of patients. Thus rules of exchange and markets can be introduced into any sort of public provision thereby mutating collective entitlements into some sort of hierarchical privileges of access (see Robinson and Le Grand, 1994: Glennester et al., 1994; Ferlie et al., 1996; Flynn and Williams, 1997 for evaluations of these changes in the NHS and elsewhere).

In general terms, societies differ in the extent to which they provide rights to citizens on the basis of collective entitlement. Welfare states as a whole exhibit wide variations in the degree to which security in unemployment, ill-health, disablement and old age is secured as a right or purchased as a commodity through private or state insurance systems. Even where security is purchased by the individual on the marketplace, there is likely to be a system of regulation which ensures a relatively higher level of protection for the consumer than would be the case in the purchase of most other commodities. However, this may still not be successful as events in Britain have shown where the regulators have revealed that over half a million people were badly advised to leave occupational pension schemes and purchase their own personal pension scheme.

What should societies allow to be traded on the marketplace? Institutional analysis can reveal the wide variations between societies and therefore the inherently ethical nature of these decisions. The 'gift' relationship in the donation of blood has been seen, since Titmuss's classic study, as indicating something deeper about the nature of collective identity – a willingness to recognize that reducing all wants and needs to a monetary value undermines certain moral and ethical principles about mutual obligation and responsibility. Organ donations given freely between relatives or after death are seen as indicative of high moral values; on the other hand, the purchase of organs from living donors which has been reported in the press raises 'moral panics' about the acceptable extent of commodification. As medical science pushes back the barriers of what is possible, societies and organizations struggle to define the acceptable line in areas like organ donations, surrogate motherhood, the definition of death and genetic engineering and selection.

The nature of trade on the marketplace is of course at the centre of debates about labour and labour power. What is actually purchased through the labour contract? The right to have control over the labourer is socially negotiated in industrial societies. Slavery and forms of indentured labour have been outlawed in the West though there are indications that they still exist in other societies, sometimes linked to the world market through the use of child labour in forms of textile and agricultural production in certain parts of the world. Even where these have been overcome the extent of the control exercised over the labourer can vary depending on many factors. Corporal punishment as well as control over the servant's body can continue to exist even where the legal basis of slavery and indenture has been abolished. The 'dignity of labour' has been primarily enforced through the combination of workers' self-help (through trade unions) and the enlightened self-interest of some employers and political parties. Thus the definitions of what is allowable in terms of control over labour can vary across societies and in different historical periods.

Conclusions

It is my argument that the institutionalist approach – whether it is based on the broad comparative and historical approach presented here or the more ethnographic style of authors examining in detail the process of management in organizations – is essential to any discussion of business ethics. It shows how morality and ethical judgements are not an outside imposition on an essentially technical process of management; on the contrary, they are the stuff from which organizations are actually built. Therefore, a more direct confrontation with how organizations and management have resolved these issues would be a fundamental first step in debates about business ethics in the current period.

However, it can reasonably be asked whether this sort of descriptive ethics take us any further than relativism (see Parker, Chapter 14 in this volume)? In other words, we can show that there have been many different approaches to the nature of property ownership and the rights of labour, but can we say anything more about which ones we would prefer to become institutionalized in the current period? Are we not then back into the philosophical domain of Kantianism and so on, albeit by a wide detour? One way to consider this is presented in Bauman's arguments concerning the nature of modernity and postmodernity, something that many of the authors in this volume have done. The tendency of modernity, in Bauman's view, is towards the creation of a uniform model of social order based on a single set of moral principles which are deemed to embody rationality. This search for a single solution to the nature of society reaches its extreme result in the Holocaust. It is the destruction of social variability (or what others might call 'political pluralism') which is a necessary if not sufficient condition for the massive immorality of the Holocaust. Whilst he recognizes that Nazi Germany and Stalin's Russia represented the most extreme attempts in the modern world to destroy variability and cultivate a single social body, he refuses to treat them as abominations, fundamental exceptions to a more civilized 'modernity' based on pluralism (Bauman, 1989). On the contrary, for Bauman, the creation of bureaucratic organizations that both literally and metaphorically distance their members from the final consequences of their actions means that modernity has perfected a system which denies the ultimate basis of moral action in the face-to-face confrontation of two individuals. Instead, it has replaced the inevitable uncertainty and anxiety of the moral act which comes from choice and freedom with the pragmatic certainty of following rules no matter what their ultimate outcome (Bauman in Barry et al., 1993; Desmond, Chapter 8 in this volume).

Postmodernity on the other hand arises from the destruction of modern certainties and the loss of faith in the idea that a 'just world' could be created by the 'legislators'. Once this faith is lost, then:

> The choice is not between following the rules and breaking them, as there is no one set of rules to be obeyed or breached. The choice is rather between different sets of rules and different authorities preaching them . . .These times offer us freedom of choice never before enjoyed but also cast us into a state of uncertainty never before so agonizing. (Bauman, 1993: 20–1)

As he states elsewhere:

> History is fraught with mass murders committed in the name of the one and only truth . . . It is hard to point out, though, a single case of a cruel deed perpetrated in the name of plurality and tolerance. (Bauman, 1997: 201)

The conceptual dualism of modernity and postmodernity becomes the peg around which Bauman hangs his epistemological, ethical and sociological arguments. Is this dualism robust enough to carry all these arguments? The institutionalist approach, for example, would point to the existence of multiple sets of ethics and values in whichever period of modernity one was examining. Indeed, it can be argued that modernity itself, through its promotion of the individual reflexive consciousness, gives rise to the further multiplication of values and beliefs. Going back to Durkheim, the problem of modernity was not the dominance of a single moral order (which was characteristic of 'mechanical solidarity') but its very opposite – the lack of such a framework and the tendency of individualism to proliferate, thereby undermining the bases of sociability. From this perspective, modernism is more accurately seen in terms of the proliferation of competing 'rationalities'; the conditions under which a single rationality becomes dominant (such as Nazism and Stalinism) are atypical rather than representative (see e.g. O'Kane, 1995 for an argument along these lines). On the other hand, Bauman's identification of the importance of face-to-face contact with the other as the basis of morality is significant for identifying the ambiguities of modernism. Much of this period can be identified in terms of the conflict between abstract principles of order and rationalities and local moralities built on face-to-face relations. Thus forms of collective self-help invariably derived from the experience of communal and family groups seeking to protect themselves against emerging forms of governmentality defined in Foucauldian terms as 'a more or less methodical and rationally reflected "way of doing things" or "art" for acting on the actions of individuals taken singly or collectively, so as to shape, guide, correct and modify the ways in which they conduct themselves' (Burchell, 1996: 19). Bauman states that:

> The downtrodden throughout the ages were morally aroused by the experience of *injustice*, rather than any prospective model of justice . . . they experienced as unjust whatever was the *departure* from the oppression they faced daily and routinely. Moral outrage was prompted by driving the screw of oppression a turn or two down, rather than by a dissatisfaction with the daily level of oppression. (1995: 42)

Resistance to oppression and regimes of governmentality is, however, inherently contradictory. In order to maintain any gains temporarily won at the local level, institutions beyond the local have to be developed and sustained. Such institutions thereby become part of the 'rationalities of government'; in simple terms, they generate new forms of control (Barry et al., 1996). The result is a continuous interplay between the local and the institutions at a distance. Certainly in some organizations, the local was effectively disempowered and vanished into the bureaucratic procedures of the formal organization. Many of the self-help financial organizations went down this route and became effectively indistinguishable from their privately owned counterparts. They no longer acted as resources which could be mobilized locally to help out individuals and their families who had hit hard times through illness, unemployment or industrial action. Their rules were dictated by market rationality and allowed little variance. In others of these institutions which had grown up locally, such as trade unions, the effect was more complex; even where the union had taken on a bureaucratic form, the local could occasionally almost spontaneously combust in response to particularly outrageous attempts by management to impose specific work conditions.

Modernism may be characterized in terms of a dialectic between projects for control, governmentality, rationality and accountability (see Munro, Chapter 9 in this volume; also Munro and Mouritsen, 1996) and local moralities based on face-to-face relationships. However, contrary to Bauman, this is a dialectic which reveals itself in many places and at many times. It does not just appear when some threshold to postmodernity is passed over. From this perspective, it is more appropriate to see this as an endemic (though perhaps increasing) struggle within the modern order. In Foucault's own writings (and life), this leads to a celebration of local resistance to governance. In others, this rediscovery of the importance of local moralities in the context of increased globalization has led to the embrace of 'communitarianism'. The stronger the local institutions and involvement within them, the more feelings of obligation and responsibility for others can be foregrounded. In this respect, the sort of institutionalism presented here links to a certain type of moral commitment based on local 'empowerment'. It represents a commitment to understanding how social institutions become forged through the confrontation between local communities and universalizing forces. Giddens expresses a similar notion when he advocates 'a concern to repair *damaged solidarities*, which may imply the selective preservation, or even perhaps reinvention, of tradition' (1994: 12). However, Bauman identifies the weaknesses of this in terms of the ways in which local 'moralities' also become forms of dominance over the individual. He argues that as the broader modernist projects slip away under the corrosive influences of consumerism and uncertainty, they are replaced by a 'new tribalism' in which individuals are trapped within traditional and non-traditional 'imagined communities' (Bauman, 1995).

Resolving these theoretical difficulties is clearly beyond the scope of this chapter. At one level, there may be convergence between the institutionalist approach to organizations and some of these broader debates in social theory. The local construction of moralities and the way in which extra-local strategies of governance impact on these is clearly an emerging field of social theorizing. In this context, institutionalism is not just a sociological/descriptive account of ethics and social values but may also arguably be said to embody a particular moral stance based on the primacy of the local community and the obligations and responsibilities founded there. It achieves the former task by pointing us to the socially embedded nature of rules of ownership and property and their range of variation. It contributes to the latter not just by relativizing current views of property and ownership but also by emphasizing the importance of local moral agreements and values in the construction of social institutions and organizations. Taking this perspective into the arena of business ethics is not just the introduction of a distinctive approach but also involves taking on a distinctive moral approach to organizations. Even so, this can only be a beginning to debate. As Bauman characteristically notes:

> The probable truth is that moral choices are indeed choices and dilemmas are indeed dilemmas – not the temporary and rectifiable effects of human weakness, ignorance or blunders. Issues have no predetermined solutions . . . There are no hard-and-fast principles which one can learn, memorize and deploy in order to escape situations without a good outcome and to spare oneself the bitter after-taste . . . Human reality is messy and ambiguous – and so, moral decisions, unlike abstract ethical principles, are ambivalent. It is in this sort of world that we must live. (1993: 32)

References

Albert, M. (1993) *Capitalism against Capitalism*. London: Whurr.
Alvesson, M. and Willmott, H. (1996) *Making Sense of Management: A Critical Introduction*. London: Sage.
Barry, A., Osborne, T. and Rose, N. (eds) (1996) *Foucault and Political Reason: Liberalism, Neo-Liberalism and Rationalities of Government*. London: UCL Press.
Bauman, Z. (1989) *Modernity and the Holocaust*. Cambridge: Polity.
Bauman, Z. (1993) *Postmodern Ethics*. Oxford: Blackwell.
Bauman, Z. (1995) *Life in Fragments: Essays in Postmodern Morality*. Oxford: Blackwell.
Bauman, Z. (1997) *Postmodernity and its Discontents*. Oxford: Blackwell.
Boyer, R. and Drache, D. (eds) (1996) *States against Markets*. London: Routledge.
Burrell, G. (1997) *Pandemonium: Towards a Retro-Organization Theory*. London: Sage.
Campbell, J., Hollingsworth, R. and Lindberg, L. (1991) *Governance of the American Economy*. Cambridge: Cambridge University Press.
Esping-Andersen, G. (1990) *The Three Worlds of Welfare Capitalism*. Cambridge: Polity Press.
Ferlie, E., Ashburner, L., Fitzgerald, L. and Pettigrew, A. (1996) *The New Public Management in Action*. Oxford: Blackwell.
Fligstein, N. (1996) 'Markets as Politics: Political-Cultural Approach to Market Institutions', *American Sociological Review*, 656–73.
Flynn, R. and Williams, G. (1997) *Contracting for Health: Quasi-Markets and the National Health Service*. Oxford: Oxford University Press.
Giddens, A. (1994) *Beyond Left and Right*. Cambridge: Polity.
Glennester, H., Matsaganis, M., Owens, P. and Hancock, S. (1994) *Implementing GP Fundholding*. Buckingham: Open University Press.
Hopkins, E. (1995) *Working Class Self-Help in Nineteenth Century England*. London: UCL.
Hutton, W. (1995) *The State We're In*. London: Cape.
Ingham, G. (1996a) 'Some Recent Changes in the Relationship between Economics and Sociology', *Cambridge Journal of Economics*, 20: 243–75.
Ingham, G. (1996b) 'The "New Economic Sociology"', *Work, Employment and Society*, 10: 549–64.
McMichael, P. (1996) *Development and Social Change*. Thousand Oaks, CA: Pine Forge.
Morgan, G. and Knights, D. (eds) (1997) *Regulation and Deregulation in European Financial Services*. London: Macmillan.
Munro, R. and Mouritsen, J. (eds) (1996) *Accountability*. London: International Thomson.
North, D.C. (1990) *Institutions, Institutional Change and Economic Performance*. Cambridge: Cambridge University Press.
North, D.C. (1991) 'Institutions', *Journal of Economic Perspectives*, 5: 97–112.
Ogus, A.I. (1994) *Regulation*. Oxford: Clarendon.
O'Kane, R. (1995) 'Modernity, the Holocaust and Politics', *Economy and Society*, 43–61.
Pauley, L. (1994) 'Promoting a Global Economy: The Normative Role of the International Monetary Fund', in R. Stubbs and G. Underhill (eds), *Political Economy and the Changing Global Order*. London: Macmillan. pp. 204–15.
Ritzer, G. (1996) *The McDonaldization of Society*, rev. edn. London: Pine Forge.
Robinson, R. and Le Grand, J. (eds) (1994) *Evaluating the NHS Reforms*. London: King's Fund.
Smelser, N. and Swedberg, R. (eds) (1994) *The Handbook of Economic Sociology*. Princeton, NJ: Princeton University Press.

Stark, D. (1996) 'Recombinant Property in Eastern European Capitalism', *American Journal of Sociology*, 101: 993–1027.
Stubbs, R. and Underhill, G. (1994) *Political Economy and the Changing Global Order*. London: Macmillan.
Titmuss, R. (1971) *The Gift Relationship*. London: Penguin.
Wade, R. (1996) 'Japan, the World Bank and the Art of Paradigm Maintenance', *New Left Review*, no. 217: 3–37.
Whitley, R. and Kristensen, P.H. (eds) (1996) *The Changing European Firm*. London: Routledge.
Whitley, R., Henderson, J., Czaban, L. and Lengyel, G. (1996) 'Continuity and Change in an Emergent Market Economy', in R. Whitley and P.H. Kristensen (eds), *The Changing European Firm*. London: Routledge. pp. 210–37.

11 The Natural Environment, Organization and Ethics

Stephen Fineman

> It's can we afford it? What will it give us in return? How long will we have to wait? Any competitive advantage? No fine moral sentiments in this. (Environmental Director, Automotives Manufacturer)

Traditional organizational theory confidently informs us that the environment is everything that lies 'outside' the organization's boundary (Lawrence and Lorsch, 1967; Aldrich, 1979; Daft, 1995). Yet the natural environment gets no mention. Indeed, in classical economics, the natural environment is literally not counted. It is there as an asset to be used as its owner wishes or, where there is no right of property (such as air, sea and common land), to be exploited as an infinite resource (Pauchant and Fortier, 1990; Daly and Cobb, 1989). What is counted is a highly particularized environment of 'contingencies' instrumental to the organization's economic performance – such as government policies, available technologies, financial regimes, labour markets, customer preferences and suppliers. Ethical responsibility conflates with market performance (see Sheldon, 1923; Friedman, 1970). The very job of economizing in business makes for social responsibility, so managers who studiously economize need not consciously deliberate the rights and wrongs of their actions.

Recently, this denatured vision of the environment has been challenged, spurred by ecological damage from industrial disasters and evidence of long term pollution from industrial processes and products. Seas, rivers, the atmosphere, forests, plants, minerals, animal and plant species, it is suggested, seem to suffer a global version of the tragedy of the commons (Hardin, 1978). The more that we grab from them for industrial and consumption purposes the less, it is argued, there is to sustain the very businesses and people that exploit them (Schumacher, 1973; O'Conner, 1983; McKibben, 1989). Their renewal cannot be taken for granted.

This raises significant moral questions for deep-green philosophers, and others in the now burgeoning field of environmental ethics. Nature becomes irrelevant unless it serves a commercial end. Its wildness is something to be packaged for consumer pleasure – such as safari parks, animal hunts and 'exotic' expedition holidays. There is a spectre of wrecking the planet and defacing its beauty while also compromising the lives of others: future generations, non-human life forms, and, some would add, rocks and mountains.

Quaintly, but evocatively, ecologist Aldo Leopold (1949) in the 1940s urged us to 'think like a mountain', a feature of a 'land ethic' which would enlarge human thinking, open our eyes and hearts to the interconnectedness of ecosystems. Such a sentiment would have been familiar to many aboriginal communities before Christian missionaries instructed them otherwise. Respect for nature is taken for granted when the spirits of one's ancestors are in birds, trees, mountains and rocks. But Judaeo-Christian thought offers a different, decidedly anthropocentric, manifesto: 'man' is at the top of the earthly pile, put there by God to tame and direct primitive nature, at best kindly, to his own ends. As planet earth is but a staging post to the hereafter, its own integrity is rather less important than how it serves the here-and-now needs of its human occupants. This is especially so for those embued with the Protestant ethic: the goodness and godliness of industriousness and the spiritual spring to much of Western capitalism.

An early, radical, reaction to industrial despoliation can be found in the 'noble savage', romantic, images of turn of the century artists and poets – such as Blake and Byron. Some present-day environmentalists are their ideological heirs: Naess (1989), Rodman (1983), Rolston (1988) and Taylor (1986) offer a stark, sometimes shocking, image of industrially ravaged nature. For example:

> I need only to stand in the midst of a clearcut forest, a stripmined hillside, a defoliated jungle or a dammed canyon to feel uneasy with the assumptions that could yield the conclusion that no human action can make any difference to the welfare of anything but sentient animals. (Rodman, 1977: 89)

> A global culture of primarily techno-industrial nature is now encroaching upon all the world's milieux, desecrating living conditions for future generations . . . For the first time in the history of humanity, we stand face to face with a choice imposed upon us because of our lackadaisical attitude to the production of things and people. (Naess, 1989: 23)

There is anxiety and outrage in such sentiments. These critics hold that social progress based on an unending materialistic quest is a myth, and a dangerous one, as it tramples on ecological laws that underpin all human existence and on which our moral systems must be based (O'Riordan, 1981). Not surprisingly, their rhetoric of rectitude bothers those in industry and science who espouse a 'rational' discourse and are committed to a moral order built upon technological progress. Apologists for industry argue that it is naive to pin the blame on industry or to underestimate the power of current institutions and technologies to heal environmental damage. At its extreme it is a dialogue of the deaf, dramatically exemplified in the mutual recriminations between 'eco warriors' and establishment representatives over the construction of new roads and river dams, and the disposal of oil rigs and nuclear waste. The rhetorics of the two parties are fundamentally incompatible.

It is plain that talk of environmental damage, and indeed of 'the natural environment', is inherently problematic. Social constructionist analyses reveal how perceiving, becoming passionate about, and taking action on environmental damage is a complex product of various social/political processes (e.g. Hannigan, 1995; Yearley, 1992). Environmental claims have to be assembled and marked off in some way. Some will be close and experiential, such as Rodman's observations above, or seeing and smelling roadside air pollution. Others will be invisible, such as 'ozone holes'; these rely on claims from science. Environmental assertions or 'findings' are contested within and across various audiences and disciplines; their popularization and dramatization adds to (or diminishes) their perceived importance. The claims that stick are often triggered by a crisis or catastrophe and amplified by the media – such as with Chernobyl, Bhopal or Shell's attempts to sink redundant oil rigs in the ocean (see Desmond, Chapter 8 in this volume). Their endurance is further reinforced when they are sponsored or coopted by high profile institutions – such as government, Greenpeace or one of the 'respectable' sciences.

So environmental risk, damage and amelioration have to be read as an unfolding, often conflictual, social and political process. Rhetoric, scientific authority and moral persuasion interact to produce legitimization. This does not detract from the possible 'realness' of environmental despoliation. But it suggests that realness – such as the death of flora and fauna, air and sea pollution, famine – is important socially in so far as it is defined and moralized by partial human actors and shaped within particular institutions – economic, legal, cultural and political (see Morgan, Chapter 10 in this volume). This means that not all environmental issues will reach the public agenda in the same way or in the same form. For example, the worth of preserving one's local wildlife habitat can look very different to the middle class citizens of Kent in the UK compared with subsistence farmers in Kenya. And, alongside Soviet style socialism, much Western capitalism glows green.

Where different environmental claims and interests are publicly expressed in direct action, such as with controversial road developments, the mechanisms of democracies can look ponderous. They are caught between rights to free expression and the maintenance of civic order. As many of the chapters in this book illustrate, most conventional tests of moral rectitude do not do too well. Where, in utilitarian language, is the greatest benefit from a particular eco-damaging industrial project? What of long term consequences? Should corporate stockholders benefit more than the local flora and fauna – the 'silent' stakeholders? How, as recently illustrated in Newbury in the UK, are we to judge the value of preserving the habitat of rare species of Ice Age snail, the size of breadcrumb, which sits exactly in the projected path of a multimillion pound road bypass? Is Kantian dignity – not to be treated as a means to an end – to be fairly afforded to the snails, plants, fields and mountains which are entwined in projects such as these? Projects already determined by powerful industrial and governmental players? And if so, how?

At the heart of the 'environmental ethic' lies the belief that natural entities have to be valued in themselves, for what they are, rather than what they deliver to us. Any morally sensitive person should be able to recognize this. It is a position that creates philosophical knots, such as whether other species and non-sentient organisms have 'needs' and what necessarily human-mediated criteria of value we should apply to them (see for example Thompson, 1990; Frederick, 1995). Given such problems, is the language of ethics essential to satisfy environmentalists' objections to despoiled landscapes? We shall return to this point later in the chapter.

Capturing the environment: inside organizations

Let us shift from the sublime to the mundane. The daily operations of businesses cannot be said to be saturated with talk of morality. Dilemmas of an ethical nature may well be embedded in certain decision processes and preferences, but they are almost all attached to local instrumentalities of business practice and to political expediencies. While managers, when prompted, may sometimes engage in larger moral and ethical debates, this is frequently a sideshow to the main organizing acts (see Jackall, 1988; Bird and Waters, 1989; Watson, Chapter 12 in this volume). This is not to suggest that industrial organizations are value-free zones. Far from it. 'Orders' of value permeate the social negotiation of space, place, power and purpose. While these may be heavily shaped by the organization's actors, they are simultaneously a product of the kind of institution it is (private, public, small, large), the industrial sector to which it belongs and the social/economic systems of which it is a part.

All organizations are in and of the natural environment, albeit much refaced through human intervention. But a manager's awareness of the natural environment as a *business* issue in part depends on which relevant stakeholders press hardest (see Sorell, Chapter 2 in this volume). Our own research in four major 'polluting' industries in the UK – automotives, power, chemicals, and supermarkets – suggests that this is often a highly partial and interpretive process on behalf of the manager (Fineman and Clarke, 1996; Fineman, 1996; 1997a). Managers were influenced by just a few stakeholders – particularly environmental campaigners and environmental regulators – because of their ability to injure or embarrass the reputation of the corporation. All other stakeholders were marginalized. The regulator was regarded as an unavoidable fact of business life, key to obtaining essential permits to operate. But the regulator was also personified as an inspector, to be matched, if not excelled, in negotiating skills. In these terms the environment was reconstructed as a political/technical issue, not a moral one, the details of which were to be negotiated between the regulator and regulated in a quasi-legal process aimed at, for the manager, cost minimization. Nature and its protection was sometimes symbolized as a BATNEEC – best available techniques not entailing excessive cost. This ambiguous rubric, set within UK environmental legislation, determines the kind of pollution control measures that govern some key industrial processes. But achieving a

BATNEEC is based on political compromise and power play. Its outcomes typically represent a massive distillation of the corporation's grand mission statements on caring for the planet, although that seldom prevents companies from making extravagant claims about their environmental achievements.

In our study, green pressure groups were given a mixed reception. For some managers they were a surrogate conscience, reminding them of responsibilities they could all too easily neglect. For others they were high-minded intruders:

> Is it right that we should be used as an economic instrument to blackmail one country into following what some people believe to be the right way forward – like banning pilot whaling? No! So PriceForce have. So they're goody two shoes. I'm *not* going to force people to a limited number of people's views on the way the world should be. (in Fineman, 1996: 489)

While this manager would huff and puff, he was amongst many others in the study who could not ignore the presence of green activists. Tales were told of embarrassing moments when concerted pressure-group action, coupled with media interest, had resulted in a highly critical portrayal of the company's environmental performance. The 'facts' were almost always disputed, but the public relations damage was very real to them. It required precautionary strategies which ranged from corporate counter-publicity – information and disinformation sheets – to cautious attempts at dialogue with the 'enemy'.

Environmental management systems were well instituted in a small number of the companies in our study; others were a patchwork of attempts. Respondents would boast of their progressive approach to environmental management. Their chief executive would champion environmental protection (although none as virtuously as the much quoted Anita Roddick of The Body Shop or Ben 'n' Jerry's eponymous chief executives). They had specially appointed environmental managers. They conducted regular environmental audits, externally validated. They audited their suppliers. They recycled waste and carefully controlled pollution. They had outreach activities into the local community, promoting environmental care and supporting local environmental projects. In all, they mirrored most of the 'best practice' systems to be found in the advice books.

In defending their 'quality' approach these managers would talk in clichés – about 'best in class' and 'turning a threat into an opportunity'. They aimed to 'get competitive advantage from the natural environment' and 'wouldn't do it if it didn't help the bottom line'. At this point deep-green critics of industry would feel edgy. Business is still, unsurprisingly, business. We tested the moral waters a little further. We asked our respondents how they felt about the view that their ultimate responsibility to the natural environment was to shift their corporate wealth away from the sort of products or processes they dealt with. The typical retort, after an uneasy silence, was that that was not their concern. They were simply supplying what the market wanted. It was their job to follow commercial pressures to grow, serving their stockholders and customers.

The grip of the customer rhetoric on moral construction was remarkable in some companies:

> Even when you've been here a short time, there's such a powerful culture that's it's rammed into you. You absorb it and can't operate outside it. We take the customer's views on cost issues, value quality – all these aspects. Sure I have a view on green pressure groups. There are things they do I believe absolutely firmly in, but there are things they also espouse I think are drivel. But it's not for me to bring personal prejudice or my own opinions into the marketplace. What's important from my point of view is to reflect my customers' requirements. So whatever I happen to think is irrelevant. I must give the customers what they require.

In such a response, from a senior manager, corporate environmentalism is revealed to be morally hollow, while ethically pragmatic. As echoed elsewhere in this book, we see shades of Bauman's (1989) views on the modern organization which encloses its members in a self-sustaining rationality, rendering morality invisible beyond a limited organizational boundary. To the above manager, moral culpability ends with the 'customers' requirements'. The customer is the benchmark of goodness. This manager was silent (as were others) on the way corporations engineer their customers' 'wants' through marketing and advertising (see Desmond, Chapter 8 in this volume). Yet there is no evidence that the people we studied were somehow evil souls, intent on environmental destruction. Most were fairly conservative, middle class citizens, who described themselves as 'light green'. At home they would 'do a bit of recycling' and respond sympathetically to their children's questions about an environmentally degrading world. But their beliefs (whether moderate or radical) and their moral agency were suspended when they slipped into their work roles. Different systems of meanings and rewards applied as the structural constraints of their jobs took hold.

Environmental business ethics

Environmental business ethicists who follow a modernist tradition have tried to fuse the economic pragmatism of organizational life, of the sort described above, with protection for the environment. In doing so they cut a path between deep-green, ecocentric values and technical/economic ones. What results is a revision of contingency theory. Despoliation of nature, goes the argument, is one of a number of social problems that organizations have to address. To do so is a mark of good citizenship as well as a necessary feature of corporate efficiency and effectiveness.

In these terms the natural environment is something to be 'managed', proceduralized with new knowledge, new political skills and, above all, new technologies: environmental audits, life-cycle analyses, eco-labelling, waste and energy control systems and product stewardship (Elkington and Burke, 1987; Beaumont et al., 1993). Basically, the classical theory of the firm remains more or less intact. Economizing is still a good thing, but with managers now in charge of the natural environment – or more precisely certain bits of it. What is 'outside' is brought 'inside' as a 'standard operating procedure' or 'strategic issue' – a cost to be internalized. The market can do the rest, serving the key goals of business profit and economic growth (Prince and Denson, 1992).

Managerialism ('man' controlling the environment) is firmly celebrated in this formulation, as are the benefits of consumerism and economic growth. Indeed, economic growth is regarded as fundamental to environmental improvement. It is enshrined in the Declaration of the Business Council for Sustainable Development (Schmidheiny, 1992) which has focused industry's eco-efficiency approaches. The view is cogently expressed by Stapleton:

> Growth is a necessary, though not sufficient, condition for achieving the higher quality of life that the world wants. In countries rich beyond the dreams of a generation ago, growth is still needed to provide the resources to clean up the pollution of old industries and to produce the technology to accommodate tomorrow's industrial processes in cleaner surroundings. In countries still miserably poor, growth which will last is essential to overcoming the ruinous impact that poverty itself has on the environment. There is, therefore, no contradiction in arguing for both economic growth and for environment good sense. (1996: 114)

These sentiments are regarded as axiomatic to enlightened self-interest in management and were frequently echoed in the rationalizations of the managers in our own study: 'Do we all want to go back to living in caves?' 'How would you feel about a life without electricity or refrigeration, or with primitive medicines?' The moral imperative is to grow economically and accumulate the riches which accrue to advanced capitalist economies. They would additionally argue that any debris created *en route* would be worth tolerating, or could be contained because we are learning new ways of preventing, or cleaning up, the mess.

Such utilitarianism has appeal to the business community and is supported by some descriptive economic studies (e.g. Grossman and Krueger, 1993). It offers one justification for the globalization of the market economy, particularly for countries where centralized economies have left bleak environmental landscapes. It is also naive. The strictly economizing firm can shift its resources and wealth to 'pollution havens', where it can escape the costs of environmental regulation – just as some will seek the cheapest labour markets. Furthermore, as Arrow et al. (1996) have shown in an unusual consensus of economists and ecologists, environmental improvements from economic growth are confined to a restricted range of indicators which fail to account for important cross-country and intergenerational pollution effects – such as from carbon dioxide emissions and persistent airborne toxins. Global trade offers free transport for biological pollutants which can cause extensive damage to native crops and forests (Schindler et al., 1996). Perhaps the most crucial omission from the growth-is-good perspective is that it ignores the carrying capacity of the planet – the depletion of resource stocks and other 'natural capital'. While the details and robustness of the 'carrying capacity' concept and content are, like those of other environmental claims, contestable, its plausibility and authority is growing amongst ecologists and 'new' economists. It raises questions such as: how many cars, fridges, aircraft, plastic products and the like, and all that is entailed in their production, maintenance and disposal, can the planet hold? Arguably each unit of production or process may eventually become greener, more 'ethical', but this simply slows the rate of ecological decline. *Titanic Earth* is still steaming towards its nemesis, if we are to believe the predictions of some ecologists. Arrow et al. shrewdly conclude:

> Economic growth is not a panacea for environmental quality; indeed it is not even the main issue. What matters is the content of growth. The content is determined by, among other things, the economic institutions within which human activities are conducted. These institutions need to be designed so that they provide incentives for protecting the resilience of ecological systems. (1996: 15)

The ecological ball is thrown squarely into the political arena with a message unlikely to please free marketeers.

Moralizing the environment

From the discussion so far we can see that industrial organizations have done a pretty good job taking on, or defending off, the natural environment on their own terms. Grand moral imperatives which appeal to the sanctity of nature and the obligations of business to care for our natural heritage have been skilfully boiled down to the pragmatics of workaday business life and its operating ethics. For some critics, such as Welford, this is a pernicious, even conspiratorial, state of affairs which locks industry into a permanent state of 'looking backwards' and moral turpitude:

> Even the population explosion is rarely considered because it does, after all, present new market opportunities . . . Business finds it almost impossible to conceive of a situation where they are selling less and the emphasis is on ecology and quality rather than growth and quantity. (1997: 8, 10)

Welford is impatient with what he sees as the arrogance of industry with its vested interests and individuals 'too frightened to explore alternatives' – which for Welford includes more communitarian, non-hierarchical, low-growth economies. I sympathize with Welford's frustration and vision. But in demonizing the managerial/industrial culture we are given little insight into (a) why certain ethical codes persist and (b) why the owners and managers of industry do not engage with new ones. If managers are indeed fearful of change which embraces significant environmental alternatives then the bases of such fears need to be understood (e.g. see Fineman, 1996). Berating them for their feelings is rather like telling a person suffering a nervous breakdown to pull him/herself together.

Industrial organizations are, in many ways, rational products of a massive social, economic and legal infrastructure which encases them. All this is unlikely to be swept away in some drastic new order – much as some eco-radicals would like it so. If anything, we see the opposite, as moderate environmentalism is absorbed into conventional business rhetoric and as market enterprise enjoys a tightening grip on world economies. Even when executives and managers accept that we may be facing ecological oblivion – which some do – this is clearly insufficient to substantively dislodge the way things are done now. There are parallels here with smokers who continue to smoke knowing that it is cancerous. There are always other social, emotional and subcultural reasons and rewards to keep an 'unhealthy' habit going. What this means is that if we want to encourage a more radical environmental agenda we cannot give up on industry; we have to find new ways of working on it, with it and around it.

Does the language of morality help? Many teachers of business ethics think it does: hence the oft-reproduced litany of philosophical 'schools' which cast managers into the role of moral agents. With adequate understanding of the great moral philosophers and their principles about harm, justice, rights and so forth, the manager, goes the argument, should be well equipped to make far-sighted decisions on environmental protection, if necessary beyond usual normative or legal constraints. In practice such prescriptions are so detached from the lived experiences and multiple interests of those in corporate/business life that they can come across as laughable. Or, as Frederick and Hoffman suggest, they appear to be 'no more than an intellectual game, a kind of karate for the mind for those lucky enough not to have to face the real world where real decisions are made. The ethics of philosophers bakes no bread and solves no problems' (1995: 708; see Parker, Chapter 14 in this volume).

When radical environmentalism is added to the moral agenda it calls for a major shift towards ecocentric thinking (see especially Shrivastava, 1995; Henderson, 1990). This kicks away many of the key props to Western philosophical thinking. It asks business, in addressing its social and moral obligations, to centre all its strategic and functional planning on pro-environmental values. I cannot dispute the sentiments of such a call. Social change, so crucial to environmental issues, requires imaginative new visions and challenges to entrenched social orders. I do, however, query the wisdom of placing the moral burden on the shoulders of the practising manager. As Watson suggests in Chapter 12 in this book, radical moral theory is vacuous if it cannot connect 'ought' with 'can', moral imperative with politically possible action.

The dominant discourse of modern organizations is saturated with the language of rationality, normal science, hierarchy, patriarchal power, cause–effect, status seeking, win–lose situations, authority, capital accumulation, profit and growth. The visions of eco-transformists, in the main, aim to produce outcomes similar to the modernists, but with a rather different set of ingredients – to include, for example, spirituality, emotions, egalitarianism, feminism, non-hierarchical structures and meaningfulness. This is an uneasy discourse to swallow for those schooled in the grand narratives of patriarchy and emotion control. Some late modern critiques ask for yet more revision, especially an abandonment of modernism's keystone – the quest for high economic growth. And talk of postmodernity – an uncontrollable, incoherent society – is likely to cap managers' incredulity.

The manager operating within the modernist tradition is not in a position to make significant moral choices outside the phenomenological and structural space that he or she inhabits, especially choices that reject certainty, toughness and control. This trap is, in part, self-designed; it is what industry has helped create. But it is also held firmly in place by many other players – banks, investors, governments, customers – who trade in industry's lifeblood, financial capital. It is unsurprising, therefore, that we find commercial organizations responding conservatively to environmentalism. Even the much lionized Body Shop and Ben 'n' Jerry's, often presented as being at the cutting edge of environmental responsibility, are firmly in the modernist mould of expansion and economic growth while also purveying products that some might regard as amongst the more frivolous of a consumerist society. It is unsurprising, also, that individual managers feel puzzled, affronted, even angry when they are told by 'outsiders' that they are on the wrong moral track and that they should radically reform their business ways for the sake of the planet (see Fineman, 1996; Brenkert, 1995). Their realities are firmly embedded in a web of short and medium term actions which are rewarded according to their contribution to the production of goods and services.

Technical responsibility, as Bauman (1989) suggests, displaces wider moral concerns. For the corporate actor the natural environment is both everywhere and nowhere. Exactly what or whom is the individual employee personally hurting or damaging when doing his or her relatively self-contained, role differentiated, task? What essence does the natural environment have to the production manager who worries about meeting his schedules, or the accountant seeking tax breaks, or the car line operator fitting dashboard after dashboard? This point was plain in the pedestrian nature of an environmental committee meeting we observed in one of the companies in our own study:

> The company manufactures trucks, and is a world-wide corporation. In a smart committee room in headquarters are seven managers from different functions and an external environmental consultant. The meeting is chaired by the manager from corporate environmental affairs. The mood of the meeting is cool; there is little sense of urgency. The agenda is a long one. The first item is entering a

national environmental award competition. The chairman says, 'we have no choice but to enter this one.' The meeting struggles for some thirty minutes with it. What could they offer? The new tyres? The energy saving in the plant? Nothing felt right, or was sufficiently outstanding to boast about. The item fizzled out.

A new agenda item. The consultant had already delivered an extensive environmental audit to the company. Now they were faced with what to do with the long, neat, list of 'actions required'. People looked glum. There was a fair amount of ducking and weaving around the table before the chairman began mechanically to tick off the items, allocating them to each manager around the table. The production manager suddenly sprang to life, slightly panicky. He rummaged in his briefcase and produced various environmental action forms and other bits of paper. He *had* been busy, he said. We should appreciate that.

Another agenda item. Plastic cups. The meeting gets excited and it turns out to be the emotional high-spot of the morning. How can they prevent people taking *two* plastic cups from the drinks machine to stop burning their hands? There are reusable cup holders provided, but people keep throwing them away. And how about recycling the cups? The committee members clearly enjoyed this item and the debate was prolonged, animated, sometimes humorous. No solution was found.

Final item: beautifying the work's grounds and physical environment. The chairman waves a brochure from the Groundwork Action Trust, a charitable organization devoted to working with industry to improve their sites. 'They have approached us before,' says the chairman, 'Maybe the time's right to do something.' The room is silent. After a while the chairman fills the uncomfortable vacuum: 'Mmm . . . planting trees and all that; not sure we're equipped to get involved with that sort of rubbish.' The item is dropped and the meeting is closed.

Here the environment is condensed into 'items' which more or less fit with the prevailing technical/bureaucratic norms. It is a routine, rationalistic, activity – largely a hollow one in the above case. It causes few ripples to the daily business of producing trucks – where the main ethical imperative of the enterprise lies and, arguably, where the main environmental problems reside. But significantly, the very structure and content of the meeting bureaucratically encapsulates those present and removes the need to think about the natural environment beyond its pale reflection in the agenda items. Rescuing the planet tends not to figure in the language and minutes of such meetings. The physical and psychological distance is considerable between what junior or middle managers daily coordinate in the production of trucks, soap powder or washing machines, and the ozone depletion, forest destruction or mineral waste that such work can eventually create. The moral muteness of these, and other, managers is less a personal character defect than a product of the social architecture of their work organizations. Such social patterns define the operational codes of work life, codes which can result in damaging, even criminal, action (e.g. see Punch, 1996).

If moral consciousness plays such a small role in corporate life, what part can moral re-education play in creating a new environmental order in industry? Probably not a lot. The very vocabulary of 'morals' and 'ethics' is not helpful, given its judgemental quality and sense of rigidity. It 'threatens the flexibility that many decision makers think is needed to adapt to fast changing situations' (Frederick and Hoffman, 1995: 707). Furthermore, 'rational', cognitive, moral language divorced from self-regulatory emotions, such as shame, pride and remorse, is like a rudderless ship. Such emotions are not simply implanted through lectures on business ethics, although it might be possible to create somewhat more sympathetic learning settings (see Fineman, 1997b; Brandt, 1979). And if effective moral debate is to occur it has to take place in a relevant moral community – where responsibility for environmental damage is 'owned'. Currently, as we have suggested, organizational indicators do not point in that direction.

Some writers see the answer in a reconstitution of environmental ethics. For example, Frederick and Hoffman (1995) argue for an approach to 'an environmental risk problem' via an enlarged concept of ethical responsibility to the environment. It would include political, economic, legal and technical considerations. These certainly reach some of the enacted moralities of organizational members, but it is far from clear how the environmental edge is maintained in relation to other business risks – such as those associated with market share and growth. And why should organizational members be bothered to take on board the ethical imperatives such as 'fairly distributing benefits and burdens' and 'treating people not merely as means to some goal' (1995: 705–6). These are fine sentiments, but curiously divorced from the pervasive instrumentality of organizational life.

Changing course?

There are economic pressures common to most business organizations which stem from their capitalist roots, producing tensions between profit, costs, competition, efficiency, growth and survival. These determine the basic shape of the organizational pot, into which different cultural and political values are stirred – and often transformed. Green values may or may not be added to the mix. At the same time big organizations play an increasing part in shaping wider institutions and voices – national and international government, school and higher education, scientific research and funding, consumer preferences. Industry's power to privilege its own economic interest is considerable, and only when it sees gain from greening does it engage in pro-environmental activity.

Behind this, as I have argued, are shifts in the legitimization of environmental care by industry with its attendant rhetorics of 'evidence' and 'concern'. But, as the basic contours of the organization have not changed, green capitalism is likely to remain fragile and mostly shallow. Yet such an approach provides a comforting gloss for those who believe we can continue to have our cake and eat it: industry *and* the environment. It also creates a compelling myth of 'trickle-down' wealth from economic growth to assuage concerns about those whose bear much of the environmental costs but receive little of the industrial benefit.

Whither change? While green capitalism will not produce a deep-green revolution, arguably it is better than nothing. We might intensify the financial and moral load on organizations, seeking out the cracks and crannies in the managerial/executive edifice. In many Western economies the combined assault from green pressure groups, environmental regulators, shifts in consumer patterns, whistle-blowers, ethical investment funding, as well as increasing green awareness amongst employees, is already weakening those organizations most wedded to a business-as-usual approach. As Morgan suggests in Chapter 10 in this book, the role of powerful environmental regulators is crucial here because, at best, they can set standards and police environmental performance. Significantly regulators do not demand a new ethical language from organizations, but home in on different ways of doing what industry already does. This, though, is more complex than it seems: some agencies are better resourced than others and they vary in their degree of capture by the industries they regulate.

The carrying capacity of the planet is not part of the daily chat of managers, or a manifest part of regulated environmental performance (although it is implicit in the framing of some environmental legislation). It is an evocative and contestable concept which has yet to enjoy popularity outside the discourse of some environmental pressure groups and scientists. Yet it sharply underlines one vision, or framing, of environmental responsibility in technocratic language – which is likely to be more persuasive to government and industry than moral exhortation. As reports multiply of eco-systems depleted through unfettered (or even greened) growth, 'carrying capacity' has the potential to be translated and popularized in ways which redefine economic policy and industrial goals. Already it has some key backers – 'new' economists and ecologists – to help it along a socially constructed path to political legitimacy.

In appealing to the workaday ethics of organizational members, should we drop all attempts at moralizing the environment? No. Moral responsibility for the institutions we help create and hegemonize should be inescapable, as heroic whistle-blowers and protest movements remind us. Some critical moral discourse is essential. If children, especially in richer economies, are not taught to question the ethic of consumption and its environmental consequences, then why should they think differently about the environment? If business courses offer at most a thin green veneer to 'market domination', then why should new recruits to business do more than light greening? And how are national politicians representing a social 'good' if they do not reflect on the long term environmental consequences of their politically expedient actions? The ideological oxygen still flows to support industrial growth, almost regardless of environmental costs. Asking questions such as these is one step towards reducing that flow and creating alternatives based on different moral orders.

References

Aldrich, H.E. (1979) *Organizations and Environments*. Englewood Cliffs, NJ: Prentice-Hall.

Arrow, K., Bolin, B., Costanza, R., Dasgupta, P., Folke, C., Holling, C.S., Jansson, B.-O., Levin, S., Maler, K.-G., Perrings, C. and Pimentel, D. (1996) 'Economic Growth, Carrying Capacity and the Environment', *Ecological Applications*, 6(1): 13–15.

Bauman, Z. (1989) *Modernity and the Holocaust*. Cambridge: Polity.

Beaumont, J.R., Pedersen, L.M. and Whitaker, B.D. (1993) *Managing the Environment: Business Opportunity and Responsibility*. Oxford: Butterworth-Heinemann.

Bird, F.B. and Waters, J.A. (1989) 'The Moral Muteness of Managers', *California Management Review,* 32(1): 73–88.

Brandt, R.B. (1979) *A Theory of the Good and Right.* Oxford: Clarendon.

Brenkert, G.G. (1995) 'The Environment, the Moralist, the Corporation and its Culture', *Business Ethics Quarterly* 5(4): 675–97.

Daft, R. (1995) *Organization Theory and Design.* Minneapolis/St. Paul: West.

Daly, H. and Cobb, J. (1989) *For the Common Good*. New York: Beacon.

Elkington, J. and Burke, T. (1987) *The Green Capitalists: Industry's Search for Environmental Excellence*. London: Gollancz.

Fineman, S. (1996) 'Emotional Subtexts in Corporate Greening', *Organization Studies,* 17(3): 479–500.

Fineman, S. (1997a) 'Constructing the Green Manager', *British Journal of Management*, 8, 31–8.

Fineman, S. (1997b) 'Emotion and Management Learning', *Management Learning*, 28(1): 13–25.

Fineman, S. and Clarke, K. (1996) 'Green Stakeholders: Industry Interpretations and Response', *Journal of Management Studies*, 33(6): 715–30.

Frederick, R.E. and Hoffman, W.M. (1995) 'Environmental Risk Problems and the Language of Ethics', *Business Ethics Quarterly*, 5(4): 699–711.

Frederick, W. (1995) *Values, Nature and Culture in the American Corporation*. New York: Oxford University Press.

Friedman, M. (1970) 'The Social Responsibility of Business Is To Increase Profits', *New York Times Magazine*, 13 September: 122–6.

Grossman, G.M. and Krueger, A.B. (1993) 'Environmental Impacts of a North American Free Trade Agreement', in P.M. Garber (ed.), *The U.S.–Mexico Free Trade Agreement*. Cambridge, MA: MIT Press.

Hannigan, J.A. (1995) *Environmental Sociology*. London: Routledge.

Hardin, G. (1978) 'The Tragedy of the Commons', *Science*, 62: 1243–8.

Henderson, H. (1990) 'From Environmentalism to Ecophilosophy: Retooling Cultures for the Twenty-First Century', in W. M. Hoffman, R. Frederick and E. S. Petry (eds), *Business, Ethics, and the Environment*. New York: Quorum.

Jackall, R. (1988) *Moral Mazes*. New York: Oxford University Press.

Lawrence, P.R. and Lorsch, J.W. (1967) *Organization and Environment*. Boston: Harvard University Press.

Leopold, A. (1949) *A Sand County Almanac*. New York: Oxford University Press.

McKibben, B. (1989) *The End of Nature*. New York: Random House.

Naess, A. (1989) *Ecology, Community and Lifestyle*. Cambridge: Cambridge University Press.

O'Conner, M. (1983) 'Is Sustainable Capitalism Possible?', in P. Allen (ed.), *Food for the Future: Conditions and Contradictions of Sustainability*. New York: Wiley.

O'Riordan, T. (1981) *Environmentalism*. London: Pion.

Pauchant, T.C. and Fortier, I. (1990) 'Anthropocentric Ethics in Organizations: How

Different Strategic Management Schools View the Environment', in W.M. Hoffman, R. Frederick and E.S. Petry (eds), *The Corporation, Ethics and the Environment*. New York: Forum.

Prince, S.J. and Denson, R. (1992) 'Launching a New Business Ethic: The Environment as a Standing Operating Procedure', *Industrial Management*, 34(6): 15–19.

Punch, M. (1996) *Dirty Business*. London: Sage.

Rodman, H. (1977) 'Liberation of Nature', *Inquiry*, 20: 89.

Rodman, J. (1983) 'Four Forms of Ecological Consciousness', in D. Scherer and T. Atteg (eds), *Ethics and the Environment*. Englewood Cliff, NJ: Prentice-Hall.

Rolston, H. (1988) *Environmental Ethics*. Philadelphia: Temple University Press.

Schindler, D.W., Kidd, K.A., Muir, D.C.G. and Lockhart, W.L. (1996) 'The Effects of Ecosystem Characteristics on Contaminant Distribution in Northern Freshwater Lakes', *Science and the Total Environment*, 160/161: 1–17.

Schmidheiny, S. (1992) *Changing Course: A Global Perspective on Development and the Environment*. Cambridge, MA: MIT Press.

Schumacher, E.F. (1973) *Small is Beautiful*. London: Abacus.

Sheldon, O. (1923) *The Philosophy of Management*. London: Pitman.

Shrivastava, P. (1995) 'Ecocentric Management for a Risk Society', *The Academy of Management Review*, 20(1): 118–37.

Stapleton, J. (1996) 'The Environmental Imperative: An Industrial Perspective', in R.M. Thomas (ed.), *Teaching Ethics. Volume 3: Environmental Ethics.* London: HMSO.

Taylor, P.W. (1986) *Respect for Nature: A Theory of Environmental Ethics*. Princeton, NJ: Princeton University Press.

Thompson, J. (1990) 'A Refutation of Environmental Ethics', *Environmental Ethics*, 12(2): 147–60.

Welford, R. (1997) 'Highjacking Environmentalism? Corporate Responses to Sustainable Development', in R. Welford, *Hijacking Environmentalism*. London: Earthscan.

Yearley, S. (1992) *The Green Case: A Sociology of Environmental Issues, Arguments and Politics*. London: Routledge.

Part 3: IMPLICATIONS

12 Ethical Codes and Moral Communities: the Gunlaw Temptation, the Simon Solution and the David Dilemma

Tony Watson

The organization and the management of work involve moral matters and ethical dilemmas from top to bottom and from beginning to end. However, issues of morality and the necessity of ethical choices are frequently pushed to one side as pressures to get results, to get the job done and to survive in a competitive or otherwise hostile world press organizational managers endlessly to seek more efficacious *means* without giving too much consideration to the *ends* to which they are oriented or to the values which are implicit in those means. This situation is increasingly being recognized and its continuation challenged. Such a recognition sometimes comes about as people conclude that, in certain circumstances, 'morality pays' or 'being ethical is good for business'. At other times it comes about as people choose to raise ethical concerns as an ethical act in itself. It is increasingly being seen as a good and right thing in itself to ask what we should do to be 'good' or 'right' in our human choices and actions.

These two imperatives – to examine the ethical bases of organizational and managerial activity on instrumental grounds and to examine them on grounds of basic human principle – are not as separate as they might at first seem. The ultimate instrumentality shared by all human beings is one of how they and their species are to survive into the future and with what quality of life. Tackling such questions inevitably raises issues of principle: questions both about how humans should relate to each other and about how they should relate to their physical environment. Principles and pragmatism are closely interwoven in practice, whether we are thinking at the higher global level or at the level of detailed organizational practice (as I shall argue later).

Increased questioning both by writers on work organization and management, and by organizational managers themselves, of simplistically and directly coercive approaches to the efficient and effective production of goods and services has focused on the 'dysfunctionality' of such a mode of organizing. There has been growing support for a more 'moral' approach to the shaping of productive enterprise – one which establishes corporate cultures and moral codes based on principles of reciprocity, trust and explicitly recognized interdependencies. In the present chapter, we see a group of managers confronting an upsurge of directly coercive management in their organization and reflecting on the need for a more moral or, as one of them puts it, a more value-based approach to managing and organizing. I use this ethnographic material, which was generated in a study where I was a participant observer within a management group, to illustrate how moral reflection on managerial practice can come about within the context of managerial practice itself.

I am anxious to show that ethical dilemmas are not the explicit concern of academic observers of organizational activities alone. And in showing this, I also hope to give some insight into the processes of social construction, contestation and institutionalization which occur within organizations. Doing this, as Morgan argues in Chapter 10 in the present volume, can be a way for the critical organization theorist to contribute to debates about the governance and regulation of organizations. A social constructionist ethnography is not simply an exercise in descriptive reporting. And just because it recognizes *relativity* does not mean that it must take us towards a moral *relativism*. It can show us the different ways in which human beings, in different social settings, both talk about and tackle issues and it can give us some idea of the outcomes and implications of people acting in various ways. Such social scientific analyses can be offered to readers to take forward into the debates which properly occur in the realm of democratic debate. Social scientific analyses should inform moral debates engaged in by the citizens of moral communities rather than be used to make ethical prescriptions. Effective moral debate, if it is to occur, has to take place in what Fineman calls the 'relevant moral community' (Chapter 11 in this volume). The uncertainties which Anthony discusses in Chapter 13 are not going to be resolved by any organization or management theorist ('critical' or otherwise).

Organizational practitioners may be no more able than academic prescriptive theorists to resolve these uncertainties, but they cannot avoid being confronted by such uncertainties from time to time. What we see in the present ethnographic episode is a set of managers experiencing such a confrontation.The managers are broadly in agreement in rejecting the type of *gunlaw rule* which they hear about from one of their number (although they are aware that there may still exist an argument for its use, in immediate corporate effectiveness terms at least – the *gunlaw temptation*). They tend to support the general 'moral community' or 'value-based management' argument of one of their number, however. This is the *Simon solution*. But Simon does not have it all his way. One of the managers presents his colleagues – and, I suggest, all of us who have been attracted to this broad approach to organizational ethics – with the *David dilemma*. This is powerfully captured in David's own words, 'You could have a death camp operating with a clear morality where all the guards trusted each other, were open and honest with each other, treated each other fairly and, well, would that be moral?' Organizational ethics, then, is a matter of more than establishing a moral base for corporate activity based on the organization as a moral community. Trust is not enough. Let us see how this argument emerged in the ethnographic episode.

The gunslingers come to town

It is early on a spring morning in the boardroom of an electronics company and the gathering is one of the company's senior personnel managers. The personnel director of the company (Martin) is chairing the meeting at which an important guest is his opposite number (Colin) from a company which is in the same group. The group's ownership has recently changed and the business in which the guest personnel director works has experienced several months of direct managerial participation by representatives of the new German co-owner. Martin, the host personnel director, his team of personnel managers (Simon, David, Roger, Timothy and Iain) and the participant observation researcher (Tony) are anxious to hear what has been happening in the other company.

> *Martin*: What's it like, then, Colin?
> *Colin*: Oh not bad you know. We are coping. Yeah coping.
> *Martin*: Why do you look so miserable every time I see you then?
> *Roger*: Come on Colin.
> *Colin*: You want to know what you might have to look forward to, don't you?
> *Iain*: Yeah, the Germans are coming. They are blitzing you aren't they?
> *Colin*: There are only two of them. I tend to think of it much more like an old Western film, though. They are a pair of ruthless gunslingers who have come to town and are firing off bullets at anything that moves. And that includes me.

At this point Colin Woodhouse explains a particular matter over which he clashed with one of the German managers who are, he says, 'determined to change the culture here'. He goes on:

> *Colin*: I don't know what sort of culture they are trying to put in. But they do seem to be determined to kill off the culture we have got, 'Bang, you're dead' ; 'Bang, I'll shoot that to pieces.' It's 'One false move and you're dead' stuff, believe me. You're in the saloon having a quiet hand of poker – you know, planning workload or something when, bang, the saloon doors crash open and there is Kurt, pistol in each hand. It's 'Under the table boys.' The bullets are whizzing over your head. You lie flat on the floor. You see your pal take one in the back. Then Kurt or maybe Gunter is standing over you, pistols smoking. You look at the whites of his eyes. 'Am I going to die?'

There is pause in the conversation, which is broken by one of the managers. He speaks in a low mock-dramatic voice.

Simon: Give us some more. I'm gripped. And scared.
Tony: But don't go too fast Colin, I'm writing all this down. It's brilliant stuff.
Colin: You think I am dramatizing? This is from the heart stuff. I am living a cheap and nasty novel at the moment. You've got to use this, Tony. It's a story of what happens when you get managers in charge who are utterly devoid of morality. It's got absolutely nothing to do with the German angle. These blokes are just total sods. It's not really important what they are trying to achieve. What I think they have been put in to do is probably reasonable. There's some real sorting out to do. I think that these two are such bastards that whatever it is they are charged with doing, they are going to fail. You just cannot manage in this amoral fashion.
Roger: Are you sure? If their mission is a death mission – a Vietnam sort of job: slash and burn, destroy the village, kill the VC – then they're doing it well.
Martin: I don't think that is what they are here for. But if it was, it wouldn't need to be done that way. They would just close down the operation.
Simon: One big surgical operation sort of thing rather than bleeding the place to death.
Iain: They're fighting a one-sided war of attrition. Is there such a thing?

The speaker looks at the researcher.

Tony: I don't know. It's interesting though how we are trying to relate war strategy to business strategy isn't it. Colin?
Colin: Yes it is. And I think, as you all know, that a business strategy has to have an ethical dimension.
Martin: Unlike war strategy.
Colin: Well I don't know. We know that baddies win battles. But do they win wars? We've had two world wars and – as we're told it – morality won both times. Evil – with all the might behind it we saw in both wars – failed.
Tony: Yes, but in the stories we were told about the Wild West, the goodies always won. Do we believe that now though?
Colin: Uhm, well. I don't think that these immoral baddies – prowling around our outfit in their black hats shooting the white hats off their white chargers – are going to win anything. They are just going to waste the place. It's worse than ever happened in the old Wild West.

Colin Woodhouse, well known in the group as a particularly articulate individual and, as we see here, an especially effective storyteller, continued to give examples of the ruthless behaviour of the two gunslingers. He tells stories of people arriving at work to find Kurt sitting at their desk, going through the drawers of their desk or filing cabinet. He speaks of Gunter removing people from their jobs overnight without consultation with anyone (including Colin, the personnel director). He reports both men arriving in the middle of meetings which they take over and leave without addressing any of the meeting's formal agenda items and he generally describes bad-tempered, rude, arrogant, secretive and impetuous behaviour and a practice of 'punishing' individuals in a variety of ways for 'offences' which they could only guess at. But Colin is not just a good storyteller and an accomplished rhetorician, and he was taking no joy in telling his tale of 'managerial murder and mayhem' – as much as he was holding his colleagues spellbound with his narrative skills. He is also known as something of a 'personnel philosopher', as one of the managers called him. And he was intent upon using his dramatic Wild West story to argue that the only outcome of a continuing management style like that he was describing would be the failure of the business.

Colin: They have seen off one or two of the people in the organization that were a problem to us. But, at the same time, they have got some of our best people looking for jobs elsewhere. I admit I am looking myself.
David: And you're one of the very best, Colin.
Colin: No, I didn't mean that. I don't know how many people are planning to go over the wall. But what I do know is that people are so utterly terrified that we can hardy expect them to do a good job for the business.
Martin: Hang on though, Colin. I've seen the sales figures, and the cost figures, you've turned in for the past couple of months. I don't doubt what you say about people being scared but this culture of coercion and bullying that you describe seems to be working.

The Timothy (gunlaw) temptation

Tim Denton took up this point and referred to examples of bullying managers he had observed. He stressed that most of these men ('and one woman, I must point out') were 'utter disasters' who tended to be seen as failures by their senior and their junior colleagues and by their peers. He argued that these people operated with 'little or no morality' and that, because 'nobody knew where they stood' with them, all their efforts to manage effectively were undermined by the 'determination of their people to trip them up whenever they could'. However, he went on, there were one or two cases where 'gunslinger types' were successful – at least in the sense that their departments 'met all their targets and kept costs under control'. He reflected on why this might have been and instigated a reaction from Martin Hillside.

Tim: I suppose you could argue that they were operating a kind of morality. It was a matter of 'What is right is what I say is right.' They were the fastest shots in town and it was, sort of, 'You don't argue with the barrel of a gun do you?'
Roger: It's 'might is right' morality.
Martin: Come off it, Tim, that's no morality is it? It is just gunlaw terror like

Colin's talking about. You can't have a morality that belongs to only one person.

Tim: Yes, that's right. But what I was getting at was that it was sort of shared. It wasn't deep down but people sort of reasoned, 'I work in this department and I know where I stand with this guy. I know the score. I'd better do what he wants.' It's a sort of moral code isn't it?

Martin: Of course it's not.

Tony: But you can see what Tim is getting at. There is some agreement – however grudging – about how things should be done, isn't there? If you accept Tim's case that these people's management style 'worked' then either you accept that there is some moral code operating or you abandon the position which you normally take – the same as Colin – that amoral management simply cannot work.

Martin: I, I . . . Colin, help me out here.

Colin: I think I can see Tim's point and why any manager might be tempted to use the heavy hand. And I do recognize that my German friends might do some positive things for the business. Now, I haven't yet worked out what Gunter and Kurt are seeking for themselves but I do see that a lot of people in management – and I bet we could name plenty of them in our own set-up – who do not intend to stay for a long time in the job they are in. They want to get results fast to show how good they are and they throw their weight around, putting aside all ethical concerns apart from the rightness of their own advancement, and they get what they want.

Martin: So in the long run Kurt and Gunter are going to be good for the business? Immorality makes the world go round. I just can't . . .

Colin: No, that's my whole point. In the *short run* they might sort some problems and even do some things that have a good long term potential – reducing the cost base on the distribution network say. But what they are doing is not good for the *long run*. The organization is not going to be a healthy one. How can we grow in the way we want to if we have got everybody continually looking over their shoulder? As soon as Kurt and Gunter get back on the plane to Deutschland everybody will lie down and go back to sleep.

Tony: You are saying, then, that management by terror, gunlaw or whatever, can work but only in the short term?

Colin: Yes, I think that is it. You need a firmer moral base to get the sort of proactive and enthusiastic business effort that you need for the longer term.

Tim: I would go along with that.

Simon: Exactly. You have got to have shared values that everybody wants to live by. Only then can people grow as people and do it in a way that makes the business grow. I at least would not want to work in a company that did not work in that kind of ethical way.

We will return later to see how Simon developed his theme. Before we look at the *Simon solution* we must look more closely at the *Timothy temptation* – the 'gunlaw temptation'. In spite of his reluctance to accept that all coercive management practice is fully immoral, Tim accepts that something more fully 'moral' is needed for long term organizational effectiveness. But he has pointed to the temptation for the individual to work in a less than fully moral way to get short term effectiveness. And Colin has pointed to certain characteristics of managerial careers which might well take people towards such a temptation. Two academic studies have dealt with the issues which arise here. We will consider what Pascale and Athos (1982) argue about how short term and long term considerations relate to management style in a moment but, first, we can note some correspondence between what Colin Woodhouse is identifying in the logic of managerial careers and what Jackall concludes from his study of the corporate 'moral maze' of a selection of American organizations.

Jackall's (1988) sociological study of managerial life in American corporations portrays a set of individuals whose consciousness, he says, is shaped by bureaucracy rather than by the Protestant ethic of an earlier period. A transformation in the 'organizational form of work itself' through the 'bureaucratization of the economy' has 'undermined' the Protestant ethic, 'even in its later, secularized form – self reliance, unremitting devotion to work, and a morality that postulated just rewards for work well done' (1988: 9). He refers to the 'enduring genius' of the bureaucratic organizational form as one which allows people to 'retain bewilderingly diverse private motives and meanings for action as long as they adhere publicly to agreed-upon rules' (1988: 6). Such rules, protocols and procedures, explicit and implicit, even govern 'for the most part' the 'personal relationships that men and women in bureaucracies . . . fashion together'. Thus:

> As a result, bureaucratic work causes people to bracket, while at work, the moralities that they might hold outside the workplace or that they might adhere to privately and to follow instead the prevailing morality of their particular organizational situation. As a former vice-president of a large firm says: 'What is right in the corporation is not what is right in a man's home or in his church. *What is right in the corporation is what the guy above you wants from you.* That's what morality is in the corporation.' (1988: 6)

This is a conclusion which Jackall draws from his study of behaviour in his selection of organizations and it is powerful in that it demonstrates the extent to which the suspension or bracketing of moral concerns other than those of the corporate jungle of career advancement are possible in the context of the modern work organization (see the various discussions of Bauman elsewhere in this volume for amplification of this point). Colin Woodhouse is recognizing this possibility in the British context but it is important to note that my own ethnographic study of managerial work and managerial thought, *pace* Jackall, suggests that moral concerns do play a role in the day-to-day life of managers (Watson, 1994a; 1996). Such issues are not generally addressed, however, separately from more pragmatic concerns. Attempts to draw out from managers the 'theories' which they applied in their managerial work produced accounts which 'typically constituted a highly integrated mixture of the principled and the pragmatic, the normative and the positive' (Watson, 1996: 332). We will return to the question of what this mixture specifically entailed later, because it takes us towards the 'Simon solution'. The difference in Jackall's analysis and my own may in part be to do with details of research method (my own participant observation style of ethnography and the lengthy confidential interviews which were done within this perhaps enabling me to get closer to the *thinking* which informs managers' actions and everyday talk) and there is inevitably a matter of international differences in corporate cultures.

One specific difference between my analysis and Jackall's is clear when we contrast the conversation which is being reported in the course of the present ethnographic analysis with Jackall's statement that 'managers do not generally discuss ethics, morality, or moral rules-in-use in a direct way with each other, except perhaps in seminars organized by ethicists' (1988: 6). Such seminars, he adds, are 'unusual and, when they do occur, are often strained, artificial, and often confusing even to managers' (1988: 6). The event examined in the present study was in no way organized by an 'ethicist'. I took part in the discussions and, as a participant member of the group, influenced its course. But this was not a significant influence. These managers wanted – one might even say 'needed' – to talk about these moral matters and would have done so whether or not the researcher was present. Further, the moral debate in this boardroom is not only far from strained and artificial, it is sophisticated and heartfelt. I would admit that on revisiting the fieldnotes of the event (which I thought I remembered clearly as an untypically and outstandingly thoughtful management meeting) I have been astonished at how articulately and penetratingly my former colleagues engaged with Colin Woodhouse's experiences. This, I believe, is significant because it counters the type of cynicism about the potential for managers to talk critically and ethically about their work which could be encouraged by a reading of Jackall's study. Those who look towards such possibilities may be encouraged (Alvesson and Willmott, 1996).

The position which our managers were approaching when we left them to look to the American research was one which saw a possible temptation offering itself in which they might seek to achieve effective performance through direct coercion rather than through negotiating a moral basis for interdependent co-operative action. They recognized, however, that this could succeed in the short term but would be problematic in the longer run. This is close to an analysis offered by two American researchers who contrast the management approach of a Japanese corporation to that of an American company which was ruled by an individual very close to Woodhouse's notion of the gunslinger. Harold Geneen of ITT is shown by Pascale and Athos to have operated a style describable as 'obsessive, compulsive, domineering, perfectionistic, paranoid, and even addictive' (1982: 78–9). He showed no trust in his managers and staff and operated something close to a reign of terror. This 'worked' however. But it only worked whilst Geneen held the reins. The absence of an institutionalized value system meant that success could only follow from constant monitoring and hectoring by the chief executive. A different level of long term success, which was not dependent on his continuing role as the dominant figure, is shown to have been achieved by Konsuke Matsushita in the Japanese corporation. The company developed a philosophy which provided a 'basis of meaning beyond the products it produces' (1982: 50). These are meanings based on a morality, we can say – if we regard morality as a matter operating within shared values – and they helped hold together this large Japanese multinational corporation, even when its founder left the helm. These values, the authors claim:

> taken to heart, provide a spiritual fabric of great resilience. They foster consistent expectations among employees in a work force that reaches from continent to continent. They permit a highly complex and decentralised firm to evoke an enormous continuity that sustains it even when more operational guidance breaks down. (1982: 51)

This argument that a corporation can be more effectively managed through values, through culture, through 'simultaneous loose–tight controls' than through traditional bureaucratic controls or management fiat is one immediately recognizable as coming from the early 1980s management thinking stable of the McKinsey consulting company, occupied in addition to Pascale and Athos by Deal and Kennedy (1982) and Peters and Waterman (1982). This broad approach to making non-Japanese, and especially American, corporations more like Japanese ones so that they could handle growing competition from the Orient was one which all of the managers in our present study were familiar with. They had all been active participants in their company's major 'culture change' programme and could all talk the language of 'managing through values'. This, though only in part, sets the context for the *Simon solution* to improving company performance through developing shared value and trust relations.

The Simon solution

We noted Simon's prescription earlier that 'You have got to have shared values that everybody wants to live by. Only then can people grow as people and do it in a way that makes the business grow.' And we noted his observation that 'I at least would not want to work in a company that did not work in that kind of ethical way'. He is explicitly connecting his preference for a value-based style of management to his personal moral preferences rather than to the ideas of any management 'guru' or executive 'flavour of the month' – something he was ambivalent about, like most other managers in these businesses (Watson, 1994b). This, again, contrasts with Jackall's (1988) analysis of managerial 'bracketing' of personal moral concerns when at work. The Simon solution, however, is one involving that combination of principle and pragmatism which I referred to earlier and which I found in the accounts produced by managers with whom I was discussing their personal 'theories' of managing.

> They would say words to the effect that you *ought* to listen to people but you will also *get better work from people* if you do. They would suggest that it is a *good thing* to encourage people to develop their skills and responsibilities at work but that people will also *do a much better job* if you do this. It was argued that it is a good and *moral* thing to set up relationships of trust with the people around you but that it also *pays off*: if people trust you they will do a lot more for you – whether they are customers, suppliers, fellow managers or subordinates. On those occasions when the question was asked of why this should be the case, answers were given such as 'isn't it what you would look for and respond to if you were the manager yourself?' By the same token, there were things which managers do which can be criticised as *wrong* such as bullying, being overly secretive and lying. Such things, it was claimed, also tended 'not to work'. One manager said, for example, 'You can get away with quite a lot by pulling wool over people's eyes – but only for so long. In the end you'll lose all authority', and another argued 'You can push and hassle, push and hassle and it will work. But it will only work whilst you're there to keep *at* people. And let's face it, you just can't be there all the time. It's not an effective way to operate – at the end of the day.' (Watson, 1996: 332)

The directly coercive style of managing is seen as 'wrong' in this perspective. Morality in the organization is basically about the way human beings relate to each other. The individual manager is able to express his or her personal identity through behaviour which they can justify to themselves as good or moral and *at the same time* operate in a way which contributes to the overall effectiveness of the organization. Simon and each of his colleagues were concerned to express themselves as moral beings who could be effective managers through acting morally. The *good manager* in the sense of the moral manager is a *good manager* in the sense of being an effective manager.

Parallel arguments to these have been developed by writers on organizations and management. Fox (1974; 1985), for example, stresses the centrality of what he calls 'trust relations' to organizations and he uses Blau's (1964) distinction between economic and social exchange. *Economic exchange* occurs when there is an expectation of immediate, carefully calculated, and tightly specified return following from whatever equivalent thing has been provided. There is little discretion about how obligations are to be met. Neither party to the exchange trusts the other. In *social exchange*, however, favours are given without expectation of immediate, specific or matching return. In this way 'diffuse future obligations' are established and, hence, relationships of trust between the parties. 'A spiral of rising trust' is created by relations based on social exchange (Fox, 1974: 71) and these relations can only develop if trust is 'embodied in the rules, roles and other policies and arrangements' made by managers.

Fox's analysis focuses on work design, procedures and broad policies which express the more 'moral' type of exchange which he believes to be a positive route towards successful 'problem-solving' at work and towards organizational effectiveness. Anthony's (1986) argument more directly addresses issues of morality and he emphasizes the extent to which an organization is a community as well as a set of work arrangements and associated contracts. He draws on research studies which have looked closely at managerial practice and interprets these as showing that 'managerial organizations . . . are held together by informal moral relationships that may be stronger than the moral order that the hierarchical superstructures seek to impose, and that moral and social relationships are cemented by myth, symbol, culture, and narrative' (1986: 188). And Anthony draws out implications for managers that closely parallel the positions taken by the managers in the piece of research we are considering in the present chapter. He says:

> If managers are to be encouraged to see themselves as maintainers of social and political networks of co-operation engaged in the practice of community maintenance they must see themselves as exercising power. If that power is to be perceived by the members of the communities they govern as authoritatively exercised, conceived to be legitimate, then managers must be taught both that their influence is real and that its exercise requires moral as well as practical significance. (1986: 194)

And:

> The authority of management must rest upon a moral base, secure in a concern for the integrity and the good of the community that it governs. That authority must be achieved, won rather than imposed; it cannot be sought by coercion or by the deceptive application of psychological tricks. (1986: 198)

We can compare this to the words of one of our personnel managers:

Simon: Your two cowboys seem to see the company as a playground which they can use to show off how tough they are, how ruthless they are in sorting people out. We are left only to guess at what they are trying to do beyond the shoot-ups. But – cue violins – people have given their lives to the business.

Martin: Well, I wouldn't . . .

Simon: Let's say, then, that a lot of people's lives are wrapped up in the company. If, as managers, we are going to put them under pressure we need to take responsibility for that.

Tony: How do you mean, 'take responsibility'?

Simon: We have got to show that what we are doing – however uncomfortable it might have to be – has got to do with how the business is going to give them a living in the future.

Iain: And provide employment for the town.

Simon: Absolutely. And we have got to share these concerns with people – win them over to the changes we have to make. We can only make changes that will stick if we do it within a framework of shared values.

There is, here, a recognition of the power that managers have and, precisely as Anthony is advocating, these managers see the need for that power to be legitimized in terms of a community. And this is a community which, as

Iain observes, stretches beyond the factory gates. The maintenance of community, then, provides moral grounds for managerial power and those moral grounds cannot be taken for granted: they have to be established through organizational relationships going beyond coercive power-wielding. The Simon solution is not just a matter of achieving performativity in the longer run (as opposed to the shorter term efficacy of the gunlaw temptation). It recognizes a deeper human interdependency and, if it is an 'instrumentalist' stance, then it is instrumental in the sense of the 'ultimate instrumentality' to which I referred earlier; that of the ways in which human beings as a species are to survive into the future.

The analysis developed by Anthony is influenced by the philosophy of MacIntyre (1981) and his rejection of a 'bureaucratic managerialism' which assumes the existence of a technically neutral body of science-like knowledge which managers can deploy to achieve their purposes. MacIntyre's attack on this 'moral fiction' (McMylor, 1994: 130) has also been taken up by Roberts who makes the claim that managers 'typically view themselves as morally neutral characters, and do draw upon social science as a source of techniques which will enhance the effectiveness of their control of others' (1984: 288). The validity of this rather bold claim is certainly questioned by the present research but this does not necessarily weaken the claim that effective managerial control in work organizations is not going to be achieved by the direct application of social science knowledge and morally neutral techniques to problems. Such techniques are 'inadequate to the task that is set for them and, only by acknowledging the moral character of their practice, will managers be able to become truly effective' (Roberts, 1984: 288). This 'true effectiveness' will be a product of people in the organization recognizing their interdependency and, for Roberts, 'this interdependence of self-conscious subjects . . . is the moral basis or condition of all social life' (1984: 299). And if the interdependence is not recognized, what will 'come into sight' is 'the self-defeating character of power dynamics' found ' in many organizations' (Roberts, 1996: 63). Is this not exactly what Colin Woodhouse was talking about when he suggested that his gunslingers 'are just going to waste the place'?

It would be very comfortable now to conclude this consideration of the place of morality in organizational practice by celebrating the parallels which I have shown between the arguments and prescriptions of some of the more morally enlightened management writers and the particular set of managers in the company I studied. Qualifications would have to be made which recognized that senior personnel managers, in a situation where they are forced by a business take-over to think about 'basic principles', are not necessarily typical of all managers in all situations. But at least the possibilities are established for managers directly considering the moral basis of what they do in their organizations. The pessimism of writers like Jackall (1988) is countered by this – as I hope it might be by my demonstration of the moral element of managerial thinking in my broader study (Watson, 1994a; 1996). But ethnographic research work rarely allows one to come to such neat and comforting conclusions. It was David Abbey who raised some awkward questions.

The David dilemma

It was my own attempt to articulate the position that his managerial colleagues were moving towards that led to David's expression of a dilemma:

Tony: Can I just see what you are all saying? Is it your view that a business can and should be run on a moral basis? [Nods all round]
Colin: You know I think that, and I don't think any of us who are aware of the importance of a strong and positive culture to management, are going to disagree.
Tony: So the idea is that all activities are influenced by a basic moral code which insists on people respecting each other, recognizing that everyone is obliged to everyone else to get the business working successfully. There is high trust between people which . . .
Simon: . . . which gives people space to innovate, take risks and commit themselves to business growth because they know that is the way that they will be able to grow themselves as individuals.
Tony: You build a high trust community . . .
Simon: . . . in which everybody gains.
David: OK, if we work like this . . .
Roger: . . . if only! . . .
David: . . . so that what we are all doing is moral because we all benefit, then . . . What I mean, is this really morality? Does something become good or right because everybody benefits?
Martin: It fits the Christian thing for me: do unto others as . . .
David: But where do the 'others' begin and end?

This question was met with some bafflement and David was asked to explain what he meant. At this stage coffee was brought into the meeting which meant that David was given time to think. He then put forward what he called 'a scenario'. This involved considering what would be widely considered to be an 'immoral' organization – the death camp. As other chapters of this book have recognized, following Bauman, the death camp is a very helpful organizational case for considering the relationship between morality and bureaucratic rationality. But David takes a different line. His dilemma derives from his recognition of the possibility of there existing a corporate *morality* within this appalling *immorality*:

David: You could have a death camp operating with a clear morality where all the guards trusted each other, were open and honest with each other, treated each other fairly and, well, would that be moral?
Timothy: I thought we were going a bit far with all the Wild West stuff – but, death camps . . .
David: All right. For the sake of argument, imagine that we set up a business to murder people.

Colin: Murder Incorporated.
David: OK, it's been done. But say we did this and we followed all the culture and empowerment stuff. We could have democratic management, lots of trust and all that. There's good pay for everybody, welfare arrangements, good pensions, Christmas parties for the kiddies. There's a moral code – just like the Mafia – that holds everything together. Everything we have said so far makes this a moral business. But we know it is not. Murder isn't moral, is it?
Iain: It's a ridiculous case, though.
Roger: But is it? What about arms companies? What about tobacco companies?

The conversation at this point became very disjointed with the main discussion being about whether morality could be a 'purely private matter' ('It is solely up to the individual whether or not they work for an arms manufacturer') or had to be universal ('If humans are going to live together in the world without wars, pestilence and all that, they have got to agree on what is right or wrong'). The subject was changed when it was pointed out, 'Hang on, we've got an agenda to get through before lunch-time.' But can *we* leave the matter there? Is there anything we can say to help solve the David dilemma?

The good organization and the good society

The position which was reached by our gathering of personnel managers (and which accords with some of the academic writing we have been looking at) prior to David introducing his dilemma is that there is the possibility of what we might term a 'local morality' at the level of the organization which can, through its recognizing and building on corporate interdependencies, encouraging mutuality, trust and effective cooperative activity, lead to a high level of corporate 'performance'. If we wish to see how moral concerns beyond those played out within organizations' own walls come to bear we can turn to resource dependence theory or strategic exchange thinking (Pfeffer and Salancik, 1976; Watson, 1994a). In the strategic exchange perspective, the basic logic of the managerial task in an organization is seen as one of working towards the organization's long term continuation through exchanging resources – material and symbolic – with all parties (internal and external to the organization) whose support it needs for its long term survival. If the state as the enforcer of the law of the land deems organizational activities 'wrong', say, or if the public as customers or members of pressure groups regard them as unacceptable, support will fall away. Thus, organizational managers will avoid acting in ways which depart drastically from the moralities which pertain in the institutional context in which the organization operates – moralities which consequently tend to become embedded in the organization's cultures and practices (Zucker, 1988; Morgan, Chapter 10 in this volume).

Organizations, then, are simply a part of the moral world in which they are located. The activities of those who have power and discretion within organizations both shape and are shaped by the societies to which they relate. Because work organizations are such significant parts of modern societies their managers could be said to have a major moral responsibility towards the members of the society which they help shape. However, they are not paid to act morally in any sense beyond that which will benefit the long term continuation of their organization. What this means is that the broad debates about what a good society or a good world should be have to be instigated and nurtured in the democratic and cultural processes of societies as a whole and in whatever international forums are devised to look at the implications of increasingly global activities and interdependencies. In an age when 'foundational' bases for morality are in doubt (Hassard and Parker, 1993) or are in competition with each other in international and inter-faith rivalry, there is perhaps nothing that we can turn to other than democratic debate (Rorty, 1989). We are not going to *find* the good society, the good life or the good organization. Moralities are social constructions – guidelines for human action which people acting socially have devised to handle the problems of their existence in a contingent world. What we might try to do, therefore, as the inhabitants of organizations, of communities, of societies and of a shared planet, is to come fully to terms with the extent of our interdependencies and set out to *create* a good world – building on everything we can learn from history, from literature, from existing traditions – to *construct* moralities which help us with the existential dilemmas we currently face. Principles of utilitarianism, Kantian categorical imperatives, Durkheimian sociological theory and ethnographic studies like the present one are all grist to this dialogical mill. They can all inform the choices we consider in our debates but they cannot make the choices for us.

A realistic starting point for many of us, of course, may well be the organizations that we work within. But what we have to recognize is that it is only as social, political and moral human beings working in organizations, rather than as managers or organizational 'experts', that we will achieve anything.

References

Alvesson, M. and Willmott, H. (1996) *Making Sense of Management: A Critical Introduction.* London: Sage.
Anthony, P.D. (1986) *The Foundation of Management.* London: Tavistock.
Blau, P. (1964) *Exchange and Power in Social Life.* New York: Wiley.
Deal, T.E. and Kennedy, A.A. (1982) *Corporate Cultures: The Rites and Rituals of Corporate Life.* Reading, MA: Addison-Wesley.
Fox, A. (1974) *Beyond Contract: Work, Power and Trust Relations.* London: Faber.
Fox, A. (1985) *Man Mismanagement.* London: Hutchinson.
Hassard, J. and Parker, M. (1993) *Postmodernism and Organizations.* London: Sage.
Jackall, R. (1988) *Moral Mazes: The World of Corporate Managers.* New York: Oxford University Press.
MacIntyre, A. (1981) *After Virtue: A Study in Moral Theory.* London: Duckworth.

McMylor, P. (1994) *Alasdair MacIntyre: Critic of Modernity.* London: Routledge.
Pascale, R.T. and Athos, A.G. (1982) *The Art of Japanese Management.* Harmondsworth: Penguin.
Peters, T.J. and Waterman, R.H.J. (1982) *In Search of Excellence.* New York: Harper & Row.
Pfeffer, J. and Salancik, G.R. (1976) *The External Control of Organisations: A Resource Dependence Approach.* New York: Harper & Row.
Roberts, J. (1984) 'The Moral Character of Management Practice', *Journal of Management Studies*, 21(3): 287–302.
Roberts, J. (1996) 'Management Education and the Limits of Technical Rationality: The Conditions and Consequences of Management Practice', in R. French, and C. Grey (eds) *Rethinking Management Education.* London: Sage.
Rorty, R. (1989) *Contingency, Irony, and Solidarity.* Cambridge: Cambridge University Press.
Watson, T.J. (1994a) *In Search of Management.* London: Routledge.
Watson, T.J. (1994b) 'Management "Flavours of the Month": Their Role in Managers' Lives', *The International Journal of Human Resource Management*, 5(4): 889–905.
Watson, T.J. (1996) 'How Do Managers Think? Morality and Pragmatism in Theory and Practice', *Management Learning*, 27(3): 323–41.
Zucker, L.G. (1988) *Institutional Patterns and Organisations.* Cambridge, MA: Ballinger.

13 Management Education: Ethics versus Morality

Peter Anthony

This discussion concerns the relationship between the ethics of organization and the education of managers. The premise is that the world is as we see it and that organizations, whether they represent the reality of that world or whether they have constructed it, are an inseparable part of it. Proposals that it should be fundamentally changed – by the now discredited aspiration for revolution or by the less immanent and verifiable creation of 'radically different' organizations based on the replacement of authority by open dialogue and the 'banning of humiliation' (Letiche, Chapter 6 in this volume) – all shift the level of discussion beyond the scope of this chapter and the possibility of a conclusion. Our concern here is merely to understand the work of managers in organizations and to consider how far it is moral and how it might be improved, leaving the work of changing the world and the perception of its inhabitants to the confident attention of others. This authoritarian, even violent, decision, rests upon the author's limitations and his idiosyncratic preference for matters that might be influenced within a limited but conceivable timespan.

That said, the relationship between morals and organization is seen here as existing within organizations which influence and are in turn influenced by managers who are the most significant actors on the organizational stage. The proposition is that their role is based on an understanding and acceptance of moral relationships and that, far from being cast as the enemies of morality, they should more accurately be seen as moral agents. If that is the case we are able to contribute to an understanding of managers by the pursuit of two academic activities: research into the extent and quality of their moral judgements, and an examination of the evidence in order to contribute to their moral education. In short, we should, like managers, keep our feet on the ground from which, it will be argued, all moral relationships grow.

Education and training

The case that managers need an education and, even if they do not know it, that society urgently requires them to be provided with one is familiar. It suggests that the preoccupation with the technical aspects of management is misplaced and redundant, on the one hand because it is not educational, and on the other because technical proficiency is both better identified and better provided by the employer. Technical training, encompassing marketing, operational control, information analysis and the like, is, in any case, not the basis of an education whether it be founded on science or the liberal arts (see the comparisons drawn by Robert Locke, 1989 and 1996, between American management education and its British colonial clone and German and Japanese educational provision). Moreover, there is an increasing recognition that the successful practice of management may be more craft-like than professional (see Watson, Chapter 12 in this volume) and that proficiency in it may be more dependent upon something resembling apprenticeship and developmental experience rather than any kind of educational foundation. If this is so, any case for the education of managers must rest on grounds other than their achievement of competence. Technical training is necessary but not sufficient to help managers to understand either the consequences of the performance of their economic tasks in the provision of goods and services for the world, or their growing importance, even domination over, the traditional sources of authority: governments.

The need for managers to be educated rests on the proposition that the establishment of authority, as distinct from their manifest power, entails the understanding and acquisition of responsibility, a requirement that becomes the more urgent as the power of management increases. The exercise of power without responsibility is notoriously dangerous both for those who exercise it and for those who have to submit to it, and the consequences of not addressing the danger go far beyond the confines of the managers' immediate perception of their role. So, whether managers know and like it or not, the rest of us in the world require them to be educated.

'Critical management'

What form should this necessary education take and what should be its purpose? These questions, where they are debated at all, are raised outside the official agendas of the business and management schools, off piste, in small but elite conferences and seminars which are unlikely to come to the notice of directors and their programme planners. The rather shady nature of the discussions contributes to a mildly dangerous excitement, largely because they are enclosed in a consensus that management education must, at all costs, not be conceived of as useful and, therefore, that it is best that the discussants' employers should not be privy to them. Explanations for discretion bordering on secrecy are all the more understandable in the face of the character of the most significant strand in the debate, the view that management education must involve an exposure to 'critical management'. In the following and brief discussion of this subject it will be enclosed in quotation marks in order to distinguish it from the orthodox and traditional view that all education must be essentially critical, a tradition extending from Plato, through Erasmus to Newman and beyond. The value of this tradition is not in question and it is not to be re-examined here. I am simply signalling that 'critical management' is something special and is to be discussed as such. 'Critical management', as well as distinct from the critical tradition of Western education, is also to be understood as different from the 'playful' engagement in the attempt to arrive at a rhetorical understanding or crafting of the experience of managers in 'shaping the organization in which they are employed' which can be achieved only if we 'understand the ways in which they shape themselves as individual human beings' (Watson, 1994: 59).

Understanding implies a degree of sympathy, a quality present in the work of Watson (1994), Mangham (1986) and Mangham and Pye (1991). It is not so apparent in 'critical management'. The absence of sympathetic understanding has been linked to a forthright suspicion amounting to contempt among teachers of management of a postmodernist persuasion. The heuristic intention of 'critical management' is to expose the unreality of management pretensions and the falsity of the texts on which they rest. From the critical perspectives of Frankfurt and Paris this is, no doubt a worthy enterprise which generates stimulating intellectual activity and work of admired opacity which acquires high academic status. There is certainly useful work to be done at a practical level in exposing the commercial exploitation of cultural foundations, particularly by consultants, a process in which meaning, along with the rich apparatus of Dionysian language; symbol, metaphor, emblem, the resonance of history, legend and myth; narrative formation and religious experience, are all put to work not merely to sell things but to form the corporate body into an apparent community which can legitimately claim the lives and spirit of its employees for as long as they are needed.

Valuable academic contributions have been made in exposing the banality of this consultant driven enterprise but the odd thing is that both the banality and its critique emerge from the business and management schools. The underlying authority that sells culture to the corporate manufacturers of visions and mission statements resides in social science and, particularly, in its latest commercial application, anthropology. But it is the business schools rather than the departments of anthropology who go out and make the sales of programmes of cultural change. And it is the same schools which maintain their academic reputation so necessary to their marketing success by demonstrating academic rigour in the exposure of the fallacies of the programmes. This bewildering deception is maintained in other and less arcane processes. The business clients of the business schools require the schools to teach what can be identified as 'management' in some recognizable and allegedly useful form. So, the standard programmes are stuffed with the post-Enlightenment paraphernalia of empirical evidence, rational and sequential argument, analysis of data and predictive planning. But at the same time the academic reputation of the schools seems to rest on or, at the very least, to be contingent with a denunciation of such modernist nonsense in a world that has left it all behind. Something is amiss.

The schools are apparently engaged in two processes at the same time: the one providing valued advice to business clients, the other critically undermining the advice. This dangerous feat, sometimes carried out within the same institution and sometimes by the same people, is made possible by the conviction that there are two quite different audiences to be addressed, the client and the collegiate: while the one provides money, the other assures reputation. The division of functions explains the familiar conundrum: how it is that some members of management schools have no interest in either management or managers. It might be thought that some discomfort would be experienced by the deliverers if not by the clients but there are some sovereign tranquillizers available. The most effective is the conviction that underlies the attack of 'critical management' on management and its innocent practitioners: neither is 'real'.

The unreality of 'critical management' takes a special form when its goal appears to be not only a questioning of the economic foundation of contemporary society but the expectation of changing it or, at least, of arriving at 'emancipatory understanding' (Sorell, Chapter 2 in this volume) as a staging post on the journey. In this sense 'critical management' seeks to persuade the functionaries of capitalism that they should break out of the gilded cage they inhabit. Some degree of resistance on their part is to be expected.

The escape from reality can be a liberating experience for the academic and consultant educators of management. The world of business is, or is believed or said to be, an immaterial world of shifting appearance whose inhabitants to survive must be surfers, engage in 'skunking', and get the annual benediction or fix from the currently approved guru. In Britain, New Age training therefore also crops up in unlikely places. For example, 'the Bank of England, British Gas, Ernst and Whinney, Mars, and Legal and General have all sent executives to be taught how to do the Whirling Dervish Dance, so as to allow their top managers to find their core of inner peace and so increase their business potential.' Then again, 'the Scottish Office sent thousands of its employees on "New Age Thinking" courses run by Louis Tice of the Pacific Institute which aimed to train the minds of workers to make them "high performance people" in their work and private lives.' Meanwhile Decision Development, a British New Age training company, was offering to boost the spiritual, emotional and creative powers of clients. The company uses the American Indian Medicine Wheel 'to take managers on a journey to discover their spiritual, emotional and creative self' (Huczynski, 1990: 54, 56, 57; see also Heelas, 1996).

'Reality'? One is reminded of a passage in Lawrence Norfolk's novel *The Pope's Rhinoceros* which describes the Abbot Jorg's attempt to prepare his monks for flight from their monastery, about to be inundated by the Baltic. He speaks to them of the world outside and its strange but natural inhabitants. Learning of the migration of quails, the monks begin to dispute their meaning; the quails are souls flying in confusion, they are angels, they are agents of the Devil. '"No! No! No!" shouted Jorg. "Can you not understand?

The quails do not mean anything. They are, quite simply, quails!"' (1996: 42) 'Reality' for employees seems to be real enough.

> 'Employee morale in the 1990s has been in freefall,' said the study by International Survey Research. 'Most employees now feel less proud to work for their companies than at the beginning of the decade.' . . . But the most dramatic fall is in the employees' identity with the company. In 1990, 42% saw a career path with their current employers. That has now more than halved to 19%. (The *Daily Telegraph,* 1 January 1997; see also Legge, Chapter 7 in this volume)

One must wonder whether it is 'in fact' – to coin a phrase – the employees or their educators who are becoming detached and who it is that remains in contact with reality.

Reality, of course, is neither finite nor reliable. Its substance, according to Plato, is shadow and, for Kant, it is constructed by the mind's 'categories of understanding'. But even the postmodernist grip on 'critical management' either approves of, or at least admits, the submission of the dignity of men and women to what, in circumstances outside the corporate control of the liberation of their spirit (and in order to increase their 'business potential'), would seem to be outrageous and barbarous indignity. Reality, we must agree, is layered and begins with our sense experience organized by perception which, although submitted to the gravest philosophical attack, is enough for most of us most of the time. These raw data are worked upon by perception and conceptual understanding and enriched or clouded by religious and traditional teaching, amended by science, distorted by language and culture until we are left with a variety of maps for finding our way in and, finally, out of the world. But even if our conviction that it *is* a real world is, as it were, groundless, we need maps that are appropriate references to our surroundings.

'Critical management' is not helpful to managers. Its stance is essentially derisive to the purpose of their enterprise and to their performance in its pursuit. Because all is vanity or rhetoric or metaphor or symbol, no comparative judgement can be made about utility or purpose. From the perspective of the manager who is busy in the world, the critic must seem as Achilles did to Ulysses, who

> . . . in his tent
> Lies mocking our designs. With him Patroclus
> Upon a lazy bed the livelong day
> Breaks scurril jests . . .
> . . . And in this fashion,
> All our abilities, gifts, natures, shapes,
> Severals and generals of grace exact,
> Achievements, plots, orders, preventions,
> Excitements to the field, or speech for truce,

Success or loss, what is or is not, serves
As stuff for these two to make paradoxes.
(Shakespeare, *Troilus and Cressida*, Act 1 Scene 3)

The education of managers must concern their reality, the practice of their complex craft, more art than science, akin often to acting in a play which they have plotted under an uncertain direction towards an unknown conclusion. Their education must help them to understand their reality and, if it is fiction, like all fiction, it must reveal its moral content.

Management and moral relations

The telling accounts of management by Jackall (1988) and the severe criticism levelled at it by MacIntyre (1981) appear to demonstrate in practice and in theory that management is no place for moral relationships. I have previously argued that this conclusion cannot be accepted if management occupies the dominant position in the contemporary world that its critics acknowledge. But that is merely a teleological argument, persuasive only if the conclusion is that, if the critics are right, then the world must be going to hell, and that is insupportable, so that the critics must be wrong. The weakness in this purported rebuttal is obvious, so, we must do better. The attempt takes us into an examination of morals and its relationship to ethics.

The terms 'morals' and 'ethics' are often taken to be interchangeable but the distinction is made clearly by Ninian Smart who defines ethics as 'the theory or philosophy which systematizes moral values' (1996: xvi). In *Postmodern Ethics*, Bauman (1993) accounts for this systematization by the individuation of modernity which heralded the separating out of morality as a special concern:

> modern legislators and modern thinkers alike felt that morality, rather than being a 'natural trait' of human life, is something that needs to be designed and injected into human conduct; and this is why they tried to compose an all comprehensive, unitary ethics – that is, a cohesive code of moral rules which people could be taught and forced to obey. (1993: 6)

This injection was administered from above, it is 'the view of those facing the task of legislating order and bridling chaos' (1993: 7). The systematization of morality is seen as issuing from 'the control desk of society' and the consequences include, says Bauman, an improper concern with order, rationality, universality and consistency, all errors issuing from the utopian and authoritarian claims of states, tribes, communities and their 'self-appointed spokesmen and prophets' and all soon to be replaced by the 'prospect of the emancipation of the autonomous moral self and the vindication of its moral responsibility' (1993: 15).

But it is surely not the case that the attempt to systematize moral relationships stems from the 'control desk' of society, wherever that is situated. There is no doubt that those holding power and exercising domination have codified laws and rules for controlling our behaviour, often for the protection of the interests of the powerful and, wherever possible, grounded in prevailing moral codes. But the effort to systematize moral relationships is distinct from the governmental project. The systematization of moral relationships is perhaps the second oldest profession in the world; it is the concern of philosophy and it has been threatened rather than developed by modernism. The evidence of oral tradition, legend and anthropology all suggest a relationship between community and the maintenance of moral relationships: that the expectation of moral behaviour, as members of a community understand it, is a function coexistent with and necessary to practical, cooperative activity and to the survival of communities. In this sense, there is a distinctly material foundation to the development of moral relationships and hence: *the derivation of any moral imperative lies in the concrete foundation of production and exchange*. The foundation of morality in production may seem more obvious, familiar to us as it is in Durkheim, than it might appear to be in the market of exchange, vulgarized as it is by economic explanations falsely derived from Adam Smith. But it can be argued that moral relationships of trust and obligation are more necessary to market activity than to production.

What has obscured the mundane foundations of moral relationships is not the distortions of power but moral philosophy itself. The intricacies of moral exchange are negotiated in changing circumstances rather than fixed and immutable and thus they are able to cope in practice with what appear to be contradiction and conundrum in theory. The everyday conviction that we 'should' do what is right and avoid what is wrong may be the result of habits acquired in our practical and communal lives, although those habits are not immune from the influence of directions given us by leaders, employers and philosophers. But habits are not subject to intellectual consistency and may be slow to adapt to sudden change in our circumstances: their utility lies in their ambiguity. They demonstrate a broad indication of the difference between right and wrong, tested, like language, against a generally understood currency of exchange, unless we are to be ostracized from the cooperation of our fellows. But they do not readily submit themselves to the tests of logic and consistency; they are working rules, generally accepted but subject to change. And they do not reveal their origins; what we perceive of them is that, generally, we share and understand them.

So, broadly speaking, we know what we 'should' do in given circumstances, despite the disturbing interventions of conflicts of interests, loyalties and the rest, but we may not perceive why we should do it. Indeed, to the confusion of systematizers, what we 'should' do seems to change with our circumstances or the context of our lives, a 'problem' referred to by Sorell (Chapter 2 in this volume) and illuminated by Watson (1994). This does not make us or managers into pragmatists, as Jackall would have it. It is possible that we see ourselves as essentially moral in circumstances that call for inconsistent behaviour. This degree of uncertainty in a sphere of great importance to our survival has been a continuing problem for philosophy, a problem that is no nearer to solution in the present day. The problem is twofold: to systematize the rules of morality and to explain the origin of the moral imperative. One of the central problems of philosophy has turned out to be the most vexing and it is no more satisfactory to explain it in terms of 'the death of God' or the decline of authority than to appeal for a return to traditional values. The most severe approach to a solution lay in the denial of the existence of the problem. Logical positivism argued that only statements about what was empirically verifiable were allowable: the rest must be dismissed as meaningless. There are two obvious objections, the first concerning some proper doubt over the reliability of empirical enquiry and the second the obstinate refusal of the rest of us to abandon moral judgement: we cannot agree that our central preoccupation consigns us to its discussion in gibberish. Nor 'should' we. The difficulty is the philosophers', not ours.

Moral expectations are instrumental to the most basic and practical relationships. Any activity which requires the cooperation or assistance of another or others depends upon an obligation for which there is an expectation of fulfilment, a fulfilment which is dutiful. Thus, acts of cooperation carry with them, from the start, moral associations. When the simplest acts of cooperation are orchestrated in the complex life of communities and organizations, acts of dutiful cooperation become complex, but they remain founded in practical necessity, enmeshed by now in obligations, expectations, duties and trusts, that is, in moral relationships. The practical and the moral are necessarily inseparable rather than distinguishable realms.

In this sense Marx was right (correct rather than morally justified, the ambiguity of the term is significant) to say that the fundamental relationships of society are determined by the relationships of production and exchange. But whether the determination extends to the penumbra of society, its art, morality and law, is another question. Morality, if it becomes an oppressive distortion produced by the 'control desk', is manufactured to a different order from the social and economic expectations that have held the society together before they became available for exploitation. The existence and persistence of oppressive regimes – of government and of production – are all too evident, but they are controlled by the bonds of force rather than morality. Marx was accused of leaving a lacuna in place of morality but, if that is the case, it is possible to fill it by an extrapolation of his detailed and accurate analysis of the production process and its development under capitalism. Each extension in the division of labour, in productivity and in the creation of surplus value, however the surplus value is subsequently divided, involves an extension in the field of cooperation and expectation. The consequence, he predicted, would be a breakdown in moral and all other relationships – alienation – but at this point his argument lost force if not conviction and has not been followed by historical verification. What reliably emerges is that the concrete base of production and exchange is also the foundation for moral as well as practical relationships.

This is not to say that moral relationships are confined to the material world of economic activity or, with Durkheim, that they are born of the division of labour and destroyed by its 'unnatural' variants. The fabric of moral and, for that matter, aesthetic judgements is richer than the material world that it covers but the relationship between them is clear: 'friendship, responsibility, leadership, love, and justice are not elements of an external ethic brought to the world like Promethean fire. They are generated by mundane needs, practical opportunities, and felt satisfactions' (Selznick, 1992: 19). It is a matter of some importance to distinguish the task of moral philosophy, of ethics, from the necessary grasp of moral relationships acquired by men and women in going about their business and their lives. The search for consistency, rationality and order is inescapable and necessary; it predates modernism by thousands of years and the consequence of its abandonment would be, since measure would be one of the tools to be jettisoned, immeasurable. But it is a distinctive, specialized and academic discipline, too rigorous for the laity. It might, however, be more open to learning from plebeian behaviour. In a proposal parallel in intention to MacIntyre's, Selznick says:

> I do not mean to deprecate or deny the larger significance of moral philosophy for human self-awareness and the life of the mind. I suggest, however, that much of moral philosophy should be more fully assimilated to social theory and should be understood as setting an agenda for more incremental, more self-corrective, more empirical enquiry. (1992: 37)

Let us turn to the agenda.

The moral education of managers

Managers have been described as 'a barbarian elite', perhaps the first such in the history of the world (Anthony, 1986). The terms contain a contradiction: membership of an elite carries authority whereas respect for barbarians is confined to fear of their power. The conclusion that followed from this description was that managers should be educated so as to acquire moral authority in order to resolve this contradiction. The problem raised by this prescription revolves around the word 'should'. It encapsulates the problem of ethics: how is 'should' to be derived? Does it refer to some ideal state of affairs – a distinction, as Selznick puts it, between moral realism and moral idealism, between 'what we can rely on from what we can aspire to' (1992: 38) – and how can 'what should be' be brought about? The questions are taxing and the separation of moral realism as the abode of practical rather than philosophical people, a distinction implied in the present argument, helps us to avoid them.

In order to make the distinction more clear, the proposed position could be exaggerated – to an indefensible degree – by deciding that the word 'should' must be removed from the vocabulary of our discussion. Having proposed that there is a material base for moral relationships, let us continue by trying to determine what those relationships *are*, not what they *should* be. We are immediately excused from the tedious and impractical business of moralizing and preaching, from trying to agree about how managers should conduct themselves and, with even greater difficulty, how they can be persuaded to conform to our programme for their improvement. The advantages of such a course are at least practical, particularly when we recognize that there is no clear agreement amongst us, the educators, as to what managers do, so that the normative gap between 'is' and 'ought' is cloudy. If that were not enough, we are left with Hume's basic puzzle:

> In every system of morality which I have hitherto met with, I have always remarked that the author proceeds for some time in the ordinary way of reasoning, and establishes the being of a God, or makes observations concerning human affairs; when of a sudden I am surprised to find, that instead of the usual copulation of propositions, *is*, and *is not*, I meet with no proposition that is not connected with an *ought*, or an *ought not*. This change is imperceptible; but is, however, of the last consequence. For as this *ought*, or *ought not*, expresses some new relation or affirmation, 'tis necessary that it should be observed and explained; and at the same time that a reason should be given, for what seems altogether inconceivable, how this relation can be a deduction from others which are entirely different from it. (1985: 521–27)

Let us at least accept a modest proposal: that we should postpone the promulgation of advice for the improvement of managerial morals while we engage more effectively in the study of their practice. The proposal has intermediate advantages. It would provide a substantial basis for the prospects of a reformed 'business ethics' as an academic study while providing some relief from what Sorell calls 'the alienation problem' (Chapter 2 in this volume). Such a study might also turn out to be a sufficient exercise for the purpose of the managers' education. The reason for this hope is that studies of managerial practice provide evidence that managers are in fact constantly engaged in a political process that requires the exercise of moral judgement. Studies of management relationships in hospitals broadly support the importance of notions of negotiated order and reciprocal obligation in maintaining necessary degrees of cooperation outside the formal structures of control (Reed and Anthony, 1993). While the significance of informal networks of obligation has long been recognized on the shop floor, their extension through supervisory to managerial levels is more recent. It cannot be claimed that management practice rests on a firm foundation of moral relations but there is sufficient evidence to suggest that they are significant. The most powerful research, evidence and argument to date are provided by Watson in supporting his conclusion that 'the moral concerns of the Ryland managers were more than matters of personal integrity and private values . . . These managers recognized the moral basis of the very work in which they were engaged' (1994: 210). Or, as he puts it in Chapter 12 in this volume, management involves moral relationships 'from top to bottom and beginning to end'. In short, we may well be justified in claiming that the moral relationship to managerial work is a matter of *is* not *ought*.

An agenda

If that is the case the moral education of managers might begin effectively with their educators learning from their students. The argument so far pursued would suggest that it is not particularly helpful to managers to tell them that 'values, moral and non-moral, can be handled systematically, and that business and industrial practices can be objectively evaluated from a moral (ethical) point of view' (Donaldson, 1989). If ethics and the systematization of morals are the proper concern of philosophers then their technical terms and classifications can be of little concern to managers: 'business ethics' may do good business but little good. The prescriptions of business ethics, as Fineman says (Chapter 11 in this volume; see also Parker, Chapter 14), are of so little relevance to business life as to be laughable. If moral relationships are to found embedded in the management process we must learn from those who practise it.

This suggests an engagement in an exchange, in a discourse in the old-fashioned sense of the word, in which the educators learn and submit what is learned to a process of conceptualization before presenting the outcome to the student, in this case, the manager. If it is reasonable to propose that moral relationships are grounded in the mundane and material world, then a necessary part of theorizing about them is that theory must keep its feet on the ground, however cerebral the concerns of its head. Such an exchange depends upon the sanction of the learner as much as it does on the authority of the learned. It might be termed reflexive in the sense that the educator reflects what is received and transmits it back to the transmitter who is regarded as a necessary source of meaning and experience.

This is a different activity from the critical project concerned with the emancipation of the manager, the exploration of his or her alienation and the – allbeit disguised – pursuit of the educator's conception of a more just society by the exposure of the hidden interests and concealed power which mask the manager's covert manipulations. Such decoding and hermeneutic dissection of the texts are, no doubt, a valuable activity but the problem in submitting managers to it is that it in turn must be suitably disguised and occluded lest it is seen as an outright attack upon its clients. The education of anyone, as we began by suggesting, must surely begin with some sympathetic understanding of the student. The agenda of management education cannot reasonably include proposals for fundamental change in society, proper though that concern might be for sociologists or political philosophers. But management education needs to be cognate, related to the reality and experience of managers while submitting it to critical examination by those best placed to conduct it: managers.

The agenda for management education and its reflexive concern with the experience of managers is not necessarily unlearned or in itself devoid of authority. It can be supported and influenced by evidence and theory. The texts that would support it might, in the British context, include Pettigrew's (1985) study of ICI (in shortened form, perhaps), Burns (1977) on the BBC, *Reshaping Work: The Cadbury Experience* by Smith, Child and Rowlinson (1990) and, of course, Watson's *In Search of Management* (1994). These are valuable contributions to what must be continuing research into the realities of management practice which would itself inform and be supported by the educational process. Finally, business history could provide valuable insights into the reality of management and might also help us to understand that it represents a tradition rather than an invention patented by Taylor and by Ford in the twentieth century.

The moral education of managers, if so conducted, might lead to an understanding of the complexity, subtlety and importance of the managerial task and might thus confer upon it the dignity and authority which it must achieve to avoid its consignment to various forms of perdition. If management is indeed the most important actor on the contemporary stage, as MacIntyre has argued, it might also turn out to be a 'practice' as he defines the term. In this case it would deserve and receive the educational attention hitherto reserved for the art of politics and government and that, in turn, might establish management education as a reputable activity.

References

Anthony, P.D. (1986) *The Foundation of Management*. London: Tavistock.

Bauman, Z. (1993) *Postmodern Ethics*. Oxford: Blackwell.

Burns, T. (1977) *The BBC*. London: Macmillan.

Donaldson, J. (1989) *Key Issues in Business Ethics*. London: Academic Press.

Heelas, P. (1996) *The New Age Movement: The Celebration of the Self and the Sacralisation of Modernity*. Oxford: Blackwell.

Huczynski, A.A. (1990) *Management Gurus: What Makes Them and How to Become One.* London: Routledge.

Hume, D. (1985) *A Treatise of Human Nature*. London: Penguin.

Jackall, R. (1988) *Moral Mazes: The World of Corporate Managers*. New York: Oxford University Press.

Locke, R. (1989) *Management and Higher Education since 1940*. Cambridge: Cambridge University Press.

Locke, R. (1996) *The Collapse of the American Management Mystique*. Oxford: Oxford University Press.

MacIntyre, A. (1981) *After Virtue: A Study in Moral Theory*. London: Duckworth.

Mangham, I. (1986) *Power and Performance in Organisations.* Oxford: Blackwell.

Mangham, I. and Pye, A. (1991) *The Doing of Management*. Oxford: Blackwell.

Pettigrew, A. (1985) *The Awakening Giant: Continuity and Change in I.C.I.* Oxford: Blackwell.

Reed, M. and Anthony, P.D. (1993) 'Southglam: Managing Organisational Change in a District Health Authority,' in D. Gowler, K. Legge and C. Clegg (eds), *Case*

Studies in Organisational Behaviour and Human Resource Management. London: Paul Chapman.
Selznick, P. (1992) *The Moral Commonwealth: Social Theory and the Promise of Community.* Berkeley, CA: University of California.
Smart, N. (1996) *Dimensions of the Sacred: An Anatomy of the World's Beliefs*. London: HarperCollins.
Smith, C., Child, J. and Rowlinson, M. (1990) *Reshaping Work: The Cadbury Experience*. Cambridge: Cambridge University Press.
Watson, T. (1994) *In Search of Management: Culture, Chaos, and Control in Managerial Work.* London, Routledge.

14 Against Ethics

Martin Parker

> I have for some time now entertained certain opinions that I have been reluctant to make public. But I have at length concluded that the time has come to air my views, clearly and without apology, and to suffer whatever consequences come my way. I am against ethics. (Caputo, 1993: 1)

In a way that I would like to align with Caputo's 'admission', this concluding chapter consists of a series of musings on the possibility and impossibility of something called 'business ethics'.[1] This writing, and my editing of this volume, have been stimulated by an interest in this wider something called the 'ethical' which followed on from a rather sociological engagement with various forms of radical scepticism, often collected together under the label 'postmodernism' (Parker, 1992; 1995). In this chapter I want to remind myself – and my readers – that these are slippery terms and that it is precisely their content which is at stake here. I want to approach 'business ethics' in the same way we might look sideways at other, rather strange, couplings. I want to keep in mind that the terms are either potentially incommensurable or unfamiliar. What I don't want to do is to assume too much. To assume that 'we' know what or where the ethical is. To assume that 'we' have some common approach that allows 'us' to begin quite a long way into the story. Also, for reasons that I will give below, neither do I want to fall easily into being either a philosopher or a business apologist. This approach will no doubt irritate many because it is unclear (to me, and others perhaps) how what I have written in any way engages with contemporary debates in conventional business ethics. But then that is rather the point.

The chapter begins with some thoughts on the tensions between moral philosophy and pragmatic managerialism that have produced the relation, or conjunction, known as business ethics. I then explore some of its elements, focusing particularly on the problems with identifying ethical and unethical behaviours, the differences between ethics and morals, and the pervasive conflict between nostalgia and modernization that characterizes so much of the writing in this area as well as much classical sociological theory. After these various excursions, I then attempt to frame the problem of ethics in terms of modern and postmodern epistemologies. Though I prefer the term 'poststructuralist' to 'postmodern', I have employed the latter as a shorthand for an intellectual attitude or style which is radically sceptical about foundational versions of truth. The chapter then leads to a (postmodern) attempt to undermine the notions of 'decision' and 'judgement' that must be central to any (modern) conception of 'ethics' by using a range of machine metaphors. The chapter concludes with inconclusion, and a series of speculations on the relevance and irrelevance of contributions like this to the project of thinking, teaching and writing business ethics.

A story so far . . .

> But surely, there is enough immorality in the world, enough unethical conduct in public and private life, without the philosophers coming out against ethics! Would it not be a better and more salutary undertaking, and certainly more in the public interest, to defend ethics against its detractors instead of implicating oneself in damaging its good name? (Caputo, 1993: 1)

Business ethics has, up to now, largely been dominated and constituted by influences from two domains – prescriptive moral philosophy (and several other organized religious movements) and the various sciences of business. Effectively this has involved the former developing arguments that seek to demonstrate how philosophical thinking either augments or destabilizes the assumptions behind business practice, or the latter developing arguments that deny the usefulness of moral philosophy in order to justify a claim that business contains ethical issues that cannot or should not be treated in classical philosophical terms. It almost seems as if much of the debate so far has been couched in terms of intellectual abstraction versus economic pragmatism, or as it is often put rather more crudely, idealism versus realism (see for example Pearson, 1995). In metaphorical terms, the ivory tower confronts the law of the jungle and there seems to be little common ground but an awful lot of fighting over who should own the terrain.

In this, rather predictable, 'two-cultures' set-up the high moral ground might appear to belong to the philosophers as missionary idealists who wish to transform business practice. It is almost as if they, through the 'unforced force' of the better argument, will be able to persuade the immoral and the amoral that certain practices must be changed, or perhaps that the same practices need to be justified in different ways. Whichever way it runs, through the application of virtue theory, or existentialism, deontology, utilitarianism, communitarianism or the strictures of some holy text, the shape of decisions and judgements will be changed and the world will become a better (or just more rational) place. However, for the business realists, the tablets from any mountain, or the arguments from the seminar room, are simply irrelevant. Not because they don't sound like good ideas, or indeed contain some good arguments, but simply because they do not translate into the language of the bottom line. Debates about reason, logic, contradiction and so on are therefore too abstract. A language of ethics is unhelpful for organization people because it does not contain references to the matters that are relevant to those who practise 'business', as opposed to those who merely preach about it. The chapters by Anthony, Fineman, Watson and Sorell explore what the last calls this 'alienation problem' in a variety of ways, but in most cases the philosopher's claimed moral high ground is implicitly or explicitly denied through reference to 'getting things done' (or some such material imperative) in the world of practice. In other words, 'we are too busy worrying about *real* problems to take your academic sophistry very seriously.' The financial bottom line is a moral bottom line too in that it allows some firm foundations to be built on what would be otherwise rather shifting sands. To be clear here, I am not suggesting that business apologists are unethical in some sense of condemnation; I simply suggest that the ethics of philosophy has little to say to someone who needs to get something done by Friday afternoon.

I think this crude sketch misses much, but it does capture something of the *agon* which I want to comment upon. Jean-François Lyotard (1988) uses the term *agon* to refer to the wrestling match between incommensurable language games. This is a match that must carry on, cannot be won or lost, because the opponents can never be resolved to each other. In Wittgensteinian terms they occupy different 'forms of life' which cannot be compared for their rightness or wrongness by some King Solomon who stands outside all other forms of life. That is why I, if I wish to do justice to either side and not to reduce one position to another, must attempt to fall on both sides – equally hard. Following the line taken in the chapters by Letiche and Munro, I cannot somehow find a position outside this *agon* and re/solve it. All that I can do is to explore it, poking and pulling at its contradictions and silences in the hope that I might produce some interesting effects.

Another way to justify this suspension of judgement about judgement is (what the philosophers sometimes call) 'descriptive' as opposed to 'prescriptive' ethics. I commented upon this in the introduction to this book and it is a division that certainly informs, for example, Watson's use of management conversations in his chapter and Anthony's condemnation of the theoretical abstractions of 'postmodernism' in his. Willmott focuses on this division explicitly in his chapter – though he also divides what I am terming 'prescriptive' ethics into 'normative' and 'analytical' modes. As many of the other chapters also note, this difference is also sometimes framed as morals – mores, norms, values – as opposed to ethics – codes, rules, tablets from the mountain. If ethics is an attempt to write an abstract grammar for the language of decision, then morals and morality are the everyday use of everyday terms. To employ this division and then turn it back on prescriptive philosophy could be to claim that ordinary life, organizational life included, is not analytically separable from the philosopher's ethics in that both involve questions of judgement and supposed moments of decision. They embody a form of life. In other words, the languages of soap operas, moral philosophers and business ethicists might differ but this does not mean that they cannot be treated as the same kind of mundane practices for the purposes of description.

I suppose this is to 'sociologize' the ethical, to draw it down from its supposed lofty place into the flow of the ordinary. This potentially means placing it in a particular time and place – a management meeting in an organization for example – and then using the specificities of that time and place to prevent the ethical from claiming a special position elsewhere. It means refusing to accept a division of labour that distinguishes the ethical from the other things that people do in particular times and places. This is hardly a new insight for economic life – let alone culture or religion. As Adam Smith, Jean-Jacques Rousseau, Emile Durkheim and many anthropologists, institutional economists, sociologists and organizational ethnographers have suggested, questions about modern organization, markets and the division of labour are matters which cannot be separated from notions of what is good and what is bad within a particular social context (see Watson, 1994; Howell, 1997; Morgan in this volume, for example). So, if we accept this social construction of the ethical, rather than insist on some form of trans-historical foundation, then this effectively presses upon us a suspension of our judgement, an attempt to go beyond any metaphysics of good and evil and gesture at relativism in the interests of a thicker description. Rather than entering into the hurly-burly of prescriptive argument we might attempt to see how others reach their conclusions about good and bad. Not of course that we can ever do this in some final sense, but rather that this is what we would like to think of ourselves doing in order that we could 'do justice' to those 'others'.

I will return to the broader implications of this ethical social constructionism later in the chapter, but for now I concentrate on doing some more description of my own. In this case, I present some further exploration of the prescriptive standoff between the ethical legislators and the economically *laissez-faire*.

Responsibilizing organization

> Against ethics? Does not the ground open up before us? Does one not shudder from the thought? Is one not visited by the worst fear and trembling? (Caputo, 1993: 1)

If business ethics is a prescriptive project then it claims to have judged business and found it wanting. Business needs ethics, in other words, because ethics claims it to be so. This might be a general judgement, a condemnation of the whole of business, but that is rare within business ethics itself – though not uncommon outside it. Marxism and Christianity are contemporary examples which seem to have persuaded many that there is something wrong with the context, not merely the content (on the former see Wray-Bliss and Parker in this volume). More usual however, from within business ethics itself, is the accusation that certain parts of business require ethical maintenance in order to function better. So, business should stop insider trading, or advertising to children, or making weapons for military regimes, or discriminating against 'diversity', or putting up cheap buildings, or using road transport, or stealing from pension funds, or polluting rivers, or 'downsizing', or selling hamburgers, or all of the above and more.

The problem, or one of the problems, is that it is rarely very clear what 'good' and 'bad' business might be as a whole and hence why business needs one cure – ethics – to address these multiple issues. Many of the chapters in this book address precisely this issue. After all, asking whether a complex fictional entity (an organization) is 'good' or 'bad' is simply confusing and invites some rather simple answers. Is McDonald's 'good' or 'bad'? It seems that any answer to that question rather depends on who you are, what you want, and which part of McDonald's you are referring to at which time. In any case, as was observed of what used to be called 'white collar crime', corporate immorality is rarely going to be like being burgled. Rather 'it' – if 'it' is an 'it' – has no clear victims, no-one is left inspecting an empty wallet, a broken window or a pool of blood. Detecting 'bad' business therefore means coming to decisions about matters that can very rarely be dramatized as self-evident rights or wrongs. Selling torture equipment to fascist dictators is rarely placed in the same category as over-pricing bread, after all. This endless series of specific 'case studies', with their ramifications, complexities and unanswerability, seems a better metaphor for business ethics than the court case, with its final demand for the accused to be led to the cells. For business ethics there seems little agreement about 'who' 'we' are asking to do 'what'. Rather there is an unending series of complaints, of small claims, which all too often seem unrelated, and which don't seem to add up to anything bigger most of the time.

Yet, notions of social crisis lurk in the background here and they help greatly to simplify both the evidence required and the sentence given. It is all too often the times that are diagnosed as awry, with 'good' fading just there in the golden past whilst the 'bad' bubbles its noxious fumes up all around us now. Just as the 'rise of street crime' is often taken to be indicative of a breakdown in something called the social fabric, so too is the 'rise of corporate immorality' taken as a sign that an older, slower and more stable business order is being swept away. The big organization has, in many ways, become articulated as a pervasive threat rather than a guarantee of social stability. It seems that global reach, massive capital resources and employees taught to sing the company song might mean that no-one is safe and paranoia about Eisenhower's 'military-industrial complex' is everywhere from *The X Files* to buying your fair trade coffee. According to many, the trans-national corporation (in cahoots with increasingly impotent states) Disneyfies, McDonaldizes and Coca-Colanizes all that once was solid and replaces older, more authentic moralities with the self-serving sophistry of the mission statement and customer service questionnaire. Community, justice, responsibility and so on are all replaced by the smile on the face of Karen Legge's crocodile – and its tears before it eats you too.

This tension between nostalgia and social change can easily be located in the holy trinity of classical sociological theory. Karl Marx insisted that the capitalist mode of production was premised upon theft, or in less ethically loaded terms, the expropriation of surplus value from the proletariat to the bourgeoisie. An authentic mode of 'species being', a real way of being human, could only be remembered from the past or produced in the future. Capitalism and capitalists are, quite simply, 'bad'. This judgement is made not with an ethical basis (though, as Wray-Bliss and Parker suggest, this was arguably the stance of the early Marx), but rather as a matter of (supposedly) self-evident scientific fact which could be deduced from the material conditions of their survival and reproduction as a 'band of hostile brothers'. Emile Durkheim, on the other hand, regarded complex societies as being a generally positive outcome of the progressive division of labour but bemoaned the lack of moral density, the normlessness, the anomie that resulted from their very constitution. A new civic religion, or social contract, could be built from the atheistic altruism already exemplified by the older professions and which might act as a bulwark against the corrosive market relationships which were so destructive of past social solidarity. Finally, Max Weber argued that modern organization – modern forms of 'ordering' – involve rationalization, or a process of placing people and things in systematic relationships. Calculability, repeatability, efficiency, accountability and so on are hence the hallmarks of the bureaucratization of the world of work. Though this rationalization is 'world changing' and often positive in its effects it also tends to produce new kinds of people who are accustomed to not seeing the bars of the iron cage that traps them into certain ways of thinking and acting.

It should not be surprising then that the *agon* of nostalgia versus modernization that I began this chapter with, of the search for the golden rule versus the search for the bottom line, can be fairly well located in the context provided by Marx, Durkheim and Weber. For the critics of the left, the rise of business ethics (like HRM, culture, quality and so on) could be seen to express the ideological mystification of capitalist interests and is hence complicit in preventing proper modernization, that is to say, the transformation of capitalism. So, what is needed is not ethics – a bourgeois conceit – but more material social change, a conclusion reached by several authors in this book (Legge is perhaps the clearest on this). On the other hand, for nostalgic liberals, modernization has produced a need for something very like business ethics which can help to resolidify an increasingly fragmented division of moralities (and perhaps Sorell exemplifies this most clearly). So what is needed is better ethics – like better community, better citizenship, better responsibility – in order to prevent the marketization of all social relationships. Perhaps however the clearest formulation of contemporary pessimism about such possible 'solutions' is found in Weber, where any attempt to found a new ethics, or recover an old one, is inevitably subject to processes of rationalization too. Indeed, any well-meaning attempt to remystify a rationalized world will inevitably be drawn back into its calculus of means as the accountants work out how much ethics costs and benefits (see Munro's chapter for example). For Weber, a conversation about values, about ends, is precisely what is required in order to prevent the narrow minded Protestant bureaucrat from colonizing the world, yet such a conversation will be (must always be) overheard and then translated into tables, examinations, rule-books and mission statements. The contemporary popularity of the Foucault of the panopticon and governmentality and Bauman's writing on the Holocaust – which runs like a thread through almost all the preceding chapters – seems to illustrate something about a current lack of faith in escape attempts.

In a sense, as Poole (1991) argues, utilitarian formulations are the most symptomatic outcome of these Weberian developments as a form of ethics that seeks to use reason to calculate benefits for a variety of stakeholders in a decision. After all, it was Bentham who first imagined the panopticon. Though we might debate who (or what) is, and is not, a member of the category 'stakeholder', the reasonableness of such an approach is evident. A rule is applied, without hatred or passion, to determine which decision should be made in which case. The scales of justice swing this way or that, without regard to their contents because justice, like the bureaucrat, is intentionally blind. This bureaucratization of the ethical is difficult to avoid for either applied philosophers or managerialist pragmatists simply because speaking of ethics within business effectively rules out many ways of formulating decision-making and responsibility that are not amenable to managerial rationalization – an inner sense of duty, a concern for authenticity or a desire for idiosyncratic ends, for example. In the same way, if we try to bring business onto the terrain of ethics then we would find it difficult to justify many of the beliefs and practices that are constitutive of modern organizations. As has been remarked many times, in this book and elsewhere, Kant's maxim that people should be treated as ends in themselves and not means to a particular goal is almost impossible to reconcile with formal organization itself.

It would seem then that the most culturally coherent way of bringing together ethics and business is through the rationalization of both and hence their reduction to a common form of life: in other words, by denying the incommensurability of the *agon*. This is what utilitarianism does so well by making all matters comparable: pleasures, pains, numbers, ends, means can be flattened out and managed. Yet, as I have suggested, there are many moral philosophers who would be unhappy with this reduction of their discipline to social engineering, and others will continue to argue about which form of utilitarianism is most appropriate in order to achieve the best kind of social engineering. So too will there be managerialists who regard even utilitarianism as an unwarranted and unjustifiable interference in the right to manage. Either way, as far as I can see, the *agon* seems likely to continue. Like double-entry bookkeeping, the accounts stack up on one side or another, but there seems to be no way of producing a final total that everyone can agree upon.

Though you might not agree with the roundabout way in which I have got there, you may well have noticed that I have done little more than restate the positions that I began with. The means–ends rationalization that ends in the practice now known as business ethics, a modern version of Niccolò Machiavelli's advice to his Prince, seems to be destroying the very possibility of ethics itself. In suggesting that business needs ethics we seem to again be in the position of suggesting that the crocodile needs feeding. The question, the quiet call, of ethics might be in danger of being drowned by the deluge of answers from various 'professionals' who wish to insist that they know how to make organizations more responsible. The warm embrace given to ethics – through professorships in business schools, conference papers, journals, course design, books like this one – could all too rapidly turn to suffocation unless we allow ethics some room to breath. Perhaps it would be better to open a window.

Postmodern descriptions

> Who, after all, wants to be found wanting in the matter of ethics? Who wants to risk having no ethics, or questioning its good name?' (Caputo, 1993: 1)

In order to free ethics from business, from the busy-ness of having to account for itself, we might want to consider the difference between what are often called modern and postmodern formulations of knowledge (Lyotard, 1984; Cooper and Burrell, 1988; Parker, 1992; Hassard and Parker, 1993; Chia, 1996). This dualism, in an evasive argument like this one, is inevitably going to be a form of shorthand which collects together elements of social constructionism, poststructuralist approaches to language, a suspicion towards liberal humanism and so on. I did promise at the start to try not to make assumptions but I'm going to use the detested word 'postmodern' to gesture vaguely towards the kind of radical scepticism which I hope this chapter exemplifies (for expansion on this see Willmott in this volume; and for examples of this kind of thinking see the chapters by Letiche and Munro).

Briefly then, for modernists, the world is supposedly knowable and certain 'machineries of judgement' guarantee some form of certainty about the entities and relations within it. Perhaps the exemplary outcome of modernizing processes is the rationalized bureaucracy and the rules it generates for managing human conduct. In this sense, much of the project of ethics in general can be seen as an attempt to develop knowledge about how we (or they) should behave through employing some version of (the scientific) method. Like a form of 'soft' human resource management on a species-wide level, modern ethics seeks to discover the sensible 'firm but fair' laws that could govern all human action. The law must rest on a foundation, a set of facts and/or relations gained empirically or through some form of thought experiment from which deductions and/or inductions can be made. Any foundationalist ethical theory seeks to persuade through reason in the expectation that 'on pain of contradiction', the reasonable person will accept the laws as prescriptions which should be followed. Once such a 'golden rule' of conduct is discovered it can be applied in (and refined for) any social context because – as with laws about temperature, motion and so on – what is known is independent of the knower. Finally, this kind of rational social engineering should equal progress, the gradual creation of a world in which 'good' is produced more efficiently than 'bad'.

On the other hand, a postmodern approach to knowledge would assume that 'knowing' is never a final state of affairs and that different knowledges can never be judged for their truth content. Science is simply one form of reason amongst others, and can claim no privilege, no trans-historical purchase which allows it to disqualify other ways of seeing. In this context, the idea of a project of ethics is simply unsustainable since there could never be any one account which was regarded as true in all places at all times and could hence be used as some kind of guide for everyone's behaviour. In other words, there are no 'golden rules' because we have different conceptions of what counts as gold and anyway apply the same rules in different ways. Ethics, then, is perhaps better dissolved in the sociological description of moralities I referred to earlier and not celebrated as the 'one best way' to achieve virtue. In any case, as seems evident to many now, the search for what John Law (1994) has called the 'hideous purity' of modernity is one that has itself justified various forms of cruelty. Zygmunt Bauman (1989) has eloquently argued that it was the very constitution of modern rational bureaucracy that allowed for the Holocaust itself. The layout of the extermination camps, the train timetables, the manufacture of gas and the distribution of responsibilities were not incidental but central to the possibility of genocide. In other words, no amount of rationality guaranteed progress and the technology of modern organization is complicit, indeed functionally necessary, in order for modern genocide to take place.

If we apply these arguments to the *agon* of philosophy and business then it becomes possible to (again) suggest that both 'sides' are effectively engaged in a set-piece example of modernist turf warfare. For the most part, both the applied philosophers and the managerialists would claim that their intellectual project is capable of producing 'better' accounts of how organizations should deal with the 'problem' of ethics. This is going to involve new behaviours, or new justifications for old behaviours, but either way is going to require the application of knowledge generated by one 'truth technology' or another. So, the argument is about who has the right answers, and the right methods for producing the right answers. The 'set-up' disallows anyone from asking any other questions, simply because then they are no longer speaking to business ethics, or perhaps even to ethics itself. Such is the power of this arrangement that reading many textbooks on the subject one might even come to believe that there was some kind of consensus about what ethics was in the first place, from its very beginning. So, perhaps radical sceptics (that is to say, those I have awkwardly termed postmodernists) might begin by asking what ethics actually means, with the general aim of suggesting that this is by no means clear. Indeed, unpicking the possibility of ethics – being 'against ethics' – might allow us to think about 'it' rather more rigorously. However, in the next section I will try to show that being against ethics is by no means simple, because it is hard to know exactly what you are up against.

Decisions and judgements

> I am, I have been – until now – when I found my nerve (or lost my senses) – quite intimidated by the word 'ethics'. Its discursive prestige has been too much for me. When I saw it coming down the street, I always greeted it with my best smile, tipped my hat and bowed in the most courteous way, offering it my warmest salutations. That halcyon time is over now. I will no longer be able to perpetrate this ruse. My neighbours will soon know that I am registered in the opposing party. (Caputo, 1993: 1)

In this section I will use various machine metaphors to 'deconstruct' some of the elements of a liberal humanist conception of ethics. These metaphors are vaguely inspired by the writings of Deleuze and Guattari (1984; 1988; see Goodchild, 1997) but also by poststructuralist philosophy more generally (Derrida, 1978; Chia, 1994). Let us begin with the idea of a decision. This is surely the end-point of business ethics, of any ethics, since it is the moment where judgements are translated into some kind of practice, some kind of action which impacts upon the world. But what is a decision? As Chia suggests, presented in terms of managerialist 'decision theory', it is the point at which human agency makes an intervention in the flow chart of conduct. On the flow chart of 'if', 'then', 'goto', 'either' and 'or' choices that diagram our various moves, the decision is the point where the lines depart from one another and stretch into the future. At this point a kind of calculation must happen, one that attempts to look backwards and forwards along the lines and then decide which to follow. This is surely the ethical moment, the time when the machinery of judgement needs to be brought out from store and the program run on the information presented.

The central metaphor here is one of division (see Hetherington and Munro, 1997). The decision is an incision both into the flow of conduct and into the arrangement of the various ideas and materials that constitute it. The decision cuts into the social, dividing like from like, this from that, and making separate piles which can be labelled 'good' and 'bad'. The key point is that these things, these outcomes, were not there before waiting to be labelled, they were made through the dividing. So, the decision has effects that constitute ethics, as well as constituting things like strategy, markets, management, the environment and so on. So decisions seem to be rather important because they produce order, they make patterns to which conduct can then be oriented.

So how do we know when decisions happen? According to the above model, they must only happen when we bring out the machinery of judgement. If they just happened without us knowing then we could not call it a decision because it would no longer be a point on a line when choices present themselves: that is to say, when we 'make' two ways from one. But surely then we must be in need of a decision as to when the machinery of judgement should be applied. In this case? Not in that case? So a decision must precede the decision. In other words, we must decide when to decide. But the same fate befalls this earlier decision, simply because we must have powered up some of the machinery of judgement in order to make that decision. And so on. Further and further back, we seem to be pushed back along the flow chart of conduct until the lines fragment under the pressure of deciding where the lines are in the first place. It would seem that the first test to be applied here is something like 'consciousness', of being reflexively aware that you are making a decision. But, problems of defining consciousness aside, even then it would seem that much of the time decisions make us. For example, in Munro's chapter see Garfinkel's description of being a member of a jury. Empirically it is difficult to imagine someone (consciously, painfully) making a decision over every movement, every thought (see the management conversations in this volume for ample illustrations). This suggests that we are often not aware of where and when the incision was made. The piles of 'good' and 'bad', of 'this' and 'that', are already there and we often negotiate over and around them without thinking very hard about 'our' decisions. Or perhaps they weren't our decisions in the first place?

Let us leave this aside for a moment and pursue another part of this fragile common sense. As I have suggested, decisions require some kind of apparatus to enable them to be made. If there was no judgement applied, then (again) how could we know that a decision was being made? The machinery must be recognizable as machinery. It could be a dice, a copy of a book on ethics or a bank balance. It doesn't need to be the same technology every time. It could be all three if there was some way of linking them together within one specific decision. The point is that the machinery provides some kind of rule, even a rule about (so-called) randomness, that allows for the possibility of things being different and for us to set off down one path or another. If there were no choice embedded inside the machine then there would be no point in bringing it out in the first place since it would merely be affirming or negating that which had already happened and was going to happen. The machine must translate, not merely transmit, and different machines must be capable of producing different outcomes, otherwise there would be no point in doing the selection. The machinery must be there so that we can provide an account – to ourselves, or others – of how the decision came to be made. If it were not there we would have no way of deciding that we had actually made a judgement which led to a decision. If the machinery had not run then conduct would not have been interrupted by any reflection and we would have missed the crucial 'either/or'.

A further problem then presents itself, one that is implicit in most of this book. How do we decide which machinery of judgement to use in a specific case? Clearly the dice, the book and the bank balance might all be appropriate in different circumstances but it implies that we have some kind of meta-machinery to adjudicate on the competing claims of different technologies. In other words, surely we need to (consciously) select a way to do the judgement work. And if this is the case, then what is the rule that is appropriate to this meta-machinery? How can we decide whether to use utilitarianism, stakeholder theory or the dice unless we have another theory machine which judges each of them in turn? And if we don't know (consciously) what the rule is that we are applying in order to decide which machine to apply, does that mean that we are still being rational? Our prejudice, our pre-judging, about different machineries must be open to question itself after all. If it is not open to interrogation then ethics seems to have disappeared into a flow of conduct informed by any number of 'unconscious', half understood and half remembered traces of what has gone before. If this is the case, then in what sense are we free to choose how to choose? Because if we can't choose how to judge then all this machinery must be clunking around in entirely determined ways, or effectively mysterious ones, that make its very operation rather futile for giving ethics some substantive content.

Finally (and bracketing the above for a moment), if decisions are the outputs from judgements, then ethics must be one of the forms of program that goes into the judgement machine. Not the only one – because it is also fed on tossing coins, books by management academics, chicken entrails and an unimaginably large range of other materials. When assessing the various forms of ethics that it is programmed with we might imagine that they work by valuing certain kinds of data more highly than others. The deontological program assesses the past lines that have led to the decision point, paying particular attention to the internal motivations of actors. The utilitarian program evaluates the future on the basis of desired states. The communitarian program looks for congruence with how other actors have behaved in the past. And so on (see Legge in this volume for expansions of all of these). In each case the machinery works by disqualifying certain inputs and valuing others and then putting the remaining data through an algorithm that gives the decision.

So, even if we get past the problem of decision, and the particular problem of judging which ethics to apply, we are then left with potentially the most depressing problem of all. We have a variety of programs for the judgement machine and no obvious reason why any version of ethics sounds that much better than betting on the National Lottery. That is to say, no obvious reason why we should celebrate one form of algorithm as being better than another *on its own terms*. If ethics is merely an equation that produces a certain result with certain kinds of data, then why should we bother to make such a fuss about it? It almost seems as if it is like arguing over the relative merits of COBOL or FORTRAN. Perhaps one is better here, another better there. One is more elegant, another is more precise. Whatever. No point in getting all steamed up about it.

Pushing decision, judgement and ultimately ethics until they tell us what they really mean, what they really have to contain (in the abbreviated way that I have here), seems to leave us with two broad alternatives. First, we could accept the machine logic of the terms and their connection in these logical and linear ways and simply ignore the problems. This allows everything to remain neat and tidy, and for us to be clear that business ethics is simply a matter of good housekeeping in a small area of human behaviour. It provides us with an account, allows ourselves and others to be rendered accountable (see Munro's chapter again). I must admit, this 'solution' to the sticky problem of ethics is a very attractive one and I don't write that with any irony intended. It would allow me to 'manage' myself and others without getting bogged down in these endless words. It solves my problems with relativism, with my deep need to celebrate some things and condemn others. It also allows the ethical to actually mean something, because the second alternative – the radical sceptical one – squeezes it so flat that it gets everywhere, and hence is really nowhere. Decisions and judgements become spread across endless networks and hence prevent us from pointing to one place and claiming ethics is there but not there. So, can 'we', should 'we' rescue ethics from this dissolution? How can we decide?

More in-conclusions

> The Instant of Decision is Madness. (Kierkegaard in Derrida, 1978: 31)

Attractive though the rationalizing, the rationing, of ethics is, it simply does not work as an empirical description of conduct or an attempt to think hard about concepts. The separations that construct decision, judgement and ethics seem to collapse if pushed even by a few pages. Any notion that we, supposedly free agents, could choose rationally an ethical framework to live our organizational lives by bears very little pressure. Indeed, every attempt to articulate what this ethical question might mean in the context of business organizations seems to lead to it being dragged into philosophy or some form of rationalized accounting. As so many of the chapters in this volume attest, though sometimes inadvertently, both of these places seem unsatisfactory and another way of putting the question is desired. The question of 'what to do' can no longer be a mad one if it ends up in either of those places and, for myself, I want the madness to remain, to acknowledge the impossibility of ethics if I am to live my life well, to reflexively 'fashion my self' as Joanna Brewis suggests in Chapter 4.

The problem that I will not address as a concluding conclusion to this book will be what options are left for a project like business ethics if all the above is accepted. It would simply be inappropriate for me to gift wrap an argument like this one. However, as a theme throughout the book, Bauman's (1993) neatly contradictory – though problematically humanist – formulation of 'postmodern ethics' has attempted to explore how we might talk about judgement and responsibility in a postfoundational style and many other social theorists have responded to this invitation. What has not been done yet, though this volume will hopefully have amended that, is to aim some of these ideas at organizations (though see Kjonstad and Willmott, 1995; ten Bos, 1997). After all, as I suggested above (via Marx, Durkheim and Weber), organizations can be articulated as one of the prime sites of modernity. In the broadest of terms I would like to suggest that losing the certainties of ethical frameworks might actually sensitize us to ethical issues in a more helpful way. At the end of the century of the Holocaust and the overpaid non-executive director 'we' (should) know that hiding behind the bureaucratic codes and laws generated by modern conceptions of the ethical is often not conducive to thinking about wider, looser, madder conceptions of cruelty and justice. This is simply because, in Weber's terms, the means can all too easily become ends in themselves, so an ethics aimed at justice becomes a code that defends injustice. If modernity does not guarantee progress, then neither does ethics guarantee the good; it merely produces accountable versions of it. Perhaps it would be better then to embrace the paradox – that being ethical requires giving up on ethics and doing justice requires giving up on the search for the law. As Derrida puts it, as soon as we speak of justice it is already gone (1978; see Letiche's chapter). Or, for Nietzsche (an older figure who also lurks behind this book), '*every* means hitherto employed with the intention of making mankind moral has been thoroughly *immoral*' (1990: 70).

Perhaps applying postfoundational thinking to our writing and teaching on organizations can suggest a rather more provisional way of thinking – one that does not encourage dangerous certainties but instead focuses on the ethical ambivalence of any action and judgement. Of course this might not mean that we stop writing and thinking about ethics in business; it might mean simply that we alter our conception of how questions on this area might be asked and then (perhaps) argue that they are best left unanswered. Encouraging the development of a sociology, or anthropology, of moralities might be the only way to avoid the bottom line and the rush to judgement that follows from 'discovering' it. However, before leaving this book dangling in the wind, I want to insist that this is not necessarily a pessimistic inconclusion. The thinking, teaching and writing I and the others in this book have been doing on ethics and on business ethics do not lead me to believe that nihilistic despair is the only outcome of radical scepticism. If those three practices are worth anything, then surely they should allow for forms of thought that encourage us to question our deeply felt beliefs, and not merely wrap us in certainties that prevent us from thinking the absurd. This does not mean that they can easily be 'applied', either to the project of moral philosophy or to management. Being 'against' both means 'in opposition' and 'leaning on'. I can't, and don't want to, make ethics or business ethics disappear, but I want to be clearer about what I'm leaning on.

Note

1 A related paper appears as 'Business Ethics and Social Theory', in *British Journal of Management* (1998), Volume 9.

References

Bauman, Z. (1989) *Modernity and the Holocaust*. Oxford: Polity.
Bauman, Z. (1993) *Postmodern Ethics*. Oxford: Polity.
Caputo, J. (1993) *Against Ethics*. Bloomington, IN: Indiana University Press.
Chia, R. (1994) 'The Concept of Decision: A Deconstructive Analysis', *Journal of Management Studies*, 31(6): 781–806.
Chia, R. (1996) *Organisational Analysis and Deconstruction*. Berlin: de Gruyter.
Cooper, R. and Burrell, G. (1988) 'Modernism, Postmodernism and Organisational Analysis', *Organisation Studies*, 9(1): 91–112.
Deleuze, G. and Guattari, F. (1984) *Anti-Oedipus*. London: Athlone.
Deleuze, G. and Guattari, F. (1988) *A Thousand Plateaus*. London: Athlone.
Derrida, J. (1978) *Writing and Difference*. London: Routledge and Kegan Paul.
Goodchild, P. (1997) 'Deleuzean Ethics', *Theory, Culture and Society*, 14(2): 39–50.
Hassard, J. and Parker, M. (eds) (1993) *Postmodernism and Organisations*. London: Sage.
Hetherington, K. and Munro, R. (eds) (1997) *Ideas of Difference: Social Ordering and the Labour of Division*. Oxford: Blackwell.
Howell, S. (ed.) (1997) *The Ethnography of Moralities*. London: Routledge.
Kjonstad, B. and Willmott, H. (1995) 'Business Ethics: Restrictive or Empowering?', *Journal of Business Ethics*, 14: 445–64.
Law, J. (1994) *Organising Modernity*. Oxford: Polity.
Lyotard, J.-F. (1984) *The Postmodern Condition: A Report on Knowledge*. Manchester: Manchester University Press.
Lyotard, J.-F. (1988) *The Differend: Phrases in Dispute*. Minneapolis, MN: University of Minnesota Press.
Nietzsche, F. (1990) *Twilight of the Idols*. London: Penguin.
Parker, M. (1992) 'Post-Modern Organisations or Postmodern Organisation Theory?', *Organisation Studies*, 13(1): 1–17.
Parker, M. (1995) 'Critique in the Name of What: Postmodernism and Critical Approaches to Organisation', *Organisation Studies*, 16(4): 553–64.
Pearson, G. (1995) *Integrity in Organisations.* New York: McGraw-Hill.
Poole, R. (1991) *Morality and Modernity*. London: Routledge.
ten Bos, R. (1997) 'Business Ethics and Bauman Ethics', *Organisation Studies*, 18(6): 997–1014.
Watson, T. (1994) *In Search of Management*. London: Routledge.

Index

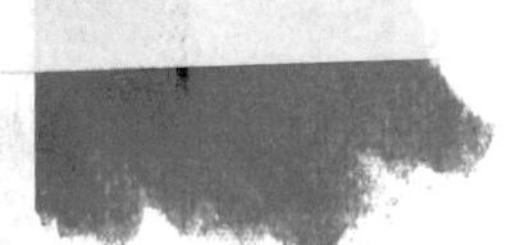

60 4040214 2